# Jewish Philosophy P

MW00852354

In this innovative volume, contemporary philosophers respond to classic works of Jewish philosophy. For each of twelve central topics in Jewish philosophy, Jewish philosophical readings, drawn from the medieval period through the twentieth century, appear alongside an invited contribution that engages both the readings and the contemporary philosophical literature in a constructive dialogue. The twelve topics are organized into four parts, and each topic and part commences with an overview of the ensuing dialogue and concludes with a list of further readings. The introduction to the volume assesses the current state of Jewish philosophy and argues for a deeper engagement with analytic philosophy, exemplified by the new contributions.

*Jewish Philosophy Past and Present: Contemporary Responses to Classical Sources* is a cutting edge work of Jewish philosophy, and, at the same time, an engaging introduction to the issues that animated Jewish philosophers for centuries and to the texts that they have produced. It is designed to set the agenda in Jewish philosophy for years to come.

**Daniel Frank** is Professor of Philosophy and Director of the Jewish Studies Program at Purdue University, USA. He has published widely in Greek and medieval Jewish philosophy, and his most recent book is *The Routledge Philosophy Guidebook to Spinoza on Politics* (co-authored, 2015).

**Aaron Segal** is Assistant Professor of Philosophy at Yeshiva University, USA, specializing in metaphysics and philosophy of religion. He has published or has forthcoming publications in *Oxford Studies in Metaphysics*, *Philosophical Perspectives*, and *Philosophical Studies*.

# Jewish Philosophy Past and Present

## Contemporary Responses to Classical Sources

**Edited by**
**Daniel Frank and Aaron Segal**

Routledge
Taylor & Francis Group

NEW YORK AND LONDON

First published 2017
by Routledge
711 Third Avenue, New York, NY 10017

and by Routledge
2 Park Square, Milton Park, Abingdon, Oxon, OX14 4RN

*Routledge is an imprint of the Taylor & Francis Group, an informa business*

© 2017 Taylor & Francis

*Library of Congress Cataloging in Publication Data*
Names: Frank, Daniel, 1955– editor.
Title: Jewish philosophy past and present : contemporary responses to
classical sources / edited by Daniel Frank and Aaron Segal.
Description: 1 [edition]. | New York : Routledge, 2016. | Includes
bibliographical references and index.
Identifiers: LCCN 2016000788 (print) | LCCN 2016006667 (ebook) | ISBN
9781138015104 (alk. paper) | ISBN 9781138015739 (alk. paper) | ISBN
9781315768564
Subjects: LCSH: Jewish philosophy.
Classification: LCC BM580 .J49 2016 (print) | LCC BM580 (ebook) | DDC
181/.06–dc23
LC record available at http://lccn.loc.gov/2016000788

ISBN: 978-1-138-01510-4 (hbk)
ISBN: 978-1-138-01573-9 (pbk)
ISBN: 978-1-315-76856-4 (ebk)

Typeset in Times New Roman
by HWA Text and Data Management, London.

Printed and bound in the United States of America by
Edwards Brothers Malloy on sustainably sourced paper

# Contents

# Contributors

**Leora Batnitzky** is Ronald O. Perelman Professor of Jewish Studies, Professor of Religion, and Chair, Department of Religion, at Princeton University. Her most recent book is *How Judaism Became a Religion: An Introduction to Modern Jewish Thought* (2011).

**Daniel Frank** is Professor of Philosophy and Director of the Jewish Studies Program at Purdue University. His most recent book is *The Routledge Philosophy Guidebook to Spinoza on Politics* (co-authored , 2015).

**Jerome Gellman** is Professor of Philosophy (emeritus) at Ben-Gurion University of the Negev. His most recent book is *God's Kindness Has Overwhelmed Us: A Contemporary Doctrine of the Jews as the Chosen People* (2013).

**Edward Halper** is Distinguished Research Professor, Department of Philosophy, at the University of Georgia. He has recently completed a three-volume study on Aristotle's *Metaphysics: One and Many in Aristotle's Metaphysics.*

**Jonathan Jacobs** is Professor and Chair, Department of Philosophy, at John Jay College, CUNY. His most recent book is *Law, Reason, and Morality in Medieval Jewish Philosophy* (2010).

**Samuel Lebens** is a Postdoctoral Fellow at the Rutgers Center for the Philosophy of Religion. He has published a number of articles on the history of analytic philosophy, metaphysics, and philosophy of religion.

**Jed Lewinsohn** is Assistant Professor of Philosophy at the University of Pittsburgh and currently a member of the Harvard Society of Fellows. He has published on Jewish philosophy and works on moral, political, and legal philosophy.

**Charles Manekin** is Professor of Philosophy and Director of the Meyerhoff Center of Jewish Studies at the University of Maryland. He has edited *Medieval Jewish Philosophical Writings* in *Cambridge Texts in the History of Philosophy* (2007).

**Yitzhak Melamed** is Professor of Philosophy at Johns Hopkins University. His most recent book is *Spinoza's Metaphysics: Substance and Thought* (2013).

**Aaron Segal** is currently Assistant Professor of Philosophy at Yeshiva University and from fall 2016 will be Lecturer in the Department of Philosophy at the Hebrew University of Jerusalem. He has published a number of articles on metaphysics and philosophy of religion.

**Kenneth Seeskin** is Philip M. and Ethel Klutznick Professor of Jewish Civilization, Professor of Philosophy, and Chair, Department of Religious Studies, at Northwestern University. His most recent book is *Jewish Messianic Thoughts in an Age of Despair* (2012).

**David Shatz** is University Professor of Philosophy, Ethics, and Religious Thought at Yeshiva University. His most recent book is *Jewish Thought in Dialogue: Essays on Thinkers, Theologies, and Moral Theories* (2009).

# Preface

The genesis of this volume gives the clearest indication of its nature, and its aims and goals. When we commenced work on a text devoted to key topics in the history of Jewish philosophy we had in mind a home in the recently launched Routledge series, *Key Debates in the History of Philosophy* (https://www. routledge.com/series/DHP). This series presents topical debates ranging across the entire history of philosophy via discussions by notable contemporary scholars on core issues. So, one finds in *Debates in Modern Philosophy* a set of lively debates on Hume on miracles and on causation, Locke on personal identity, and Kant on the synthetic a priori. The volumes that have so far appeared in the series are engaging. We hoped we would be able do the same for Jewish philosophy. But it was not possible to do so, and it is important to understand the reason why. Given the relative unfamiliarity of Jewish philosophy and its history, we could not reasonably ground our volume on secondary texts devoted to familiar issues in the history of philosophy. Rather, taking nothing for granted, we decided to present as 'essential readings' on a specific topic the primary (historical) texts themselves, and then, and only then, on this foundation to turn to important recently published scholarly work and specially commissioned new essays responding to that work and to the 'essential readings' as well. Proceeding as we do, by not detouring around the classic texts, but by debating with them, we hope to establish a certain agenda in engaging with the Jewish philosophical tradition. The tradition is a commentarial one, and our volume stresses tough reflection on perennial issues. If this volume achieves its goals, it shall offer a solid introduction to the whole history of Jewish philosophy and, in keeping with the spirit of the *Key Debates* series, "[t]he result is a new kind of introduction—one that enables students to understand philosophy's history as a still-living debate."

Briefly then, this volume is divided into four parts, Language and Interpretation, Epistemology and Metaphysics, Philosophical Theology, and Practical Philosophy. Each of the four parts is subdivided into three subsections on specific topics. Each of the twelve topical subsections commences with a brief introduction and concludes with a short list of further readings, inclusive of both Jewish and non-Jewish sources. We have been determined from the outset to set Jewish philosophy in the context of general philosophy, so as to overcome any parochialism that might hover over the project.

Our task has been facilitated by the timeliness of our contributors and their enthusiasm for the project. DF assembled the sections on Language and Interpretation, and Practical Philosophy, while AS put together the sections on Epistemology and Metaphysics, and Philosophical Theology. Both of us have vetted the whole and inspected each other's work.

A stalwart quartet of Yeshiva University students deserve special mention for their help on the volume: David Naggarpowers and Daniel Rhodes assisted with the further readings and the general bibliography, and Benjamin Apfel and Doron Levine prepared the previously published material and compiled the index. We would like to express our deep appreciation for the award of a Dr. Kenneth Chelst Book Grant (from Yeshiva University), which supported their efforts.

Routledge (New York) has been a pleasure to work with, and we signal the special assistance and encouragement of Andy Beck.

Daniel Frank and Aaron Segal
October 2015
Cheshvan 5776

# Acknowledgments

The editors and publishers wish to thank the following for permission to use copyright material:

Hermann Cohen, *Religion of Reason Out of the Sources of Judaism*, trans. S. Kaplan, 1995. Reprinted with permission of Scholars Press, Atlanta.

Hasdai Crescas, *The Light of the Lord*, trans. W. Z. Harvey, 1973. Reprinted with permission of the translator.

Daniel Frank, "What is Jewish Philosophy?" 1997. Reprinted with permission of the author.

Gersonides, *The Wars of the Lord*, trans. S. Feldman, 1987. Reprinted with permission of the Jewish Publication Society.

Lenn E. Goodman, *On Justice: An Essay in Jewish Philosophy* (2nd ed.), 2008. Reprinted with permission of Yale University Press, New Haven.

Moshe Halbertal, "'Ones Possessed of Religion': Religious Tolerance in the Teachings of The Me'iri," 2000. Reprinted with permission of the author.

Moshe Halbertal and Avishai Margalit, *Idolatry,* 1992. Reprinted with permission of the President and Fellows of Harvard College.

Judah Halevi, *The Book of Refutation and Proof on Behalf of the Despised Faith (The Kuzari)*, trans. B. Kogan and L. Berman, 2000. Reprinted with permission of the translator.

Moses Maimonides, *The Guide of the Perplexed*, trans. S. Pines, 1963. Reprinted with permission of University of Chicago Press, Chicago.

Moses Maimonides, *The Guide of the Perplexed*, abridged J. Guttmann, trans. C. Rabin, 1995. Reprinted with permission of Hackett Publishing Company, Inc. All rights reserved.

Moses Maimonides, *Shemonah Perakim (Eight Chapters)*, trans. R. Weiss and C. Butterworth, 1983. Reprinted with permission of Dover Publications, Mineola.

Moses Mendelssohn, Open Letter to Lavater, in M. Gottlieb (ed.), *Moses Mendelssohn: Writings on Judaism, Christianity, and the Bible*, 2011. Reprinted with permission of University Press of New England, Hanover.

Steven Nadler, *Spinoza's Heresy: Immortality and the Jewish Mind,* 2001. Reprinted with permission of Oxford University Press, New York.

Leon Roth, "Is there a Jewish Philosophy?" in Roth, *Is There a Jewish Philosophy? Rethinking Fundamentals*, 1999. Reprinted with permission of Littman Library of Jewish Civilization.

Daniel Rynhold, *Two Models of Jewish Philosophy: Justifying One's Practices*, 2005. Reprinted with permission of Oxford University Press, New York.

Saadia Gaon, *The Book of Beliefs and Opinions*, trans. S. Rosenblatt, 1948/1976. Reprinted with permission of Yale University Press, New Haven.

Kenneth Seeskin, "Job and the Problem of Evil," 1990. Reprinted with permission of SUNY Press, Albany.

David Shatz, "Freedom, Repentance, and Hardening of the Hearts," 1997. Reprinted with permission of *Faith and Philosophy*, Wilmore.

Joseph Soloveitchik, "Moses and the Redemption," 2006. Reprinted with permission of Toras HoRav Foundation.

Benedict (Baruch) Spinoza, *Theological-Political Treatise*, trans. E. Curley, 1995. Reprinted with permission of Princeton University Press, Princeton.

Howard Wettstein, "Poetic Imagery and Religious Belief," in D. Shatz (ed.), *Philosophy and Faith: A Philosophy of Religion Reader*, 2002. Reprinted with permission of McGraw-Hill Education, New York.

Howard Wettstein, "The Significance of Religious Experience," in H. Wettstein, *The Significance of Religious Experience*, 2012. Reprinted with permission of Oxford University Press, New York.

Michael Wyschogrod, *The Body of Faith: God in the People Israel*, 1983. Reprinted with permission of the author.

# Introduction
## Jewish Philosophy: Past, Present, and Future

## I

This volume is designed to simulate one conversation and to stimulate two others. It simulates a conversation between the Jewish philosophical past and its present. For each of twelve topics in Jewish philosophy, a contemporary philosopher contributes an original response to several classic works of Jewish philosophy, works that are in turn opposed to one another on the topic at hand. Each contributor engages in the twin tasks of clarifying the opposing views of his/her predecessors and proffering a view of his/her own. While the balance between the executed tasks differs from contributor to contributor, in no case is either task neglected entirely. The intended effect is a virtual conversation between participants from different eras and very different philosophical persuasions. None of the classic works are treated as a museum piece, and none as a mere mouthpiece. Jewish philosophy is presented here as a living, growing enterprise.

At the same time, we would like to stimulate two related conversations, one between Jewish philosophers and the wider Anglophone philosophical community, and the other among Jewish philosophers themselves. PhD-granting philosophy departments in North America, the United Kingdom, and Australia have long been dominated by so-called analytic philosophy. Analytic philosophy is itself a rather diverse discipline. Practitioners hold widely divergent views on matters of substance: empiricism, rationalism, skepticism, utilitarianism, deontologism, virtue ethics, idealism, theism, physicalism, platonism, nominalism, moral realism, and moral anti-realism are just some of the views that have prominent adherents. And there is no consensus on proper philosophical methodology: some analytic philosophers champion linguistic or conceptual analysis, while others deride it (as many have noted, 'analytic philosophy' is something of a misnomer!); some construct and select philosophical theories based on their explanatory power, while others eschew explanation entirely. Notwithstanding that diversity, analytic philosophers are more-or-less unified by an objective, a manner of philosophizing, a set of prized virtues, and a group of philosophical role-models.[1] The objective, at least usually, is to get to the bottom of some relatively general feature of reality: to determine whether anything has that feature, what it consists in, and what its scope is. The manner of philosophizing at least ideally involves putting forward theses in a logically perspicuous form, offering arguments to defend them, and carefully considering objections. Clarity, rigor, and literal expression are usually thought to be virtues rather than vices. And those prominent philosophers, particularly from the late nineteenth and early twentieth centuries, who share the same objective, philosophize in roughly the same manner, and prize the same philosophical virtues, constitute philosophical role-models.

Few Jewish philosophers, however, have 'done' Jewish philosophy in the analytic mode or interacted substantially with the work of analytic philosophers. For the last century or more, Jewish philosophy has almost exclusively consisted either in contextualizing and explicating its own history – it has been, to use Bernard Williams's (2006) distinction, more history of ideas than history of philosophy – or in so-called Continental philosophy, or in a combination of both. It is open to speculation as to why this is so, but it is hard to deny that it is so. Over twenty years ago Kenneth Seeskin (1991) noted that the "analytic movement that dominated Anglo-American departments for the greater part of this century had little impact on Jewish thought. There is no one who stands to Jewish philosophy as Alvin Plantinga, Philip Quinn, or Ninian Smart stand to Christian." Not much has changed since then. One would be hard pressed to find a piece of analytic Jewish philosophy in the *Journal of Jewish Thought and Philosophy* or *DAAT*, two leading journals in Jewish thought and philosophy. The annual Association for Jewish Studies conference and the quadrennial World Congress of Jewish Studies regularly host sessions on Jewish philosophy, but analytic philosophy rarely makes an appearance; at the American Philosophical Association divisional meetings and the Joint Session of the Aristotelian Society and the Mind Association, on the other hand, where analytic philosophy is de rigueur, papers on Jewish philosophy are hard to come by.

To be sure, there have long been pockets of analytic Jewish philosophy, and such pockets are slowly growing. Without mentioning names, for fear of inadvertently omitting some who ought to be mentioned, a handful of senior philosophers have over several decades done substantial and important work in analytic Jewish philosophy. As a result, one can find a smattering of articles in general philosophy journals and some monographs and edited collections dedicated to analytic Jewish philosophy. (Nearly all of these works are cited in the essays in this volume or appear in the lists of further readings after each subsection.) More recently, a younger cohort of analytically-trained Jewish philosophers has coalesced around the Association for the Philosophy of Judaism, a nascent organization that has sponsored several conferences, symposia, and essay prizes to promote analytic Jewish philosophy (http://www.theapj.com/). But a conversation between Jewish philosophy and the broader Anglophone philosophical community is still in its infancy. Analytic Jewish philosophy lags behind its Christian counterpart in both scope and sophistication.

We wish to deepen the dialogue between Jewish philosophy and analytic philosophy, and this volume is intended to be a substantial step in that direction. The classic selections are drawn primarily from outside the contemporary Continental canon of Jewish philosophy (Rosenzweig, Buber, Cohen, Levinas, etc.), and, as noted above, the invited contributors treat the classics as bona fide interlocutors in the search for the truth about philosophical matters, rather than as mere historical artifacts. Most of the invited contributions are written in an analytic mode and many of them explicitly engage with an analytic literature. It is hopefully not unreasonable to expect, therefore, that much of this volume will speak to such philosophers in a 'language' that they can understand and address questions they share. Our intended scholarly audience decidedly encompasses analytic philosophers of many backgrounds, including those who are unfamiliar with Jewish philosophy.

But our intended audience also encompasses Jewish philosophers, including those who are unfamiliar with, or perhaps even dismissive of, analytic philosophy. We want to spark a conversation about the direction Jewish philosophy ought to take. As we see it, Jewish philosophers would likely benefit from exploring and interacting with a much broader range of philosophical figures and works than many of us do at present. In particular, we stand to gain a wealth of insights by attending to what has been the regnant form of philosophy in much of the world for the past century; and we have much to lose by essentially ignoring it. The essays collected here give some sense of what is to be gained. More work will hopefully give an even better sense.

## II

As noted, it is open to speculation as to why Jewish philosophy has eschewed analytic trends. Part of the answer is historical and we suspect that another part is rooted in the propensity to perpetuate the status quo and cleave to the familiar. As for history, modern academic Jewish philosophy (maybe even "Jewish philosophy" itself) is a German-Jewish phenomenon. It was born as a subfield within the 19th-century movement known as Wissenschaft des Judentums ("Science of Judaism") – a movement that featured close historical and philological analysis of classical texts – and it grew up together with post-Kantian German philosophy. As a result, historicist and Continental trends played a formative role in modern Jewish philosophy.

More specifically still, many modern Jewish intellectuals, like their non-Jewish contemporaries, repudiated the medieval philosophical project. Modern science dealt a decisive blow to medieval Aristotelianism, and Kant was widely held to have rendered natural theology and metaphysics impracticable. With medieval Jewish philosophy in disrepute, modern Jewish philosophers naturally turned to the Hebrew Bible and, to a much lesser extent, the Rabbinic corpus.[2] The Hebrew Bible is, however, pre-philosophical. It evinces little concern for careful doctrinal formulations, or consistency, with respect to the nature of ultimate reality and our knowledge of it. The text is shot through with evocative imagery, symbolism, and narrative, and its subject matter is often the interpersonal relationships between God and humans and among humans themselves.[3] The Hebrew Bible was thus a fertile ground for phenomenology, existentialism, hermeneutics, and typological interpretation, less so for a rigorous defense of a carefully expressed thesis about some general feature of reality.[4] Compounding matters, a substantial majority of modern Jews abandoned traditional religion while remaining squarely within the Jewish community. This made it wholly unclear what would count as a 'Jewish thesis' worth defending, and reduced the number of Jewish philosophers who had 'Jewish theses' to defend. The entrenchment of a turn to the Hebrew Bible and an abandonment of traditional doctrines thus conspired to make analytic philosophy singularly unwelcome when it came on the scene. There were simply too few theses to defend and too few philosophers to defend them. By contrast, scholarly history of medieval philosophy, shorn of any commitment to its truth, and the phenomenological, existentialist, and hermeneutical streams of Continental philosophy thrived.

Finally, the current academic zeitgeist probably plays a role. As several leading Christian analytic philosophers note with some dismay, many of their co-religionists in theology and religion departments have resisted the introduction of analytic philosophy into Christian theology. This resistance appears to be at least partly based on a commitment to a thoroughgoing, global anti-realism and relativism, a commitment shared by many in the humanities and perceived to be inimical to analytic philosophy.[5] (Very roughly, anti-realism is the view that everything is the way it is in part due to how we think about it, and relativism is the view that nothing is true tout-court, only relative to a given point-of-view.) Many contemporary academic Jewish philosophers hold these views as well, with a resulting antipathy to analytic modes of philosophizing.

Our historical explanation of the current state of Jewish philosophy may of course be taken as a reason, even a justification, for perpetuation of the status quo. But is it a good reason? Should the status quo, which has too little engaged with analytic trends in general philosophy and with the rich argumentative veins in the medieval Jewish philosophical tradition, be perpetuated? These are normative questions and answers will depend on what Jewish philosophers aim at, or ought to aim at. But if even Yitzhak Melamed's very broad suggestion, that the aim of Jewish philosophy is "to provide a well-argued and informed account of Jewish religious and cultural beliefs and practices," is deemed reasonable,[6] then we see no reason not to broaden the scope of Jewish philosophy so as to include constructive, philosophical-truth-seeking interaction with both analytic philosophy and the entirety of the Jewish philosophical tradition.

Jewish religious and cultural beliefs and practices have evolved over the history of Judaism, a history that was not arrested after the close of the Biblical period. Of course, Jewish intellectual, religious, and cultural history includes the Hebrew Bible, and it cannot be ignored in giving a philosophical account of Judaism. But that history includes much else – halakha (Jewish law), medieval Jewish philosophy, and works of mussar (nineteenth- and twentieth- century ethical literature), for example – and these other elements cannot be ignored, at the risk of unmooring Jewish philosophy from Judaism. Halakha is ripe for exploration using the tools of analytic philosophy, as several recent essays have demonstrated.[7] Medieval Jewish philosophy, like medieval philosophy more generally, is in many ways continuous with contemporary analytic philosophy, especially given the resurgence over the past four decades of grand-old metaphysical theorizing: even Aristotelian teleology has made a comeback![8] And a classical mussar text can be the source of rich philosophical insight in the hands of a brilliant analytic philosopher.[9] There might not be "thirteen principles" at the core of Judaism, but there are plenty of claims and practices that were or are central to the way Jews experienced their Judaism for an extended period of time. A well-argued reconstruction of any of them would be aided by employing analytical philosophical tools and methods.

We believe that the methodology regnant in Jewish philosophy at present comes at a considerable cost. The cost is a manifest loss of the kind of clarity and argumentative rigor that is the hallmark of the analytic tradition, and even more importantly of the greatest Jewish philosophers themselves, such as Maimonides. In our work we treat Maimonides as our contemporary interlocutor, precisely because he is such a fine philosophical mind. There is absolutely no reason to debar him from participation in a dialogue with analytic thinkers focusing on canonical issues in religious language, epistemology, metaphysics, philosophical theology, and moral and political philosophy. Not to participate in such dialogue is to marginalize the best minds in the Jewish philosophical tradition from broader philosophical trends.

Our aim in this volume is partisan, but it is not parochial. We do not intend to close off conversation. To the contrary, we would very much like to open up a conversation about the nature and future of Jewish philosophy. Indeed, we offer a whole section on the nature of Jewish philosophy, and our contemporary commentator in certain ways opposes the general perspective that we are delineating in this introduction. The future of Jewish philosophy and philosophizing is open-ended, and our goal is an inclusive one, to encourage the development of rigorous analytic Jewish philosophy. If this volume is able not only to display to analytic philosophers some of the richness of the Jewish philosophical tradition but also to encourage future Jewish philosophers to expand the literature with which they interact and the range of modes in which to philosophize, our purposes will have been served well enough.

## Notes

1 See Soames 2003, Rea 2009, and Zimmerman 2007.
2 See Melamed 2009 who argues that the Protestantization of modern German Jewish intellectuals led to a nearly exclusive focus on the Bible as a source of philosophical reflection.
3 See Wyschogrod 1983 and Wettstein 2002 (reprinted in this volume).
4 We do not mean to imply that it is impossible to read the Hebrew Bible philosophically in an analytic mode and informed by contemporary analytic philosophy. It can be done, and done well; see, e.g., Stump 2010. But it does not come naturally. (See also Samuel Lebens's contribution to this volume, in which he explicitly attempts to ease the tension between traditional philosophical theology and fidelity to the Biblical portrayal of God.)
5 See the essays collected in Wainwright 1996, along with Zimmerman 2007 and Rea 2009. Note that some of their discussion is focused on analytic theology, which forms but a part of what analytic Jewish (or Christian) philosophy is and can be.
6 Melamed ibid. (translation is from an unpublished English version of the same article).
7 See Lewinsohn 2006–7, Hirsch 1999 and 2006.
8 See Nagel 2012 and Kroll (forthcoming).
9 See Steiner 2000.

# Part I
# Language and Interpretation

# 1 Religious Language

In this general section on *Language and Interpretation* we focus on three related interpretive issues: the nature of religious language, the correct interpretation of Scripture, and finally, the historiography of Jewish philosophy. The Bible and its memorable imagery seem to ill consort with the propositional structure of theological doctrine developed by medieval religious philosophers intent on squaring reason with revelation. **Howard Wettstein** presses the point, and draws a very strong contrast between biblical discourse (imagistic poetry) about God and theological doctrine that abstracts God from such imagery so as to iron out 'poetic' inconsistencies. The anthropomorphic descriptions of God that we find in the Bible and the rabbis of the Talmudic period are, according to Wettstein, not a misguided attempt to understand divinity, but rather a perfect vehicle to capture His disparate roles in history, as creator, lover, judge, etc., and to give meaning to the vibrancy of religious life. For Wettstein, it is the theologians who, in demanding consistency and uniformity, miss the point of the story and flatten out the contours of religious life and practice.

Wettstein has thrown down the gauntlet, and it is natural to turn straightway to two of the greatest Jewish religious philosophers, **Maimonides** and **Gersonides**. We present the classic debate between them concerning human discourse about the divine. For Maimonides, the utter simplicity of God, His metaphysical unity, entails the impossibility of describing God in any direct way. Periphrases are necessary, and even they must be interpreted aright. We are able only to say of God what He is not, and such negation is a denial of the applicability of the property in question. So, for Maimonides, "God is one" means "God is not not-one," the negation of the privation, and this latter is understood as the denial of the applicability of the very property in question. It is a category mistake to say of God that He is the kind of being who is one (or even "not many"), precisely because God is not the sort of being for whom this property applies.

Gersonides finds this *via negativa* unintelligible. Such absolute equivocation would render us mute and uncomprehending, and though Maimonides himself praises silence and human incapacity to describe the divine, Gersonides argues that in fact univocality is assumed in the negation itself. Contra Maimonides, if anything can be inferred from God's being "not not-one," then "one" must be used in its normal sense. For Gersonides, a kind of analogy obtains between divine and human nature. For example, God has knowledge ("is wise") in a primary, perfect way, and is the cause, the grounds, for human knowledge, which exists in a lesser degree. Aquinas lodged the same objection against Maimonides (*ST* I q. 13, art. 2).

**Samuel Lebens** rounds out the section with a response to Wettstein, and a way to understand biblical imagery and language. In reconciling poetic imagery with philosophical doctrine, Lebens points to the way metaphorical imagery works. While not translatable in so many words, while not expressive in propositional form, metaphors depend for their efficacy upon a "core set of background beliefs." The multifarious images of God (lover, judge, etc.) all work against the background of a life lived according to certain principles and beliefs. This doxastic element gives metaphorical imagery its power to move us. Metaphors "point" or hint in ways that reach beyond our discursive capacities, but are not untethered from them. In countering Wettstein, Lebens defends the *via negativa* as a way that, like metaphor itself, illuminates in spite of its literal falsehood.

## HOWARD WETTSTEIN

### "Poetic Imagery and Religious Belief" (1997/2000), in D. Shatz (ed.), *Philosophy and Faith: A Philosophy of Religion Reader* (2002)

Religions are systems of thought. So we tend to suppose. What certainly qualify as systems of thought are the products of philosophical theology. But there is some tension between such constellations of theological doctrine and the primary religious works—in the tradition on which I will be focused, the Hebrew Bible as understood through, and supplemented by, the Rabbis of the Talmud.

This tension is a product of the genesis of philosophical theology, the application of Greek philosophical thought to a very different tradition, one that emerged from a very different world. The primary religious works speak of God impressionistically. Their mode of description is as remote from definition as poetry is from mathematics. Their imagery is strikingly anthropomorphic.

Medieval religious philosophy, by contrast, disparages anthropomorphic description. While not quite an abstract entity, God is described, even defined, in abstract terms. The flavor of this is perhaps best conveyed by an example from the Christian philosophic tradition, St. Anselm's characterization of God as "the most perfect being." This is no mere honorific supplement to the anthropomorphic characterizations. It is a definition, one that subsumes specific divine perfections.

My aim here is to explore this tension with an eye to the fate or ultimate status of the doctrinal output of the philosophers. I will argue that theological doctrine is not a natural tool for thinking about Judaism, and insofar as Judaism is in this way representative, it's not a natural tool for thinking about religion. The "system of thought" model applies only with the application of force.

A. J. Heschel, an important American Jewish scholar and thinker, comments that much of his career was devoted to elucidating distinctively Jewish—as opposed to medieval Greek-inspired—modes of religious thought. "It is not an easy enterprise," Heschel notes.

The Hellenization of Jewish theology actually goes back to Philo [first century B.C.E] ... The impact of Philo on theology was radical. To oversimplify the matter, this approach would have Plato and Moses, for example, say the same thing, only Plato would say it in Greek. ... This view has had a great impact on much of Jewish medieval philosophy. They talk about God in the language of the Greeks.

(1997, 155–6)

Perhaps we should not suppose any failure on the part of the medievals to discern the distance between biblical-rabbinic and Greek-inspired modes of theological thought. Rather, for the medievals, this was the only way to make sense of the God of the tradition; the only way to square revealed and philosophic truth. One who wants to make philosophical sense of biblical-rabbinic remarks about God will inevitably do so in terms of one's own idiom and conceptual repertoire. It might seem, then, that the medievals only did what we all do, what is inevitable.

Still, as Heschel sees it, Philo's innovation violates something at the heart of the tradition. The introduction of Greek modes of philosophical thought encouraged the minimization or outright rejection of anthropomorphism. The God of the Hebrew Bible is, among other things, loving, nurturing/merciful, just, even angry. The Bible speaks of relations between people and God in the language of personal relationships. What grounds obligation to God, for example, is nothing very abstract. It is rather the community's historic and personal relation to God.

Such robustly anthropomorphic characterizations of God play an apparently indispensable role in the religious life. That God loves and cares are, for the religious practitioner, no throwaways. To attempt to relegate anthropomorphism to the status of a mere surface level phenomenon is to engage in an uphill battle. The burden of proof, given the character of religious life, surely seems on the other side. On the face of it, the distance between biblical/rabbinic and medieval philosophic thinking is enormous.

## *I. Poetic Imagery and Religious Belief*

### *1. Poetic Imagery*

Let's consider a somewhat lengthier list of anthropomorphic images of God in biblical/rabbinic literature: loving and nurturing, even if demanding, parent; benevolent judge/ruler who does not forget acts of loving kindness and generously and lovingly passes on the rewards to one's progeny; righteous judge who has access to our deepest secrets and who rewards and punishes accordingly; king of the universe, to be treated with lordly deference; bridegroom; husband; woman in labor; angry, regretful, even vengeful, remembering the sins of the parents and visiting them upon distant generations. When one scans this panoply of images, doctrine seems far away. Many of the images fail to yield anything like a characterization of God that could figure in doctrine. Among the images, moreover, are striking dissonances, hardly a phenomenon friendly to doctrine.

Clearly, conceptual refinement and coherence is not a high priority in the Bible and *Aggada* [nonlegal portions of rabbinic literature]. One has the sense that one is dealing with something more like poetry; sometimes poetry per se, as in Psalms, other times poetic, image-laden prose.

The virtues of this poetry, any poetry, do not include the discursive articulation characteristic of philosophy. The sorts of things one seeks from poetry are brilliance and depth of perception, suggestiveness; these inextricably bound with beauty of formulation. A collection of poetry on the subject of, say, love might include pieces reflecting different attitudes, moods, experiences. The poet seeks to illuminate the phenomena, sometimes casting them in a positive light, sometimes in a negative light. Many of the images, perhaps even the most beautiful and suggestive ones, do not yield easily to anything like a philosophically adequate idea. Nor would the images presumably constitute a coherent set. Imagine the folly of trying to derive any sort of theory of love from such poetry.

Doctrine—the theory of God, as it were—is equally remote from biblical/ rabbinic characterizations of God. The point holds not only for Psalms and the like; one of the fundamental ideas of Genesis, that humans were created in God's image, provides an example from biblical prose. The idea of reflecting divinity is potent, pregnant with meaning. But it is imagery, not doctrine. Its very magnificence— literary and religious—seems to place it at some distance from doctrine.

## 2. The Language of Poetry

One should not suppose that literary or poetic "imagery," any more than other forms of discourse, is necessarily connected with visual or mental images. Perhaps literary imagery is more likely than is, say, a weather report, to stimulate one to form an image in one's mind. But that is not essential. We do not refer to these figures of speech as imagery because they induce mental images. How to characterize literary imagery—why exactly we call it "imagery"—is more difficult, something I won't explore here. But simple examples of metaphor, one form of such imagery, make it clear that mental imaging is not essential. "Sea of troubles," mentioned below, will do.

Here's *The American Heritage Dictionary*'s definition of metaphor: A figure of speech in which a word or phrase that ordinarily designates one thing is used to designate another, thus making an implicit comparison, as in "a sea of troubles." When we explain metaphor to our students—say, in connection with some philosophical metaphor—metaphorical language, we suggest, is second best. We revert to it when we are not in a position to provide literal description, when we can't do better than mere analogies, implicit comparisons. What we don't mention—because we are not really thinking about poetry and literary language—is that in literary contexts, metaphor is often used for its own sake; it is not second best.

Why is metaphorical language sometimes preferable? It goes to the heart of literary imagery—here we go beyond metaphor—that the words resonate. One might speak about this phenomenon in terms of levels or layers of meaning. But "resonance" better conveys the lingering intimations, the echoes, the movement of the mind. In poetry or poetic prose, a single word or phrase may have multiple resonances. Sometimes one predominates, comes to the fore; others linger in the background. Other times one finds oneself moving between them, sometimes repeatedly. Resonances have many determinants: the occurrence of the expression in famous literary contexts; or other contexts, or other ways, in which the words are customarily used; or other words that sound alike or that come from the same root—these are a sample.

Where does meaning, significance, come in? We should not try to say what the meaning of a word in poetry consists in—a bad idea even in, as it were, straight philosophy of language. Instead, let's say that an expression's significance has everything to do with the networks of resonance in which it is embedded. A host of just such miscellaneous considerations, for example, figures in the significance of "God."

### 3. Mere Poetry?

Have I distanced the biblical/rabbinic literature too far from theological doctrine? If imagery is at the heart of biblical/rabbinic characterization of God, then what becomes of religious belief, of the tenets of religion?

Heschel writes, "In Biblical language the religious man is not called believer, as he is for example in Islam (*mu'min*), but *yere hashem* [one who stands in awe of the Lord]." (1959, 77) In the present context this is extremely interesting; it suggests that in thinking about religion we make too much of the doxastic dimension and too little of the affective. What I take from this is not that the concept of religious beliefs has no purchase in Judaism. Or that the religious life does not require appropriate beliefs. Rather belief is not at the heart of the matter; one gets a misleading picture of Jewish religiosity if one's focus is a set of beliefs. There is an analogy with the question of linguistic meaning in poetry. It's not that a linguistic expression in poetry does not mean what it ordinarily does, say, in a newspaper article. But that dimension of its meaning is often not at the heart of its function in poetry.

What then do I make of religious belief, given my emphasis on poetic imagery? My answer is that likening biblical/rabbinic remarks to poetry certainly does not imply or even suggest that these remarks involve no beliefs, no real commitments; that they are, as one might say, "just poetry." For such commitment-neutrality is surely not true of poetry itself.

Poetry may assume, for example, straightforward factual information about the world, that there are people, that they behave in certain ways, and so on. Second and more interestingly, poetry may be committal even where there is no way to formulate the relevant belief in straightforward, literal language. If we wish to formulate such belief, we do one of two things. We can approximate, extracting a piece of the picture, one that is propositionally manageable, and attributing that piece. Alternatively, we can mimic the poet, attributing belief using the very imagery she used—or related imagery. This may be a philosophical no-no; it will strike some as bizarre to suppose that such a thing counts as belief. Here as elsewhere, as Wittgenstein urged, philosophy would do well to look at actual practice rather than think about what it must be like.

In the religious literature that is my focus, many things are assumed about the world, many beliefs can be distilled from the imagery. All the old standards, as it were: belief in God, in God creating the world, creating people in his image, freeing his people from Egyptian bondage, revealing himself to Moses and giving the Torah on Mount Sinai, and the like. How should we think about these beliefs? Are they like the straightforward propositional claims that we can often distill from poetry or are they of the second variety mentioned, claims that remain at the level of imagery? When we report someone as having such and such religious belief, to what extent are we discursively articulating propositional content; to what extent are we ourselves using religious imagery?

I'm intrigued by the idea that in speaking of the divine, intimation is the rule. Religious belief, one might then say, lives at the level of imagery. Belief ascription would then be a matter of utilizing the believer's imagery in characterizing his belief. However, I am doubtful that things are this simple and uniform, that there is a single story to tell about religious belief per se. Clearly, the matter requires much more thought, with detailed scrutiny of examples.

To return to my philosophic heterodoxy, what sort of belief is it that has no propositional content? In fact, on grounds that are completely independent of the current discussion, I think that the usual sort of philosophic thinking about belief—the propositional content model—is misconceived. Indeed, that the propositional content model is not consonant with my emphasis on religious imagery is fine with me. This is not the place to motivate my contrary conception. But we can at least see how it works for the case of religious belief.

Let's distinguish two different ways of appreciating, say, the ideas, for example, the idea that we reflect God's image. One may appreciate this powerfully suggestive idea from the outside, as it were. Call this the Bible-as-literature approach; here one is sensitive to the idea's significance for one's religious tradition. Alternatively, one may make the divine reflection idea one's own, see the world through its imagery, declare it, for example, in prayer. The question is whether one signs on, as it were; whether the poetic resonances reflect one's own take on the world.

If one wholeheartedly endorses the divine reflection idea, then we may use this imagery to characterize her approach to the world. That is what we do when we ascribe belief, when we say, for example, that she believes that human beings reflect God's image. Don't think of this as pinning on the believer belief in another fact; it is rather using her preferred imagery to characterize her mind.

To attribute a belief is thus to kidnap a piece of the person's favored imagery, to absorb it into a different genre. It's to use the image in a new way. To ascribe such a belief to someone is like saying "This image plays a fundamental role for her."

Involved here is a sliding scale, from those parts of the imagery that are more serious and fundamental to those that are less so. Consider the imagery of God's right arm. It's as if one kidnaps the imagery of God's right arm, and then learns that one can't make straightforward use of it; it fails to go quietly into the belief ascription genre. This is so because it is an image we are happy to let go. At least we are after we learn from it. Religious Jews believe that God created the world, but not that he has a right arm. The latter is not part of the imagery with which they approach the world. It is not a constituent of the story that serves as a backdrop to their lives. So, as our belief reporting practices go, it is inappropriate to use this imagery to keep track of their religious whereabouts. This is not to say that the image has no power for them.

## II. Theology

### 1. Philosophical Ambition

The medievals, blessed with a more-or-less stable first philosophy, lived philosophically charmed lives. There is some parallel in our attitude to, say, physics. We are not sure of the details of our physics, not confident that we have final answers, but pretty sure we are in the ballpark, playing by the right rules, very confident of some general outlines. Perhaps the medievals were even more confident about philosophy. They were, after all, looking backward towards the philosophers, while we are looking forward to a somewhat uncertain future, humbled by the history of past scientific upheavals.

Possession of philosophic truth grounded in a stable first philosophy makes many things possible: philosophy providing foundations for religious belief, philosophy clarifying the content of revealed religions, philosophy determining the nature of God, or perhaps determining that God's nature is demonstrably, as it were, beyond us. Doctrine, the propositional articulation of religious fundamentals, is at home in such a setting.

A doctrine approach need not deny what I've been arguing about the impressionism of biblical/rabbinic characterizations of God. One might argue—as Maimonides indeed suggests—that it is only because of philosophically available truths about God that we are in any position to discriminate among the images, to know which to take seriously and which not. The ordinary person has no independent access to God, so how can he discern biblical talk of God's unity and God's creation of the world from the merely figurative attribution of bodily properties to God? Absent our access to philosophical truth and we would be religiously deprived.

This seems an extreme view, one that gives more independent weight to philosophy than many of the medievals, and probably more than Maimonides himself in other moods, or literary modes. But it nicely dramatizes the contrast with our own philosophic environment. The medieval conception (or cluster of them) of how religion and philosophy might join forces seems to many of us inapplicable nowadays. The crucial philosophic truth complement seems missing in action. It is not only that the traditional proofs of God's existence are in disrepute. Nor is it merely the lack of a received view—or even a widely accepted consensus—in philosophy, substantively or methodologically. For many of us philosophy simply cannot be brought to bear on religion the way that the medievals supposed.

One might assume that this makes it natural for us to think with the Rabbis, who also carry on without a first philosophy. However, the tradition, as we have it, has acquired much medieval philosophy, much doctrine, at least semi-officially. This of course was Heschel's gripe. If we follow his lead, trying to recover what he called Jewish as opposed to Greek ways of thinking about Judaism, we are indeed led straight back to a biblical/rabbinic mode of religious expression.

To reject medieval philosophic ambition is not to suggest that philosophic training is irrelevant to the understanding of religious thought, Jewish or other. In philosophy we are trained to think carefully, analytically, to be sensitive to conceptual distinctions, to extend our thinking, as it were, both vertically, persistently pressing beneath the surface, and horizontally, taking a comprehensive view of the domain. There is no reason why such virtues would be irrelevant to the understanding of religion and religious ideas. But this is a far cry from the sort of access to philosophic truth that fuels the medieval project.

## 2. Poetic Inconsistency

Why not start from the imagery and try to figure out what's going on with the leading figure? One of the aims of such theorizing would be to make sense of the tremendous multiplicity of roles that God plays in the imagery. What is this all about? What sort of being underlies these images and why are they fitting images for this being?

I begin with an example that shares some features with our situation. In both we begin with ideas that stand in conflict with one another. In both something short of theoretical resolution seems natural and satisfying. Indeed, theoretical resolution seems out of place.

There is a Hasidic adage that a person should carry in his pocket two pieces of paper with dissonant messages: "I am but dust and ashes," and "The world was created for me." I have often thought that the really difficult trick is to get both on the same piece of paper; to live a life that is not so compartmentalized, that integrates the superficially incompatible messages.

Maurice Friedman suggested to me that it would be better to leave them on separate sheets, maybe even in different pockets. The imagery of a single piece of paper suggested to Friedman what he took to be a bad idea: that the philosophic job is to render these insights coherent, to articulate an inclusive principle. What one needs is rather a kind of practical skill, the ability to negotiate experience respecting both truths—that is, both images, each of which illuminates human experience.

This example (and others like it) exhibits two features that are salient for us. First, there are conflicting ideas, each of which possesses a kind of truth or validity. Second, the tension is resolved not by discovering a higher order principle, but the acquisition of a practical ability or skill, a kind of "knowing how." The agent develops a sense of balance, the ability to call upon the idea appropriate to the situation at hand.

How does the first feature apply to the sundry characterizations of God? Think of the diverse, sometimes conflicting, images of God as profiles, as views from a perspective. Each profile is crucial for the religious life. Each has validity. Each illuminates in its own way. There are situations in which the image of God as nurturing parent is salient. In other situations other imagery may be salient, perhaps God as an impartial judge, or as a friend, or as creator of heaven and earth, or as one you have wronged, or as the parent of one you have wronged.

There are still other situations in which two or more profiles of God are somehow salient. Some of these may be very pleasant; as if one were taking in several varieties of beauty at once, or through several sensory modalities. Some of these situations, though, may be troubling, confusing. Such situations, as Moshe Halbertal and Avishai Margalit point out in the first chapter of their excellent discussion in *Idolatry* (1992), are analogous to one who works for his father-in-law, who also happens to be his teacher, landlord, and plays unnamed other roles in his life. One can readily imagine situations that become quite complicated and confusing. One doesn't quite know where one stands.

Let's turn to the second highlighted feature: the resolution of the tension between the ideas takes place on the plane of action rather than theory; it involves a practical ability or skill. Theoretical resolution in the form of a comprehensive principle seems unnecessary. This is of course the critical issue in the present context. For theoretical resolution—at least a leading candidate for such a resolution—would involve an account of the entity that lies behind the profiles, an account of how these could possibly be perspectives on the same being.

How does this apply to biblical imagery? The story here is more complicated than in the two examples. The religious life involves a combination of practical abilities or skills that are grounded in understanding, intuitive if not articulate. The religious life also involves habits, behavioral and affective. All of this requires education, training, and practice. As is our way with such things, some are more given to it, more gifted at it, some will take to it more easily than others, others may come along more slowly, but may attain greater heights in the end.

One stage in religious development is understanding the many different human relationships in terms of which these profiles of God are formulated: developing a sense of what it is to relate to another as child to parent, as the subject to monarch, as defendant to judge, as creature to creator, as lover, as friend, and so on. Developing a sense of ease with their directions reversed is also of great utility: parent to child, monarch to subject, and so on. The more vivid one's grasp, the more deeply one sees into these relationships, the farther along one is in this stage of the training. Some of this understanding requires the accumulation—sometimes years—of experience. This education is a lifelong affair.

The next step—not that these need to be separated in time—is the application of this growing understanding to the relationships between people and God. One needs to think about and practice seeing oneself in relation to God as child to parent, with the variety of complications that entails; and to think about it from both sides of the relationship. And as lover to lover, friend to friend, judge to judge, and all the rest.

The payoff of one's work—the propriety and caring for others, the comfort and solace, the elevation and dignity that are the concomitants of developed religious character—depend upon one's ability to negotiate the world feeling and acting in ways appropriate to just such relationships. One needs to feel and act as if one has a Godly parent, a Godly lover or friend, a Godly judge who sees all, a creator of inexorable laws of nature that proceed as if we didn't exist, even—I suspect—an angry, even vengeful Godly ruler—this last being more complicated and controversial.

Of course, one doesn't feel and act in these ways all the time, or all at the same time. Part of the skill—what takes training, practice, and experience—is to call upon, or be called upon by, the appropriate image at the appropriate time, sometimes a single image, sometimes multiple ones. The latter can be confusing, disconcerting, as Halbertal and Margalit point out, and it can be wonderful, sometimes both. At the death of a parent, for example, many of these images may strike: God as creator of inexorable laws of nature; God as friend and comforter; (and since belonging and community becomes so important at such times) God as focal point—glue, as it were—of Jewish community, a community that extends horizontally– the present community—and vertically—the community over time; and perhaps others.

Ritualized prayer—something that also takes training and practice if it is to be more than mechanical (and even if it is merely mechanical)—provides another example of the sometimes confusing but wonderful multiplicity. In prayer, when it works, many of the magnificent images are summoned. One is provided with the opportunity of experiencing these relationships and of reflecting upon them, seeing more deeply into them, seeing new aspects all the time.

That there are multiple images, that they seem discordant—properties that make theories seem very far away—are thus rationalized. We don't do so by finding a theoretical account of God that puts the images in their right place. Rather the miscellany, the mixed multitude of robustly anthropomorphic ideas and images, facilitate the religious life.

I will conclude with a brief return to the concept of religious belief. As I explained my approach to religious belief, the imagery that plays a fundamental role for the believer finds its way into the report of the person's belief. Belief lives at the level of imagery. I want to integrate that idea with what we have been exploring most recently, the multiplicity of discordant images. The transition from the imagery as it functions for the religious person to the imagery as it functions in the report of her belief is a very significant one. For in the original context of poetry, or image-laden prose, consistency of imagery is hardly a virtue. Indeed, the very multiplicity and variety facilitate the religious life. But once the imagery has found its way into the context of belief, into a report of someone's belief, inconsistency becomes a substantial liability. This reflects the utility of belief talk, what it does for us.

The belief idiom is a fundamental tool for locating people cognitively, for tracking their cognitive whereabouts, their take on how things stand. For that very reason, it is quite sensitive to matters of consistency. To see this, don't think of beliefs about religious matters, but about the weather, or about history, or elementary particles. When, however, we speak of belief with respect to a domain in which imagery plays such a fundamental role, the idiom has limitations. Along with talk of belief comes the suggestion that it's not a good thing to have conflicting ones. And that simply is not true, at least not in an unqualified way, of the domain in question.

I have been exploring a perspective according to which doctrine is not the heart of the religious sensibility. Indeed even religious belief—and even when not viewed as doctrinal—is not at the core. What bearers of a religious tradition have been given are directions for living the religious life. The essential constituent of such a life is a system of communal and individual practice, both ritual and ethical, informed by a narrative history interwoven with religious imagery. The imagery, in all its variety and inconsistency, along with the historical narrative provide many dimensions of meaning to the otherwise abstract and elusive imagery. The constellation of practices, historical narrative, and imagery issue in a distinctive kind of life with its own substantial virtues and rewards. It seems reductive and misleading to represent this as a system of doctrine, a set of well-formed beliefs, a system of thought.

## MOSES MAIMONIDES (1138–1204)

### *The Guide of the Perplexed* (1190)

#### *Book 1, Chapters 57–8* (tr. **Rabin**)

*Religious Language and Divine Attributes*

CHAPTER 57

It is obvious that existence is an accident affecting that which exists. It is, therefore, a concept superadded to the essence of that which exists. This is an incontrovertible fact. Whenever the existence of a thing is due to a cause, its existence is a concept superadded to its essence. But whatever possesses an existence not due to any cause—and such is God alone, for this is what we mean when we say that God exists necessarily—the existence of such a thing is its essence and character and its essence is its existence. Such a thing is not subject to the accident of existing, so that its existence should be a concept superadded to its essence. He exists necessarily and perpetually, not because existence came to Him from without or affected Him as an accident. He therefore exists without existence, and similarly lives without life, is powerful without power, and knows without knowledge. All these derive from a single concept without any multiplicity, as we shall explain later on.

It must also be clearly realized that unity and multiplicity are accidents affecting the thing which exists insofar as it is many or one. This is proved in the *Metaphysics* [5.6, 10.2]. As number is not the thing counted, so unity is not the thing which is one. All these are accidents of the class of discrete quantity which affect the numerable things in existence, because they are subject to such accidents. As for that which exists necessarily and is truly simple without being in any way liable to compositeness, as it is absurd to think of it as affected by the accident of plurality, so it is absurd to think of it as affected by the accident of unity. I mean to say by this that His unity is not a concept superadded to His essence, but He is one without unity.

These subtle concepts, which almost pass the comprehension of our minds, are not readily expressed by words. Words are altogether one of the main causes of error, because whatever language we employ, we find the restrictions it imposes on our expression extremely disturbing. We cannot even picture this concept except by using imprecise language. When we desire to indicate that the Divinity is not plural, all we are able to say is that He is one, although both, 'one' as well as 'many,' are terms of quantity. We must therefore compress our meaning and guide the mind to the proper understanding of our intention by saying 'one, but not by unity.' It is just the same when we use the word 'ancient' to indicate that He did not come into being. The lack of precision in our use of 'ancient' is obvious, since one can only apply the term to something affected by time, which is an accident supervening to movement, which implies a body. Furthermore it belongs to the class of relative terms. When you use 'ancient' of the accident of time, it is like saying 'long' and 'short' with regard to the accident of one-dimensional extension. One cannot really employ the terms 'ancient' and 'come into being' of anything to which the accident of time does not apply, any more than one can say of sweetness that it is either crooked or straight, or of a sound that it is salty or unseasoned. Such things are evident to one who has some practice in assessing the true meaning of ideas and expresses them with full rational comprehension, if he isolates them properly and does not employ the vague sense suggested by the words in common usage.

Wherever you find the words 'first' and 'last' employed in Scripture in speaking of God [e.g., Isa. 44:6], this is to be taken in the same way as the passages where He is described as having eyes or ears. The meaning of those terms is that God is not affected by change and in no way ever acquires new properties, not that He falls under the category of time, so that some analogy might result between Him and things subject to time, and it can be said of Him that He is first and last. All these terms are 'according to the parlance of men' [Berakhoth 31b]. So, too, when we say one we mean thereby that He has no peer, not that His essence is affected by the concept of unity.

CHAPTER 58

You must understand that the description of God by means of negative terms is the only sound description which contains no element of loose terminology, and implies altogether in no circumstances a lack of perfection in God. His description by positive terms, on the other hand, comports polytheism and a lack of perfection in God in the way we have demonstrated.

First I must explain how negative terms can in a manner be attributes, and in what way they differ from positive attributes. Then I shall show how it is that we have no way of describing Him except by negative terms and no others. An attribute is not something specifying the thing described in such a way that it cannot share the attribute with anything else. On the contrary, an attribute may describe something even if it shares that attribute with other things and is not peculiar to it. For instance, if you see a man from a distance and ask: what is that which is visible? the reply may be: some living being. This is without any doubt a correct description of the thing seen, though it does not set it aside as a peculiar thing from all others. Some specification does, however, result, namely, that the thing seen is not an object of the vegetable or mineral class. In the same manner also, if there is a man in a certain house, and you know that there is some object in it, but not what it is, you may ask: what is in this house? and may receive the reply: there isn't a vegetable or mineral object in it. Then you obtain some specification and know that a living being is in the house, though you do not know what kind of living being it is. From this point of view the negative attributes have something in common with positive attributes, because they must necessarily produce some specification, even though this specification means merely the removal of the negated items from among those that we had before imagined un-negated. The difference between negative and positive attributes is in this, that positive attributes, even when they do not specify, indicate some part of the totality of the thing which we desire to know. This may be either a part of its substance or one of its accidents. The negative attributes do not in any manner tell us anything about the essence of the thing which we wish to know as it is, except incidentally, as in our example.

After these prefatory remarks I state that it has been proved that God exists by necessity and that He is non-composite, as we shall prove, and we can apprehend only that He is, not what He is. It is therefore meaningless that He should have any positive attribute, since the fact that He is is not something outside of what He is, so that the attribute might indicate one of these two. Much less can what He is be of a composite character, so that the attribute could indicate one of the parts. Even less can He be substrate to accidents, so that the attribute could indicate these. Thus there is no scope for any positive attributes in any way whatsoever.

It is the negative attributes which we must employ to guide our mind to that which we ought to believe concerning God, because from them no plurality can result in any way. They can guide the mind to the utmost limit of what man can apprehend of God. For instance, it has been proved to us that something must exist apart from those objects which our senses apprehend and which our reason can encompass with its knowledge. We say about this thing that it exists, meaning that it is absurd to say that He does not exist. Then we apprehend that its existence is not like the existence of, say, the elements, which are lifeless bodies, and consequently say that He lives, meaning that God is not subject to death. Then we apprehend that this being is also not like the existence of heaven, which is a living body, and consequently we say that He is not a body. Then we apprehend that this being is not like the existence of an Intelligence, which is neither a body nor subject to death, but is due to a cause, and consequently say that God is eternal, meaning that there is no cause which called Him into being. Then we apprehend that the existence of this Being, which is its essence, is not only sufficient for that Being itself to exist, but many existences emanate from it. It is, however, not like the emanation of heat from the fire or the automatic connection between light and the sun, but it is an emanation which He perpetually keeps going, giving it a constant flow arranged according to a wise plan, as we shall show. We shall say on account of these arrangements that He is omnipotent, omniscient, and possessed of will. By these attributes we mean to say that He is neither powerless nor ignorant nor distracted or disinterested. When we say He is not powerless, we mean that His existence is sufficient to bring into existence things other than Himself. When we say He is not ignorant, we mean that He apprehends, i.e., lives, for whatever apprehends lives. When we say He is not distracted or disinterested, we mean that all those existing things run along an ordered and planned course, not without supervision and coming into being just by chance, just like anything which a person possessed of will plans with purpose and will. Then we apprehend that there is no other being like this one. When we, therefore, say He is One, we mean thereby to deny any plurality.

Thus it becomes clear that every attribute with which we describe Him is either an attribute of action or has the purport of negating its own absence if our intention thereby is to apprehend His essence rather than His works. These negative terms are also not used absolutely of God, but only in the manner mentioned before, that one denies of a thing something that by the nature of things could not exist in it, as when we say of a wall that it does not see.

You know well, dear reader, that the heaven is a moving body, and that we have measured it in yards and feet and have complete data on the extent of its parts and of most of its movements, and yet our minds are completely unable to apprehend what it is, although we know that it must necessarily possess matter and form, but not matter of the kind that is with us. For this reason we can only describe it by indefinite nouns, not by definite positive terms. We say that the heaven is not light and not heavy, does not suffer action and is therefore not receptive to impressions, it has no taste or smell, and similar negative terms. All this is because we are ignorant of that kind of matter. What will be the position then of our minds when they endeavor to apprehend that which is free from matter, non-composite to the utmost degree, of necessary existence, has no cause and is not attained by anything additional to its perfect essence—the meaning of its perfection being the denial of all shortcomings, as explained before? We can only apprehend that He is; that there exists a Being unlike any other being which He brought into existence, having nothing whatsoever in common with them, who has no plurality in Him, and is not powerless to bring into existence things other than He himself, and that His relation to the world is that of the captain to the ship. This also is not a true relation, and not even remotely resembles the real one, but it serves to guide the mind to the idea that God governs the universe, meaning that He supports it and keeps its order as it should be. This point will be explained in a more concrete manner.

Praise be to Him who is such that when our minds try to visualize His essence, their power of apprehending becomes imbecility; when they study the connection between His works and His will, their knowledge becomes ignorance; and when our tongues desire to declare His greatness by descriptive terms, all eloquence becomes impotence and imbecility.

## GERSONIDES (1288–1344)

### *The Wars of the Lord* (1329)

### *Book 3, Chapter 3* (tr. Feldman)

*A Critical Examination of the Arguments of Maimonides on Divine Attributes*

It is proper that we determine whether Maimonides' efforts to counter all the possible arguments of the philosophers who differ from him are successful before we examine whether or not these arguments are correct and, if they are correct, whether [or not] they entail what the philosophers concluded from them. For if Maimonides' replies to these arguments are adequate, there will be no need for us to examine them by means of another method.

We claim that the first thing to do is to examine whether the term "knowledge" is equivocal with respect to divine and human knowledge, such that the difference between them is as Maimonides thought—i.e., that divine knowledge is the opposite of our knowledge, so that what we consider to be opinion, error, or confusion is knowledge with respect to God—or whether the equivocation involved here is such that this difference cannot be such [as Maimonides claimed]. It seems to us that Maimonides' position on this question of divine cognition is not implied by any philosophical principles; indeed, reason denies this view, as I will show. It seems rather that theological considerations have forced him to this view. The question of whether the Torah requires this doctrine will be considered after our philosophical analysis of this problem.

That philosophical argument rules out Maimonides' position on this topic will be demonstrated as follows. It would seem that God's knowledge is equivocal with respect to our knowledge in the sense of prior and posterior predication, that is, the term "knowledge" is predicated of God *primarily* and of others *secondarily*. For in God knowledge is identical with His essence, whereas in anyone else knowledge is the effect of God's knowledge. In such a case the term is applied to God in a prior sense and to other things in a posterior sense. The same is true with respect to such terms as "exists," "one," "essence," and the like, i.e., they are predicated of God primarily and of other things secondarily. For His existence, unity, and essence belong to Him essentially, whereas the existence, unity, and essence of every [other] existent thing emanate from Him. Now when something is of this kind, the predicate applies to it in a prior sense, whereas the predicate applies in a posterior sense to the other things that are called by it insofar as they are given this property directly by the substance that has the property in the prior sense. All of this is obvious to the reader of this treatise, and it will be discussed in detail in Book 5. Hence, it seems that the difference between divine and human cognition is a difference in terms of greater perfection, for this is what is implied by prior and posterior predication. Now if what we have said is true, and since it is obvious that the most perfect knowledge is more true with respect to specificity and determinateness, it would follow that God's knowledge is more true with respect to specificity and determinateness. Hence, it cannot be that what is considered knowledge with respect to God can be called "belief," "error," or "confusion" with respect to man.

We can show in another way that the difference between divine and human cognition is not as Maimonides thought. It is evident that we proceed to affirm attributes of God from that with which we are familiar. That is, we say that God knows because of the knowledge found in us. For example, since we apprehend that the knowledge belonging to our intellect is a perfection of our intellect—without which it could not be an intellect in act [i.e., perfect]—we predicate of God that He knows by virtue of the fact, which we have demonstrated concerning Him, that God is indubitably an intellect in act. It is self-evident that when a predicate is affirmed of some object because it is true of some other thing, it is not predicated of both things in an absolutely equivocal sense, for between things that are absolutely equivocal there is no analogy. For example, just as it would be impossible to infer that man is intelligent from the fact that body is a continuous magnitude, so, too, would it be impossible [even] if we were to posit [arbitrarily] a term that is predicable of both [attributes] *intelligent* and *continuous* in an absolutely equivocal sense. Hence, it is clear that the term "knowledge" is not completely equivocal when applied to God and man. Since this term cannot be applied univocally with respect to God and man, it must be predicated in the sense of priority and posteriority. The same holds for other attributes that are predicated of both God and man. Thus, the difference between divine and human knowledge is one of greater perfection, albeit exceedingly so, and this type of knowledge is more precise and clear. In general, the kind of equivocation with respect to divine and human knowledge is analogous to the equivocation involved in the attribute of essence in God and in the acquired intellect among men, since the knowledge and the knower are numerically identical (as has been previously explained). And just as God's essence is more perfect than the essence of the acquired intellect in us, so, too, is His knowledge [more perfect] than our knowledge. . . .

Indeed, it can be verified that the attributes of God are predicated of Him primarily but of other things secondarily, even though it be conceded that there is no similarity between God and His creatures. There are several predicates that are predicated of some things primarily and others secondarily in this way [i.e., even though these things are not similar]. For example, the term "existent" is predicated of a substance primarily but secondarily of accidents, as has been shown in the *Metaphysics*; yet it is evident that there is no similarity between substance and its accidents. It is important to realize that there are attributes that *must* be attributed to God, for example, that He is a substance. The term "substance," however, is not predicated of God and other beings univocally but [of God] primarily and of everything else secondarily. For, that which makes all things describable by some attribute in such a way that they are [truly] describable by that attribute— [namely], by virtue of what these things have acquired essentially and primarily [i.e., directly] from it—is itself more appropriately called by that term. Now God makes all other things in such a way that they are substances, for He endows them with their substantiality; accordingly, He is more appropriately describable as "substance." Moreover, the divine substance is self-subsistent, whereas all other substances derive their existence from something else, and whatever is self-subsistent is more appropriately described as "substance" than something whose existence derives from another thing . . .

On the basis of this entire discussion, it is now evident that reason shows that the term "knowledge" is predicated of God primarily and of creatures secondarily, not absolutely equivocally, and that the principles [of religious language] adopted by Maimonides in order to remove the objections of the philosophers concerning the problem of divine knowledge are not acceptable.

## SAMUEL LEBENS

## "Reconciling Imagery and Doctrine"

### *Introduction*

For Howard Wettstein (2002), the imagery of the Hebrew Bible, Talmud, and Midrash does not sit well with the doctrines of medieval Jewish philosophy. Since Jewish imagery is inconsistent, Wettstein fears that it is going to serve as a shaky foundation for a body of coherent theological doctrine. Wettstein's response – the response that this paper questions – is to jettison the entire project of building a coherent body of doctrine. For Wettstein, a healthy religious life is fueled by its imagery and not by its doctrine; unlike doctrine, imagery does not need to be consistent.

### *Profiles of God*

Wettstein counsels us to think of the conflicting images of Jewish lore as 'profiles', or 'views from a perspective'. One is reminded of the Indian story of the blind men and the elephant. They have been told that they are all touching the same object. The first man, holding the elephant's leg, concludes that they are holding the trunk of a tree. The second man, holding the elephant's trunk, disagrees, thinking it to be a large snake. The third man, touching the elephant's side, argues that they are touching a great big wall. Sometimes God appears to us as a lover, and sometimes as a ruler. That is because we are like the blind men in the story; we cannot see the whole of God and cannot arrive at an 'inclusive principle' to describe discursively what it is that is causing these disparate appearances.

But what we can do, Wettstein counsels, is to cultivate a set of practical skills: (1) understanding the various relationships mentioned by our imagery (the relationship of lover, parent, ruler, etc.); (2) seeing God in terms of these relationships, and thinking 'about [God] from both sides of the relationship'; and (3) the skill to 'call upon, or be called upon by, the appropriate image, at the appropriate time, sometimes a single image, sometimes multiple ones'. For Wettstein, a theoretical answer to the question as to what sort of God can underwrite so many profiles is beyond us. Our perspectives are inherently limited like the men in the story. But even if we cannot arrive at a full answer to the question, perhaps we can say more than Wettstein does.

### Meaning and Pointing

Let us turn to a Midrash from *Shir ha-Shirim Raba* (1:8) about the power of Solomon's metaphors:

> R. Hanina said: it [metaphor] is like a deep well full of water. And its waters were cold, and sweet, and good. But nobody was able to drink from it. A man came along and tied string to string, and rope to rope, and drew from the well and drank. Thereafter, everybody began to draw and drink. So too, [moving] from word to word, and from metaphor to metaphor, Solomon was able to understand the secrets of the Torah.

The content of the Torah lies beyond the reach of any word; and even beyond the reach of any metaphor.[1] You have to tie metaphor to metaphor, and only then will you be able to access the water. Let us call an *entrenched* metaphor any metaphor that cannot be faithfully cashed out without reference to other metaphors. 'Thomas has a cold heart', translates pretty cleanly to, 'Thomas lacks compassion'; thus, the cold-heart metaphor was not entrenched. But when Romeo describes Juliet as the sun (Act 2, Scene 2), he says something that we struggle to translate without recourse to other metaphors: she sustains him; she gives him warmth and light; life without her would be dark. A metaphor is entrenched when its explanation requires at least one other metaphor.

The chain of metaphors initiated by an entrenched metaphor supervenes upon a chain of associations: the mind moves from the sun, to warmth and light, and from there to sustenance, etc. A chain of associations moves in an order; it is, in some sense or other, a *directional* affair. This gives rise to the notion that a chain can *point* towards something. One metaphor might not be able to express the inexpressible, but a chain of metaphors can point one in the right direction, just as a chain of ropes can reach the water that lies beyond the grasp of any individual rope.

For Donald Davidson (1978), words have only a *literal* meaning. Romeo's words mean that Juliet is numerically identical to the big burning ball of gas that seems to rise above the eastern horizon every morning. To ask, in addition, for the *metaphorical* meaning of Romeo's utterance is to expect some new words in return. But if there were words that Romeo could have said in order to express literally what he was trying to say, he would not have been forced into using a metaphor.

How many facts or propositions are conveyed by a photograph? None, an infinity, or one great unstatable fact? Bad question. A picture is not worth a thousand words, or any other number. Words are the wrong currency to exchange for a picture.

(Davidson 1978, 46–7)

Words mean just what words mean – Juliet is a burning ball of gas – but what we really want to know is, what was Romeo's *point*? What sort of great unstatable fact, or ineffable truth, or truths, was Romeo pointing towards? And of course, we cannot put the answer, literally, into words; for (literal) word use is the wrong currency. There is not always a neatly delineated and accessible meaning to be expressed, even if there is always a *point*. It is not what Romeo's words meant that really mattered here – for their meaning is obvious and absurd – what matters is what Romeo was trying to *point* to with the use of his words. We must distinguish between the meaning of an utterance, and its point, and between the meaning of an utterance and what that utterance points to.

In the story about the blind men, each person's statement had a kernel of truth at its heart. The elephant is not a tree, but its leg is certainly tree-like. On Wettstein's suggestion, God is not a King, but some profiles of his are certainly King-like. Rabbi Hanina can deny that. The content of religious imagery might be completely false, with no kernel of truth at its heart whatsoever. God is no more King-like than Juliet resembles the star at the center of our solar system. Rather, something about *saying* 'God is king,' in the right circumstances, despite its falsehood, can point you and your audience in the direction of certain ineffable theological truths.

### The First Hint of a Resolution

Apophaticism is the view that language cannot say very much, or perhaps anything at all, about God. Negative theology (the *via negativa*) can be treated as a special and distinct branch of apophaticism, according to which one cannot say anything about what God *is*, but *can* say a lot about what God *isn't*; and thus, via a series of negations, God can be described (negatively).

We should note that the *via negativa* of Maimonides proceeds in a very specific order. First we deny that God has eyes, recognizing that the Bible's talk of his eyes is supposed to indicate, to the vulgar, that God can see. Then we deny that God can see, recognizing that our earlier claim was merely indicating, to the slightly less vulgar, that he has knowledge of our actions.[2] Then we deny that he has particular knowledge of our actions, recognizing that our earlier claim was merely intended to communicate, to the still less vulgar, his perfection.[3] By telling us all of the things that we *should not* be saying about God, and by doing so in a specific *order*, we are led in a direction of ever-diminishing vulgarity that transcends the limits of language, towards a God who cannot be spoken about discursively. Where Maimonides *points* with a chain of negations, R. Hanina thinks that religious imagery *points* with a chain of associations; both point to that which cannot be said. Already, the divide between Jewish lore and philosophy seems less wide.

## Concerns with Apophaticism

There is good reason to be concerned when one commences to talk about something that cannot be spoken about. If it cannot be spoken about, then what is one doing speaking about it? In brief, this is Alvin Plantinga's main concern with apophaticism (Plantinga 1980, 2000).

Initially, Plantinga seemed content to exempt the *via negativa* from his general criticism of apophaticism. The *via negativa* does not say that one cannot say/know anything about God. That would be absurd. Instead, the *via negativa* accepts that we *do* know things about God, but that what we know is 'essentially negative'; that is to say, 'there are no properties such that we know of God that he has them, although there are some properties that we know he lacks' (Plantinga 1980, 19). If one couples this view with the view that there are only positive properties, and not negative ones, such that 'there is such a thing as the property of being a horse, but no such thing as the property of not being a horse' (Ibid.), then, as far as Plantinga is concerned, the *via negativa* is safe from the charge of incoherence. One is not saying that God has the property of having no properties, since there is no commitment to the existence of negative properties.

Plantinga's attack has grown stronger over the years. In his *Warranted Christian Belief* (2000), he considers John Hick's attempt to formulate a coherent kind of apophaticism. For Hick, if there were an infinite, transcendent, and ultimate being, then the only properties it could have of which we could have a grasp are (a) formal properties and (b) negative properties. Plantinga attacks this suggestion on a number of fronts.[4] Foremost is his doubt that one can coherently draw a distinction between negative and positive concepts. Hick wishes to say that being infinite is a negative property, defined as not having limits. But isn't it equally intuitive to say that *being infinite* is a positive property and that *having limits* is negative?

The positive-negative distinction is hazy. This threatens the coherence of Hick's whole thesis. But it also threatens the *via negativa* that Plantinga (in 1980) had initially exempted from his critique. If one cannot make the distinction between positive and negative concepts, then one will not have the resources to sustain the claim that negative properties don't exist, and thus one will not have the conceptual resources to prevent the position from collapsing into the paradoxical thesis that God has the property of having no properties.

## A Plantinga-Proof Apophaticism

Elsewhere I have argued that Plantinga is unduly critical of apophaticism.[5] I accept that apophatic discourse about an indescribable God is absurd. But so also is the claim that Juliet is the sun. Sometimes by the power of metaphor, and sometimes via other, under-researched mechanisms, falsehood has the power to be, in some sense or other, *illuminating*.

For Hilary Putnam (1982, chap. 1), a brain in a vat, who has had no contact with brains outside of the vat, or with the 'unenvatted' world, is unable to say that she is a brain in a vat. She speaks a different language from ours. When she says, 'I am a brain in a vat', she is speaking vat-English, not real English. Her use of the word 'vat' does not refer to earthly vats, because she has had no direct causal contact with them. A skeptical brain in a vat might have the suspicion that all she experiences is an illusion organized by other-worldly scientists. She has the feeling that she might be a brain in a vat. Accepting Putnam's arguments, she realizes that she does not actually have the linguistic apparatus necessary for expressing the situation she thinks she might be in; she cannot even mentally represent to herself the situation she wants to represent, because she can only utter the vat-English sentence, 'I am a brain in a vat', and not the relevant English sentence. But she might still feel that her false utterances of 'I am a brain in a vat' somehow gesticulate in the direction of the true proposition that she wants to assert but cannot. She might feel that her false utterance, though false, is somehow illuminating. It points in the direction of what she really wants to say and think.

One way to save Maimonides and other Jewish apophatic theologians from absurdity, and contradiction (since, on the one hand, they often say a great deal about God and his nature, and on the other hand, they say that we cannot say anything about God) would be to refuse to take their apophatic discourse at face value. Maimonides makes all kinds of positive claims about God. He believes them too. But perhaps he also believes that engaging with the *via negativa*, and uttering the absurd claim that we cannot know anything positive about God, can point one towards important ineffable truths. His apophaticism may have been adopted as an illuminating falsehood.

Interpreting Maimonides in this way saves him from an old puzzle. Gersonides could not understand why, as Maimonides thought, it is acceptable to say that God is not ignorant, but unacceptable to say that God is not wise. If Maimonides were serious about negative theology, he should accept both negations: God is neither wise nor ignorant.[6] But perhaps both are false, while only one is illuminating. To arbitrate that discussion, we would need a test for a sentence's illuminating powers. That, I'm afraid, is beyond me. But there is good reason to think that only some theological falsehoods are going to be illuminating, just as only certain metaphors have the power to illuminate what it is one really wishes to point out.

### *Resolution #1*

Golda believes that on Rosh Hashana, God judges humanity and inscribes them into either the book of life or the book of death. Is she asserting the proposition <*God judges humanity and inscribes them into the book of life or into the book of death on Rosh Hashana*>? No. God's writing names into books is clearly a metaphor. Golda knows that. Is she then asserting the proposition <*On Rosh Hashana God judges humanity, and their lives depend upon the outcome of the judgement*>? Is that the proposition that she is asserting? Not necessarily. Does she think that God is a temporal being such that he can do a specific action at a specific time, or does she think that he lives outside of time and can act, but never at a specific point in time? Perhaps, like many Jews who claim to believe that God judges people on Rosh Hashana, she has no worked-out metaphysics of God's relationship to time. So, what is Golda really asserting in her alleged belief that God judges humanity on that auspicious day?

Wettstein's insight is that there is no propositional attitude here. Golda is merely assenting to the *imagery* of Rosh Hashana, with its books of divine justice. She is agreeing to structure her life through the prism of that narrative; to engage her emotions with it; to make it hers. When one says, 'Golda believes that God judges humanity on Rosh Hashana', perhaps one is not really reporting her to have a propositional attitude, so much as to, 'kidnap a piece of [her] favored imagery', using it as if it functioned as a proposition that she believed in, but really meaning to say: 'This image plays a fundamental role [for her]'.

Despite the strength of Wettstein's insight, it cannot be that *all* of our religious beliefs can be reduced to the assenting to an image. The power that the imagery of Rosh Hashana has over me has a great deal to do with my background beliefs in God. When I say that 'I am a theist,' I do not merely mean that I assent to the imagery of theism (although that might be part of what I mean).[7] I (also) mean that I assert the proposition that God exists. If I didn't assert *that* proposition, and a number of other propositions, I am not sure what power the imagery of Rosh Hashana would continue to hold over me.

Thus, I think that one of the key tasks for the philosophy of religion must be isolating, for any given religion, the core set of genuine beliefs (or a family of equally sufficient sets of beliefs), that are necessary (or sufficient) for making sense of the choice to choreograph one's life according to the symbolic landscape of the rest of the claims of the religion. The task would be to isolate the core of religious beliefs that give life to the religious *images* that orbit those beliefs.

We believe in a God that transcends our abilities to describe him exhaustively. Beyond those limits of description, we believe that certain images have more power than others to point in his direction, towards his grace, so that we should experience his presence and the moral and religious inspiration that that induces in us. Perhaps, if we are more orthodox and traditional, our core beliefs will contain certain historical claims, for instance, that the Jewish people experienced a mass revelation at the dawn of their identity, bestowing a unique Divine sanction upon the religious narratives and rituals that evolved from that moment; and one will believe, for instance, that Jesus is not the Messiah, and that Muhammad was not sent by God to correct the forgeries of the Rabbis.

But if one's core set of beliefs are internally consistent, one will not be bothered by conflict between beliefs and images, or between one image and another. One only really countenances the core beliefs, and merely quasi-believes in the images; and the images are allowed to contradict one another, since two different signs are able to point in the same direction – two metaphors with conflicting meanings can still have the same *point*, or point to the same ineffable features of the world. We might even find out that some of what passes as religious doctrine from the medieval period, such as the doctrine of the God of whom nothing can be said, will turn out not to be doctrine at all, but just new and powerful imagery, that, despite its falsehood, continues to point us ever closer to the God that we long to know.

### *Resolution #2*

Perhaps a consistent image of God could emerge from the Biblical text if we had some sort of hermeneutic for deciding which images to take literally, and which images to treat as metaphor. Many Jews would argue that the Bible does not commit us to God having a body, because all such Biblical talk is clearly metaphorical, just as Romeo calling Juliet the sun is metaphorical. The audience of the Bible is no different from the audience of *Romeo and Juliet*, both are supposed to be able to understand when something is a metaphor and when not. But most religious Jews would say: the Bible *does* commit us to the existence of a God who created the world, made certain promises to Abraham, and brought us out of Egypt.

On such a view, a consistent picture of the Deity is supposed to emerge from a reading of the Bible, when one pays close attention to which parts are supposed to be metaphor and which parts are not. It is clearly going to be difficult to establish rules for determining when a verse should be read literally and when metaphorically, but let us put that aside for a moment. Even if we adopt a hermeneutic that tames Jewish imagery and gives rise to a consistent picture of God, a new version of Wettstein's problem still emerges.

The God of the Bible does not seem to have the properties of the God of the philosophers. Even if one accepts that the God of the Bible does not have a body, he does seem to change his mind, which contradicts the philosopher's conception of an impassible God; he seems to be ignorant about certain matters, which contradicts the conception of Divine omniscience; at times he seems hurt by the actions of the Jewish people, which contradicts the conception of Divine omnipotence. Even in harmonizing Jewish imagery, there is a real fear that the body of theological propositions that emerges from that imagery will be inconsistent with the propositions of classical Jewish philosophy. The only way to reconcile Biblical theology with Maimonidean theology is to do too much violence to the Biblical text.

In his novel *Timequake* Kurt Vonnegut meets Kilgore Trout. But Kilgore Trout is a fictional character. It is not possible that Kurt Vonnegut could have met him. Rather, what is true of Kurt Vonnegut in the story – that he met Kilgore Trout – is false of him outside of the story. Of course, we might want to say that there are two Kurt Vonneguts – the author who wrote *Timequake*, and the fictional representation of the author, who is a mere character in that book. But this seems unattractive. To assume that there is one, rather than two, Kurt Vonneguts is ontologically parsimonious. When you go to Baker Street, you get excited to be on the very same street where Sherlock Holmes fictionally lived. This excitement is based upon the intuition that there aren't two Baker Streets – the fictional one and the real one – but only one Baker Street; and there aren't two Kurt Vonneguts either. And thus, we can say that the very same Kurt Vonnegut has things true of him outside of *Timequake* that are not true of him inside the story, and vice versa.[8]

If we adopt the *prima facie* bizarre assumption that the history of the world is a story in the mind of God, an assumption that lies at the heart of certain Hassidic philosophies,[9] then there may be things that are true of God inside the story that are not true of him outside of it, and vice versa. The God that emerges from a harmonized appraisal of Jewish religious imagery may be an accurate description of God as he appears to us in this world, while the more abstract, philosophical conceptions of an impassible, omnipotent, omniscient God may be attempts to sketch what God must be like *outside* the story, outside history. This is no more a contradiction than the one seemingly posed by the fact that Kurt Vonnegut both did and did not meet Kilgore Trout.

In two very different ways, then, we have addressed the tension that Wettstein has diagnosed between Jewish lore and doctrine.

## Notes

1　Compare R. Hanina's position here with what he says in *BT* B'rachot 33b.
2　'[W]e say that [God] has eyes, ears, hands, a mouth, a tongue, to express that He sees, hears, acts, and speaks; but seeing and hearing are attributed to Him to indicate that He perceives' (*Guide* 1.46, tr. Friedländer).
3　'[P]hysical organs are ascribed to the Most Perfect Being ... [as] indications of the actions generally performed by means of these organs. Such actions being perfections respecting ourselves, are predicated of God, because we wish to express that He is most perfect in every respect ...' (Ibid.).
4　See Lebens 2014 for a full account of Plantinga's attack on Hick's apophaticism.
5　See Lebens 2014.
6　Gersonides, *Wars of the Lord*, 3.3 (and Feldman's comment in his edition, vol. 2, p. 79).
7　I argue in Lebens 2013 that while theistic belief accompanies a commitment to the relevant imagery, the cognate propositional beliefs are likewise necessary for being a theist.
8　Currie (1990, §1.2) advances the same argument at length.
9　See Lebens 2015.

## Further Reading on Religious Language

Alston, W. *Divine Nature and Human Language: Essays in Philosophical Theology* (Ithaca, NY: Cornell University Press, 1989), 17–81.
Alston, W. "Aquinas on Theological Predication: A Look Backward and a Look Forward," in *Reasoned Faith*, ed. E. Stump (Ithaca, NY: Cornell University Press, 1993), 145–178.
Davidson, D. "What Metaphors Mean," *Critical Theory* 5 (1978), 31–47.
Halbertal, M. *Maimonides: Life and Thought* (Princeton, NJ: Princeton University Press, 2014), 277–311.
Jacobs, J. D. "The Ineffable, Inconceivable, and Incomprehensible God: Fundamentality and Apophatic Theology," *Oxford Studies in Philosophy of Religion* (forthcoming).
McFague, S. *Metaphorical Theology* (Philadelphia, PA: Fortress Press, 1982).

Min, A. "D. Z. Phillips on the Grammar of 'God'," *International Journal for the Philosophy of Religion* 63 (2008), 131–146.

Phillips, D. Z. *Wittgenstein and Religion* (New York: Palgrave Macmillan, 1994), 22–79.

Sagi, A. "Yeshayahu Leibowitz—A Breakthrough in Jewish Philosophy: Religion without Metaphysics," *Religious Studies* 33 (1997), 203–216.

Scott, M. "Religious Language," *Philosophy Compass* 5 (2010), 505–515.

Stern, J. *The Matter and Form of Maimonides'* Guide (Cambridge, MA: Harvard University Press, 2013), 18–96.

# 2  The Interpretation of Scripture

It is unarguable that Scripture, the Word of God, means different things to different readers. Some understand God as a powerful being, like a circus strongman. Some believe that miraculous events actually happened. Some take the foregoing to be absurd, indicative of a gullible literalism. **Maimonides** and **Spinoza** square off on the interpretation of Scripture. Maimonides understands Scripture as somehow inclusive of all truth, and if it is not immediately apparent that it contains deep metaphysical truths, that is exactly as it must be, given that Scripture is for all members of the community. To reveal the deepest truths unadorned is dangerous for most, and thus Maimonides' *Guide of the Perplexed,* his philosophical magnum opus, written to assuage the perplexity of a religious person who has studied science and philosophy, shows only such a person the 'real' meaning of certain biblical terms and parables. The section of the *Guide* we present shows Maimonides creatively at work on analyzing some celebrated passages in Genesis.

For Spinoza, whose biblical criticism in Chapter 7 of the *Tractatus Theologico-Politicus* was greeted with scorn and disbelief, Maimonides' 'creativity' with the biblical text is question-begging. Presuming the inerrancy and divinity of Scripture, Maimonides reveals Scripture as *au courant* with science and philosophy. But for Spinoza, this presumption of inerrancy and polymathy "should emerge from a critical examination and understanding of Scripture … and [cannot be] assumed at the very beginning as a rule of interpretation." By contrast, Spinoza proposes to interpret Scripture *sola Scriptura.* Such a historical-critical method debunks the inerrancy and divinity of Scripture, and reveals the text as written solely for moral and political purposes, with obedience not scientific insight as its goal.

**Daniel Frank** brings Maimonides and Spinoza into debate with one another. He understands Maimonides' *Guide* in its own terms as a biblical commentary *more philosophico,* and as such as a part of a tradition of interpretation as old as Philo. Maimonides' goal in the *Guide,* "the true understanding of the Law," reveals itself as a foundational project for ascertaining the reasons for and trajectory of the Law (*ta'amei ha-mitzvot*), and *this* entails nothing less than a full study of God and His creation. Metaphysics and cosmology undergird morals and politics. This Platonic and Hellenistic trajectory of the project is shared by Spinoza in his own *Ethics* and *Tractatus Theologico-Politicus.* Even as Spinoza debunks the divinity of Scripture and eviscerates Maimonides' dogmatism and a priori theorizing, he presents his own major works as 'practical' in just the way Maimonides does. A fine irony pervades Spinoza's critique. The "true understanding of the Law" and the "natural history of Scripture" are both guides on a path toward wisdom and freedom.

## MOSES MAIMONIDES (1138–1204)

### *The Guide of the Perplexed* (1190)

*Introduction; Book 1, Chapters 1–2; Book 2, Chapter 25* (tr. Rabin)

*On the Interpretation of Scripture*

INTRODUCTION

This treatise has as its principal object to clarify the meaning of certain terms in the Bible. Of these, some are words bearing several meanings (homonymous), and ignorant people persist in taking them always in one of those meanings. Others are used in a metaphorical sense: these same people take them in their primary sense. Others again are of an ambiguous (amphibological) character, making sometimes the impression of being employed in their conventional sense, and sometimes of possessing several meanings.

The aim of our treatise is, however, not to explain all these terms to the vulgar crowd or to mere beginners in philosophy, or even to those who study nothing but the Law – i.e., the legal and the ritual aspects of our religion (since the whole purpose of this and similar treatises is the true understanding of the Law). It's aim is rather to stimulate the mind of the religious man who has arrived at deep-set belief in the truth of our faith and who is perfect in the religious and moral sense. If such a man has also made a study of the philosophical sciences and grasped their meaning, and feels attracted to rationalism and at home with it, he may be worried about the literal meaning of some scriptural passages as well as the sense of those homonymous, metaphorical, or ambiguous expressions, as he has always understood them, or as they are explained to him. He will thus fall into confusion and be faced by a dilemma: either he follows his reason and rejects those expressions as he understands them: then he will think that he is rejecting the dogmas of our religion. Or else he continues to accept them in the way he has been taught and refuses to be guided by his reason. He thus brusquely turns his back on his own reason, and yet he cannot help feeling that his faith has been gravely impaired. He will continue to hold those fanciful beliefs although they inspire him with uneasiness and disgust, and be continuously sick at heart and utterly bewildered in his mind.

This treatise has a second purpose, namely, to throw light on some exceedingly recondite similes which appear in the prophetic books without it being made clear that they are similes. It therefore seems to the ignorant and unwary that these are to be taken in their literal sense without any hidden implication. When a person acquainted with the truth considers such similes, taking them at their face value, he again experiences utter bewilderment. Only when one explains them to him, or at least points out that they are similes, can he find the right way and be relieved of his perplexity. This is the reason why I have called this treatise *Guide of the Perplexed...*

*Book 1, Chapter 1*

> Let us make man in Our image
> (Genesis 1:26)

People think that the word *tzelem* (image) in Hebrew refers to the outward shape and contours of a thing. This has been a cause of crass anthropomorphism because of the verse: *Let us make man in Our image after Our likeness* (Genesis 1, 26). They think that God is of the image of man, i.e., his shape and outline, and thus fall into unalloyed anthropomorphism, in which they firmly believe. It appears to them that by abandoning this belief they would deny Scripture, nay, the very existence of God would be called in question unless they imagine Him as a body with face and hands like themselves in shape and design, only – as they deem – bigger and brighter, and its substance not of flesh and blood. That is the highest degree of incorporeality they are prepared to grant to God.

You will find in the course of this treatise the complete demonstration of the falsity of anthropomorphism and the arguments for the true unity of God, which makes no sense without the rejection of anthropomorphism. In this chapter we intend to explain only the terms *image* and *likeness*. I maintain that 'image', as it is used in current speech to denote the shape and outline of a thing, is in Hebrew *to'ar* (form) as used in the phrases: *beautiful of form and beautiful of appearance* (Genesis 39, 6), *what form is he of?* (1 Samuel 28, 14), *like the form of princes* (Judges 8, 18). This word is also applied to the image or form which the craftsman produces, as in *he formeth it (yeta'arehu) with red chalk ... he formeth it with a compass* (Isaiah 44, 13). That is a term which cannot, God forbid, under any circumstances whatsoever be applied to the Almighty Lord.

The word 'image', on the other hand, is applied to [the natural] form, i.e., the essential feature of a thing by which it becomes what it is, which constitutes its true character in so far as it is that particular thing. In man this feature is the one from which springs human [apprehension]. It is because of this intellectual [apprehension] that the words *in the image of God He created him* (Genesis 1, 27) are used. For the same reason Scripture writes: *thou wilt despise their image* (Psalms 73, 20), because 'contempt' attaches to the soul, i.e., the [species] form, not to the shapes and outlines of the limbs. I suggest further that the idols are called 'images' because what is intended by them is their supposed function, not their shape and outline. I maintain the same with regard to the images *of your hemorrhoids* (1 Samuel 6, 5), because what was intended by those was their function of dispelling the disease of hemorrhoids, not the shape of hemorrhoids. If however you do not accept my explanation of these two phrases, and take *image* in both in the sense of shape and outline, then *image* is a term of several meanings or one of amphibological signification, which can be applied to [species] form as well as to the form of an artifice and shapes and outlines of natural bodies. In the phrase 'we shall make man in our image' the [species] form is intended, that is intellectual [apprehension], and not the shape and outline.

Thus we explain the difference between *image* and *form* and the meaning of *image*. As for *demuth* (*likeness*) it is a noun derived from *damah* 'to be like', which again is applied to function or character. The phrase *I am like a pelican of the wilderness* (Psalms 102, 6) does not imply that he had wings and feathers like the pelican, but that he was sad like the pelican. Similarly, *nor any tree in the garden of God was like unto him in his beauty* (Ezekiel 31, 8) refers solely to the feature of beauty. So too, *they have venom in the likeness of the venom of a serpent* (Psalms 58, 5), and *his likeness (dimyono) is as a lion greedy of his prey* (Psalms 17, 12), all imply resemblance in function, not in shape and outline. Similarly *the likeness of the throne* (Ezekiel 1, 26) only implies resemblance with regard to the function of being elevated and exalted, not that of being square or thick or having long legs, as some poor spirits think. The same applies to *the likeness of the living creatures* (Ezekiel 1, 13).

Since man is distinguished by a very remarkable function, which does not exist in anything else beneath the sphere of the moon, namely intellectual [apprehension], which is not exercised by any of the senses or outer limbs or inner organs, this is compared with divine perception, which needs no tool – though this is not a true comparison, but a superficial first impression. Because of this function the divine intellect bestowed upon him, it is said of man that he is in the image and the likeness of God, not because God is a body and therefore possesses a shape.

*Book 1, Chapter 2*

Ye shall be as Gods knowing good and evil
(Genesis 3:5)

Some years ago a certain man well versed in the sciences set me a strange problem. It is worthwhile here to study both the question and the answer I gave in solving it. Before I mention the problem and its solution I want to state the fact well-known to every Hebrew scholar, that the noun *Elohim* has the meanings of God, angels, and judges who govern states. Onkelos the proselyte – on whom be peace – has rightly seen that in the verse *and ye shall be as* Gods *knowing good and evil* (Genesis 3, 5), the last meaning is intended, since he says 'ye shall be like lords'. Having thus agreed that the term is homonymous, let us begin with relating the problem.

My enquirer said that from the simple meaning of Scripture it appeared that at first it had been intended for man to be like the other animals without intellect and thought and without any ability to distinguish between good and evil. When he had rebelled, that very fact of his rebellion brought him that immense perfection which makes man so unique, that he should possess this discernment which we have. It is the noblest function found within us and it constitutes our human character. This, my correspondent said, was the astonishing thing, that his punishment for rebellion should be to give him a perfection which he did not possess before, namely the intellect. What else is this than the story we are told of a man who was rebellious and exceedingly wicked, and in the end was transformed into a star and placed into the sky?

This was the general sense of the question, though not the exact words. Listen now to the arguments of my reply. I said: You go in for philosophy with your half-baked ideas and brainwaves, and you think you can understand a book, which has guided ancients and moderns, in passing, in a few moments snatched from drinking and lovemaking, just as you would glance at a book of histories or of poetry? Stay and think, for the matter is not as it appears to you at first blush, but as will emerge when we give our full consideration to the passage. The intellect which God bestowed on man as his ultimate perfection was the one which was given to Adam *before* his disobedience. It is that one which is meant by saying that Adam was made *in the image and likeness of God.* Owing to it he could be addressed (by God) and receive commands, as is said *and the Lord God commanded the man* (Genesis 2, 16). Such instructions cannot be given to animals or beings not gifted with intellect. By his intellect man distinguishes between truth and falsehood. This faculty existed in him to its full extent. The distinction between good and bad, however is a matter of general agreement, not of intellectual activity. One does not say 'it is good that the sky is spherical' or 'it is bad that the earth is flat', but one applies to such statements the terms true and false. In our tongue one expresses true and false by *emeth* (truth) and *sheqer* (falsehood), while good and bad are expressed by *tov* (good) and *ra'* (evil). By his intellect man knows truth from falsehood, a distinction which he applies in all intellectual activities. With regard to this, man had reached the highest stage of development with nothing but his natural sense and his innate intellectual concepts, so that because of these it was said of him: *Thou hast made him lack but little of being God* (Psalms 8, 6). At the same time he possessed no faculty for dealing with the generally agreed in any manner, and had no sense for it. Not even the most obviously bad thing from the point of view of the generally agreed, that is the uncovering of one's private parts, was bad in his eyes, nor would he have grasped that it was bad.

When, however, he became disobedient and turned towards the lusts of his imagination and the pleasures of his physical senses, as is indicated by the verse *that the tree was good for food and was a lust for the eyes* (Genesis 3, 6) – then only he was punished by being deprived of intellectual [apprehension]. This was the reason why he disobeyed the command of God which had been given to him by virtue of his intellect. He thus acquired the sense for the generally agreed, and became absorbed in judging things as to their being good and bad. Now he realized what he had lost, and into what state he had fallen. For this reason Scripture says: 'Ye shall be as *Elohim* knowing good and evil', not 'knowing truth and falsehood', or rather '[apprehending] truth and falsehood'. Good and evil are not logically necessary at all, but truth and falsehood are. Just consider the passage:

*And the eyes of them both were opened and they* knew *that they were naked.* It does not say the eyes of them both were opened and they *saw* that they were naked, because what he *saw* then was the same that he had seen before. There was no covering on his eyes that was removed, but his state of mind changed so that he considered bad what he had not considered bad before.

It may be remarked that the word *paqah* 'to open' always refers to the bestowal of mental awareness, never to a bodily act of seeing, as in the verses: *God opened her eyes* (Genesis 21, 19), *then shall the eyes of the blind be opened* (Isaiah 35, 5), *opening the ears, he heareth not* (Isaiah 42, 20), in which last passage the sense is as in *that have eyes to see, and see not* (Ezekiel 12, 2).

## Book 2, Chapter 25

PHILOSOPHY AND TORAH: CREATION VS. ETERNITY OF THE WORLD

It should be clearly understood that our reason for rejecting the eternity of the world is not to be sought in any text of the Torah which says that the world is created. The passages which indicate that the world is created are no more numerous than those that indicate that God is a body. The method of allegorical interpretation is no less possible or permissible in the matter of the world being created than in any other. We would have been able to explain it allegorically just as we did when we denied corporeality. Perhaps it would have been even much easier. We would in any case not have lacked the capacity to explain those texts allegorically and establish the eternity of the world just as we explained those other texts allegorically and denied that God was a body. If we have not done this and do not believe in it, this is for two reasons: one is that it is conclusively proved that God is not a body. We must of necessity explain allegorically all those passages the literal sense of which is contradicted by evidential proof, so that we are conscious that they must be allegorically interpreted. The eternity of the world is not conclusively proved. It is therefore wrong to reject the texts and interpret them allegorically because of preference for a view the opposite of which might be shown to be preferable for a variety of reasons. This is one reason; the other is that our belief that God is not a body does not destroy in our eyes any of the ordinances of our Law or belie the statements of any prophet. There is nothing contrary to Scripture in it, except that the ignorant think it is. As we have explained, there is no contradiction, but this is the real intention of the text. If, on the other hand, we believed in the eternity of the world according to the principles laid down by Aristotle – that the world exists by necessity, that the nature of no thing ever changes and that nothing ever deviates from its customary behavior – this would destroy the Law from its very foundation and belie automatically every miracle, and make void all hopes and fears the Law seeks to inspire, unless, of course, one chooses to interpret the miracles as well allegorically, as did the *Batiniyya* sect among the Moslems. In this way we would end up in some kind of idle prattling.

Again if we believe in the eternity of the world according to the second theory we have expounded, that of Plato, namely, that the heavens themselves are transitory, such a view would not upset the ordinances of the Law, nor would its consequence be the belying of miracles, which, on the contrary, would be possible. The various passages could be interpreted in accordance with it. One might even discover many equivocal passages in the text of the Torah and elsewhere with which it could be connected and which might even be considered to argue for it. However, there is no cogent incentive for us to do so unless that theory were proved. Since it is not proved, we shall neither allow ourselves to be beguiled by this theory nor pay the slightest attention to that other theory, but shall take the texts in their literal meaning. We say, therefore, that the Law intimates to us a thing which we have no power fully to apprehend. The miracles bear witness that our claim is true.

It must be clearly understood that once we believe in the world being created, all miracles become possible and the Law itself becomes possible, and any question that might be asked in this connection is automatically void, even such questions as the following: why did God accord a revelation to this one and none to others? Why did God prescribe this Law to a certain nation and not to others? Why did He give the Law at the time He gave it and not before or after? Why did He ordain these positive and those negative commandments? Why did He distinguish any particular prophet by those miracles that are mentioned, and no others took place? What did God intend by this act of lawgiving, and why did He not implant these commandments and prohibitions in our nature, if that was His purpose? To all these questions, answers can be made by saying: thus He wanted, or: thus His wisdom decreed it. Just as He brought the world into existence when He willed and in this form, without our being able to analyse His will in this connection or the principles by which His wisdom selected these particular forms or that time, so we do not know His will or the motives of His wisdom in determining all the things concerning which we have just asked. If one says that the world necessarily had to be as it is, all these questions must be asked, and cannot be disposed of except by reprehensible replies which both contradict, and make nonsense of, the literal sense of all those Scriptural passages concerning which no sensible person can doubt that they are to be taken in their literal sense.

This, then, is our reason for recoiling from that theory. This is why people of worth have spent their lives, and others will go on spending their lives, in speculating on this problem. For if it were proved that the world is created – even in the manner this is stated by Plato – all the objections of the philosophers to us would fall to the ground. If, on the other hand, they would succeed in providing a proof for its eternity according to Aristotle's view, the Law in its entirety would fall to the ground and other manners of thinking would take its place, for I have made clear to you that the whole of it hangs on this one point. Give it, therefore, your most earnest consideration.

BENEDICT (BARUCH) SPINOZA (1632–77)

## *Theological-Political Treatise* (1670)

### *Chapter 7* (tr. Curley)

*On Interpreting Scripture*

[6] Now ... to liberate our minds from theological prejudices, and not to recklessly embrace men's inventions as divine teachings, we must treat and discuss the true method of interpreting Scripture; for so long as we are ignorant of this, we cannot know anything with certainty about what either Scripture or the Holy Spirit wishes to teach.

To sum it up briefly, I say that the method of interpreting Scripture does not differ from the method of interpreting nature, but agrees with it completely. [7] For just as the method of interpreting nature consists above all in putting together a history of nature, from which, as from certain data, we infer the definitions of natural things, so also to interpret Scripture it is necessary to prepare a straightforward history of Scripture and to infer the mind of the authors of Scripture from it, by legitimate reasonings, as from certain data and principles. [8] For if someone has admitted as principles or data for interpreting Scripture and discussing the things contained in it only those drawn from Scripture itself and its history, he will always proceed without any danger of error, and will be able to discuss the things which surpass our grasp as safely as those we know by the natural light.

[9] But to establish clearly that this way is not only certain, but also the only way, and that it agrees with the method of interpreting nature, we must note that Scripture very often treats of things which cannot be deduced from principles known to the natural light. For historical narratives and revelations make up the greatest part of it. [10] But the historical narratives give a prominent place to miracles, that is, (as we have shown in the preceding chapter) narratives of unusual things in nature, accommodated to the opinions and judgments of the historians who have written them. Moreover, the revelations were also accommodated to the opinions of the prophets, as we have shown in the second chapter, and they really surpass man's power of understanding. So the knowledge of all these things, that is, of almost everything in Scripture, must be sought only from Scripture itself, just as the knowledge of nature must be sought from nature itself.

[11] As for the moral teachings also contained in the Bible, although they can be demonstrated from common notions, still it cannot be demonstrated from common notions that Scripture teaches them. This can only be established from Scripture itself. Indeed, if we wish, without prejudice, to certify the divinity of Scripture, we must establish from it alone that it teaches true moral doctrines. Only from this can we demonstrate its divinity. For we have shown that the prophets' own certainty was established principally by the fact that they had a heart inclined toward the right and the good. So to be able to have faith in them we too must establish the same thing.

[12] Moreover, we have also demonstrated already that the divinity of God cannot be proven by miracles, not to mention that miracles could also be performed

by false prophets. So the divinity of Scripture must be established only by the fact that it teaches true virtue. But this can only be established by Scripture. If it could not be done, it would only be as a result of great prejudice that we would embrace it and testify to its divinity. Therefore, all knowledge of Scripture must be sought only from Scripture itself.

[13] Finally, Scripture does not give definitions of the things of which it speaks, any more than nature does. So just as the definitions of natural things are to be inferred from the different actions of nature, in the same way [the definitions of the things spoken of in Scripture] are to be drawn from the different narratives occurring in the texts concerning them.

[14] Therefore, the universal rule in interpreting Scripture is to attribute nothing to Scripture as its teaching which we have not understood as clearly as possible from its history. But now we must say here what sort of history that must be and what things it mainly relates.

[15] First, it must contain the nature and properties of the language in which the books of Scripture were written, and which their authors were accustomed to speak. For in this way we shall be able to find out all the meanings which each utterance can admit in ordinary conversational usage. And because all the authors, both of the Old Testament and the New, were Hebrews, it is certain that the history of the Hebrew language is necessary above all others, not only for understanding the books of the Old Testament, which were written in this language, but also for understanding those of the New Testament. For although they have been made common to all in other languages, nevertheless they express themselves in a Hebrew manner.

[16] Second, it must collect the sayings of each book and organize them under main headings so that we can readily find all those concerning the same subject. Next, it must note all those which are ambiguous or obscure or which seem inconsistent with one another. I call these sayings clear or obscure here, insofar as it is easy or difficult to derive their meaning from the context of the utterance, not insofar as it is easy or difficult to perceive their truth by reason. For we are concerned only with the meaning of the utterances, not with their truth.

[17] Indeed, we must take great care, so long as we are looking for the meaning of Scripture, not to be preoccupied with our own reasoning, insofar as it is founded on the principles of natural knowledge (not to mention now our prejudices). But lest we confuse the true meaning with the truth of things, that meaning must be found out solely from the usage of language, or from reasoning which recognizes no other foundation than Scripture.

To make all these things clearer, I shall illustrate them with an example. [18] These sayings of Moses—that *God is a fire* and that *God is jealous*—are as clear as possible, so long as we attend only to the meaning of the words. Therefore, I put them among the clear sayings, even though they are very obscure in relation to truth and reason. Indeed, although their literal meaning is contrary to the natural light, unless it is also clearly opposed to the principles and foundations derived from the history of Scripture, that literal meaning will nevertheless have to be retained. And conversely, if these sayings, according to their literal interpretation, were found to be contrary to principles derived from Scripture, even though they agreed completely with reason, they would still have to be interpreted differently (i.e., metaphorically).

[19] Therefore, to know whether or not Moses believed that God is a fire, we must not in any way infer our answer from the fact that this opinion agrees with reason or is contrary to it, but we must rely only on other sayings of Moses himself. Since Moses also teaches clearly in a great many places that God has no likeness to any of the visible things which exist in the heavens, on the earth, or in the sea, either this saying or all of those are to be explained metaphorically.

[20] But because we must depart as little as possible from the literal meaning, we must first ask whether this one sentence, *God is a fire*, admits another meaning beyond the literal one, that is, whether the term *fire* signifies something other than natural fire. If [that term] is not found, according to linguistic usage, to signify something else, then this sentence also is not to be interpreted in any other way, however much it may be contrary to reason. On the contrary, all the others, although in agreement with reason, would still have to be accommodated to this one. [21] If this also could not be done according to linguistic usage, then these sentences would be irreconcilable, and therefore we would have to suspend judgment about them. But because the term *fire* is also taken for anger and jealousy (see Job 31:12), these sentences of Moses are easily reconciled, and we infer legitimately that these two sentences, *God is a fire* and *God is jealous*, are one and the same sentence [i.e., express one and the same opinion].

[22] Next, since Moses clearly teaches that God is jealous, and nowhere teaches that God lacks passions *or* passive states of mind, from this we must conclude without reservation that Moses believed this, or at least that he wished to teach it, however much we may believe that this opinion is contrary to reason. For as we have already shown, it is not permissible for us to twist the intent of Scripture according to the dictates of our reason and according to our preconceived opinions. The whole knowledge of the Bible must be sought from the Bible alone.

[23] Finally, this history must describe fully, with respect to all the books of the prophets, the circumstances of which a record has been preserved, namely, the life, character, and concerns of the author of each book, who he was, on what occasion he wrote, at what time, for whom, and finally, in what language. Next, it must relate the fate of each book: how it was first received, into whose hands it fell, how many different readings of it there were, by whose deliberation it was accepted among the Sacred Books, and finally, how all the books which everyone now acknowledges to be sacred came to be unified into one body.

The history of Scripture, I say, must contain all these things. [24] For in order for us to know which sayings are put forward as laws and which as moral teachings, it is important to know the life, character, and concerns of the author. Moreover, the better we know someone's spirit and temperament, the more easily we can explain his words. Next, if we are not to confuse eternal teachings with those which could be useful only for a time or only for a few people, it is important also to know on what occasion, at what time, and for which nation or age all these teachings were written. [25] Finally, it is important to know the other things I have mentioned in addition, in order to know also, beyond the authority of each book, whether or not it could have been corrupted by illicit hands, and whether errors have crept in or whether they have been corrected by men sufficiently expert and worthy of trust. It is very necessary to know all these things so that we are not carried away by a blind impulse to embrace whatever has been thrust upon us, but embrace only what is certain and indubitable.

[26] Now after we have this history of Scripture and have firmly decided to maintain nothing with certainty as the teaching of the prophets which does not follow from this history, or is not derived from it as clearly as possible, then it will be time for us to get ready to investigate the mind of the prophets and of the Holy Spirit. But for this purpose we also require a method and order like the one we use for interpreting nature according to its history.

[27] In examining natural things we strive, before all else, to investigate the things which are most universal and common to the whole of nature—namely, motion and rest, and their laws and rules, which nature always observes and through which it continuously acts—and from these we proceed gradually to other less universal things. In just the same way, the first thing to be sought from the history of Scripture is what is most universal, what is the basis and foundation of the whole of Scripture, and finally, what all the prophets commend in it as an eternal teaching, most useful for all mortals. For example, that a unique and omnipotent God exists, who alone is to be worshiped, who cares for all, and who loves above all those who worship him and who love their neighbor as themselves, and so on.

[28] Scripture, I say, teaches these and similar things everywhere, so clearly and so explicitly that there has never been anyone who disputed the meaning of Scripture concerning these things. But what God is, and in what way he sees all things, and provides for them—these and similar things Scripture does not teach openly and as an eternal doctrine. On the contrary, we have already shown above that the prophets themselves did not agree about them. So concerning such things we must maintain nothing as the doctrine of the Holy Spirit, even if it can be determined very well by the natural light.

[29] Once this universal teaching of Scripture is rightly known, we must proceed next to other, less universal things, which nevertheless concern how we ordinarily conduct our lives and which flow from this universal teaching like streams. For example, all the particular external actions of true virtue, which can only be put to work on a given occasion. Whatever is found to be obscure *or* ambiguous in the texts about these things must be explained and determined according to the universal teaching of Scripture. But if we find any things which are contrary to one another, we must see on what occasion, and at what time, and for whom they were written...

[43]...Since this method of ours, which is founded on the principle that the knowledge of Scripture is to be sought only from Scripture, is the only true method [of interpreting Scripture], whatever it cannot furnish for acquiring a complete knowledge of Scripture, we must absolutely give up as hopeless. [44] But we must now say what difficulty this method involves, or what is to be

desired in it, for it to be able to lead us to a complete and certain knowledge of the Sacred Texts.

To begin with, a great difficulty in this method arises from the fact that it requires a complete knowledge of the Hebrew language. But where is this now to be sought? [45] The ancient cultivators of the Hebrew language left nothing to posterity regarding its foundations and teaching. At least we have absolutely nothing from them: no dictionary, no grammar, no rhetoric. Moreover, the Hebrew nation has lost all its adornments and marks of distinction—this is no wonder, after it has suffered so many disasters and persecutions—and has retained only some few fragments of its language and of a few books. For almost all the names of fruits, birds, fish, and a great many other things have perished in the unjust treatment of the ages. Again, the meaning of many nouns and verbs which occur in the Bible is either completely unknown or is disputed.

[46] We lack, not only all these things, but also and especially, a phraseology of this language. For time, the devourer, has obliterated from the memory of men almost all the idioms and manners of speaking peculiar to the Hebrew nation. Therefore, we will not always be able, as we desire, to find out, with respect to each utterance, all the meanings it can admit according to linguistic usage. Many utterances will occur whose meaning will be very obscure, indeed, completely incomprehensible, even though they are expressed in well-known terms. . . .

[65] These are all the difficulties I had undertaken to recount arising from this method of interpreting Scripture according to the history we can have of it. I judge them to be so great that I do not hesitate to affirm that in very many places we either do not know the true meaning of Scripture or are divining it without certainty. [66] On the other hand, we should note again that all these difficulties can only prevent us from grasping the intention of the prophets concerning things which are incomprehensible and which we can only imagine, but not concerning things which we can grasp with the intellect and of which we can easily form a clear concept. For those things which, by their nature, are easily perceived can never be said so obscurely that they are not easily understood, according to the proverb: to one who understands a word is enough.

[67] Euclid, who wrote only about things which were quite simple and most intelligible, is easily explained by anyone in any language. For to grasp his intention and to be certain of his true meaning it is not necessary to have a complete knowledge of the language in which he wrote, but only a quite common and almost childish knowledge. Nor is it necessary to know the life, concerns, and customs of the author, nor in what language, to whom, and when he wrote, nor the fate of his book, nor its various readings, nor how nor by whose deliberation it was accepted.

[68] What I have said here about Euclid must be said about everyone who has written about things by their nature comprehensible. So we conclude that concerning moral teachings we can easily grasp the intention of Scripture from the history we have of it and that in this case we can be certain of its true meaning. For the teachings of true piety are expressed in the most familiar words, since they are very ordinary and no less simple and easy to understand. And because

true salvation and blessedness consists in true peace of mind, and we truly find peace only in those things which we understand very clearly, [69] it is evident that we can grasp with certainty the intention of Scripture concerning things salutary and necessary for blessedness. So there is no reason why we should be so anxious about the rest. Since for the most part we cannot embrace these other things by reason and the intellect, such concern would show more curiosity than regard for our advantage.

## DANIEL FRANK

## "Meaning, Truth, and History: Maimonides and Spinoza on the Interpretation of Scripture"

We may begin to get our bearings on the interpretive issue before us with this comment by Hourani, in the introduction to his classic edition of Ibn Rushd's (Averroes') *Fasl al-Maqal* (*On the Harmony of Religion and Philosophy*): "It may be suggested that if agreement with philosophy is made one of the criteria for the correct interpretation of Scripture, the meaning of Scripture is prejudged. Does the *Qur'an* really say the same things as Greek philosophy, or has Ibn Rushd "cooked" his results, predetermining the *Qur'an*'s meaning by a requirement that is extrinsic to it?" (Averroes/Hourani 1961, 27) The issue here is the use of and the justification for employing philosophical categories and arguments in ascertaining the (true) meaning of Scripture. Hourani is quite explicit that such philosophical categories and arguments are "extrinisic" to Scripture, and their outsider status is immediately problematic, for it raises an issue of we might call "interpretive disingenuousness", the real possibility of prejudging the meaning of Scripture ("cooking the results"). Is the exegete genuinely interpreting Scripture *sola Scriptura*, or rather, is he imposing upon the text alien categories and results? Must Scripture say *x* just because Philosophy says *x* (and Philosophy is presumed to be true)? Further, we should note straightway that whether or not Scripture agrees with Philosophy, whether or not they are intensionally equivalent, there is presumed in Hourani's analysis to be two 'texts' before the interpreter, Scripture and Greek philosophy, and we are to imagine the interpreter as having to find some way to render them commensurable. *Prima facie* there is no hint here that Scripture *itself* may be philosophical. The presumption is that philosophical analysis is alien to Scripture, and must be brought to bear upon it from the 'outside.'

The problematic that Hourani poses is directly transferable to the modern period and the severe critique that Spinoza makes of the "theologians" (including Maimonides) with respect to the correct way to interpret Scripture. Spinoza writes in his celebrated chapter seven of the *Tractatus Theologico-Politicus* (*TTP*), "… his [Maimonides'] position assumes that the sense of Scripture cannot be established from the Bible itself; for the truth of things is not established from Scripture since it offers no demonstration of anything, and does not teach the things about which it speaks by means of definitions and their own first causes. According to Maimonides, therefore, its true sense cannot be established from itself and should not be sought from the Bible itself." (*TTP* 7/115) For Spinoza, Maimonides, much like Ibn Rushd according to Hourani, appeals to philosophy to wrest Scripture's "true sense", and as a result, Spinoza would answer affirmatively with regard to Maimonides (and the "theologians") to the second half of the question that Hourani poses of Ibn Rushd above: Yes, Spinioza would say, Maimonides has "cooked" the results, by understanding and interpreting Scripture by a standard extrinsic to it. In this essay we shall adjudicate this dispute. Maimonides shall have his say in reply, and we will hopefully be in a better position at the end to determine if indeed Maimonides is guilty of interpretive disingenuousness, of prejudging the meaning of Scripture.

### *"Apples of Gold in Settings of Silver": Maimonides on the Interpretation of Scripture*

Maimonides understands Scripture to be addressing a variety of human concerns and as a text written for audiences with different intellectual capacities and interests. He lays this out explicitly at the very beginning of the *Guide of the Perplexed*, his philosophical magnum opus, when he describes the audience for the treatise. Maimonides addresses the *Guide* to "one who has philosophized and has knowledge of the sciences, but believes at the same time in the matters pertaining to the Law and is perplexed as to their meaning because of the uncertain terms and the parables." (*Guide* introduction/3a) Maimonides' project is to dispel the perplexity of a philosophically-minded one ("perfect in his religion and character"), who puzzles at the literal meaning and sense of Scripture, by clarifying the true meaning of the text. Only such a one is perplexed, for those not philosophically-inclined will more readily take the text at face value. A strong dichotomy is drawn by Maimonides between those who can derive benefit from a 'deeper' reading of Scripture and those whose faith may be shaken by such a course of study. Maimonides cautions on innumerable occasions against letting the *Guide* fall into the wrong hands. But for those for whom such a deeper reading is beneficial, Maimonides is adamant that they undertake this project. He understands this project, and the goal of the *Guide* itself, as "the true understanding of the Law" ("the science of Law in its true sense", tr. Pines), and by this he means a foundational study of Torah in the broadest sense, inclusive of both the oral and the written Law. Such a foundational study will result in a true understanding of the reasons for and the trajectory of the Law. Not merely following the Law, but also comprehending what the Law is for and precisely how it achieves its ultimate goals is the *summum bonum*.

Maimonides offers a memorable image to facilitate understanding of the multivocality (the parabolic nature) of Scripture. "The Sage has said: 'A word fitly spoken is like apples of gold in settings of silver'" (Prov 25:11). For Maimonides, this image well captures the way Scripture is written, on two levels, an external level ("beautiful as silver") and a deeper, internal level ("more beautiful than the external one"; *Guide* introduction/6b–7a). As Maimonides sees it, a single text, analogous to a single jewelry setting, holds *within* it a multiplicity of readings.

Scripture is polysemous. Given that the Scriptural text *itself* has this 'deeper', more theoretical level, we should be wary in describing the "science of Law in its true sense", Maimonides' express goal in the *Guide*, as a 'philosophical' project. In so describing the *Guide*, we run the risk of understanding the exegetical method employed as one that imports or imposes an interpretive dimension "extrinsic" to Scripture, in precisely the way Spinoza (and Hourani) have suggested. As they read and understand Maimonides (and Ibn Rushd), the true sense or meaning of Scripture cannot be established from the text itself, but requires a source external to it. And this alien wisdom parading about as Scriptural truth is the "disingenuousness" referred to above. For Spinoza, Maimonides has cooked the results in 'making' Scripture say what philosophy says, and Maimonides' disingenuousness is his pretending that this is not so.

But Maimonides doesn't see his project in the *Guide* as a 'philosophical' one in the way just described. He doesn't think of himself as standing outside an exegetical tradition as he goes about his work. The "science of Law in its true sense", the means whereby the perplexed student is enabled to overcome his dilemma and understand the trajectory of the way of life of the religious community, is presented as *commentary* on Scripture, as glosses on "uncertain terms and the parables." Maimonides is hardly the first in the rabbinic tradition to proceed in this general way, indeed the entire rabbinic tradition is a commentarial one. So, for present purposes, it is very important to understand the genre of the Maimonidean project of explicating "uncertain terms and the parables" as biblical commentary (*more philosophico*).

Understanding such a foundational study of the Law as a species of biblical (halakhic) commentary allows one to see the Maimonidean project as a traditional one (and more proximately as a direct successor and response to *Emunot ve-De'ot* (*Book of Doctrines and Beliefs*) of Saadia Gaon, some two centuries earlier in Baghdad). Scripture was from rabbinic times, and even before in the time of Philo, mined for its 'deeper' (allegorical) meanings. The text allowed for, indeed demanded, interpretation, halakhic, aggadic, and even philosophical. The *Guide* is part of this commentarial tradition, and this is what Maimonides is indicating when he describes his project as aiming at "the science of the Law in its true sense." Maimonides does not envision himself as importing alien categories and conclusions into the text, but rather as revealing the deepest meaning of the text for those able to comprehend it. He is working *within* an interpretive (rabbinic) Scriptural tradition of long standing. It is reasonable to describe Maimonides as like an archaeologist unearthing the subterranean foundations and the substructure, and the *Guide* as in its own way a part of the traditional commentarial genre intent on unlocking the deepest secrets of Scripture. It is an imaginative tour de force to see nested in the rabbinic tradition, in the Law itself, an injunction, an obligation, to engage in all manner of philosophical and scientific interpretation for those capable of so doing. Maimonides avers over and over again the difficulty and danger of the project, and he is clear that the *Guide* is for just a few. But for those few, the project is obligatory. There is a duty to philosophize, to reflect on the deepest foundations of the Law. The very same point is also made by Ibn Rushd.

To debar the 'intellectual' from engaging with the text at a deep, subterranean level is unjustifiable. It is to withhold water from a thirsty person (*Fasl al-Maqal* 1.6).

To speculate on the foundations of the Law might seem to be a narrowly juridical enterprise, an exercise in legal philosophy. For Maimonides, however, the "science of Law in its true sense", as it is presented over the course of the *Guide*, is far broader in scope than that. For Maimonides, divine Law is inclusive of all human wisdom (*hokhmah*), and over the course of the three parts of the *Guide*, Maimonides presents discussions in what we would characterize as philosophy of language, philosophy of nature, cosmology, philosophical theology, metaphysics, epistemology, philosophical psychology, philosophy of law, political philosophy, and moral philosophy. The "science of Law in its true sense" ramifies across all these domains, and the reason the Maimonidean project takes on the form it does, and is presented in the order it is, is because Maimonides considers the way of life of the (perplexed) reflective believer as clarified and fully motivated by a deep understanding of the nature of the divine and its relation to nature. The model is a Platonic and Hellenistic one. Moral action and human felicity depend upon an understanding of the workings of the world, and the divine role in it. Peace of mind and relief from perplexity are functions of intellectual insight. Spinoza is part of this tradition as well, even as he is a fierce critic of his own ancestral tradition.

This 'intellectualist' predilection in Maimonides is manifest in the passages from the very beginning of part one of the *Guide* included in this section. Maimonides explicates certain passages from Genesis, and in both cases understands divinity as mind and its highest exercise as theoretical contemplation. Such divine repose is problem free, and acts as a regulative ideal for the post-lapsarian period in which we all now live. To achieve now a level of contentment depends upon an understanding of the divine creation and its order. An understanding of the Law, now in the narrow sense of the social and political regulations that govern or ought to govern human interactions, is part of this understanding of the divine order of creation. In tenth-century Baghdad Saadia Gaon, influenced by the Mu'tazila, engaged in the philosophical project of *ta'amei ha-mitzvot*, ascertaining the reasons for the commandments or Laws, and Maimonides is in his debt. But Maimonides outpaced him and all others in the kalamic tradition by his contextualizing of the Law in the very broad way suggested here. For Maimonides, law in the narrow juridical sense is to be understood as part of the divine order of creation, and a full understanding of the Law ("science of Law in its true sense") requires rectification of belief and rational excellence. Such insight is achieved through science and philosophical speculation. In sum, the "science of Law in its true sense" is indistinguishable from the attainment of Wisdom, and Maimonides' interpretive strategy is to unearth Wisdom from Torah, and in so doing to dissolve perplexity and reposition the reflective believer in the community.

We thus return to our starting point. Maimonides understands his *philosophical* project as the "science of Law in its true sense". For him, the study of the Law is all encompassing, there is nothing 'outside' it. The hermeneutical project does not lead him to "cook" the results by subordinating Scripture to Philosophy. Maimonides is not being disingenuous in looking *in* Scripture to find truth. Philosophical truth is embedded in Scripture at a subterranean level and for Maimonides, there are those whose task it is to unearth it, and in so doing to alleviate their perplexity.

As we have seen, Spinoza's critique of Maimonides in chapter seven of the *Tractatus Theologico-Politicus* takes him to task for "his view assumes we are permitted to explain and distort the words of Scripture according to our own preconceived opinions" and for being willing "on the basis of reason ... to bend Scripture to devise an interpretation that would ultimately render it saying apparently the same thing [as reason]" (*TTP* 7/115, 114). We will turn to Spinoza's own interpretive project momentarily, but for the present we note that he takes Maimonides to be willing to "distort" (or "bend") the plain meaning of the text to fit a more philosophical one. In context, the specific conundrum is a cosmological one, the eternity or creation of the world (*Guide* 2.25). Maimonides opts for creation, but

> It should be clearly understood that our reason for rejecting the eternity of the world is not to be sought in any text of the Torah which says that the world is created. The passages which indicate that the world is created are no more numerous than those that indicate that God is a body. The method of allegorical interpretation is no less possible or permissible in the matter of the world being created than in any other. We would have been able to explain it allegorically just as we did when we denied corporeality. Perhaps it would have been even much easier. We would in any case not have lacked the capacity to explain those texts allegorically and establish the eternity of the world just as we explained those other texts allegorically and denied that God was a body. If we have not done this and do not believe in it, this is for two reasons: one is that it is conclusively proved that God is not a body. *We must of necessity explain allegorically all those passages the literal sense of which is contradicted by evidential* [demonstrative] *proof,* so that we are conscious that they must be allegorically interpreted. The eternity of the world is not conclusively proved. It is therefore wrong to reject the texts and interpret them allegorically because of preference for a view the opposite of which might be shown to be preferable for a variety of reasons.
>
> (*Guide* 2.25/54b, tr. Rabin; emphasis added)

Maimonides is explicit that in the particular instance of divine corporeality and in general "we must of necessity explain allegorically all those passages the literal sense of which is contradicted by evidential proof..." Truth cannot contradict truth. Although in the particular case concerning the creation or eternity of the world allegorization is not mandated (because eternity has not been proved), Maimonides' serious consideration of both sides of the cosmological debate and his willingness to allegorize ("interpret figuratively", tr. Pines), "if its literal sense is found to conflict with reason" (*TTP* 7/113), convinces Spinoza that Maimonides is committed to an 'external' norm in adjudicating the issue. But why assume that postulating *reason* as an authoritative guide ipso facto prejudices the project? Why assume that the employment of philosophical reflection and taking the latest science into account is ipso facto to move 'outside' Scripture itself?

Perhaps the text is 'deep' in ways Spinoza does not allow, even though Spinoza himself allows that Scripture employs metaphorical language (e.g., *TTP* chap. 1 *passim*; 7/101). In the final analysis, the argument between Maimonides and Spinoza appears to hinge on the nature of Scripture (and religion) itself, and the goals it is meant to serve. For Maimonides, the Law serves a two-fold purpose, political and supra-political (*Guide* 3:27); it is meant to instill obedience, *and* moral and intellectual edification. For Spinoza, Scripture serves just political ends, with obedience not scientific insight as its goal. Maimonides finds in Scripture (the Law) *all* truth, and the means to pry it out. Spinoza does not.

In sum, let us consider Maimonides as a biblical commentator *more philosophico*, in his own way engaged in a project not unlike that of Philo or Saadia. He is not juggling two 'texts', he is not trying to put Humpty-Dumpty back together again. He is not caught between Athens and Jerusalem. For Maimonides, there is but a single truth (Torah), inclusive of human wisdom, expressed in manifold ways, each one in accord with the intellectual abilities of the audience.

### *Spinoza on Meaning, Truth, and Method*

For Spinoza, faith and philosophy are clearly distinguished, in such a way that the kind of deep theoretical insights that Maimonides finds embedded in Scripture is not there. This is why Spinoza believes that Maimonides distorts Scripture when he unearths in Scripture a variety of philosophical views. Spinoza does not countenance a 'science' of the Law that adjudicates philosophical or scientific disputes. These are resolved by natural science itself. We must be cautious here. Sometimes one reads that for Spinoza there is no truth in Scripture, that it is just a fairy tale for the simple-minded. This is not true. While it is true that Scripture is not a repository for scientific and cosmological truth, Spinoza holds that Scripture is a purveyor of *moral* (and political) truth. For Spinoza, universal moral teachings such as the Golden Rule are the true Word of God and accessible through the natural light (*TTP* 11/156; 14/174). Such truths are guides for living, and in their own ways, the prophets of old are bona fide moral teachers instilling obedience to the Law.

Spinoza is not the first to call attention to the unphilosophical nature of Scripture and to dichotomize faith and philosophy. If one thinks of Scripture as a species of imaginative rhetoric, designed to motivate the simple-minded, one can look back to Plato, and his distinction between philosophy and rhetoric, to find an early instance of the dichotomy. But while sharply critical of Maimonides and his 'dogmatic' project, Spinoza is not dismissive of Scripture. He wishes to understand it and its nature on its own terms, scientifically. No less than Maimonides, Spinoza wishes to ascertain the goals and ends that Scripture serves, and, as importantly, can be made to serve in a functional republic.

Spinoza is a very careful reader of Scripture, no less than Maimonides. We should not think that his critique of Scripture is meant to lead to its demise. He firmly holds that Scripture has an important role to play in political life, inculcating virtue and obedience to the law. This is not the place for a full analysis of Spinoza's political philosophy, but it is important in this context to signal Spinoza's careful presentation of Israelite history. Throughout the *Tractatus Theologico-Politicus*, Spinoza shows himself to be a keen student of human nature and political history, by drawing lessons and cautionary tales from Jewish history. While not a repository of scientific truth, there is much to learn of *political* truth in Scripture.

Spinoza brings to the text a *method* for interpreting it. The scientific revolutions of the seventeenth century saw an explosion of universal methods and methodologies to facilitate discovery, understanding, and presentation of truth. Bacon, Galileo, and Descartes come to mind immediately. In working to understand and interpret nature (the natural world), the student of nature adopts a method, an empirical tool to assay the data. Analogously, Spinoza writes,

> I hold that the method of interpreting Scripture does not differ from the method of interpreting nature, but rather is wholly consonant with it. The method of interpreting nature consists above all in constructing a natural history from which we derive the definitions of natural things, as from certain data. Likewise, to interpret Scripture, we need to assemble a genuine history of it and to deduce the thinking of the Bible's authors by valid inferences from this history, as from certain data and principles.
>
> (*TTP* 7/98)

The analogy is exact. Spinoza means what he says. Just as the natural scientist uses an empirical method to interpret the data and derive general principles of nature, so the biblical critic, the student of the text, will need a method by which to proceed to gain an understanding of the text and its lessons. Scripture is the subject for study, and a natural history of Scripture demands philological and linguistic expertise, as well as historical and psychological insight. Spinoza writes, "The universal rule for interpreting Scripture is to claim nothing as a biblical doctrine that we have not derived, by the closest possible scrutiny, from its own history" (*TTP* 7/99). To interpret Scripture with such historical sensitivity is the counter to a Maimonidean 'dogmatism' that *presumes* the inerrancy of Scripture, instead of patiently sifting the evidence. Just as we must not bring to bear supra-natural causes to explain nature, so for Spinoza, we must not import supra-historical causes to understand Scripture. Scripture is a historical text written at a certain time, in a certain place, and by certain people, and to understand it we need to understand fully the context of its composition. In quick succession supra-historical (and supra-natural) events and causes like miracles and divine revelation go by the boards. As nature is understood *sola Natura*, so Scripture must be understood *sola Scriptura*. Philosophy and science are of no help for the latter project.

We may be tempted to draw a distinction between Maimonides and Spinoza here, between one position that (illicitly) interprets a field or subject using principles *extraneous* ("extrinsic") to it and one that does not. We might be minded of Aristotle who famously remarks that "precision is not to be sought for alike in all discussions", and that it is "the mark of an educated man to look for precision in each class of things just so far as the nature of the subject admits." (*Nicomachean Ethics* 1.3). From Spinoza's perspective, Maimonides' "science of Law in its true sense" is misguided by virtue of its importation of philosophical categories into the Scriptural context. For Spinoza, Maimonides forces Scripture to cohere with Philosophy. For Spinoza, by contrast, Scripture and Philosophy each have their own respective principles and starting points, and the better part of wisdom, and the antidote to a dangerous dogmatism, is to realize this and to adopt a principled methodological pluralism.

What are we to make of this point? I think this plea for a methodological pluralism is in general a reasonable one, but it is not clear that Maimonides is guilty of the dogmatism with which he is charged. I offer one example. In *Guide* 3.32 Maimonides presents a brilliant analysis of the laws concerning sacrifices (*korbanot*) and their role in extirpating idolatrous worship. Maimonides' discussion evinces a keen understanding of history and human nature, and why in fact there are (and were) laws of sacrifice. Maimonides writes that a ban on animal sacrifices "would in those [idolatrous] days have been quite inconceivable ... seeing that human nature is always happy only with that to which it is accustomed" (*Guide* 3.32/70a). As a result, sacrifices continued, but sacrifices were now re-directed to God. I highlight Maimonides' discussion here, and I urge all readers to turn to this text [see the section on Idolatry for this text], to get a sense of Maimonides as a keen student of religious *history*, as one reading the text as a student of *natural* religion would. He explains the laws of sacrifice in a way that is attentive to historical context and human nature. The discussion here is as empirical as anything one finds in Spinoza or Hume. There is no distortion or bending of the text, and the rationale and purpose for sacrifices is derived from the empirical data of history and human nature.

In general, for all of Spinoza's complaining about Maimonidean dogmatism, there is much in common between Spinoza and Maimonides. As we have noted, the "science of Law in its true sense" is for Maimonides a foundational project of ascertaining *ta'amei ha-mitzvot*, the reasons for and general trajectory of the Law. This explanatory project is a 'naturalistic' one, illustrating precisely the (divine) teleological functionality and purposiveness that Maimonides sees operative throughout creation. So, when Spinoza writes, in response to the dogmatists, "I hold that the method of interpreting Scripture does not differ from the method of interpreting nature, but rather is wholly consonant with it", we may wish to come to Maimonides' defense by calling to mind the very *empirical and historical* foundations of the Maimonidean project of ascertaining the reasons for and general trajectory of the Law.

The ultimate goal of the Law (and the *Guide* itself) is rational excellence, and it is important to understand this excellence as the *summum bonum* of a certain way of life. Maimonides is engaged in his own way in a traditional moral philosophical project of detailing the best life for a human being. As he sees it, the purpose of the Law is to provide an outline for a fulfilling life. An understanding of the Laws has *practical* import, and the *Guide* should be seen in this perspective. In this regard it is not really different from Aristotle's ethical project, whose goal is "not in order to know what virtue is, but in order to become good" (*Nicomachean Ethics* 2.2). For all of the theoretical work on display in the *Guide*, theory serves practice in the sense that it informs and motivates practice and is the finest activity (praxis) in a good life. The very end of the *Guide* (3.54/134a) clarifies this, and in explicitly asserting that the philosophers and the prophets are in complete agreement on the *summum bonum*, Maimonides underscores the importance of speculation in an understanding of the Law and in achieving the human good—knowledge and love of God.

Viewed from this angle, Spinoza's philosophical projects bear comparison with Maimonides'. They too serve a practical end. Maimonides' goal in the *Guide* is to deliver from perplexity a student alienated from the community, and in so doing to reposition that one actively back in the community, in full knowledge that the scientific and philosophical studies he has undertaken are in fact mandated by the Law for one such as himself. For his own part, Spinoza's goal in both the *Tractatus Theologico-Politicus* and the *Ethics* is in its own way practical. In historicizing Scripture and countering religious dogmatism Spinoza hopes to weaken the grip of fear and superstition, and in delimiting the role of institutional religion in the state, Spinoza optimistically asserts that the state is able "to free everyone from fear so that they may live in security so far as possible ... to allow their minds and bodies to develop in their own ways in security and enjoy the free use of reason ..." (*TTP* 20/241). And Spinoza's *Ethics*, by its very title as well as the order of presentation, clarifies that project as one of providing the metaphysical and psychological foundations for comprehending and achieving well-being and the *summum bonum*—knowledge and love of God.

Both Maimonides and Spinoza are avid readers and interpreters of Scripture because they find Scripture, if read in a comprehending way, inordinately helpful in living well. Holy Writ (Torah) may or may not be a repository of all wisdom and timeless truth, but its power to motivate cannot be gainsaid.

### Further Reading on Interpretation of Scripture

Averroes (Ibn Rushd) *On the Harmony of Religion and Philosophy (Fasl al-Maqal)*, trans. and comm. G. F. Hourani (London: Gibb Memorial Trust, 1961).

Carmy, S. "A Room with a View, but a Room of Our Own," *Tradition* 28 (1994), 39–69.

Carmy, S. and D. Shatz. "The Bible as a Source for Philosophical Reflection," in *History of Jewish Philosophy*, eds. D. Frank and O. Leaman (London: Routledge, 1997), 13–37.

Golding, J. "On the Limits of Non-Literal Interpretation of Scripture from an Orthodox Perspective," *The Torah U-Madda Journal* 10 (2001), 37–59.

Halivni, D. W. *Peshat and Derash: Plain and Applied Meaning in Rabbinic Exegesis* (New York: Oxford University Press, 1991).

Lancaster, I. *Deconstructing the Bible: Abraham Ibn Ezra's Introduction to the Torah* (New York: Routledge, 2002), 142–176.

McCall, T. "On Understanding Scripture as the Word of God," in *Analytic Theology*, eds. O. Crisp and M. Rea (Oxford: Oxford University Press, 2009), 171–186.

Plantinga, A. *Warranted Christian Belief* (Oxford: Oxford University Press, 2000), 374–421.

Preus, J. S. *Spinoza and the Irrelevance of Biblical Authority* (Cambridge: Cambridge University Press, 2001), 154–202.

Rudavsky, T. M. "The Science of Scripture: Abraham Ibn Ezra and Spinoza on Biblical Hermeneutics," in *Spinoza and Medieval Jewish Philosophy*, ed. S. Nadler (Cambridge: Cambridge University Press, 2014), 59–78.

Shatz, D. "The Biblical and Rabbinic Background to Medieval Jewish Philosophy," in *The Cambridge Companion to Medieval Jewish Philosophy*, eds. D. Frank and O. Leaman (Cambridge: Cambridge University Press, 2003), 16–37.

Stump, E. and T. Flint (eds.) *Hermes and Athena: Biblical Exegesis and Philosophical Theology* (Notre Dame, IN: University of Notre Dame Press, 1993).

# 3 Jewish Philosophy and its History

The historiography of Jewish philosophy is a peculiarly modern topic, for only from the nineteenth century do we find histories of Jewish philosophy. At once the question arises about the nature of the subject, Jewish philosophy. **Leon Roth** asks the obvious question: Is there a Jewish Philosophy? As obvious as the question is, a moment's reflection engenders problems. Shall we understand Jewish philosophy as a kind of inquiry into Judaism and the principles that underlie it? Or shall we understand the subject as a way of philosophizing? Again, is the *philosophy of Judaism* an inquiry into the nature of the religion or a set of answers that the religion gives to fundamental philosophical problems? Roth asks the pertinent questions, and his final answer is: "The philosophy of Judaism is the thinking and rethinking of the fundamentals of Judaism." "Rethinking" is key here, for the inquiry into Judaism, teasing out its commitments, is an on-going project. Judaism is not a fossil, nor is its philosophy.

Agreeing with much of Roth's diagnosis, **Daniel Frank** adds a historical dimension to the discussion. He suggests that Jewish philosophy itself, the very subject, did not exist before nineteenth-century academic historians of philosophy invented it. Jewish philosophy is a projection onto certain Jewish thinkers, and is modeled on regnant historical categories. Frank argues that no pre-modern 'Jewish' philosophers (say, Maimonides or Gersonides) identified as or were such, except in the trivial sense of being Jews and being philosophers. But being a Jew and being a philosopher does not entail that one is engaged in Jewish philosophy. Maimonides' project in the *Guide* is a general philosophical one, and just here Spinoza offers his strong critique that this project ill consorts with biblical interpretation. Frank suggests that Jewish philosophy, the subject itself, emerges only in the nineteenth century, and is a response to and a sign of Enlightenment, and a desire to assimilate to European academic life.

**Leora Batnitzky** suggests that the nature of Jewish philosophy, and by this she means the interconnections between Judaism and philosophy, is clarified by inspecting its history. The history of Jewish philosophy reveals that those engaged in 'Jewish philosophy,' in both the pre-modern and modern periods, do not, and cannot, recognize this category as descriptive of their activity. Neither Maimonides nor Gersonides, nor Cohen, Rosenzweig, Levinas, Heschel, and Strauss are Jewish philosophers. From the side of philosophy, Batnitzky notes that "[w]hile

Cohen, Rosenzweig, and Levinas agree that Jewish sources and ideas provide important occasions for philosophical reflection, from their perspectives these foundations do not make their philosophies Jewish." For them, their philosophies could be 'Jewish' only if (*per impossibile*) they harmonize with reason and are not inflected in any non-philosophical way. And from the side of Judaism, Judah, Halevi, Heschel, and Strauss stress the irresolvable contrast between religion and philosophy, thus precluding the possibility of Jewish philosophy. So, where does this leave us in understanding Jewish philosophy? For Batnitzky, the historical lesson offers no definitive answers, but provides a challenge to reflect on the universality of philosophy and its connections to historical Judaism.

## LEON ROTH (1896–1963)

### "Is there a Jewish Philosophy?" (1962), in *Is There a Jewish Philosophy? Rethinking Fundamentals* (1999)

#### *I The Problem*

I take my text from the concluding words of Husik's standard work on the history of Jewish medieval philosophy (1916): 'There are Jews now and there are philosophers; but there are no Jewish philosophers and there is no Jewish philosophy.'

Let me read that again: 'There are no Jewish philosophers and there is no Jewish philosophy.' You will note that he is talking about the present ('There are Jews *now* and there are philosophers'), with the implication (presumably) that the matter was not always so: after all he had just concluded a big volume on Jewish medieval philosophy himself. But even among the philosophers whom he describes there would seem to be some who would not merit the title *Jewish* philosophers even though they lived long ago. You may recall, for example, the remarks prefaced by the editor to the first edition (1560) of Gersonides' *Wars of the Lord*: 'His words seem to contradict our Torah and the wise men of our people. ... But he has explained in his Introduction and the last chapter of his First Part that the Torah is one thing and philosophy another, and each occupies itself with its own affairs ...' Since the sixteenth-century editor does not seem to be shocked by this avowal of Gersonides, it would seem that in Renaissance Italy too it could be said that there are Jews now and there are philosophers, but that it does not follow from the fact that a philosopher happens to be a Jew and even writes in Hebrew that his philosophy is necessarily Jewish.

So the problem is fairly set. In what sense can we talk about Jewish philosophy, and what can we expect to find if we look for it? ...

#### *III The Nature of the Subject*

The year 1933 saw, among other things, the publication of the last product in the direct line of the authentic Judaeo-German 'Science of Judaism'. I refer to Julius

Guttmann's *Philosophie des Judentums.* Julius Guttmann was the distinguished son of a distinguished father. Guttmann the elder, Jacob Guttmann, rabbi of the community of Breslau, had gone patiently through the classical Jewish philosophers from Isaac Israeli to Abrabanel and summarized clearly both their own teachings and the influence they exerted on others; Guttmann the son, Julius, a student of economics as well as of philosophy, had started his career as a lecturer in general philosophy in the University of Breslau, and as Professor of Jewish Philosophy in the Jüdische Hochschule in Berlin he had by his comprehensive and independent studies of the whole field rounded off the results of his father's labors into one coherent and systematic whole. It was this which appeared in Munich in 1933, a Hebrew version with some additional chapters being published in Jerusalem after the author's death in 1951.

The significant thing about Julius Guttmann's volume was its title, *Die Philosophie des Judentums*, The Philosophy of Judaism. Earlier books on the subject, for example that of Moritz Eisler in German and of Husik in English, had all borne as their title or part of their title the words 'Jewish philosophy'. Some of them, indeed, taking advantage of the German partiality for compound terms, had squeezed in the word 'religious' before philosophy. The pioneer work of David Kauffmann, for example, on the attributes of God, and that of S. Horovitz on the psychology of man, are named specifically contributions to 'Jüdische *Religions*-philosophie', that is, the Jewish philosophy of religion. The great Munk, however, in his celebrated *Mélanges*, was content to speak of Jewish (and Arabic) philosophy; and in this he was followed by most students of his own time and indeed is so followed today. Some scholars ventured even further. The brilliant and original, if unconventional, David Neumark entitled his Hebrew edition of his German history the *History of Philosophy among the Jews.*

The only book on the subject written originally in Hebrew, that of S. Bernfeld, adopted a different name altogether. Its title is *Da'at elohim*, The Knowledge of God; and whether or not Bernfeld's use of this phrase coincides with that of Hosea, it made a title of great interest. For it suggested at least that the philosophers with whom it dealt had something to communicate rather about the nature of God than about the universe in general, and that that something was connected, in however distant a way, with the doctrine found in the Hebrew Scriptures.

### IV Philosophical Interpretation of Judaism

So we have before us, reflected in these various titles, a variety of possibilities as to the nature of our subject. At the one extreme we may place Neumark with his *History of Philosophy among the Jews*, then Munk and the generality of students with their histories of Jewish philosophy. The intermediate position is occupied by the histories of the Jewish philosophy of religion. The other extreme is held by Bernfeld with his *Knowledge of God* and, more explicitly, Julius Guttmann with his 'Philosophy of Judaism'. You will remember that, broadly speaking, the matter of all these books is the same. Even Neumark's highly suggestive, and highly controversial, writings cannot do more than cover the usual list of thinkers—

Philo, Saadya, Maimonides and the rest; and one sees even with him a recognition of the fact that, even when we speak of the history of philosophy among the Jews, we are not really considering a series of attempts to rethink fundamentals in general and to give freely the results arrived at. We have, rather, the restricted interests commonly covered by religion and in particular by historical Judaism, and a series of attempts to work out, in the light of specific historical data, its basis and presuppositions. It is this fact which is recognized clearly by Guttmann and expressed in his title. The genuinely philosophical side of the so-called Jewish philosophers, he explains, is derived from without, that is, from the non-Jewish culture of their time. What they did was to select from that culture such ideas as would offer an account of Judaism which should be consonant with the spirit, or, if you like, the vocabulary, of the age.

We may perhaps put the matter thus. There is an old talmudic saying, made much of by medieval writers, that the Torah spoke in the language of men. Since the men in whose language the Torah spoke passed away long ago, it would seem to rest with each successive generation to provide the Torah with a new vehicle of expression. This, historically, was the task and achievement of the philosophers (or at least of most of them), and their work is therefore quite fairly described as the, or a, philosophy of Judaism; as indeed emerges clearly if they are considered soberly one by one, even Gersonides' *Wars of the Lord* which we noticed before being admissible, and admitted, under the rubric 'Wars *against* the Lord'.

It is this which is the subject of later lectures in this series, and I shall not attempt to anticipate them except in order to illustrate my present point. At the head of the long line of thinkers to be presented to you there is set generally the name of Philo, the Alexandrian Jew who lived in the early days of the Roman Empire and whose recorded public appearance was on the mission to Caligula in the years 39–40 of the Common Era. Philo was a great Jew and an original and interesting thinker, too; but he thought and breathed Plato and the Stoa, and it was his interpretation of Judaism in the light of these non-Jewish systems which constituted his 'philosophy'. True, he came to some surprising conclusions, and these conclusions led to conclusions yet more surprising; but they were the result not of thinking out the nature of things in general but of a Hellenized thinking on the nature of Judaism. The greatest figure we have is undoubtedly Maimonides, but he would be a rash man who would speak of a Maimonidean philosophy. For did not Maimonides himself state explicitly that so far as philosophy, that is, the wisdom of man, is concerned we must all go back, as to a sole source, to Aristotle? True, as Philo used Plato, so Maimonides used Aristotle, in an original way with original results. But the originality consisted not in his philosophy, which was that of Aristotle (or rather, of the Arabized Aristotle), but in what resulted when he applied his Aristotelianism to Judaism. In the same way the German Jewish philosopher Mendelssohn reflects the political thinkers of the seventeenth, and the theologians of the eighteenth century; Lazarus and (in his own fashion) Hermann Cohen set out from the philosophical foundations laid down by Kant. The same holds true today. Students of contemporary Judaism in the United States know how influential a figure is Mordecai Kaplan. But Kaplan took his philosophical ideas from John Dewey; and he then proceeded, in the light of Dewey's ideas, to produce what can only be called, not a Jewish philosophy but a philosophy of Judaism. Similarly, the work of one of the all-too-few Jewish theologians of this country, Dr. Ignaz Maybaum, is based on the thinking of the existentialists; but the result is an existentialist philosophy of Judaism, not a Jewish existentialism.

## *V The Philosophy Offered by Judaism*

At the risk of tiring you I shall push this contrast home as it is important. I spoke earlier of the analogy to Jewish philosophy presented by a hypothetical Jewish physics and Jewish mathematics, and I suggested to you that all such terms are nonsense. Let us consider now the further analogy offered by a phrase often heard recently, *Christian* philosophy. In the twenties or early thirties there was a grand debate on this phrase in the French Société de Philosophie. (The minutes were published in their Bulletin and make interesting reading.) Many different views were expressed, from that of the extreme religionists that there is no genuine philosophy which is not Christian to that of the extreme secularists that philosophy and Christianity have no connection with one another whatsoever. The honors of the debate went to the secularists; but the religionists made the excellent point that religion poses certain fundamental problems which all philosophies must attempt to meet, and suggests certain answers. This was in essence Neumark's position in his *History*. There are, he said, specific problems like that of the origin of the world, of the constitution and destiny of man, of the nature of truth and right action; and on all of these, Neumark held, Judaism gave an intelligible and coherent answer which, implicitly or explicitly, in different stages of development, and in different degrees of conscious articulation, can be found in texts and documents throughout the course of Jewish literary history and more particularly in the writings of the philosophers and especially in those of Moses Maimonides. The world as such, Neumark would seem to be saying, poses its questions and Judaism, when properly understood, that is, as understood by Maimonides as understood by Neumark, gives the answers; just as the proponents of Christian philosophy would say that the world as such presents its questions and that the answers to them are given by Christianity as understood by, say, Thomas Aquinas.

Buddhists or Taoists could be forgiven if they were skeptical about these claims, although they might concede that any religious system might embody some truth or offer some persuasive account of some element in experience. And here, I think, we may leave the matter. We have seen enough to suggest that, however much we may use the term 'Jewish philosophy', the most we should intend by it is a philosophy of Judaism, that is, a discussion of the answers offered by Judaism to some of the general problems of life and thought; and we must recognize that this is not philosophy in the authentic historical sense of a *universal* curiosity and a *universal* questioning into the *widest* aspects of human experience. It is on the contrary a restricted study of certain historical ideas severely limited in relevance and space and time. Now it may possibly be that these historical ideas are of a universal interest, even of a universal importance. But this is a matter of enquiry and discussion. It is not a self-evident truth.

### VI Jewish Philosophy: An Enquiry into Judaism

And we may go even further. The Neumarkian view is, as I have said, that the world poses its problems and Judaism offers the solutions, of course the right solutions. The philosophy of Judaism is therefore the philosophy *offered by* Judaism. 'Of' in this case is a possessive: the philosophy of Judaism is equivalent to Judaism's philosophy.

But are we sure we know what Judaism is? In our generation, a generation (I am afraid) of little learning and less understanding, it is just the nature of Judaism which we need to study and enquire into. So I suggest we take the term a little differently, rather after the model of the 'philosophy of science' than of that of the 'philosophy of Kant'. The philosophy of Kant is the philosophy *held by* Kant. The philosophy of science is the philosophical enquiry *into* science. Science is not the inventor but the object of the philosophy. Philosophy, as we saw at the outset, is the thinking and rethinking of the fundamentals, and when an object is attached to it, the sphere of its application is restricted. The philosophy of science is the thinking and rethinking of the fundamentals of science. The philosophy of Judaism is the thinking and rethinking of the fundamentals of Judaism.

And that, I think, is the historical fact of the matter. When Philo faced the Jewish Hellenists, when Saadya argued against the Karaites, when Maimunists and anti-Maimunists excommunicated one another, when Jacob Sasportas fought his lonely battle against the followers of Shabbetai Zevi, when S. D. Luzzatto extolled Rashi and Yehudah Halevi against Maimonides and Ibn Ezra—the object of discussion was not the nature of the world at large but the nature of Judaism.

So at long last we have found our proper subject. Jewish philosophy, or rather the philosophy of Judaism, is the thinking and rethinking of the fundamental ideas involved in Judaism and the attempt to see them fundamentally, that is, in coherent relation with one another so that they form one intelligible whole.

## DANIEL FRANK

### "What is Jewish Philosophy?" in *History of Jewish Philosophy* (1997)

In his introduction to the English translation of Julius Guttmann's monumental *Die Philosophie des Judentums* (first edition, 1933), Zwi Werblowsky writes:

> Philosophers and historians may be at variance on the question of the nature, or even of the very existence, of constant factors or structures making up an "essence" of Judaism. It is not only philosophies – including philosophies of Judaism – that may change, but also the historian's views on the nature and historical function of earlier philosophical expressions. Perhaps sometime in the near or more distant future, a new history of Judaism will have to be written.

We believe the time has come, and not only because of advances in historical scholarship. There has also been a reconsideration of the nature of the (essentialist) foundations upon which histories such as Guttmann's are written. As Werblowsky already noted in the 1960s, there is debate among philosophers and historians about the "very existence" of an essence of Judaism. This foundational debate is ongoing and now includes discussion of the nature or essence of philosophy itself. At present everything seems unsettled. Little wonder, then, that the question before us – What is Jewish philosophy? – appears particularly timely, indeed timely in two senses. One sense has to do with the obvious relevance of the question in current debates; the other, foreshadowing a point I shall later stress, is perhaps best hinted at by Werblowsky himself at the end of his introduction:

> Guttmann's work stands out, not only as a reliable study which condenses sound and subtle scholarship, and a unique survey of the history of Jewish scholarship; it also represents the fruit and the summing up of an important period in the history of Jewish scholarship. As such, it will remain a lasting monument of a significant phase in the history of Jewish philosophy and its attempt to elucidate not only Judaism, but also itself.

What Werblowsky, writing approximately thirty years after Guttmann, is here penning is an obituary, an obituary to the kind of historical scholarship which Guttmann represents, as well as the presuppositions upon which it is based. In this "terminal" sense, then, the question before us is a timely one, wearing its lineage on its sleeve, as it were. The questions of our forebears remain, relevant to current concerns and yet evocative of a bygone era in the annals of scholarship.

The question, What is Jewish philosophy? is not a perennial one, although in the way it has often been discussed it may appear to be so. Usually it is supposed that the question is a query into the essence of Jewish philosophy, a property or set of properties that Jewish philosophy has always possessed and that distinguishes it from all other branches of philosophy. The discussion of the issue demands that one should isolate common strands in the thought of Philo, Saadia, Maimonides, Crescas, (maybe) Spinoza, Mendelssohn, Cohen, Buber, Rosenzweig, Levinas, and others. This may or may not be possible to do, but it is important to realize at once that reflection on the nature of Jewish philosophy is of comparatively recent vintage. We are fooled into thinking that the question, What is Jewish philosophy? is a perennial one, because its subject matter, Jewish philosophy, extends far into the past in a unified and connected way. But so characterized, the subject matter is question-begging, for the supposition that all the thinkers we have listed are Jewish philosophers, in some non-trivial sense, and that they are together engaged in something called "Jewish philosophy" is a construct we impose upon the past by virtue of the very question we are asking. Such a construction may or may not be legitimate, indeed may or may not be inevitable, but we ought at least to be aware of what we are doing when we ask about the nature of Jewish philosophy.

Much the most important part of any answer we give to our initial query into the nature of Jewish philosophy is that Jewish philosophy is an academic discipline. It is an invention, for reasons important to ponder, of nineteenth-century historians, intent on bringing together certain thinkers, while simultaneously excluding others. Before the invention of Jewish philosophy as an academic discipline no one asked or wondered about the nature of Jewish philosophy, quite simply because the subject did not exist. Put another way: a certain Platonism holds us captive. In the particular case before us, we think that there is a certain essence "out there," namely Jewish philosophy, awaiting study and analysis by historians. But that is not the way to understand the relation that obtains between a subject and the study of it. The discipline itself "makes" the subject as much as it studies it. What counts as relevant and essential is not transparent. Liminal cases are important here and establish the point I am trying to make. In Jewish philosophy, Spinoza comes readily to mind as the paradigm of a figure who wrecks any attempt to derive a definition or essence of the subject. Try as one might, as Wolfson more than others did, Spinoza reveals himself as a protean person for all seasons, defying any attempt at a neat categorization. And what this shows is that Jewish philosophy and its study are much more intimately related to one another than a simple-minded Platonism would have it. And with the demise of such a Platonism we free ourselves to ask about the motivation of those engaged in the study of Jewish philosophy, the impetus which led to the development of the academic discipline.

No one in pre-modern, indeed in much of modern times understood Jewish philosophy as a subdiscipline of philosophy, as a way of philosophizing. No one felt the need to ascertain the essence of Jewish philosophy – "philosophy among the Jews" as it was invariably (and reductively) construed – distinguishing it from every other kind of philosophy or mode of theological interpretation. Note that the claim here about the relative lack of interest in earlier times in a category of Jewish philosophy is not a claim about the status of philosophy in pre-modern times, although it is important to remember that such demarcations as we make between philosophy, science, and theology were not always so. In the Islamic world, wherein one finds the efflorescence of medieval Jewish philosophy from the tenth century on, there existed a branch of wisdom called *falsafa*; presumably those engaged in it had an image of themselves as philosophers (*falāsifa*). Once again, the claim is not that the philosophers had no image of themselves as such, but rather that neither they nor anyone else had an awareness of them as Jewish (or Muslim) philosophers. Neither Maimonides nor Gersonides nor even Mendelssohn, in the modern period, thought of himself as a Jewish philosopher. To the extent that they thought of themselves as philosophers, they imaged themselves as providing an interpretation of the biblical and rabbinic tradition according to universal, philosophical categories. For them, the Bible is a philosophical book, and they interpret it accordingly. But such an interpretation of the tradition hardly amounts to what we call "Jewish philosophy," if by the latter we mean to refer to an inquiry that is "by a Jew and for Jews," with no universal implications whatsoever. For the classical Jewish philosophers, there is a duty for those able to philosophize to do so. And so they do. They philosophize about Judaism, they interpret the tradition in philosophical terms, discussing such (general) issues as divine language, creation, providence, and prophecy. But such a philosophical interpretation of the tradition is in essence not an enterprise specific to Judaism. Consider Philo, the first Jewish philosophical commentator on the Bible, and his influence upon the early Church Fathers. Wolfson considers Philo and his exegetical method as foundational for religious philosophy in all three monotheistic traditions. Again, Maimonides was a Jew and a philosopher, but he did not engage in something called "Jewish philosophy," and the *Guide* is not, except in the most trivial sense, "a Jewish book." Maimonides did not philosophize in a certain, Jewish, way; rather he speculated about his tradition in philosophical terms, about issues of general import embedded in the traditional texts. In essence Averroes did the same thing, and little is to be gained by distinguishing the Maimonidean project from the Averroean one.

What begins to emerge from all this is that not only do we err in thinking that Jewish philosophy is some sort of natural kind, but we are also misled by the surface grammar of the phrase. To the extent that Jewish philosophy has any relevance to the classical thinkers, and here I would include some modern thinkers like Hermann Cohen, it must be parsed as "philosophy of Judaism." Jewish philosophy is not a branch of philosophy, a sub-discipline. Rather, it is, as previously noted, a way, among others, of interpreting the tradition, the philosophical way. The detractors of the *Guide* were surely wrong in thinking that what Maimonides was up to was at variance with the tradition. On the contrary, it was part of it, a way of understanding the tradition – the philosophical way. So construed, the understanding of a particular religious tradition becomes the vehicle for speculation about a host of general philosophical issues. The project is analogous to that of any creative thinker's use of the past for present purposes. One thinks of MacIntyre's use of Aristotle, Murdoch's of Plato, and Gauthier's of Hobbes. History of philosophy becomes philosophy. Similarly, textual exegesis subserves theoretical (and practical) concerns.

If Jewish philosophy, understood as requiring a self-consciousness of itself as an idiosyncratically Jewish enterprise, cannot be imposed upon pre-modern times, it seems, not surprisingly, that one ought to turn to the modern period to fix the genesis of our initial question. Only with emancipation in the eighteenth and nineteenth centuries does the (consequent) fear of assimilation and loss necessitate the need to forge an identity, an identity, in the present context, of subject matter. And so one sees the emergence in the nineteenth century in Germany and, to a much lesser extent, in France of the writing of the history of the nominal subject matter of this book, Jewish philosophy.

To ask, then, about the nature of Jewish philosophy is to position oneself in a certain historical framework, one in which there is the felt need to establish a boundary, a marker whereby the definiendum gains legitimacy. Again, to ask about the nature of Jewish philosophy is to accede to a certain characterization of thinkers, ideas, and texts. And this may, of course, be a false characterization, false in the sense that it is insufficiently attentive to the historical context in which the grouped thinkers and their ideas were originally nested. Indeed, if I am right, there is no Jewish philosophy before the nineteenth-century historians of Jewish philosophy invented the subject. Husik's famous and oft-quoted remark at the end of his influential *A History of Mediaeval Jewish Philosophy* (1916), "there are Jews now and there are philosophers, but there are no Jewish philosophers and there is no Jewish philosophy," seems to me just backwards. For now there are Jewish philosophers, or at least individuals who imagine that they are engaged in something called "Jewish philosophy," whereas before the modern period, before the nineteenth century, there was no one who had such a thought. Again, this is not to suggest that there were no philosophical influences upon Jews – of course, Plato and Aristotle influenced Halevi, Maimonides, Gersonides, and del Medigo, and Kant influenced Mendelssohn (and vice versa). Nor is it to suggest that we are wrong in understanding and even interpreting the medieval Jewish thinkers and their immediate successors as part of the philosophical tradition. Rather the point is that their being influenced by current philosophical trends and the plain fact of their being Jews writing from within the tradition does not mean that they were engaged in something called "Jewish philosophy" or that in some non-trivial sense they were themselves Jewish philosophers.

As noted, Jewish philosophy came into being as a disciplinary response of Jewish academics to a particular historical condition, one which threatened the very identity and being of Jewish culture. Jewish philosophy came into being as an attempt to delineate, along standard academic lines, a certain body of literature. Perforce Jewish philosophy quickly came to exclude those elements which did not fit the regnant academic model. Mysticism was excluded from the discipline because of its (supposed) arationality, even though we come to learn of its *philosophical* (Neoplatonic) antecedents. Again, to gain a foothold of academic respectability, Jewish philosophy quickly began to parallel, even ape, current trends. It still does.

But there is no a priori reason why Jewish philosophy must parallel non-Jewish philosophy. Why does it? Is it part of an assimilationist ideology, to which Scholem more than anyone else drew our attention? It was Scholem's general charge against the proponents of Wissenschaft des Judentums that they, historians of Judaism, whitewashed the past in the service of a liberal, assimilationist, ultimately anti-Zionist agenda. Ought the great historians of Jewish philosophy to stand accused of the same charge? Why really has the history of mysticism been so notably absent in histories of Jewish philosophy? To answer in a positivist way that its absence is due to its unphilosophical nature is, first, to be historically misinformed and, second and most importantly, to evince a way of doing the history of philosophy which is patently derivative, driven by current or recent trends.

Let us return to the initial question. At first it gave the appearance of an essentialist inquiry into the nature of the subject. Now I hope we see that such an inquiry is a non-starter and that in fact the question is ill-formed or, at least, admits of a radically different answer than it originally suggested. For now the simple answer to the question, What is Jewish philosophy? is: Jewish philosophy is an academic discipline invented in the nineteenth century by scholars intent on gaining a foothold of academic respectability. I pass no value judgement here whatever. I hope merely to provide a bit of genealogy. In this regard I stand with Nietzsche in attempting to "historicize" what too often is taken in an atemporal sense.

LEORA BATNITZKY

## "The Nature and History of Jewish Philosophy"

The term "Jewish philosophy" suggests that such an enterprise must do justice to both Judaism and philosophy. This means that, as Leon Roth remarks, thinking about Jewish philosophy requires that we contemplate not only the nature of Judaism but also the nature of philosophy. But what does it mean to do philosophy from the point of view of Judaism? Is Jewish philosophy applicable to non-Jews as well as to Jews? If Jewish philosophy articulates Judaism in a philosophical medium, then which has more weight in this effort at translation, Judaism or philosophy? If the answer is Judaism, how can Jewish philosophy still be philosophy, which is usually defined as a universal means to truth? And if the answer is philosophy, how can Jewish philosophy claim to be an authentic portrait of Judaism, which, however one defines it, is constituted by specific texts and traditions, not to speak of a special, if not unique, relationship with God?

We can add to these complications the fact that, as Daniel Frank notes, "Jewish philosophy" is a category that only emerged in the nineteenth century. Among other things, this would suggest that seminal figures whom we today call Jewish philosophers, such as Maimonides or Gersonides, thought of themselves simply as philosophers, and not as Jewish philosophers. This brings us to another set of questions. Does the historical particularity of "Jewish philosophy" suggest then that there is a significant divide between modern philosophers who might do Jewish philosophy and pre-modern thinkers who knew of no such enterprise? And can we really talk about Jewish philosophy as if it is one particular type of enterprise?

In what follows, I will suggest that thinking about the history of Jewish philosophy can help us think about the nature of Jewish philosophy. I begin by examining the relationship between Judaism and philosophy from the point of view of "philosophy," after which I turn to examine the relationship between philosophy and Judaism from the point of view of "Judaism." The conclusion reflects on what all of this means for thinking about what Jewish philosophy might or might not be.

Let us begin by considering the relationship between Jewish philosophy and other categories of philosophy. Is the gap between the self-understanding of thinkers often labeled Jewish philosophers and the category of Jewish philosophy any larger than, for instance, the disparity between ancient philosophers who didn't think of themselves as ancient and the category of ancient philosophy? Like the modifier "Jewish" to philosophy, the modifier "ancient" to philosophy is a modern academic construction. Ancient philosophers would not have thought of themselves as ancient philosophers simply because they were not ancient from their point of view. While the particularities of their histories are different, "ancient philosophy" and "Jewish philosophy" are alike in that both categories came into being with the development of modern university education. The curious thing about "Jewish philosophy," however, is that it is not just pre-modern "Jewish philosophers" who did not think of themselves as doing Jewish philosophy. Modern philosophers writing after the academic invention of "Jewish philosophy," who have been canonized as Jewish philosophers, also do not recognize themselves as such. In this way, it does indeed seem that the gap between the self-understanding of philosophers called Jewish philosophers and the category of Jewish philosophy is wider than the gap between the self-understanding of philosophers and other modern categories of philosophy.

But this is not entirely true. Questions surrounding the nature of Jewish philosophy are not any different in kind from questions surrounding, for instance, the natures of Islamic philosophy or Buddhist philosophy. We could ask almost all of the same questions about the nature of Jewish philosophy described in the first paragraph of this essay about Islamic or Buddhist philosophy. This point may tell us more about the definitions of philosophy in modern universities, and perhaps especially in American universities, than it does about the natures of Jewish, Islamic, or Buddhist philosophies. Take for instance the categorization of Immanuel Kant, a seminal figure for both continental and analytic philosophy. While interpretations of Kant rage on, Kant is for the most part classified not as a Christian philosopher, but just as a philosopher. Yet it is also clear, though generally not acknowledged in philosophical circles, that Kant's philosophy depends on a number of Christian, and particularly Lutheran, assumptions.

Christian assumptions are not accidental but essential to Kant's philosophy. Kant defines autonomy and morality in terms of a self-legislating law: "the will is not merely subject to the law but subject to it in such a way that it must be viewed as giving the law to itself and just because of this as first subject to the law (of which it can regard itself as the author)."[1] As John Rawls put it a bit more clearly, "Kant's main aim is to justify and deepen Rousseau's idea that liberty is acting in accordance with a law we give ourselves."[2] Yet as Hermann Cohen (arguably the most important modern Jewish philosopher and a great admirer of Kant) recognized, Kant's concept of law (as well as of Judaism) is indebted to a "Pauline prejudice."[3] Like Paul, Kant defines actual laws as coercive and heteronomous while defining the moral law as free and autonomous. These assumptions are implicitly part of Kant's views of law and morality, but he also offers a particularly explicit statement regarding the intimate connection between his philosophy and Paul's theology in *Religion within the Limits of Reason Alone*. Kant writes: "To become free, 'to be freed from bondage under the law of sin, to live for righteousness'—this is the highest prize he [the morally well-disposed man] can win."[4] Note that Kant's statement paraphrases Paul's famous words in Romans 6: 15–18: "Are we to sin because we are not under law but grace? By no means! Do you not know that if you yield yourselves to any one as obedient slaves, you are slaves of the one whom you obey either of sin, which leads to death, or of obedience, which leads to righteousness? But thanks to God, that you who were once slaves of sin have become obedient from the heart to the standard of teaching to which you were committed and, having been set free from sin, have become slaves of righteousness."[5]

One of Cohen's neo-Kantian philosophical tasks is to move Kant's philosophy beyond this prejudice and make law the center of ethics. Of course, there is much to be debated about Kant's views of law and autonomy as well as about Cohen's corrective. For the purposes of understanding the nature and history of Jewish philosophy, however, the important point is that Kant, like all philosophers, begins with non-philosophical opinions and attempts to move towards philosophical truth. The fact that Kant's notions of autonomy and law are at least in part dependent on "Pauline" assumptions does not invalidate Kant's philosophy. Cohen's claim is not that Kant is actually a Christian and therefore not a philosopher but rather that some of Kant's assumptions about law do not hold up philosophically. The question of whether Kant is right about self-legislation depends on whether or not he can defend his arguments on the basis of reason.

We can now offer a preliminary definition of Jewish philosophy. Jewish philosophy, like any philosophy, begins with non-philosophical opinions and attempts to move toward truth not by necessarily disregarding these opinions but by refining them. The non-philosophical opinions that are the beginnings (though not necessarily the exclusive beginnings) of something we might call Jewish philosophy are not any different in kind from, for instance, the non-philosophical beginnings of Greek philosophy, Islamic philosophy, or Kantian philosophy. In content, the non-philosophical beginnings of Jewish philosophy may or may not bring new insights into philosophical conversation. But the point of Jewish philosophy, described in this very minimalist way, is to allow non-philosophical opinions, derived from Jewish texts or experiences, to enter into philosophical conversation.

In this way, considering the nature of Jewish philosophy allows us to question what may be described as a distinctly modern philosophical prejudice, which is that philosophical universality requires the discarding of all human particularities. As Leo Strauss put it in regard to Socrates, "Socrates implied that disregarding the opinions about the nature of things would amount to abandoning the most important access to reality which we have, or the most important vestiges of truth which are within our reach."[6] Or as Franz Rosenzweig mused in a diary entry, "One's own eyes, to be sure, are only one's eyes. But it would be stupidly bourgeois to believe that one had to pluck out one's own eyes in order to see clearly."[7] We can also now appreciate why properly speaking there can be no single Jewish philosophy but rather Jewish philosophies. The pre-philosophical stuff of Judaism and Jewishness is in no way homogeneous. The sources of Judaism as well as Jewish lived experience are and historically have been diverse and in some cases even contradictory. This is not to suggest a kind of relativism with regard to Judaism or philosophy. Instead, part of the work of Jewish philosophy is arguing about which sources or which experiences ought to count as the right starting point for philosophizing.

Somewhat paradoxically, however, these very reasons also indicate why many philosophers called Jewish philosophers would not describe themselves as such. Emmanuel Levinas illustrates this well. Levinas distinguishes between his philosophical and confessional writings, the latter of which are largely readings of the Talmud. As he puts it, "I always make a clear distinction in what I write, between philosophical and confessional texts ... I would never, for example, introduce a talmudic or biblical verse into one of my philosophical texts to try to prove or justify a phenomenological argument."[8] The key words in these sentences are "prove" and "justify." Levinas's claim here is about philosophical authority, and not about whether Judaism, in the form of the Talmud or the Bible, can enter into philosophical thinking. Levinas develops many religious, and specifically Jewish, themes, such as election, transcendence, and "the messianic." But Levinas never claims validity for these ideas on the basis of their religious authority. Rather, he uses these notions as starting points for a vigorous phenomenological investigation into the meanings of humanity as such.

Levinas describes his approach as follows: "I have never aimed explicitly to 'harmonize' ... both traditions [philosophy and religion]. If they happen to be in harmony it is probably because every philosophical thought rests on pre-philosophical experiences, and ... the Bible has belonged to these founding experiences."[9] And as he puts it even more explicitly, "philosophy derives [*dérive*] from religion. It is called for by religion adrift [*en dérive*], and in all likelihood religion is always adrift."[10] Philosophy and religion thus exist in a relation of mutuality. Philosophy derives from religion but philosophy also gives direction and purpose to religion. Judaism and philosophy do not need to be harmonized for Levinas, because they are already in fundamental harmony with one another. Judaism or what Levinas, perhaps following Hegel, elsewhere calls "religiosity" ["*le religieux*"] is the pre-philosophical stuff out of which philosophy arises. For Levinas, Judaism has something important, if not essential, to contribute to philosophy. But once Judaism has contributed to his philosophical thinking, Judaism as such is not relevant to his philosophy any longer since philosophy must stand or fall only by virtue of its own authority.

Similarly, Cohen also would not consider himself a Jewish philosopher. As we saw above, Cohen recognizes religious categories in philosophical thinking. But for Cohen, as for Kant and Levinas, these categories only derive their authority from philosophical reflection. The title of Cohen's posthumous work, *Religion of Reason out of the Sources of Judaism*, a philosophical corrective to *Kant's Religion within the Limits of Reason Alone*, makes this clear. The sources he considers may be Jewish, but what matters is whether or not they can produce not a religion of reason, i.e., a rational Judaism, but religion of reason as such (Cohen of course argues that they can). While his conception of philosophy departs from Cohen's, Franz Rosenzweig makes a similar point about his magnum opus, *The Star of Redemption*, which he maintains: "is not a 'Jewish' book, at least not in the sense that those buyers, who were so angry with me, think of a Jewish book; for while it deals with Judaism, it deals with it no more comprehensively than it deals with Christianity, and barely more comprehensively than it deals with Islam." For Rosenzweig, *The Star* is an attempt to develop what he calls the "new thinking," which bridges philosophy, defined in terms of Nietzsche's perspectivalism, and theology, defined not in specifically Jewish terms but in terms of a wholly universalized notion of revelation that he describes as neighbor love.

I have suggested that just as pre-modern thinkers often labeled as "Jewish philosophers" did not and would not recognize the term, so also Cohen, Rosenzweig, and Levinas do not and would not describe themselves as such. While Cohen, Rosenzweig, and Levinas agree that Jewish sources and ideas provide important occasions for philosophical reflection, from their perspectives these foundations do not make their philosophies Jewish. For them, their philosophies are Jewish only if one assumes that philosophy as such begins with reason, and without pre-philosophical commitments. But this is a steep price to pay, for such a 'modern' (Enlightenment) view of philosophy is problematic. We see then that what is at stake in these considerations about the history and nature of Jewish philosophy is the very understanding of philosophy itself.

While we have just examined questions about the history and nature of Jewish philosophy from the point of philosophy, we now turn to consider some of these questions from the point of view of Judaism. Again, we begin with an historical point. Whereas an engagement with philosophy has historically been integral to both the Christian and Buddhist traditions, an engagement with philosophy has not been central to the Jewish or Islamic traditions. As Leo Strauss puts it, "For the Christian, the sacred doctrine is revealed theology; for the Jew and the Muslim, the sacred doctrine is, at least primarily the legal interpretation of the Divine Law (*talmud* or *fiqh*). The sacred doctrine in the latter sense has, to say the least, much less in common with philosophy than the sacred doctrine in the former sense."[11] Strauss's characterization suggests that Judaism and philosophy are two very different kinds of enterprises. As such, the category of "Jewish philosophy" would be, from this point of view, oxymoronic.

Although he is often characterized as a Jewish philosopher, Judah Halevi, in his most philosophical work, the *Kuzari*, implicitly rejects the possibility of such a category. The *Kuzari* is an imagined dialogue between the King of the Khazars, a philosopher, a Muslim, a Christian, and a Jew. The King dreams that his way of thinking is pleasing to God but that his way of acting is not. Determined to act in a way agreeable to God, the King asks the philosopher, Muslim, Christian, and Jew each to offer a defense of his respective beliefs and practices. The King begins with the philosopher but quickly dismisses him. The King says to the philosopher: "Thy words are convincing, yet they do not correspond to what I wish to find. I know already that my soul is pure and that my actions are calculated to gain the favor of God. To all this I received the answer that this way of action does not find favor, though the intention does. There must no doubt be a way of acting, pleasing by its very nature, but not through the medium of intentions."[12] The King maintains that philosophy is concerned with the intellect while religion concerns action. And having been convinced that Christianity and Islam are merely derivative from Judaism, the King eventually converts to Judaism.

This is of course nothing but the most cursory reading of the *Kuzari*, but for our purposes it suffices to make an important point. Halevi's argument that Judaism and philosophy are two distinct approaches to life is not a claim that Judaism is irrational and that philosophy is rational. After all, it is on the basis of reasoned argument that Halevi puts his position forward. The claim that Jewish philosophy is oxymoronic suggests that Judaism and philosophy have fundamentally different answers to the question of what constitutes the good life. Philosophy is contemplative, while Judaism is action-oriented. This of course does not mean that philosophers don't act or that Jews don't think. But it does mean that philosophy begins and ends with thought, while Judaism begins and ends with acting as God demands. Yet there is something more than this. While insisting on the difference between philosophy and Judaism, Halevi nonetheless implicitly suggests that philosophy can make a contribution to Judaism in the form of a kind of negative argument. The *Kuzari* demonstrates, through philosophical argumentation, philosophy's own limits. In so doing, Halevi uses philosophy to show not what Judaism is but what Judaism is not.

Abraham Joshua Heschel, who is also often labeled a Jewish philosopher, similarly contends that Judaism and philosophy are fundamentally different from one another. Heschel describes the divide somewhat differently than Halevi. Heschel writes:

> Not only are the problems of philosophy not identical with the problem of religion; their status is not the same. Philosophy is, in a sense, a kind of thinking that has a beginning but not end ... the awareness of the problem outlives all solutions. Its answers are questions in disguise; every new answer giving rise to new questions. In religion, on the other hand, the mystery of the answer hovers over all questions.[13]

Heschel's reference to mystery is not an endorsement of irrationalism. He is not suggesting that Judaism is irrational while philosophy is rational, but rather that Judaism begins and ends with the mysterious yet real relation between the Jewish people and God. There can of course be reasoned arguments about what constitutes this relation, but the relation itself can only be a given—it can neither be demonstrated philosophically nor transcended for the sake of a higher philosophical truth or even a philosophical question. Within this framework, Heschel outlines the contours of a constructive relationship between Judaism and philosophy, which he does not call Jewish philosophy but rather "a philosophy of Judaism." A "philosophy of Judaism," Heschel proposes, understands the term Judaism as a subject, that is, as a "source of ideas we are trying to understand," and not as an object of philosophical critique.[14] Like Halevi, Heschel maintains that philosophy does have something to contribute to Judaism. Yet also like Halevi, philosophy's contribution serves to clarify the ultimate difference between philosophy and Judaism.

Leo Strauss is perhaps the most vocal, and controversial, modern proponent of the position that Judaism and philosophy are fundamentally irreconcilable. Strauss boldly states that "being a Jew and a philosopher *are* mutually exclusive."[15] Strauss's tone may be strident, but his position is not very different from Halevi's or Heschel's. Contrary to the ways in which he is often interpreted, Strauss never claims that Judaism is irrational or that it consists in blind obedience. The difference between philosophy and Judaism is their respective starting points. The philosopher begins and ends with his own sense of wonder, and hence the philosopher's own questions are stimulated by wonder. In contrast, the Jew, Strauss maintains, "is not master of how to begin; before he begins to write he is already confronted with writings, with the holy writings, which impose their law on him."[16] Like Halevi, Strauss contends that Judaism is about acting, while philosophy is about contemplation. And like Heschel, Strauss maintains that unlike philosophy, Judaism begins and ends with the mystery and reality of God's relation to human beings. But this does not mean that there is no questioning and reasoning within the framework of obedience and mystery, or that philosophy has nothing to contribute to Judaism. As Strauss stresses, one can be a Jew challenged by philosophy or a philosopher challenged by Judaism.[17] But one cannot be a Jewish philosopher. For Strauss, such an identity falsely claims to resolve what is in fact an irresolvable religious *and* philosophical problem: that the answer to the question of what constitutes the good does not admit of only one solution.

Where do we go from here? I've suggested in this essay that two historical points offer us entry into contemplating the nature of Jewish philosophy. First, most pre-modern and modern Jewish thinkers would not call themselves Jewish philosophers. I have suggested that this has to do with changing and disputed understandings of philosophy. Second, philosophy has not historically played the kind of central role in Jewish traditions that it has in Christian traditions. This suggests that debates about philosophy's proper relation to Judaism have to do with disputed understandings of Judaism. While the first set of thinkers we explored (Cohen, Rosenzweig, and Levinas) would not call themselves Jewish philosophers because of their understanding of philosophy, the second set of thinkers we explored (Halevi, Heschel, and Strauss) would not call themselves Jewish philosophers because of their understanding of Judaism. Nevertheless, all these thinkers implicitly agree that there is great value to thinking about philosophy and Judaism together. What does this all mean for thinking about the nature of Jewish philosophy?

By way of conclusion, I suggest that "Jewish philosophy" is a modern academic construct whose subject is the examination of the ways in which different thinkers have explored the relationship between "Judaism" and "philosophy." Understood in this way, Jewish philosophy does not provide neat solutions to questions about the definitions of "Judaism" or "philosophy." This means that Jewish philosophy will be a frustrating subject for those seeking ultimate philosophical answers or even final agreement on questions of interpretation. But it also means that considering questions about Jewish philosophy offers an interdisciplinary and creative challenge to those who wish to understand the complexities involved in historical and philosophical constructions of Judaism and philosophy.

## Notes

1  Kant 1999, 81.
2  Rawls 2001, 225.
3  Cohen 1984, bd. 7, 227–28.
4  Kant 1960, 57.
5  Translation of the New Testament is from *The New Oxford Annotated Bible with the Apocrypha*, Revised Standard Version (New York: Oxford University Press, 1964).
6  Strauss 1964, 124.
7  Rosenzweig 1974–1984, GS I: 2, 587.

8  Kearney, in R. Cohen (ed.) 1986, 18.
9  Levinas 1985, 24.
10  Levinas 1977, 156.
11  Strauss 1952, 18–19.
12  Halevi 1964, 39.
13  Heschel 1976, 4.
14  Ibid, 22.
15  Strauss 1952, 19.
16  Strauss 1997, 374.
17  Strauss 1979, 111.

## Further Reading on Jewish Philosophy and its History

Hughes, A. *Rethinking Jewish Philosophy: Beyond Particularism and Universalism* (New York: Oxford University Press, 2014).

Morgan, M. and P. Gordon, "Modern Jewish Philosophy, Modern Philosophy, and Modern Judaism," in *The Cambridge Companion to Modern Jewish Philosophy*, eds. M. Morgan and P. Gordon (Cambridge: Cambridge University Press, 2007), 1–13.

Nadler, S. and T. M. Rudavsky, "Introduction," in *The Cambridge History of Jewish Philosophy: From Antiquity through the Seventeenth Century*, eds. S. Nadler and T. M. Rudavsky (Cambridge: Cambridge University Press, 2009), 1–4.

Plantinga, A. "Advice to Christian Philosophers," *Faith and Philosophy* 1 (1984), 253–271.

Rynhold, D. *An Introduction to Medieval Jewish Philosophy* (London: I. B. Tauris, 2009), 8–13.

Seeskin, K. *Jewish Philosophy in a Secular Age* (Albany: SUNY Press, 1990), 1–29, 213–225.

# Part II
# Epistemology and Metaphysics

# 4    Belief, Knowledge, and Theism

In this general section on *Epistemology and Metaphysics,* we focus on three issues: the sources of religious belief and knowledge, idolatry, and, in particular, the misrepresentation of God and/or the natural world that idolatry essentially involves, and the nature and ultimate destiny of human persons.

Philosophers of religion have often grappled with the grounds for religious beliefs. On what are those beliefs based? And if religious believers at least sometimes have religious *knowledge,* how do they come to have it?

**Saadia Gaon** directly confronts these questions. He enumerates three generally accepted sources of warrant—observation, intuition, and logical inference—but notes that the "community of monotheists" adds "authentic tradition" as a fourth. And it is on the basis of such an authentic tradition, tracing back to the Exodus and the Revelation at Mt. Sinai, that Saadia and his contemporaries can know the theological and normative claims taught by traditional Judaism.

But, like Locke and Hume, Saadia maintains that you know the deliverances of a given testimonial chain only if you have available an argument for the reliability of that chain, all of whose premises are known in a non-testimonial way. Saadia thinks there is such an argument here. Whatever the merits of that argument, Saadia evidently maintains the fourth source of warrant is in principle dispensable. Indeed, he believes that even had there been no chain of Jewish tradition or divine revelation at all, we would have been able on the basis of observation and reason alone to argue our way to the theological and normative claims of traditional Judaism. God kindly provided us with a shorter and easier route, so that we would not be left in the dark for too long.

The next two selections, from **Judah Halevi** and **Maimonides**, are more skeptical about the powers of unaided human reason and observation. Halevi (or, Judaism's spokesman in Halevi's dialogue, *The Kuzari*) offers an epistemological explanation of his preference for referring to God using an historical, rather than cosmological, description. We know God and much about Him from history: primarily from the events of the Exodus and the Revelation at Mt. Sinai, and traditions about those events. But we can know very little about Him based on reason and ordinary observation alone: demonstrative arguments are rare in natural theology, and nearly all natural theological arguments are beset by interminable and intractable disputes. And while Maimonides often insists that we can satisfactorily prove God's existence and unity, in our selection he maintains that there are important theological issues, such as the eternity of the world, which cannot be settled by any cogent demonstration. They are matters beyond the point at "which the intellect stops," and we are forced to rely on tradition.

**Howard Wettstein** goes further still. He contends that there are no good arguments at all for God's existence, or, for that matter, for any substantive theological claims. This includes the argument, of more recent vintage, from religious experience. Perhaps there is a good argument that a believer has "no epistemic duty to reject" her religious convictions. But for Wettstein, such a concern is altogether too refined. He is more concerned that his belief is "dumb," and he is aware of no argument that it isn't. Wettstein's proposed way forward looks backward to the Bible and Rabbinic literature. It's not that these texts contain good arguments for the truth or intellectual rectitude of religious beliefs— belief in God and such matters was as obvious to them as "belief in the weather," and so such questions never arose. Rather, we find in them a religious attitude that is primarily experiential, affective, and behavioral, and only derivatively doxastic. We can learn from them to see "the life as fundamental and the doctrinal side of one's tradition as more like the furniture in the living room, importantly expressive of the specifics of the tradition's sensibility, rather than the foundations of the edifice." And once metaphysics is dethroned from its position as foundational, we no longer need a supporting epistemology.

**Charles Manekin** closely examines the medieval views and Wettstein's far-reaching critique, and makes common cause with the former. He argues that even biblical characters were concerned with having warranted religious beliefs; and that the medieval search for supporting arguments stemmed not from a desire for unshakeable foundations, but from a laudable aspiration for theological understanding and intellectual honesty.


## SAADIA GAON (882–942)

### *The Book of Beliefs & Opinions* (933)

#### *Introductory Treatise, v, vi; Treatise I, exordium* (tr. Rosenblatt)

*Sources of Knowledge*

INTRODUCTORY TREATISE

*V*


Having concluded now what we thought fit to append to our first statement, it behooves us to give an account of the bases of truth and the vouchers of certainty which are the source of all knowledge and the mainspring of all cognition. Discoursing about them in keeping with the aim of this book, we declare that there are three [such] bases. The first consists of the knowledge gained by [direct] observation. The second is composed of the intuition of the intellect. The third comprises that knowledge which is inferred by logical necessity.

Following up [this] enumeration with an explanation of each of these roots of knowledge, we say that we understand by the knowledge of observation whatever a person perceives by means of one of the five senses; that is, by means of sight or hearing or smell or taste or touch. By the intuition of the intellect, we mean such notions as spring up solely in the mind of a human being, such as approbation of truthfulness and disapproval of mendacity. By the knowledge derived from logical necessity, again, is meant conclusions, which unless they are accepted by the individual as true, would compel his denial of the validity of his rational intuitions or the perception of his senses. Since, however, he cannot very well negate either of these two, he must regard the said inference as being correct. Thus we are forced to affirm, although we have never seen it, that man possesses a soul, in order not to deny its manifest activity. [We must] also [agree], although we have never seen it, that every soul is endowed with reason, [merely] in order not to deny the latter's manifest activity.

Now we find that there are many people who deny [the reliability of] these three sources [of knowledge]. A small minority of them reject the first source. Of these we shall give an account in the first treatise of this book, together with a refutation of their view. By rejecting the first source, they have automatically rejected the second and the third, since the latter two are based upon the first. More numerous than this group are those that acknowledge the validity of the first but reject the second and the third [sources]. Of their thesis, too, we shall make mention in the first treatise and refute it. Most numerous of all, however, are those who acknowledge the validity of the first two sources [of knowledge] and reject the third. The reason for the difference in their rating of these [various sources of knowledge] lies in the fact that the second [type of] knowledge is more recondite than the first, and likewise the third more so than the second, and that whatever is invisible can more readily be denied than what is visible.

Again there are people who reject the validity of this [last type of] knowledge in certain instances and recognize it in others, each group among them affirming what its opponent negates. Their argument [in each case] is that logical necessity led them to the particular conclusion. Thus there is he who affirms that all things are at rest. He consequently denies the reality of motion. Another, again, affirms that all things move, and by virtue thereof denies the reality of rest. Each one declares the evidence adduced by his opponent dubious and unconvincing.

As for ourselves, the community of monotheists, we hold these three sources of knowledge to be genuine. To them, however, we add a fourth source, which we have derived by means of the [other] three, and which has thus become for us a further principle. That is [to say, we believe in] the validity of authentic tradition, by reason of the fact that it is based upon the knowledge of the senses as well as that of reason, as we shall explain in the third treatise of this book.

At this point, however, we remark that this type of knowledge (I mean that which is furnished by authentic tradition and the books of the prophetic revelation), corroborates for us the validity of the first three sources of knowledge. Thus it enumerates the senses in connection with the denial of their functioning in the case of idols, making them a total of five with two more added to them. It says, namely: *They have mouths but they speak not; eyes have they but they see not ... neither speak they with their throat* (Ps. 115:5–7).

## VI

...God's statement, moreover, *Have I not announced unto thee of old?* (Isa. 44:8) refers to the prophetic revelations concerning the future. His remarks again, *And I declared* (ibid.) has reference to the prophetic revelations concerning the past. Thus, too, does He say elsewhere: *The former things, what are they? Declare ye, that we may consider, and know the end of them; or announce to us the things to come* (Isa. 41:22).

When, furthermore, He says: *And ye are My witnesses* (Isa. 44:8), He alludes to the marvelous signs and the manifest proofs witnessed by the [Jewish] people. These [were revealed] in many forms, such as the visitation of the ten plagues and the cleaving of the [Red] Sea and the assemblage at Sinai. Personally, however, I consider the case of the miracle of the manna as the most amazing of all miracles, because a phenomenon of an enduring nature excites greater wonderment than one of a passing character. Aye it is hard for the mind to conceive of a scheme whereby a people numbering something like two million souls could be nourished for forty years with nothing else than food produced for them in the air by the Creator. For had there been any possibility of thinking up a scheme for achieving something of this nature, the philosophers of old would have been the first to resort to it. They would have maintained their disciples therewith, taught them wisdom and enabled them to dispense with working for a livelihood or asking for help.

Now it is not likely that the forbears of the children of Israel should have been in agreement upon this matter if they had considered it a lie. Such [proof] suffices, then, as the requisite of every authentic tradition. Besides, if they had told their children: "We lived in the wilderness for forty years eating naught except for manna," and there had been no basis for that in fact, their children would have answered them: "Now you are telling us a lie. Thou, so and so, is not this thy field, and thou, so and so, is not this thy garden from which you have always derived your sustenance?" This is, then, something that the children would not have accepted by any manner of means.

His statement, again, *Is there a God beside Me?* (ibid.) means: "If, now, perchance you be afraid that some of the things, about which I have told you that they had come to pass or some of those concerning which I have told you that they would come to pass, are not true, [that fear on your part might be justified] if a creation had been effected by someone else than Me. In that event I might perhaps not have been posted on what he was making. But inasmuch as I am One, My knowledge embraces everything that I have made and that I will make."

Finally under His statement, *And there is no rock (sur) that I do not know* (ibid.) are subsumed the distinguished men of the human race and its sages. For the expression *sur* may be applied to great men. Scripture says, namely: *Look unto the rock (sur) whence ye were hewn and to the hole of the pit whence ye were digged. Look unto Abraham your father, and unto Sarah that bore you* (Isa. 51:I, 2). It says also: *Yea, thou makest the rock (sur) turn back his sword, and hast not made him to stand in the battle* (Ps. 89:44). What is meant by the verse under discussion is therefore: "There is no wise or distinguished man that I do not know. Hence it is impossible that he should be able to produce an argument against you in the matter of your religion or do injury to your creed, because My knowledge is all-embracing and I have imparted it to you."

In this way, then—may God be merciful unto thee—do we conduct our speculation and inquiry, to the end that we may expound concretely by means of rational intuition and logical inference what our Master has imparted unto us. With this thesis, however, there is intimately bound up a point that we cannot avoid [bringing up]. It consists of the question: "Inasmuch as all matters of religious belief, as imparted to us by our Master, can be attained by means of research and correct speculation, what was the reason that prompted [divine] wisdom to transmit them to us by way of prophecy and support them by means of visible proofs and miracles rather than intellectual demonstrations?"

To this question we should like to give, with the help of God, exalted be He, an adequate answer. We say, then, [that] the All-Wise knew that the conclusions reached by means of the art of speculation could be attained only in the course of a certain measure of time. If, therefore, He had referred us for our acquaintance with His religion to that art alone, we would have remained without religious guidance whatever for a while, until the process of reasoning was completed by us so that we could make use of its conclusions. But many a one of us might never complete the process because of some flaw in his reasoning. Again he might not succeed in making use of its conclusions because he is overcome by worry or overwhelmed by uncertainties that confuse and befuddle him. That is why God, exalted and magnified be He, afforded us a quick relief from all these burdens by sending us His messengers through whom He transmitted messages to us, and by letting us see with our own eyes the signs and the proofs supporting them about which no doubt could prevail and which we could not possibly reject. Thus He said: *Ye yourselves have seen that I have talked with you from heaven* (Exod. 20:19). Furthermore He addressed His messengers in our presence, and made it an obligation to believe him forever, as He said: *That the people may hear when I speak with thee, and may also believe thee forever* (Exod. 19:9).

Thus it became incumbent upon us immediately to accept the religion, together with all that was embraced in it, because its authenticity had been proven by the testimony of the senses. Its acceptance is also incumbent upon anybody to whom it has been transmitted because of the attestation of authentic tradition, as we shall explain. Now God commanded us to take our time with our speculation until we would arrive thereby at these selfsame conclusions. We must, therefore, persevere in this standpoint until the arguments in favor of it have become convincing for us, and we feel compelled to acknowledge God's Torah [that has already been authenticated] by what our eyes have seen and our ears have heard.

So then, even if it should take a long time for one of us who indulges in speculation to complete his speculation, He is without worry. He who is held back from engaging in such activity by some impediment will, then, not remain without religious guidance. Furthermore women and young people and those who have no aptitude for speculation can thus also have a perfect and accessible faith, for the knowledge of the senses is common to all men. Praised, then, be the All-Wise, who ordered things thus. Therefore, too, dost thou often see Him include in the Torah the children and the women together with the fathers whenever miracles and marvels are mentioned.

Next I say, in further elucidation of this matter, that one might compare the situation to that of a person who out of a total of 1,000 drachmas weighs out 20 to each of five men and $16^{2/3}$ to each of six, and $14^{2/7}$ to each of seven, and $12^{1/2}$ to each of eight, and $11^{1/9}$ to each of nine, and who wishes to check with them quickly on how much money is left. So he tells them that the remainder amounts to 500 drachmas, supporting his statement by the weight of the money. Once, then, it has been weighed by them quickly and found to be 500 drachmas, they are compelled to credit his statement. Then they can take their time until they find out [that] it [is really so] by way of calculation, each one according to his understanding, and the effort he can put into it and the obstacles he might encounter.

One might further compare this case to that of a person who, upon being informed about an illness accompanied by certain pathological conditions, designates it by a natural symptom [whereby it may be] immediately [recognized], until the diagnostician is able by means of [his] investigations to check the matter.

It behooves us also to believe that even before the era of the children of Israel God never left His creatures without a religion fortified by prophecy and miraculous signs and manifest proofs. Whoever witnessed the latter in person was convinced of their authenticity by what he had perceived with his sense of vision. He, again, to whom it was transmitted, was convinced by what he had grasped by means of his sense of hearing. Thus the Torah says about one of these [who lived before the rise of a Jewish nation]: *For I have known him, to the end that he may command his children* (Gen. 18:19).

TREATISE I: CONCERNING [THE BELIEF] THAT ALL EXISTING THINGS HAVE BEEN CREATED

*Exordium*

The author of the book said: "This treatise starts out with the preliminary observation that whoever ventures into it is seeking [light on] something that has never been beheld with human eyes nor been perceived by the senses, but which he is nevertheless anxious to ascertain by means of rational deduction. [The problem I have reference to] is: 'How did all things come into being before our time?' Now the principal object of his investigation is something so subtle and fine that the senses are unable to grasp it. He therefore endeavors to attain it intellectually. Since, then, it has all along been the intention of the investigator to achieve the object of his investigation in just this manner, therefore once he has found it in the form in which he has sought to find it, it would be improper for him to reject it or to desire to attain it in any other form."

Now as far as the knowledge of how things came into existence before our time is concerned, that is a phenomenon that no rational being has ever personally witnessed. Yet we all strive to attain with our minds things distant and remote from our senses, as the saint has remarked thereon: *That which is far off, and exceeding deep, who can find it out?* (Eccles. 7:24). When, then, we reach the conclusion that all things were created out of nothing, although our senses have never experienced anything like it, it is not meant for us to reject that conclusion or to say frivolously: "How can we acquiesce in anything the like of which we have never seen?" For our investigation was from the very start of such a nature as to yield for us something the like of which we have not seen. We should rather welcome it and rejoice in it, since we shall thereby have attained what we have sought. ...

Therefore, O thou that seekest the truth, may God be gracious unto thee, if our discussion yield to thee any conclusion of such a nature as [for example] the doctrine of *creation ex nihilo*, do not hasten to reject it, since it was precisely something like this that thou didst look for from the beginning of thy quest and [since] whoever else goes in search of the truth does likewise. Hear, rather, and realize that thy proofs are stronger than those of the others and that thou art in possession of arguments by means of which thou canst refute any faction of them. Furthermore thou hast over them the advantage of being in possession of miracles and marvels that have been established for thee [as trustworthy]. Therefore hold on to the following three points in every chapter of this book: namely, *(a)* that thy proofs are stronger than those of others, *(b)* that thou art able to refute anyone who disagrees with thee, and *(c)* that the miracles of thy prophets are a part of thy advantage.

## MOSES MAIMONIDES (1138–1204)

### *The Guide of the Perplexed* (1190)

#### *Book 1, Chapter 71* (tr. Pines)

*Theological Knowledge and Its Limits*

Know that the many sciences devoted to establishing the truth regarding these matters that have existed in our religious community have perished because of the length of the time that has passed, because of her being dominated by the pagan nations, and because, as we have made clear, it is not permitted to divulge these matters to all people. For the only thing it is permitted to divulge to all people are the texts of the books. You already know that even the legalistic science of law was not put down in writing in the olden times because of the precept, which is widely known in the nation: "Words that I have communicated to you orally, you are not allowed to put down in writing" (Gittin 60b). This precept shows extreme wisdom with regard to the Law. For it was meant to prevent what has ultimately come about in this respect: I mean the multiplicity of opinions, the variety of schools, the confusions occurring in the expression of what is put down in writing, the negligence that accompanies what is written down, the divisions of the people who are separated into sects, and the production of confusion with regard to actions. All these matters should be within the authority of the Great Court of Law, as we have made clear in our juridical compilation and as the text of the Torah shows. Now if there was insistence that the legalistic science of law should not, in view of the harm that would be caused by such a procedure, be perpetuated in a written compilation accessible to all the people, all the more could none of the mysteries of the Torah have been set down in writing and be made accessible to the people. On the contrary they were transmitted by a few men belonging to the elite, to a few of the same kind, just as I made clear to you from their saying: "The mysteries of the Torah may only be transmitted to a counsellor, wise in crafts" (Hagigah 14a), and so on. This was the cause that necessitated the disappearance of these great roots of knowledge from the nation. For you will not find with regard to them anything except slight indications and pointers occurring in the Talmud and the Midrashim. These are, as it were, a few grains belonging to the core, which are overlaid by many layers of rind, so that people were occupied with these layers of rind and thought that beneath them there was no core whatever.

As for that scanty bit of argument regarding the notion of the unity of God and regarding what depends on this notion, which you will find in the writings of some Geonim and in those of the Karaites, it should be noted that the subject matter of this argument was taken over by them from the Mutakallimun of Islam and that this bit is very scanty indeed if compared to what Islam has compiled on this subject. Also it has so happened that Islam first began to take this road owing to a certain sect, namely, the Mutazila, from whom our coreligionists took over certain things walking upon the road the Mutazila had taken. After a certain time another sect arose in Islam, namely, the Ashariyya, among whom other opinions arose. You will not find any of these latter opinions among our coreligionists. This was not because they preferred the first opinions to the second, but because it so happened that they had taken over and adopted the first opinions and considered it a matter proven by demonstration.

As for the Andalusians (Spaniards) among the people of our nation, all of them cling to the affirmations of the philosophers and incline to their opinions, in so far as these do not ruin the foundation of the Law. You will not find them in any way taking the paths of the Mutakallimun. In many things concerning the scanty matter of which the later ones among them had knowledge, they have therefore approximately the same doctrine that we set forth in this treatise.

…There is no doubt that there are things that are common to all three of us, I mean the Jews, the Christians, and the Muslims: namely, the affirmation of the temporal creation of the world, the validity of which entails the validity of miracles and other things of that kind. As for the other matters that these two communities took the trouble to treat and were engrossed in—for instance, the study of the notion of trinity into which the Christians plunged and the study of the Kalam into which certain sects of the Muslims plunged—so that they found it requisite to establish premises and to establish, by means of these premises that they had chosen, the conceptions into the study of which they had plunged and the notions that are peculiar to each of the two communities, having been established in it: these are things that we do not require in any respect whatever.

...When I studied the books of these Mutakallimun, as far as I had the opportunity—and I have likewise studied the books of the philosophers, as far as my capacity went—I found that the method of all of the Mutakallimun was one and the same in kind, though the subdivisions differed from one another. For the foundation of everything is that no consideration is due to how that which exists is, for it is merely a custom; and from the point of view of the intellect, it could well be different. Furthermore, in many places they follow the imagination and call it intellect. Thus when they propound the premises that we will let you hear, they found by their demonstrations the [affirmative] judgment that the world is created in time. And when it is thus established that the world is created in time, it is likewise undoubtedly established that it has a maker who has created it in time. Then they adduced arguments in favor of the inference that this maker is one; whereupon, basing themselves upon his being one, that he is not a body. That is the way of every Mutakallim from among the Muslims in anything concerning this subject. Thus also do those belonging to our community who imitate them and follow their ways. While the ways in which they adduce the arguments in favor of the inference as to, and propound the premises with regard to, the establishment of the temporal creation of the world or to the refutation of its pre-eternity, differ from one another, the universal thesis of all of them consists in the first place in the affirmation of the temporal creation of the world. And by means of its temporal creation, it is established as true that the deity exists.

Now when I considered this method of thought, my soul felt a very strong aversion to it, and had every right to do so. For every argument deemed to be a demonstration of the temporal creation of the world is accompanied by doubts and is not a cogent demonstration except among those who do not know the difference between demonstration, dialectics, and sophistic argument. As for those who know these arts, it is clear and evident to them that there are doubts with regard to all these proofs and that premises that have not been demonstrated have been used in them. The utmost power of one who adheres to a Law and who has acquired knowledge of true reality consists, in my opinion, in his refuting the proofs of the philosophers bearing on the eternity of the world. How sublime a thing it is when the ability is there to do it! And everyone who engages in speculation, who is perceptive, and who has acquired true knowledge of reality and does not deceive himself, knows that with regard to this question—namely, the eternity of the world or its temporal creation—no cogent demonstration can be reached and that it is a point before which the intellect stops...

## JUDAH HALEVI (1075–1141)

### *The Book of Refutation and Proof on Behalf of the Despised Faith* (*The Kuzari*) (c. 1140)

#### *Book 1, Sections 11–25* (tr. Kogan and Berman)

*Religious Knowledge: Revealed and Transmitted*

[The Jewish Sage's Creed]

(1:11) Accordingly, [the Jewish sage] said to him: I put [my] faith in the God of Abraham, Isaac and Israel who brought the children of Israel out of Egypt with signs and miracles, provided for them in the wilderness, and gave them the land of Syro-Palestine after they had crossed the Sea [of Reeds] and the Jordan [River] miraculously. He sent Moses with His Law, [and] then thousands of prophets after him to support his law by means of promises [of reward] to whoever observed it and threats [of punishment] to whoever disobeyed it. Our faith [pertains] to all that was included in the Torah, but the story is long.

(1:12) The Khazar said: I had [originally] decided not to ask a Jew because I knew about the destruction of their traditions and the inferiority of their opinions, since their misfortune has not left them [anything] worth praising. Why then didn't you say, O Jew, that you put your faith in the creator of the world, [who] orders it and governs it, and in Him who created you and provided for you, and [use] similar such descriptions, which constitute proof for everyone who has a religion? Because of descriptions like these, people pursue truth and justice in order to imitate the Creator in His wisdom and justice.

(1:13) The sage said: What you are referring to is [really] the syllogistic, governmental religion to which speculation leads, but it contains many doubtful points. Ask the philosophers about it, and you will not find them agreeing on a single action or a single belief because they are [merely] claims. Some of them they can demonstrate. Some of them they can show to be persuasive; but some of them they cannot [even] show to be persuasive, let alone establish by demonstration.

(1:14) The Khazar said: I think your speech [now], O Jew, is more likely [to persuade me] than the opening part of it was before, and I would like [to hear] more.

(1:15) The sage said: On the contrary, the opening part of my speech is the demonstration. What is more, it is [based on] direct observation and doesn't need proof and demonstration.

(1:16) The Khazar said: How is that [possible]?

(1:17) The sage said: Permit me to make some preliminary comments, because I see that you are showing disdain for my [opening] statement and making light of it.

(1:18) The Khazar said: Make your preliminary comments so that I may hear [them].

(1:19) The sage said: If you were told that the ruler of India is virtuous and that you should revere him, praise his name and count his exploits because of what had come to you[r attention] about the justice of the people of his country, [signifying] both the excellence of their character traits and the justice of their conduct towards one another, would this compel you [to do so]?

(1:20) The Khazar said: How could it compel me, when there is doubt as to whether the justice of the people of India is due to their own nature and they have no king or [whether in having one] their justice is due to their king, or [whether] the fact is due to both causes taken together?

(1:21) The sage said: But then, if his messenger came to you with [typically] Indian gifts, about which you have no doubt that they are found only in India, in the palaces of kings, along with a message in which it is attested that it is from him [that is, the king] and accompanied by medicines that cure you of your illnesses and preserve your health, as well as poisons for your enemies and those who wage war against you, with which you may confront them and kill them without [either] preparation or [superior] numbers, would you be obligated to obey him?

(1:22) The Khazar said: Yes, of course [I would]. My previous doubts as to whether India has a king or not would have disappeared, and I would believe that his dominion and his command (*amr*) extend to me.

(1:23) The sage said: If you were asked about him, how would you describe him?

(1:24) The Khazar said: By means of those attributes that, in my opinion, were well established on the basis of direct observation. Then I would follow them up with those [other attributes] that are generally accepted and have become evident by means of these last ones [I mentioned].

(1:25) The sage said: Well, I answered you in [exactly] the same way when you questioned me; and Moses began addressing Pharaoh in the same way too when he told him, 'The God of the Hebrews has sent me to you', meaning, the God of Abraham, Isaac and Jacob, since their story was well known among the nations as well as [the fact] that a divine order (*amr ilāhī*) accompanied them, took interest in them, and performed wonders for them. He did not tell him, 'The Lord of heaven and earth [sent me]', or 'My Creator and your Creator sent me'. And God also began His address to the multitude of the children of Israel in the same way [by saying], 'I am [the] God, whom you worship, who brought you out of the land of Egypt. ...' He did not say, 'I am the creator of the world and your creator'. Accordingly, I began [to speak to] you this way, O commander of the Khazars, when you asked me about my faith. I answered you in terms of what is compelling for me and for the community of the children of Israel for whom that [which I have described] is well established on the basis of direct observation and subsequently, through uninterrupted tradition, which is as valid as direct observation.

HOWARD WETTSTEIN

## "The Significance of Religious Experience" (2011)

> His kind of faith is a gift.
> It's like an ear for music or the talent to draw.
>
> Woody Allen, *Crimes and Misdemeanors*

### I. Introduction: Proofs, Old and New

Occasionally one meets or reads about people who were, as we say, born at the wrong time or place. Their gifts, tendencies, and ways, awkward in the context of their lives, would have seemed natural at some other time or place. The classical proofs for the existence of God suffer a different fate. Born at precisely the right time and place, they now seem out of context, no longer compelling in the way they must have been. At least they seem that way to many of us.

The natural habitat of the proofs was the medieval philosophical world, an intellectual culture in which philosophical justification of the religious fundamentals was just what was needed. If one moves back some centuries to ancient Israel and its Jewish and arguably early Christian aftermath, rational justification of religion is not on the horizon. To defend belief in God's existence would have seemed bizarre, like defending belief in the existence of the weather.

Indeed, strange as this seems to our ears, belief itself is never mentioned in the Hebrew Bible. There is talk of believing *in* God, i.e., trusting, relying upon God. But no talk of believing doctrines, believing that something is the case; no commandment—no explicit one at least—to believe anything. However by the early middle ages in Jewish religious culture—earlier in Christianity—beliefs, thoughts, and the like become very much the center of attention, and there is a felt need to justify religious belief.

The medieval attitude to belief's centrality has become the norm. We identify the belief that God exists as a *sine qua non* of religious commitment. The Hebrew Bible's interest is rather in one's overall stance, the essential components of which are affective and behavioral, most importantly awe/fear and love of God as realized in lived experience.

But while belief has become central, the proofs of the medievals—the classic philosophic defenses of that belief—have lost their punch. The considerations to which they appeal—like the order and beauty of the universe—have by no means lost their suggestiveness, their relevance to and significance for religious thought and feeling. But proof is another thing.

My aim here is to reflect on a relatively new style of proof—a distant relative of the classical arguments—current throughout the twentieth century and in recent decades even more vital, the argument from individual religious experience. Here too, or so I will argue, we should distinguish the proof's cogency from the religious significance of the considerations to which the proof appeals, my topic at the conclusion of this paper.

The focus on individual religious experience brings to mind the Protestant religious orientation. Not that individual religious experience is a mere afterthought in the other monotheisms. Indeed the proof's advocates appeal to religious experiences in a variety of traditions. Likewise, advocates of the argument include philosophers as diverse as William Alston and Richard Swinburne on the Protestant side, Gary Gutting, a Catholic, and Jewish thinker Jerome Gellman. For the most part, however, contemporary discussions of proofs of God's existence in the Catholic, Jewish, or Muslim traditions—as I say, they are hardly the central topic nowadays—are of the classical arguments.

My aim here is to explore the fundamental ideas of the argument, this as opposed to the numerous sophisticated variations that have emerged. I begin with William James, early in the twentieth century. Whatever the specifics of his religious views, James emerges from the American Protestant world and gives such proofs a great deal of respect. It is good to begin with James moreover since he has a gift for raising fundamental questions in an intuitive, technically unencumbered way. In this way, he is like later philosophers P. F. Strawson and Harry Frankfurt; penetrating minds whose insights give rise to rather technical literatures.

## *II. Gifts to the Spirit*

James characterizes experiences that purport to be of God—he includes them in the category of mystical experiences—as "gifts to our spirit." "No account of the universe in its totality can be final which leaves these ... forms of consciousness quite disregarded."

Such experiences for James bespeak quite literally another form of consciousness. It is an open question, he supposes, as to whether such forms reveal worlds, as it were, that are ordinarily beyond our reach. It is difficult to know what to do with James's seemingly extravagant notion of forms of consciousness. This raises issues of the paranormal; James was a founder of the American Society for Psychical Research in 1885.

Whatever one thinks about the paranormal, James's remarks about "gifts to the spirit" are themselves gifts. Here, James evinces an appreciation of religion that is nowadays lost to many. John Dewey, a similarly sympathetic critic of religion, writes:

A writer says: "I broke down from overwork and soon came to the verge of nervous prostration. One morning after a long and sleepless night ... I resolved to stop drawing upon myself so continuously and begin drawing upon God. I determined to set apart a quiet time every day in which I could relate my life to its ultimate source, regain the consciousness that in God I live, move and have my being. That was thirty years ago. Since then I have had literally not one hour of darkness or despair."

This [life story constitutes] an impressive record. I do not doubt its authenticity nor that of the experience related. It illustrates a religious aspect of experience. But it illustrates also the use of that quality to carry a superimposed load of a particular religion. For having been brought up in the

Christian religion, its subject interprets it in the terms of the personal God characteristic of that religion.

(1934, 11–12)

Dewey's expression, "a religious aspect of experience" is no throwaway; he emphasizes the reality and significance of such aspects. In this passage he suggests and in the sequel he greatly expands upon the power of religion and its potential for influencing positively the course of life. At the same time he much more clearly and forcefully than James rejects the supernaturalist metaphysics associated with traditional religion. Nevertheless I suspect that James's phrase "gifts to the spirit" would sit well for Dewey.

Speaking for myself, I very much like James's characterization. This is in part because I think with Dewey that such peak moments, and religious life more generally, can have a beneficial influence, including one's psychological balance, ability to negotiate life's challenges, the significance one accords to one's life, and the dignity one assigns to others. But there is another and perhaps deeper reason, albeit one that I find difficult to express.

What makes "gifts to the spirit" so difficult to explicate is "spirit." I could explain James's idea if I could explain the concept of the spirit, and related idea of the spiritual. There is significantly more to these ideas than the largely psychological dimension that Dewey emphasizes—the various beneficial effects mentioned above as well as "the unification of the self" of which Dewey speaks.

The quotation from *Crimes and Misdemeanors* at the head of this paper suggests that an affinity for things of the spirit is grounded in a natural gift, a human capacity, analogous to, in the aesthetic domain, having an ear for music or the talent to draw. I will begin with the latter and return to religion shortly. As we will see, there is more to mine here than a mere analogy. The aesthetic dimension has its own ties to matters of the spirit.

One obstacle to establishing the link I am after is that "aesthetic" is often heard in a reductive way; ascriptions of beauty, for example, are sometimes thought of, dismissed as, merely subjective. This is a function, I believe, of thinking too abstractly about this sphere. Consider by contrast actual aesthetic gifts, like musical talent or even having an ear for music. These abilities are far along the continuum from subjective toward objective, which is not to suggest that this distinction is either sharp or clear. Surely musical talent, an ear for music, and the like are no less aspects of the world than other abilities—including those in the domain of athletics—to perform, to discern and appreciate, etc. The "tone deaf" idiom suggests that one, otherwise sound in auditory capacities, can systematically miss something important.

One who is musically advanced may hear the same performance as the rest of us but may alone penetrate to profound levels of appreciation. Similarly, one advanced in the appreciation of the visual arts may bring something very different to, and take something very different from, a painting, or indeed a natural scene, for example a landscape with its play of light, shadow, color, and the like.

Profound aesthetic experiences, no less than the religious experiences of which James wrote, deserve to be thought of as gifts to the spirit. They may engender a sense of awe and mystery, and of the sublime; they may provoke a feeling of being privileged and so of gratitude. The experience may be at once elevating and humbling. These represent important points of contact with religious moments.

The points of contact are not limited to such reactions. Artistic and religious virtuosity both involve, even begin with, natural aptitude, as noted in the quotation from *Crimes and Misdemeanors*. Some are more given to these things than others. And in both domains, hard work, genuine focus—at times single-minded—is essential if one is to approach one's potential. We are less apt to think this way about the religious domain than the artistic. But a religious giant, a Mozart of the spirit, is a rare find; she is (certainly typically) one who has labored strenuously in pursuit of excellence. And just as one who is tone-deaf can appreciate the musically gifted as responding to something of substance, one who is less able than another in matters of the spirit can recognize the latter's accomplishment. Needless to say, being tone-deaf is a rare condition in either domain. Ordinarily people occupy an intermediate position within a wide spectrum of which being tone-deaf is at one extreme.

I have been emphasizing the analogies between the two domains, and the quasi-religious character of profound aesthetic experience. Now consider one who has undergone considerable development in both domains. A religious orientation—bringing God into the picture—may heighten and deepen one's reactions to beauty. Explaining this is another matter, and not a trivial one. There may be no single story. God may play the role of an object of gratefulness, someone as it were on whom one bestows one's gratitude. Sometimes the felt presence of God links experiences that would otherwise feel discrete; one comes to see an array in place of discrete dots. The points in the array seem to accrue added significance; aesthetic experience can thus partake of something analogous to what is sometimes called intertextuality. Sometimes it may be God's role as a partner and, as it were, friend with whom to share the wonder. There are no doubt other dimensions, and the experience of several of these at once adds considerable power. One shares the wonders with their source, takes pleasure in their array.

Consideration of the aesthetic domain may be illuminating. Still, in much religious experience the aesthetic dimension is marginal or not present. All sorts of things can stimulate religious reflection and feeling: another's death, or the prospect of death—one's own or that of others, various sorts of horrors or extreme ugliness, witnessing simple acts of particularly touching human kindness, childbirth, the intellectual and/or moral growth of one's child or simply of another person, to name a few. It seems too much of a stretch to assimilate the religious reactions that may be prompted to reactions in the aesthetic domain.

And finally, there are James's favorite examples of gifts of the spirit, quasi-perceptual experiences of God's presence. There is no reason to assimilate these—certainly not all of them—to the aesthetic. They represent a spiritual achievement, the sense of being in God's presence. Of course, many experiences can provoke a sense of the divine presence, for example, some of the aesthetic ones discussed above. But the quasi-perceptual experiences are quite another thing, face to face with God, as James puts it.

To approach religious sensibility with James is to bring to center stage the experiential side of the religious orientation. But what of religious belief? James, while he writes that religion is fundamentally a phenomenon of the gut rather than of the head, argues forcefully that the experiential aspect has important implications for the doxastic side of religion.

### III. What, If Anything, Do Religious Experiences Prove?

James and many of the more recent advocates of the argument from religious experience treat such experiences on the model of perception; James calls them, "face to face presentations." They are, he says, "absolutely authoritative."

> Our own more "rational" beliefs are based on evidence exactly similar in nature to that which mystics quote for theirs. Our senses, namely, have assured us of certain states of fact; but mystical experiences are as direct perceptions of fact for those who have them as any sensations ever were for us.
>
> (1987, 382)

This powerful "warrant for truth" does not however extend to those who have not themselves had such experiences. Testimony about religious experiences, according to James, is vitiated by what would seem to be a very powerful consideration, the great variety of such reports of experiences, testifying as it were to many different gods, non-gods, various metaphysical realities, and the like. Here James sounds a bit like Hume who famously denies that claims to miraculous experiences have epistemic value for those who merely hear testimony about them. By contrast, some more recent advocates maintain that such "perceptual" experiences constitute objective evidence, evidence for all of us, not only for participants.

By way of reaction to James's "absolutely authoritative" claim, it seems important that the experiences in question are not phenomenally like ordinary sense perception. Consider one of James's examples:

> God is more real to me than any thought of thing or person. I feel his presence positively, and the more as I live in closer harmony with his laws as written in my body and mind. I feel him in the sunshine and rain; and awe mingled with a delicious restfulness most nearly describes my feelings. I talk to him as to a companion in prayer and praise, and our communion is delightful. He answers me again and again, often in words so clearly spoken that it seems my outer ear must have carried the tone, but generally in strong mental impressions. Usually a text of scripture, unfolding some new view of him and his love for me, and care for my safety. I could give hundreds of instances, in school matters, social problems, financial difficulties, etc. That he is mine

and I am his never leaves me, it is an abiding joy. Without it life would be a blank, a desert, a shoreless, trackless waste.

(ibid., 81)

For the most part the people James quotes are not claiming literally to see or hear God. Their sense is that they are experiencing God—in some way that is difficult for us (and them) to define. The experiences are to be sure various, ranging from ones that involve a deeply felt sense of God's presence, God's love, etc. to quasi-sensual "almost seeings, almost hearings," and the like. In the quotation just given, there is only one reference to actual hearing, and it may well be that the writer is speaking of an as-if hearing. The closer to claims of actual perceptual experience, the more likely we are to take them to be a bit crazy. Interestingly, St. Teresa of Avila, the sixteenth-century mystic, suggests, according to Rowan Williams, that as a rule of thumb "the closer such perception is to ... actually supposing the object of vision to be present to the senses ... the less likely it is to be genuinely of God." (2000, 147)

The differences with ordinary perception are not limited to the phenomenal aspects. The religious experiences in question are for most of the subjects once (or at most several) in a lifetime experiences. There are those mystics who more regularly enjoy such privileges but it would be surprising in the extreme if they could call them up at will. Ordinary, everyday perception, by contrast, is reliably repeatable. One can return to a room and typically see exactly what one expects to see.

In addition to the matter of repeatability, there is the question of whether what one perceives—and indeed one's perceiving it—is available to other normal perceivers. The question is not only whether others can have similar experiences, but also whether what one takes in on a particular occasion is open to others' perception. In the example above, the person talks with God and receives answers—in the special "as-if perception" mode. Whatever else one thinks about the give and take, no one takes the interaction to be available to others.

These differences do not themselves imply that anything short of veridical perception is occurring. But they do strain the analogy with ordinary sense perception. While it is less than clear that James's is exactly an argument from analogy, it is worth keeping our eyes upon these differences.

Perhaps more important, though, is James's Hume-like point about testimony, what we might call "the many-gods problem." Indeed it is difficult to understand why James supposes that the agent's "warrant for truth" survives the agent's own knowledge of the many-gods problem. After all, if one were having a notoriously unreliable sort of sense perception one would do well, despite the appearances, to question what one seems to be seeing. In the case of religious experience, the Jamesian agent would not trust another's testimony. Why then should she not apply this lesson to her own case?

Finally, and perhaps most important of all, these religious experiences do not involve sensory apparatus. This seems to me—but evidently not to James and his followers—perhaps the most important point of all, one that puts the other points mentioned into proper perspective. I will linger a bit on it.

The accumulated experience of humankind gives much weight to the senses as yielding more or less reliable information about the environment. However this is to be rationalized, understood, theorized, all but the most strident skeptic is on board here. Indeed the rough outline of how this all works is well known. One does not need contemporary neuroscience; Locke had something like the basic idea.

So sense perception has for us a privileged epistemic status. But this has everything to do with the idea that our senses are trained on aspects of the environment. There are other experiences that are in a wider sense "perceptual," experiences like the religious ones we are considering, but also mental images, hallucinations, dreams. These are phenomenally more like perception than like, for example, conceptual thinking. But they do not therefore somehow automatically inherit the epistemic credentials of sense perception.

James's contrary contention, apparently, is roughly that any sufficiently vivid (if that is the right word) presentation has as much claim as any other to being veridical, the disclosure of an independent reality. But why should vividness, *pace* Hume, or the sense that one is making genuine perceptual contact, bridge the gap between actual perception of the environment and these other sorts of "perceptual" experiences?

It is as if, under the influence of the Cartesian tradition, one were working from the inside. Sufficiently vivid perceptual states are on a par unless one can find grounds to distinguish them. And from such a perspective, working one's way from inside to outside—finding such grounds—is the major undertaking. But this is not the only way to approach these matters. It is plausible that as human beings in perceptual touch with our surroundings, we are already outside. We begin, as Quine says, with ordinary things. But such perception of the environment is a very different business than perceptual experience of the wider variety, including quasi-perceptual religious experience.

Accordingly, a reflective person, privileged to have an intense religious moment of the sort in question, might bracket the epistemology of the experience. It means ever so much, she might well say, but it proves little. My own certainly fit this pattern. They were at once powerfully significant—even if relatively tame—and epistemically inert. The question of what the experience verified never so much as arose.

Here I am not alone. Rowan Williams writes:

> [For Teresa] the mysticism is demystified, and mystical experience as such is accorded no particular authority. Its authority ... has to be displayed in the shape of the vocation of which it is part. [Still, ... ] there is good reason for intensified phenomenological interest in the varieties of preternatural or paranormal occurrence in prayer, especially when (as in Teresa's case) these are to some extent organized as an ascending series. Teresa herself is fascinated by her experiences....
>
> (2000, 148)

Teresa and her contemporaries would have found this [the idea of trying to validate doctrine] in light of such mystical experiences surprising. For all Teresa's interest in the visionary and paranormal, she is not disposed to use it as evidence for the way the universe is. "Do mystical states establish the truth [of religious claims]?," asks William James in the course of a discussion of Teresa. Teresa herself would never have imagined that "mystical states" could do such a job... [or that they] had any part whatever to play in doctrinal discussion. So far from "mystical states" being a sort of paradigm of certainty, they have authority only within a frame of reference which is believed in on quite other grounds, and are therefore properly to be tested according to their consistency with this.

(ibid., 149)

St. Teresa, then, brackets her experiences in epistemological terms. This does not, in her view, however, militate against their being religiously significant. Indeed, she seems to measure spiritual progress, at least of one significant variety, by something like the intensity and perhaps the frequency of the experiences.

Such epistemological neutrality does not entail metaphysical neutrality. I am sure that St. Teresa believed she was making contact with God in mystical experience. Unlike a Jamesian, however, she did not presume that one could, from reflecting on the perceptual character of the experience, rationally conclude that it really was contact with God.

Imagine now another grade of removal from the Jamesian picture. One undergoes a powerful religious experience but is less than sure about, even skeptical about, any sort of real contact with the supernatural. "I know," he might say, "that this experience reflects my deep religious involvement, but whether I've actually achieved contact with God is hard to say." Another example is provided by the advocate of a perfect being theology and some associated anti-anthropomorphism. Divinity, on such a view, might be taken to be beyond our perceptual (or even conceptual) reach. But such a theological position historically has not led to giving up prayer. And such a person might indeed be subject to various sorts of religious experiences. Whatever these experiences are, she might reflect, they are powerful, elevating, and humbling; their intensity and regularity a measure of one's spiritual situation. In short, one who departs from metaphysical/epistemological claims about the experiences might still adopt St. Teresa's Jamesian attitude about their religious value.

### IV. Interlude: Epistemic Legalism

James's treatment of these phenomena—and even more so later advocates of the argument from religious experience—exhibits what I will call "epistemic legalism." What I have in mind here is analogous to what Bernard Williams and others have called "scientism," roughly the misapplication to philosophy of modes of explanation that have their home in scientific theorizing.

In Charles Griswold's recent book, *Forgiveness*, he speaks frequently of warranted and unwarranted resentment, of the *obligation* to forgive, to forswear *unjustified* resentment, of the question of who has *standing* to forgive. In remarks on Griswold's book in a 2008 Pacific APA symposium, I called attention to what seemed to me like an invasion of legal terminology/conceptualization into the ethical domain. The legalism, or so I argued, does not do justice to our experience of forgiving and being forgiven.

Of course the whole matter is controversial; for deontologists the legalistic terminology is apt. But that it is apt does not go without saying, and it is worth noting that it does not. Here too, in discussions of the epistemology of religion by James and his followers, notions like justification, warrant, and obligation are central. Since we are in the domain of epistemology, perhaps you will think that all this indeed goes without saying, that these are inevitably the pivotal notions. But perhaps not.

I spent my college years increasingly engaged with and committed to Orthodox Judaism. Religious practice and the sense of spiritual/intellectual community were extremely compelling. At the same time part and parcel of the life were beliefs: that a supernatural God exists, that he revealed the Torah to Moses on Mt. Sinai, and the like. Given that one could not be sure of such things was there something like evidence or a good reason to think that these things were actually true? Doesn't intellectual responsibility require more than just the powerful feeling that attends to the life? Such were my pangs of intellectual conscience.

One could no doubt put these questions in terms of justification, warrant, intellectual duty/obligation and the like. And surely at the time I was not making distinctions between theoretical approaches in epistemology. But the description in terms of virtues like intellectual honesty, integrity, and responsibility seems more in line with my thinking.

Some years ago I was speaking with my then Notre Dame colleague, Fred Freddoso. We were discussing the attempt by our colleague Alvin Plantinga to show that belief in God was rational. Plantinga once commented there were many good arguments for the existence of God, thirty-two if I remember correctly. (I quipped that I knew the five famous ones and they didn't do it.) I believe that Plantinga was thinking of a good argument in a different way than I. When he spoke and wrote about the rationality of belief in God, he meant something quite refined, something like—if I have him right—one way one might proceed without irrationality. To establish that belief in God was rational was something like establishing that one had no epistemic duty to reject it. In discussing this, Freddoso, an Aquinas scholar, commented that in St. Thomas's treatment, such a sophisticated (and legalistic) conception of rationality is not at issue. What St. Thomas asks is (something like) "Is belief in God dumb?" The force of that question I can feel.

Thinking in terms of intellectual honesty, integrity, and responsibility may lead in a direction very different from that of the epistemic legalism that has been in vogue for so long. As with other issues in philosophy, switching vocabulary is no guarantee of a substantially different approach. It depends, of course, on what one makes of the virtue talk. And of course this is a large topic at which I am merely glancing here.

Justification is the concept from the legalistic framework that I am most concerned with at present. Justification often has a defensive flavor, in philosophy and more generally. In philosophy it is as if a Pyrrhonian homunculus were perched on one's shoulder, repeatedly whispering in one's ear, "How do you know; are you certain?" And providing a non-question-begging answer is a very difficult business even for the most pedestrian beliefs; witness Descartes. This is of course not to say that one cannot theorize about justification without the skeptic in mind. But there is often the scent of skepticism in the air, perhaps especially in discussions of justifying religious belief.

## V. Swinburne et al.

I propose that we characterize the religious experiences we have been exploring as neutrally as possible (with respect to what they indicate about God's existence), as experiences "as of God." This lacks poetry; but not to worry, it won't come up much in conversation. Richard Swinburne, also in search of a non-question-begging description, proposes that we speak of them as "epistemic seemings." For Swinburne, apparently following Chisholm, "seems epistemically that $x$ is present" means roughly that the agent believes (or is inclined to believe) that $x$ is present on the basis of the experience.

There is one respect in which Swinburne's terminology seemingly fails to achieve the non-question-begging character he seeks. For it presupposes that to have such an experience is to believe (or be inclined to believe) that God exists on the basis of the experience. But as we have seen, on St. Teresa's approach, the experience fails to provide a ground for the belief. The agent's belief is grounded elsewhere. And on the alternative I mentioned above—a further grade of removal from James—the agent can take the experience to be religiously momentous without believing that he is making perceptual contact with God. Again, the experience will hardly provide a ground for his belief.

Still, surely some people do experience such "epistemic seemings," religious experiences on the basis of which they ground their religious beliefs. Swinburne, a super-Jamesian, attempts to extend their justification to the rest of us: given the religious experiences of some people, rationality requires that we all believe that God exists. The following "principle of credulity" is at the heart of his argument:

> It is a principle of rationality that (in the absence of special considerations) if it seems (epistemically) to a subject that $x$ is present, then probably $x$ is present; what one seems to perceive is probably so.

> (1991, 254)

Swinburne argues for this principle on grounds that denying it would "land one in a skeptical bog" about ordinary perception. Here we have not just the scent of skepticism, detected in the emphasis on justification. Skepticism constitutes a crucial link in the argument.

Swinburne's approach to the epistemology of individual religious experience represents an important trend in twentieth-century Christian philosophy. Respect for skepticism is one important aspect of the trend, but it is not the only one or the deepest. That honor belongs to an idea to which I now turn.

My first encounter with the idea was as a college freshman, overhearing a conversation in a coffee shop. "We all have premises," offered a defender of religion. "These are mine." I didn't know a lot of philosophy at the time, but even then this sort of defense had very little appeal for me. Surely, I thought, we want more than that from philosophy. In such a fashion, one could defend just about anything one felt strongly enough about.

There is another way to take this sort of defense of religious belief. Perhaps the idea is that religious belief does not stand in need of philosophical justification; that religious belief is something with which one comes to philosophy. I myself, while I do not so approach religious belief (at least as it is usually construed—see later), I very much do so approach other matters, for example, our common sense beliefs about the world: that my dog is lying at my feet as I write these words, that he is a dog and I am human, and the like. As I have said, we start with ordinary things; we start out in and with the world.

To maintain that religious belief is something that one brings to philosophy is to give religious belief the status of common sense. But this is to deny a striking intuitive gap between ordinary and religious beliefs; between on the one hand the belief that I am a human being and on the other that a supernatural God exists outside of time and space. With respect to the former, it takes some sort of philosophical skepticism to generate concern. Not so for the latter. A normally reflective person, religious or not, will recognize that there is an issue here. Or so we often suppose.

The denial of the intuitive gap is at the heart of the trend represented by Swinburne's approach. It is the meeting ground for James and his contemporary followers. Various philosophic strategies have been utilized to eliminate the gap. The freshman—post-Philosophy 1—comment above was one way. Closely related is the idea that religious belief is in effect (or can have the status of) common sense. Then there is James's: to grant the special "as of God" experiences the epistemic status of sense perception. Still another way to eliminate the gap is by way of skepticism.

Here the idea is to place great weight on the skeptic's claims. One begins with the idea that some ordinary belief is in epistemological trouble given the weight of the skeptic's claims. Early along Alvin Plantinga emphasized belief in other minds. Swinburne, in the work cited, speaks more generally of beliefs based on ordinary sense perception. How are we to deal with the skeptic? How might we, in the face of the skeptic's good questions, account for our everyday knowledge? Only by adopting a very strong epistemic principle, for example, Swinburne's principle of credulity. But then, strong epistemic principle in hand, religious belief is no worse off than the most ordinary, pedestrian beliefs. Skepticism levels the playing field.

To the extent that one is moved by the skeptical starting point one will want to scrutinize the idea that something like the principle of credulity is the only way to rescue ordinary beliefs. From my perspective, while I worry about my beliefs being responsible, as discussed above, that constitutes no problem for ordinary beliefs and remains an issue for the religious beliefs in question.

I have explored a number of attempts to eliminate the intuitive epistemic gap I have been discussing. And of course, one needs to have a look at each such proposal in detail. But something seems questionable with the general idea, with the very attempt to eliminate the gap.

Philosophy is notorious for solutions the brilliance of which outshines their contact with good sense. Russell reminded us to maintain our sense of reality "even in the most abstract studies." The intuitive gap I have been discussing is one that presents itself to many religious and non-religious people. Some of our forebears who produced elaborate rational proofs for the existence of God were presumably moved to do so by the sense that their passionately held convictions were indeed controversial, and not only in the sense that some people believed otherwise. Surely a reasonable defense would reveal good reasons to believe without suggesting that the gap was illusory.

### VI. Conclusion: Making Sense of Religion

Our modern sensibilities distance us from the ancients for whom God, like the weather, was hardly optional. We have well-known options. And even if one's own way is to take God for granted almost like the weather, the question of whether this makes sense almost inevitably arises at some point in one's life, certainly in the lives of those around one. In what follows I will sketch an alternative to the approach taken in so much twentieth- and twenty-first-century work, by defenders of religion as well as by critics.

One thing that is striking—and new—in the Jamesian arguments we have been exploring is the idea that the experiential side of religion can serve as the foundation, specifically the epistemic foundation, of religious belief. At the same time, James is hardly interested in religious experience only for its epistemic implications. James called his book *The Varieties of Religious Experience*, and the varieties and their meanings—meanings in the broadest sense—are its main focus.

To thus emphasize the experiential side is to make contact with the mystical tradition, and to diverge from the spirit of medieval rationalist theology. It is also to converge with the approach of the Hebrew Bible with its emphasis on what Buber calls faith, a matter of living a life characterized by an intimacy with God.

The ancients lived their faith without the help of our concept of belief. But this is not to say that there is something illegitimate about the use of our notion to characterize them, although it does require a certain delicacy. Surely there were things in the religious domain that they took to be true: the historical events described in the Bible for example, with God's role in them, as well as that God is good, forgiving, at times angry, and the like. There is no harm in the cautious ascription of belief here.

Here is one reason for caution: The language in which many of these beliefs are expressed is poetically infused, the way of the Bible. And where not poetic, the language is often anthropomorphic, and so problematic as to its ultimate import. We may speak of belief here, but we are quite far from the philosophers' conception of assent to a well-defined propositional content. Max Kadushin, reflecting on such belief, refers to it as "uncrystallized," an arresting image.

Religious belief can engender philosophical pique from another direction as well, the not inconsiderable inconsistency in the biblical characterization of God, an inconsistency that reflects our own sense of these things. To focus on our own case, we believe passionately in how much He cares—we feel or almost feel His touch—and then, turning a corner, we feel His absence acutely, sometimes almost a sense of cruelty. Or for another dimension of inconsistency, our experience of God, as just described, essentially involves God's feelings, thoughts, and the like. At the same time, we experience God as somehow beyond all that.

The lack of clarity, the anthropomorphism, the inconsistency, these are things that while smoothly accommodated within religious life drive the philosophic mind to drink. Or to purify. When Greek philosophy enters into contact with the Israelite religious tradition there ensues a rationalizing of these earlier modes of religious thought. The literary rendering, so apt for the religious life as it was (and largely still is) lived, is seen as inadequate, as in need of translation into a non-poetic idiom, as in need of a metaphysical foundation and attendant epistemological support. And making sense of religious life comes to be seen as defending the religious metaphysics, in part by supplying a supporting epistemology. Which brings us to proofs of the existence of a God.

What, though, if we maintain our focus on lived experience rather than on any allegedly necessary metaphysical underpinning? Without a religious metaphysics and epistemology we may well be accused of not knowing of what we speak. But is it not a genuinely religious intuition that with respect to understanding God we are over our heads, that central to religious life is an intimacy, the other party to which is as it were seen through a glass darkly?

Making sense of one's commitment to a religious life is not and should not be a trivial matter. But there is a world of difference between defending supernaturalist metaphysics and making sense of the form of life. That the life genuinely speaks to one is, for example, germane to the latter project. An aspect of this, stronger for some participants than others, is a sense of God's presence. And one may reflect that one has more confidence in the wisdom of the life than in any philosophical interpretation of what it all comes to.

The effect of my approach is to reduce substantially the gap between ordinary and religious belief. The gap upon which I have insisted earlier, the gap that we ordinarily feel, is the product of a philosophical interpretation of religion, a metaphysics that we have come to think of as at the heart of a religious orientation. But this is not to suggest that there is no gap, that religious belief is somehow just common sense.

To proceed in this direction is to dethrone philosophy as the provider of foundations in this domain. This is not, however, to deny philosophy the exploration of fundamentals. Here religion provides a rich field. To provide one example, I spoke above of the ancients' (and our) religious beliefs that, I said, drive a philosopher to drink. At the same time, the religious utility of such uncrystallized beliefs is enormous; in that regard we couldn't ask any more of them. Uncrystallized belief is an idea that cries out for philosophical clarification.

We are not the ancients, and philosophy has made its mark on us, one that we do not wish to eschew. But it is one thing to see religious life as riding on a metaphysical picture, quite another to view the life as fundamental and the doctrinal side of one's tradition as more like the furniture in the living room, importantly expressive of the specifics of the tradition's sensibility, rather than the foundations of the edifice.

## CHARLES MANEKIN

### "Warrants for Belief, and the Significance of Religious Experience"

If there exists a distinction between the Biblical "believing in God" and the medieval-philosophical "believing that God exists," as is claimed by many, including Howard Wettstein in the selection above, then that distinction does not lie in the need for epistemic warrant. Belief in God was never taken for granted, certainly not in the Bible. Whoever did not encounter God directly had to be convinced in some way that He was, well, *God*. "And when Israel saw the wondrous power which the Lord had wielded against the Egyptians, the people feared the Lord; they believed in the Lord and His servant Moses." (Exodus 14:31). On that day the Israelites had to be provided with a powerful demonstration that God could be relied on to save them from the Egyptians. Without this demonstration they would have little warrant to believe that God exists *as their God*, a being powerful enough to vanquish their enemies and provide for them in times of need.

So the Bible assumes that the doxastic states possessed by one who believes in God need to have some sort of warrant, even if the Bible's approach to belief is, as Wettstein suggests, affective. And this is also true of the medieval tradition. When the Jewish sage is queried by the Khazar King as to his belief, he answers, "I believe in the God of Abraham, Isaac, and Israel," and then proceeds to justify his faith by an appeal to the historical evidence.[1]

Moreover, believing that God exists may also indicate that the believer puts her faith in God. After all, if a child believes *that* Santa exists, she generally believes *in* Santa, i.e., trusts that Santa will reward her if she has been good because that's just what Santa does. True, believing that God exists does not *entail* believing in God, in the sense of putting one's trust in Him. A small child may believe that the man dressed in a red suit in the mall is Santa, without relying on him.[2] Likewise, one may believe that other gods beside the Lord exist without putting faith in them; indeed, the ancient Israelites were prohibited from having other gods besides the Lord. And in the Greek philosophical tradition, belief in the existence of an impersonal First Cause or First Mover certainly does not imply putting one's trust in it. Still, the point remains that belief in the Bible presupposes doxastic states[3] and is not detached from epistemic concerns, and this brings it closer to the way belief is used in medieval philosophy.

But there is a further similarity because the medieval philosophical project of providing explanation and justification for religious fundamentals is more than an attempt to give "the sort of foundations that intellectual virtue requires of a reputable theology."[4] To be sure, philosophers like Saadia and Maimonides are anxious to purify correct, and to refute heretical beliefs. But for Saadia the goal of their efforts are to produce people "whose prayers are pure," who "improve in their inner being as well as their outer conduct," who "tend towards the realm of wisdom and feel no inclination for anything else."[5] And for Maimonides the acquisition of true beliefs about God and His world produce the states of love, awe and obedience of God.[6] To be sure, Maimonides' understanding of what those states are will be different from that which emerges from the Bible. Nevertheless, the overarching goal of *knowing* God for Maimonides is not simply to have well-grounded beliefs, but to be within His presence and to imitate God's actions of loving-kindness, judgment, and righteousness within the earth.[7]

The Bible and the medieval philosophers do not differ so much in the *need* for a warrant for belief in God but rather over *what kinds* of warrant are appropriate, and indeed, how one comes to believe in or know God. In the Bible, one comes to possess first-hand knowledge of God through direct encounter, either *immediately*, through the prophesying of a prophet, or *mediately* through witnessing signs of his power; the latter evidence can be temporary (as in the splitting of the Red Sea in Exodus 14), or regular (as in the movements of the heavens in Psalm 91). Prophets may initially doubt whether the voice they hear is from God (as in the call to young prophet Samuel in 1 Samuel 2), but the prophet is ultimately certain of the prophetic message.[8] In any event, the Bible assumes that direct experience of God's power clearly warrants belief in God's claims to be God; those who doubt it (e.g., Pharaoh, the Israelites, on occasions) need more demonstrations of His power to be convinced, and in the absence of those demonstrations may cease believing it altogether.[9]

The Bible also teaches that one can come to have second-hand knowledge of God through belief in prophets and prophecy. Belief that Moses speaks in the name of God is warranted through prior acceptance of Moses as God's prophet, which itself needs to be warranted, since there are false prophets. The criteria for authenticating a prophet is dealt with cursorily in Deut. 18:18–22, and at greater length in medieval sources. Once a prophet is authenticated, one is warranted, indeed, obligated to believe that his or her message is Divine, although here, too, there are conditions that are discussed by the medievals. And finally, one can learn of God's power simply through hearing reports (as in the case of Jethro in Exodus 18, who presumably believed in the Lord's power without relying upon Him).

In sum, beliefs concerning God in the Bible are warranted through prophetic experience, witnessing miracles, hearing directly from an authenticated prophet, or receiving reports from a reliable contemporary source, which ultimately rests on one of the first three warrants.

Medieval Jewish philosophers expanded this last warrant to include a reliable chain of tradition that transmitted the reports of the eyewitness testimonies. Generally, this warrant consisted of two elements: the claim that a miracle was witnessed, or experienced, by a large number of people, and second, that the miracle report was reliable. The miracle could be a single event that was witnessed on a grand public scale, such as the splitting of the Red Sea, or the revelation at Sinai, or it could be a miracle that occurred over a large period of time, like the falling of the manna that fed the Israelites in their wanderings through the wilderness. What was said to guarantee the reliability of the tradition was the sheer unlikelihood that an invented story would be accepted by subsequent generations. In recent years this has become known as the "Kuzari argument" for the truth of some claims of Judaism,[10] but it appears in different versions in writers besides Judah Halevy, such as Saadia and Maimonides, and is used for different purposes.

According to Saadia, prophetic revelation transmitted reliably is indubitable because it is ultimately based on the testimony of eyes and ears, and sense knowledge is likewise indubitable. Since reason is such a reliable source of knowledge, both theoretical and moral, the question arises for Saadia why prophetic revelation was necessary at all? He provides several answers. First, since the art of speculation takes time to master, and some possess an "inborn defect," God did not leave his people without religion, but rather sent the prophet who announced the revelation publicly. "He thus made us see with our own eyes the signs and the proofs that support them indubitably ..." and did it in such a manner that even "women and young people" would understand, and be at no disadvantage. Second, prophetic knowledge as found in the Torah acts as a check on our scientific and philosophical researches since the Torah provides the "answer key" that guides us in the discovery of truth. Third, the reliability of prophetic tradition answers some of the doubts posed by proponents of other religions and other creeds, as well as the doubts that to which our incomplete investigations gives rise. And fourth, reason can discover general principles, but not particular details of many of the laws.[11]

For Maimonides, the public experience of revelation at the Gathering at Mount Sinai vouchsafes the uniqueness of the Torah and guarantees that it will not be superseded. It was not witnessing Moses' miracles that led the Israelites to believe in his mission, for putative miracles cannot be easily distinguished from magic and sleight-of hand. Rather, it was only the unique, public experience "which our eyes saw, and not the stranger's, and our ears heard, and not another's" that removed all doubts from the mind of the believer.[12]

Both Maimonides and Saadia describe the experience at Sinai in the first person, as if they themselves were there. In contrast, Halevy's Jewish sage establishes his beliefs first on the basis of direct observation of others, and then on an "uninterrupted tradition which is the equal of direct observation". The term Halevy uses for "uninterrupted tradition" appears in classical Arabic in connection with the transmission of reliable reports about the prophet Muhammad, and indeed, the Muslim provenance of the Jewish sage's argument should be noted. While rabbinic Judaism has always validated its teachings through appeal to an uninterrupted prophetic and legal oral chain of tradition stretching back to Moses, Halevy's claim that an uninterrupted tradition is *equal* to direct observation provides him a polemical weapon with which to answer the philosophical objections of the Khazar king, Halevy's stand-in for the acculturated twelfth-century Andalusian intellectual. When the philosophers offer arguments why God would not be concerned with human beings, or reveal to them His will, the Jewish sage replies that these arguments are based on insufficient data, since the philosophers lacked the prophetic knowledge that was publicly witnessed and reliably transmitted. The philosophers are to be excused for their errors, since the Greek tradition was not privy to the prophetic tradition available to the ancient Israelites, *nor can reason come up with it*.[13]

Halevy is often portrayed as a critic of philosophy because he points to the inability of unaided reason to penetrate the deep structures of reality, and because he claims that belief in God is warranted through an appeal to prophetic tradition and not through philosophical demonstration. Maimonides, by contrast, is often portrayed as a supporter of philosophy because he identifies those deep structures with Aristotelian physics and metaphysics and adopts the methods and doctrines of the philosophers. But there are points of commonality: Halevy's Jewish sage doesn't so much reject philosophy as devalue it, while simultaneously incorporating many medieval scientific and philosophical doctrines into his worldview. According to Maimonides "all [the Andalusian Jews] cling to the affirmations of the philosophers and incline to their opinions," himself, presumably, included. But he adds the important proviso, "in so far as these do not ruin the foundations of the law."[14] Because Maimonides is convinced of a well-attested prophetic tradition, such as the occurrence of scriptural miracles, he is led to reject the philosophical doctrine of the eternity of the world, since, he believes, miracles are incompatible with the world's eternity. In this acceptance of the historicity of some Biblical miracles, which, he believes, presupposes a transcendent Creator, he is in Halevy's camp.

Still, there is an important difference between Halevy and Maimonides on the question of the epistemic value of historical knowledge. While Maimonides holds that the public revelation at Sinai validates the prophecy of Moses for those present, he does not consider uninterrupted tradition to be the equal of direct experience. Even direct witness to a historical event conveys certainty only for the time it occurs. Thus miracles are certain in the opinion of one who witnesses them, but "at a future time their story becomes a traditional narrative, and there is a possibility for the hearer to consider it to untrue."[15] Epistemically speaking, there is difference between warranting a belief on the basis of direct experience, and on the basis of a report or hearsay; the latter is inferior to the former because it is subject to doubts. And if this is true with respect to the witnessing of miracles, how much more so is it true with respect to receiving the tradition of esoteric wisdom revealed to Moses and transmitted "in chapter headings" to subsequent students, until it was extant only in occasional hints in the received texts. According to Maimonides, this tradition, which includes physics, metaphysics, and theology, needs to be reconstructed with the aid of science and philosophy. So if Halevy bases his belief in Jewish teachings on a reliable prophetic tradition, Maimonides adds that the true meaning of this tradition can only be discovered with the aid of reason, and with the aid of those predecessors who have discovered the truth outside of the Jewish prophetic tradition, i.e., the philosophers.

To the enthusiastic embrace of reason by Saadia and its wary acceptance by Halevy, Maimonides offers a third approach, one that focuses on choosing the appropriate method of confirmation for different kinds of true beliefs, distinguishing between the epistemic value of those methods, and criticizing the Kalam theologians (and, in the case of creation, the followers of Aristotle) for failing to do the same. Since the possession of true beliefs is considered by him to be both vital for human happiness and mandated by the Torah, the uneducated, or those incapable of following philosophical argument, are taught to accept certain true beliefs, including beliefs in the existence, unity, and incorporeality of God, on the basis of traditional authority.[16] Beliefs warranted through traditional authority possess two defects: they are not well-understood, and they are not held with certainty; still, they are *true* beliefs, and represent an epistemological bottom line from which some believers may ascend. For those educated in and capable of following rational argument, the highest method of believe-acceptance is conclusive proof, either discursive, as in demonstration, or through something like intuition, as in the case of prophets; below that is probable proof, which is the province of dialectic. Conclusive proof not only confirms the truth of a belief but renders it demonstrably certain, which carries the highest epistemic weight. Not all beliefs are capable of being demonstrated due to the limitations of human knowledge, and in those cases we have to be content with near-certainty. Maimonides claims that the existence, unity, and incorporeality of God can be proved conclusively, and further he claims to have done so.[17] The creation of the world can be proved with arguments approximating a conclusive proof, and so the belief that the world is created can be held with near-certainty.

We saw above that direct experience also renders beliefs certain, as when the Israelites believed in the existence of God at the Gathering at Mount Sinai. So what is the epistemic difference between a certain belief warranted by sense experience and one warranted by rational proof? Maimonides touches on this question indirectly when he distinguishes between the experiences of the Israelites and Moses, respectively, at the Gathering at Mount Sinai.[18] Through their sensory experience of the fires, the thunder, the created voice of God, they came to believe without a doubt in the existence and uniqueness of God. But "their rank was not equal to the rank of Moses," despite their being present at the same event, because while they experienced the created voice of God, and *inferred* from that God's existence and incorporeality, Moses understood these directly through an act of prophetic intuition, which he appears to understand as a rational intution of a unique kind. So the indubitability conferred by the experience of God's unity and incorporeality differed in the case of the Israelites and Moses, because the nature of their experience of the deity differed. Even within the prophets there are different gradations of experience, ranging from one who prophesizes once in his lifetime to the one who is constantly in God's presence, a level reserved by Maimonides to Moses.

In light of Howard Wettstein's essay on the significance of religious experience, it may seem odd that what started out as a discussion of the appropriate method of confirmation of true beliefs has led us to the question of different ways of experiencing the deity. What do the possession of beliefs, the affirmation of a creed, have to do with religious experience of the divine? And how can subjective religious experience confirm the reality of what is putatively experienced? Let us begin with the latter question first, as we consider Wettstein's fruitful idea of comparing religious experience with aesthetic experience: Like an artist who has a sense of beauty that others may lack, a gift or a talent that needs to be developed through hard work, but nonetheless enables her to create things of beauty, the religious individual is endowed with a certain "gift to the spirit" or talent that allows her to experience certain things. Wettstein argues that while that religious experience is or can be deeply significant in the lives of those who have this gift, it cannot warrant the rest of us, who may lack this gift, to accept any claims of the reality about what has been experienced. Religious experience may not be used even by the believer as a warrant for her own belief, as in the case of St. Teresa he cites. This is not to suggest that religious belief cannot be considered foundational, i.e., fundamentally important, by those who possess it, in ways similar to other foundational beliefs, such as the belief in universal human rights. But it is difficult for many, even very religious people, in today's world, to consider these beliefs as epistemically basic as some of our ordinary beliefs, such as the belief in the reliability of the senses and the beliefs in other minds.

Has it ever been different? Wettstein suggests that the ancients lived their faith without the concept of belief, by which he means that they did not seek for a "metaphysical foundation and attendant epistemological support." If by this he means that, *pace* Maimonides, the Biblical prophets were not philosophers, he is of course correct. But if he means that, unlike the medieval Jewish philosophers, the Biblical prophets were not concerned with what we call "epistemic warrant" for their affective *attitudes* towards the deity, then I would ask the reader to consider two further points.

First, both the Biblical prophets and the medieval Jewish philosophers lived in intellectual settings where there were *alternatives* to their teachings. In the case of the Bible, the alternative was not atheism but idolatry, but it was a very real alternative, as we know from the speeches of the Biblical prophets. In the case of medieval Jewish philosophers, the alternatives were either different forms of Judaism that did not recognize Greek philosophy as a source of truth, or different forms of religion, including the religion of philosophers. But in both cases, thinkers had to justify their views and to convince by means of arguments. The modes of justification were different, but there has always been a need for epistemic warrant; that seems to be a constant in the human condition. It would indeed be bizarre for the Biblical prophets to defend belief in God's existence, but it was not at all strange for them to argue on behalf of worshipping the Lord rather than other gods, and that's what they spent a lot of their time doing, to judge from the writings attributed to them.

Second, there is indeed something foreign, almost inimical to contemporary sensitivities, in the medieval Jewish philosophical approach to religion, with its emphasis on intellectual achievement as the chief way in which one comes close to God. Maimonides was quick to brand ways of thinking about God that were incompatible with scientific demonstration as idolatrous, and were it not for his conviction that "even women and children" could be brought to have a rudimentary correct conception of God "on the basis of traditional authority," it would seem as if he consigns uneducated Jews to the ranks of inadvertent idolaters (at times, he speaks of them as beasts.) When one combines this elitism with Maimonides' adherence to a certain picture of the universe and conception of God, it is understandable why this understanding of religion would be considered unattractive today. It is not merely that Maimonides' picture of the universe is Aristotelian and his conception of God largely intellectual. It is also that he assumes that science and religion are inconceivable without each other, and while this view is shared by many religious scientists, it cannot be said to be the *bon ton* in departments of philosophy.

But as I suggested above, the deeper project of medieval Jewish philosophy was not so much to provide epistemic warrant for belief in God against the atheist, or to make those beliefs intellectually respectable, but to deepen one's understanding of God and the world in order to know the proper way to love and worship Him, and to be within God's presence. For the medieval Jewish philosophers, the Biblical prophet was endowed with certain gifts and talents that, with the proper training, and the fulfillment of various conditions, would allow her to experience Divine overflow, even union with God. The problem was how was this encounter possible in an age when prophecy had ceased? And the solution, according to the Jewish Aristotelians like Maimonides, was through an intellectual/moral experience that involved a cleaving or conjunction with God. Through perfection of the intellect, through knowledge of the ways God acted in the world (i.e., the natures of things), humans achieved a certain attachment to the Divine. And here I would like to return to Wettstein's analogy between religious experience and aesthetic experience, and suggest how it could apply to the medieval Jewish philosophical conception of religious experience. If, for the medieval philosopher, a Biblical prophet could be likened to an aesthetic genius like Beethoven, then Jewish sages who are not philosophers could perhaps be likened to lesser composers and artists. They possessed native intellectual gifts in various degrees, which allowed them to achieve some measure or "immortality" much the way artists do. And because the medieval Jewish philosophers thought, with Aristotle, that humans are by nature rational and desire to understand, they believed that all could be given the rudimentary elements for *some* sort of encounter with the Supreme Intellect, much the way that music teachers believe that "music appreciation" can be taught to all who possess hearing. The possession and contemplation of truths *was* their religious experience.

A final note – although the medieval Jewish philosophical understanding of religious experience offered by Maimonides may strike some moderns as overly "theological," Maimonides' views on the "ethics of belief" in *Guide* 1:70 are worthy to be remarked upon. Maimonides demands that one recognize the epistemic value of the arguments used to establish a belief, and that one never uses a bad argument to establish even a foundational belief. Although he felt that belief in the creation of the world was a principle of Judaism second only to the unity of God, he refused to establish it on the basis of the Kalam arguments that he considered to be unscientific and tendentious, and when he did provide warrant for his belief in creation, he conceded that he had not conclusively proved it or refuted his opponent. This demand for intellectual honesty goes beyond the desire to make a dogma "intellectually" respectable. In the service of God, who is Truth, nothing less than a well-founded adherence to the truth will do.

## Notes

1  *Kuzari* 1:11 (trans. Barry Kogan, with a modification, in Frank, Leaman, and Manekin, 2000, 206).
2  Think of the child who tells the department store Santa that he doesn't want anything for Christmas because he is Jewish.
3  This is conceded by Wettstein in "Against Theology" (Wettstein 2012, 109).
4  Wettstein, "The Significance of Religious Experience" (Wettstein 2012, 130 n.1).
5  *The Book of Beliefs and Opinions*, Introductory Treatise (Saadia 1948, 9).
6  See *Mishneh Torah, Basic Principles of the Torah* 2:2.
7  See *Guide of the Perplexed* 3:54.
8  At least according to Maimonides; see *Guide* 3:24.
9  There are cases of human deception in scripture, but in general "seeing is believing."
10  It has been much discussed on the web under this name as well as the "Kuzari principle."
11  In addition to the reading in this volume, see *Book of Beliefs and Opinions* 3:3–4,6 (Saadia 1948, 145–50, 154–7).
12  See *Mishneh Torah, Basic Principles of the Torah* 8:2.
13  See *Kuzari* 1:63, 2:66.
14  *Guide* 1:71 (Twersky 1972, 276).
15  *Guide* 3:50, 615–6 (Pines).
16  See, for example, *Guide* 1:35, 1.77–81 (Pines).
17  See *Guide* 1:71 and 2:2.
18  See *Guide* 3:33.

## Further Reading on Belief, Knowledge, and Theism

Adams, R. M. *The Virtue of Faith* (Oxford: Oxford University Press, 1987), 9–47.
Alston, W. P. *Perceiving God: The Epistemology of Religious Experience* (Ithaca, NY: Cornell University Press, 1991).
Alston, W. P. "Belief, Acceptance and Religious Faith," in *Faith, Freedom, and Rationality: Philosophy of Religion Today*, eds. J. Jordan and D. Howard-Snyder (London: Rowman & Littlefield, 1996), 3–27.
Buber, M. *Two Types of Faith: A Study of the Interpenetration of Judaism and Christianity*, trans. N. Goldhawk (Syracuse, NY: Syracuse University Press, 2003).
Carmy, S. "'The Gate Matches the Home': On R. Lichtenstein's Depiction of Faith," *Tradition* 47 (2015), 211–222.
Frank, D. "New Introduction," in Saadya Gaon, *The Book of Doctrines and Beliefs*, abridged and trans. A. Altmann (Indianapolis, IN: Hackett, 2002), 1–10.
Golding, J. "The Rational Defensibility of Being a Religious Jew," *Religious Studies* 35 (1999), 391–423.
Halbertal, M. "On Belief and Believers," in *Faith: Studies in the Concept of Faith and its History in the Jewish Tradition*, eds. M. Halbertal, D. Kurzweil, and A. Sagi (Tel Aviv: Keter Press, 2005), 11–38 [Hebrew].

Plantinga, A. *Warranted Christian Belief* (Oxford: Oxford University Press, 2000).

Ross, J. J. "The Hiddenness of God: A Puzzle or a Real Problem," in *Divine Hiddenness: New Essays*, eds. D. Howard-Snyder and P. Moser (Cambridge: Cambridge University Press, 2002), 181–196.

Schlesinger, G. *New Perspectives on Old-Time Religion* (Oxford: Clarendon Press, 1988), 100–164.

Segal, A. "'The Source of Faith' Examined," *Tradition* 47 (2015), 192–210.

Soloveitchik, J. B. "The Yearning Heart," in J. B. Soloveitchik, *And From There You Shall Seek*, trans. N. Goldblum and eds. D. Shatz and R. Ziegler (Jersey City, NJ: Ktav, 2009), 7–17.

Swinburne, R. *The Existence of God*, 2nd ed. (Oxford: Clarendon Press, 2004).

Wolterstorff, N. "The Migration of the Theistic Arguments: From Natural Theology to Evidentialist Apologetics," in *Rationality, Religious Belief, and Moral Commitment*, eds. W. Wainwright and R. Audi (Ithaca, NY: Cornell University Press, 1986), 38–81.

# 5  Idolatry

The previous part examined whether religious knowledge is possible and if so, on what grounds. This section is in a sense the other side of the coin. In what ways might one's religious convictions or conceptions be inaccurate, and what might underlie such inaccuracies?

The Bible frequently rails against the worship of 'other gods' and foreign modes of worship. As a normative matter, one could easily get the impression that the choice between right and wrong worship is as stark as Elijah portrayed it at Mt. Carmel (1 Kings 18): the distinction between proper and improper religious attitudes and behavior is crystal clear and the biblical opposition to idolatry makes no accommodations. As a practical matter, one could reasonably think that idolatry belongs primarily to the distant past, hardly to be found in contemporary Judaism.

The contributions in this section suggest otherwise. Each contribution in one way or another narrows the gap between right and wrong ways of approaching God and the natural world. **Maimonides** is as emphatic as anyone about the Torah's opposition to idolatry. The first purpose of the Mosaic law, Maimonides tells us, "is to remove idolatry and to wipe out its traces and all that belongs to it." Remarkably, however, Maimonides contends that God conceded something to the idolatrous habits of the Israelites. Since it is "not in keeping with human nature for man to abandon suddenly all he has been used to," God permitted the *modes* of foreign worship to continue so long as God was the *object* of that worship. While firmly opposed to pagan religion, God reluctantly accommodated certain of its practices.

If for Maimonides the Israelites were attracted to paganism due to their historical circumstances, for **Spinoza** the masses of every era and every area are by nature attracted to superstition. Humans are by nature *afraid*, and that fear breeds irrational beliefs and behavior. Fear explains superstition. But it also thereby explains conventional religious practice, since the latter, Spinoza contends, is nothing but an institutionalized version of the former.

**Moshe Halbertal** and **Avishai Margalit** find in Maimonides and Spinoza another feature of human nature that explains our tendency toward an idolatrous misrepresentation of reality: the imagination. It feeds our deepest fears (we imagine much worse outcomes than we should rationally expect) and wildest hopes (we imagine much better turnarounds than we should rationally expect), which in turn motivate superstitions, and even idolatry. Moreover, the imagination "leads to the two main elements of idolatrous thought about God: corporeality and multiplicity." The trouble is that "it is impossible to avoid making use of it [the imagination] in religious instruction directed at the masses."

In the same vein, **Yitzhak Melamed** notes that for Maimonides, it is rather easy for intelligent people to fall into idolatry. For Melamed, though, this is a conceptual point, not just a psychological one. Given the correct conception of idolatry—and of God's relationship to everything else—idolatry already encompasses much more than we might have thought. Absolute veneration for the Torah amounts to idolatry, Spinoza claims, and nationalist sentiment is often idolatrous, Melamed contends. Thus, unlike Maimonides, Melamed thinks the Rabbinic obituary for idolatry was premature. Idolatry is alive and well.

## MOSES MAIMONIDES (1138–1204)

### *The Guide of the Perplexed* (1190)

#### Book 3, Chapters 29, 32 (tr. Rabin)

*Idolatry's History and Mosaic Law*

CHAPTER 29

It is a well-known fact that our father Abraham was brought up in the religion of the Sabians, who believed that there was no God other than the stars. When I shall have finished telling you in this chapter about their books – which we now possess in Arabic translations – and their ancient tales, and exposing their beliefs and history to you from those sources, you will realize that they openly asserted that the stars are God and that the sun is the supreme God. They also claimed that the other planets were gods, but considered the two luminaries to be the greatest. You will also find that they expressly asserted that the sun is the one that governs the upper and the lower world. These are the actual words they used.

You will also find that in those books and tales of theirs they mention our father Abraham and say literally the following: As for Abraham, who was brought up at Kutha, when he proclaimed opinions contrary to the general belief and asserted that there was a Maker other than the sun, they adduced such-and-such arguments against him. Among their arguments they mentioned a number of effects of the sunlight such as are plainly perceived. Abraham then said to them: You are quite right; the sun is like the axe in the hand of the carpenter. Then they go on to mention some further arguments he employed against them. In the end of that story they tell how the king imprisoned our father Abraham and how he continued to argue with them in prison for some days. Finally the king became afraid that Abraham would make orderly government impossible for him and turn people away from their accustomed beliefs. He therefore exiled him to the other end of Syria, having first confiscated all his property. Thus they relate. You can find this story in full detail in the *Nabataean Agriculture*. They make no mention of the events related in our more reliable documents or of the revelations he received, because they deny the truth of his words, for the reason that he contradicted their pernicious doctrine. I have little doubt that when he came out in opposition to the beliefs of all his compatriots, those poor misguided people reviled and reproached him, and spoke ill of him. When he bore all this for the sake of God and preferred truth to honor, it was said to him: *And I will bless those that bless thee, and him that curseth thee I will curse, and in thee shall all families of the earth be blessed* (Genesis 12, 3). The outcome of his story was that, as we can see today, most of the inhabitants of the earth are agreed in holding his memory dear and blessing themselves with his name. Even those who are not of his progeny derive their origin from him. No one now is against him or ignorant of his greatness, except for the last remnants of that extinct religion, who have remained in the remote corners of the earth, like the heathen Turks in the far north, and the Indians in the far south. These are the last remnants of the Sabians.

The highest peak the philosophers of those times reached in their speculations was the following phantasy: God is the spirit of the heavenly sphere, i.e., the heavens and the stars are the body and God its spirit. Abu Bakr al-Sa'igh mentions this belief in his commentary on Aristotle's *Physics*. For this reason all Sabians believed in the uncreated world, since God in their view was identical with the sky.

They also assert that Adam was a person born from a male and a female like all other men, but they hold him in high esteem and say that he was a prophet, the emissary of the moon, and that he preached the worship of the moon; also that he wrote books about agriculture. The Sabians further maintain that Noah was an agriculturist and did not approve of idolatry. All Sabians disparage Noah because of this, saying that he never in his life did obeisance to any idol. They also say in their books that he was beaten and imprisoned for his worship of God, and suchlike stories more.

And because of those Sabian ideas they put up statues for the stars: golden statues for the sun and silver statues for the moon, etc., and divided the metals and the climes among the stars, saying this or that region had as its god to this or that planet. They built temples and placed images in them. They claimed that the powers of the planets were emanated onto those images, and those images spoke, understood what was spoken to them, reasoned, gave revelations (oracles) to people and gave them useful information. They said similar things about the trees which belonged to the division of those planets. If such a tree were dedicated to that particular planet and was planted in its name, and certain things were done for it and with it, the spirituality of that planet would emanate onto that tree. It would then give oracles to people and speak to them in their dreams. You will find all this in their books, which I shall name later on.

These then were the prophets of Baal and the prophets of Asherah, who are mentioned in our books, and in whose minds those ideas had got such hold that they *forsook the Lord* (Isaiah 1, 4) and cried: *O Baal, answer us* (1 Kings 18, 26), all this because such views were then generally held. At that time ignorance was widespread, and much nonsense and phantasy of that kind was current in the world, and all kinds of ideas arose, and there rose among them *one who useth divination, one who is an observer of times, an enchanter, a conjurer, a charmer, a consulter with familiar spirits, a wizard, and one who inquireth of the dead* (Deuteronomy 18, 10–11). In our major work, *Mishneh Torah*, we have explained that our father Abraham set about combating these ideas by argument and mild preaching, by friendly persuasion and by attracting them by means of kind deeds to the worship of God. Then the prince of prophets (Moses) was sent forth and completed the work, commanding to kill those people, to wipe out their very traces and to extirpate their progeny: *their altars shall ye pull down*, etc. (Judges 2, 2). He issued a prohibition against following any of those customs of theirs, saying: *and ye shall not walk in the customs of the nation*, etc. (Leviticus 20, 23).

You know well from the express statements of the Torah in a number of passages that the first purpose of the whole law is to remove idolatry and to wipe out its traces and all that belongs to it, even its memory, and everything that leads to carrying out some action connected with it, such as consulters of familiar spirits, wizards, passing through fire, diviners, observers of times, enchanters, conjurers, charmers, and inquirers from the dead, and to warn of doing anything that is like any of their deeds, leave alone imitating them. It is clearly stated in the Torah that all the things which they considered acts of devotion to their gods and means of obtaining their favor are things hated and loathed in the sight of God: *For every abomination to the Lord, which he hateth, have they done unto their gods* (Deuteronomy 12, 31).

This is the thing regarding which the true prophets say: *for after vain things which cannot profit, they have gone* (cf. 1 Samuel 12, 21). How immense therefore is the benefit of every commandment that liberates us from that terrible heresy and guides us back to the path of true faith, namely that there is a God who created all this and that it is He who must be worshipped and loved and feared, not those imaginary divinities, and this true God does not require for coming near to Him and gaining His favor anything onerous, only love for Him and fear of Him, which are the highest degrees of worship, as we shall show: *And now, o Israel, what doth the Lord thy God require of thee, but to fear the Lord thy God, to walk in all His ways, and to love Him* ... (Deuteronomy 10, 12). We shall follow up on this subject later on.

Now, however, let me return to my present subject. I say that the meaning and causes of many laws became fully clear to me only when I studied the beliefs, views, actions, and methods of worship of the Sabians, as you will see when I come to explain the motives of those commandments which are wrongly assumed to have no reason. I shall now enumerate the books from which you will be able to learn all I know about the Sabians' beliefs and views, so that you will be able to convince yourself of the correctness of my statements concerning the motives of those laws. The most extensive book on the subject is the *Nabataean Agriculture*, translated by Ibn Wahshiyya. That book is full of the figments of the idol-worshippers and of such things to which the common people feel somehow attracted and attached, such as the fabrication of talismans, the attraction of star-spirits to earth, magic, jinns and ghouls who populate the deserts. More such fables are spread abroad in that book which make sensible people laugh. Their purpose is to discredit the clear signs and wonders by which the people of the world know that there is a God who judges the inhabitants of the earth, as it is said: *in order that thou mayest know how that the earth is the Lord's* (Exodus 9, 29), and *to the end thou mayest know that I am the Lord in the midst of the earth* (Exodus 8, 22).

All those that I have mentioned to you are books of idolatry which have been translated into Arabic. No doubt they are only a small proportion compared with those that have not been so translated, or do not exist any more, but have perished and been lost in course of time. Those that we possess now, however, contain most of the views and actions of the Sabians. Some of these are still known today in the world, such as the building of temples, the placing of statues of cast metal and stone inside them, the building of altars on which either animal sacrifices or various kinds of food are offered, festive rites and meetings for prayer and other forms of worship in those temples – in which they institute some very sacred spots which they call temples of intellectual forms – the placing of statues *upon the high mountains,* etc. (Deuteronomy 12, 2), the worship of Asheroth, the erection of Masseboth, and other things about which you may inform yourself from those books which I have indicated. The knowledge of those views and actions is an important step in the enterprise of finding reasons for the commandments. The very root and linchpin of our law is the extirpation of those ideas from our minds and the erasing of those monuments from existence. To wipe them from our minds, as it is said: *that your heart be not deceived* (Deuteronomy 11, 16), and *whose heart turneth away this day from the Lord our God* (Deuteronomy 7, 5), and *ye shall destroy their name out of the same place* (Deuteronomy 12, 3). These two points are repeated in a number of passages. This was the primary and general aim of the whole law, as our Rabbis teach us in the comment handed down in their name to the verse: *All that the Lord hath commanded you by the hand of Moses* (Numbers 15, 23), where they say 'thus you learn that everyone who acknowledges idol-worship denies the whole law, while everyone who denies idol-worship acknowledges the whole law' (Horayoth 8a, etc.). Take good note of this.

CHAPTER 32

When you consider the works of God as seen in nature, you will become conscious of God's subtlety and wisdom in creating the animal body with the interlocking functions of its organs and their complicated layout. You will also realize how wisely and subtly He arranged for the successive stages of development of the whole individual.

Many items in our Law exhibit the same careful planning, being, of course, the work of that same planner, God. It is impossible to pass all at once from one extreme to another; it is therefore not in keeping with human nature for man to abandon suddenly all he has been used to. This was so when God sent Moses to make us a *kingdom of priests and a holy nation* (Exodus 19, 6) through the knowledge of God – as has been explained before – and said: *Unto thee it was shewed, that thou mightest know, that the Lord he is God in the heavens above,* etc. (ibid. 39). He also sent him to invite us to devote ourselves exclusively to His worship, as it is said: *and to serve him with all your heart* (Deuteronomy 11, 13); *And ye shall serve the Lord your God* (Exodus 23, 25); *and him shall ye serve* (Deuteronomy 13, 4). At that time the generally accepted custom all the world over, and the common method of worship in which we ourselves had grown up, was to offer sacrifices of various animals in those temples in which the statues had been placed, to prostrate oneself before them, and to burn incense before them. The religious and godly men of that time were those who dedicated themselves to service in those temples which had been erected for the stars, as we have related. This being so, God's wisdom and subtlety, evident in all His creation, did not decree that He should proclaim in His law a complete ban on all these kinds of worship, and their abolition. It would in those days have been quite inconceivable that such a thing should have been accepted, seeing that human nature is always happy only with that to which it is accustomed. Such a step at that time would have been as if a prophet should appear in our own time to preach the worship of God, and would say: God enjoins upon you not to pray to Him, not to fast, and not to call upon His help in misfortune, but to let your worship consist in thought only, to the exclusion of all works.

For this reason God permitted those methods of worship to continue, but instead of their being directed to created beings and figments of the imagination devoid of any reality, He caused them to be directed to Himself and enjoined us to carry them on in His name. He commanded us to build Him a temple: *And let them make me a sanctuary* (Exodus 25, 8), in which the altar should be dedicated to His name: *An altar of earth shalt thou make unto me* (Exodus 20, 24). The sacrifices were to be offered to God: *If any one of you wish to bring an offering unto the Lord* (Leviticus 1, 2). Also prostration and incense-burning were to be carried out only before Him. He prohibited that any of these acts should be done for anyone else: *He that sacrificeth unto any God, save unto the Lord only, shall be utterly destroyed* (Exodus 22, 20); *For thou shalt not prostrate thyself to another God* (Exodus 34, 14). He also set aside priests for the service of the Sanctuary, and said: *that they may be priests unto me* (Exodus 28, 41). It was, of course, necessary that dues should be paid to them in sufficient quantities for their livelihood, because their own time was taken up by the service of the temple and the sacrifices; these are the tithes payable to Levites and Priests. By this subtle disposition on the part of God the very memory of idolatry was in course of time wiped off the earth. The essential and real principle of our faith, the existence and Unity of God, was thus established without people being shocked and dismayed by the abolition of the forms of worship to which they had been accustomed, since no other form of worship was then known.

This type of worship, i.e., the sacrifices, was for a secondary purpose, while private and public prayer and such like acts of worship were closer to the primary purpose and indispensable in attaining it. Therefore an important difference has been made between the two types. The first type of worship, viz. the sacrifices, though carried out in the name of God, was not made obligatory upon us to the extent that it had been practiced before. Sacrifices were not to be brought in every place and at every time, neither was a temple to be erected wherever accident would have it, nor was anyone who happened to be present entitled to offer sacrifices, *whosoever desired it he consecrated* (1 Kings 13, 33). All this was forbidden. One temple was to be established *unto the place which the Lord shall choose* (Deuteronomy 12, 26), and no sacrifices were to be offered anywhere else, *that thou offer not thy burnt-offerings in every place which thou mayest see* (ibid. 13). No one was to be a priest but the descendants of a particular family. All this was designed to diminish this type of acts of worship and to prevent there being any more of it than divine wisdom had thought inadvisable to abolish altogether.

Private and public prayer, on the other hand, were to be offered in every place and by whoever happened to be there. The same applies to the Fringes, the *Mezuzah*, the Phylacteries and other forms of worship of that kind. Because of this distinction which I have just pointed out to you, there are found in the books of prophets so many passages of reproof for the people because of their zeal in sacrifices. They were told that these were not in themselves of any essential value and that God had no need for them. Thus Samuel said: *Hath the Lord as much delight in burnt-offerings and in sacrifices, as in obeying the voice of the Lord?* (1 Samuel 15, 22). Isaiah said: *For what serveth me the multitude of your sacrifices, saith the Lord* (Isaiah 1, 11). Jeremiah said: *For I spoke not with your fathers, and I commanded them not on the day of my bringing them out of the land of Egypt, concerning burnt offering or sacrifice; but this thing did I command them, saying, Hearken to my voice, and I will be unto you for a God and ye shall be unto me for a people* (Jeremiah 7, 22–23). This passage has been a source of difficulty for every one whom I have so far read or heard. They ask how Jeremiah could assert that God did not command us concerning burnt offering and sacrifice, since a large part of the commandments deal with just this matter: The meaning of the passage is as I have explained it to you: namely, that the primary purpose was that you should apprehend Me and not worship anyone but Me, 'and I will be unto you for a God and ye shall be unto me for a people'. All those laws concerning sacrifices and pilgrimages to the Temple were merely in order to achieve that principle. For its sake I have transferred those acts of worship to Myself, until the traces of idolatry should be extinguished and the principle of My unity established. You, however, have come to dismiss that purpose, and cling to those things that were merely instituted for its sake. You have attached doubt to My existence: *They have denied the Lord and said, he existeth not* (Jeremiah 5, 12). You have worshipped idols: *will ye ... burn incense to Baal and walk after other gods ... and then come and stand before my presence in this house?* (Jeremiah 7, 9–10): you still visit the temple of God and offer sacrifices, though these were not intended as a primary purpose.

That very same idea which is here expressed by Jeremiah, is also put forward in the Psalms as a reproof for the whole people, because they ignored at that time the primary purpose and made no clear distinction between it and the secondary purpose: *Hear, o my people and I will speak; o Israel and I will testify against thee: God, thy God, am I. Not because of thy sacrifices will I reprove thee, and thy burnt-offerings are continually before me. I will not take a bullock out of thy house, nor he-goats out of thy folds* (Psalm 50, 7–9). Wherever this idea is expressed it has this meaning. Think this well over and take it to heart.

## BENEDICT (BARUCH) SPINOZA (1632–77)

### *Theological-Political Treatise* (1670)

*Preface, sections 1–4, 7–10, 14–20; Chapter 1, sections 13–16* (tr. Curley)

*Superstition and Idolatry*

PREFACE

[1] If men could manage all their affairs by a certain plan, or if fortune were always favorable to them, they would never be in the grip of superstition. But since they are often reduced to such straits that they can bring no plan into operation, and since they generally vacillate wretchedly between hope and fear, from an immoderate desire for the uncertain goods of fortune, for the most part their hearts are ready to believe anything at all. While they are in doubt, a slight impulse drives them this way or that; and this happens all the more easily when, torn by hope and fear, they are at a loss to know what to do; at other times they are too trusting, boastful, and overconfident.

[2] Everyone, I think, knows this, though most people, I believe, do not know themselves. For no one has lived among men without seeing that, when they are prospering, even those who are quite inexperienced are generally so overflowing with wisdom that they believe themselves to be wronged if anyone wants to give them advice. In adversity, on the other hand, they do not know where to turn and humbly ask advice of everyone. They hear no advice so foolish and so absurd or groundless that they do not follow it. They hope now for better things, and then again fear worse, all for the slightest reasons.

[3] For if, while they are tormented by fear, they see something happen which reminds them of some past good or evil, they think that it portends either a fortunate or an unfortunate outcome, and for that reason they call it a favorable or unfavorable omen, even though it may deceive them a hundred times. Again, if they see something unusual, and wonder greatly at it, they believe it to be a portent of disaster, which indicates the anger of the Gods or of the supreme God. Prey to superstition and contrary to religion, men consider it a sacrilege not to avert the disaster by sacrifices and votive offerings. They create countless fictions and interpret nature in amazing ways, as if the whole of nature were as insane as they are.

[4] In these circumstances, we see that it is particularly those who immoderately desire uncertain things who are thoroughly enslaved to every kind of superstition, and that they all invoke divine aid with votive offerings and unmanly tears, especially when they are in danger and cannot help themselves. Because reason cannot show a certain way to the hollow things they desire, they call it blind, and human wisdom hollow. The delusions of the imagination, on the other hand, and

dreams and childish follies they believe to be divine answers. Indeed, they believe God rejects the wise, and writes his decrees not in the mind, but in the entrails of animals, or that fools, madmen, and birds foretell his decrees by divine inspiration and prompting. Thus does fear make men insane...

[7] Whatever some may say, who think that superstition arises from the fact that all mortals have a certain confused idea of divinity, from the cause of superstition I have given, it follows clearly, [first,] that all men by nature are liable to superstition; next, that, like all delusions of the mind and impulses of frenzy, it must be very fluctuating and inconstant; and finally, that it is preserved only by hope, hate, anger, and deception, because it arises, not from reason, but only from the most effective of affects.

[8] As easily, then, as men are taken in by any kind of superstition, it is just as difficult to make them stand firm in one and the same superstition. Indeed, because the common people always remain equally wretched, they are never satisfied for long, but are most pleased by what is new, and has not yet deceived them. This inconstancy, indeed, has been the cause of many outbreaks of disorder and bloody wars. For as is evident from what we have just said, and as Curtius noted very aptly, "Nothing sways the masses more effectively than superstition." That is why they are easily led, under the pretext of religion, now to worship their Kings as Gods, now to curse and loathe them as the common plague of the human race.

[9] To avoid this evil [of inconstancy], immense zeal is brought to bear to embellish religion—whether true or false—with ceremony and pomp, so that it will be considered weightier than every [other] influence and always worshiped by everyone with the utmost deference. The Turks have succeeded so well at this that they consider it a sacrilege even to discuss [matters of religion] and they fill everyone's judgment with so many prejudices that they leave no room in the mind for sound reason even to suggest a doubt.

[10] But if the great secret of monarchic rule, and its whole interest, is to keep men deceived and to cloak in the specious name of religion the fear by which they must be checked, so that they will fight for slavery as they would for salvation, and will think it not shameful, but an honorable achievement, to give their life and blood that one man may have a ground for boasting, nevertheless, in a free state nothing more unfortunate can be contrived or attempted. For it is completely contrary to the common freedom to fill the free judgment of each man with prejudices, or to restrain it in any way. ...

[14] I have often wondered that men who boast of their allegiance to the Christian religion—that is, to love, gladness, peace, continence, and honesty towards all—would contend so unfairly against one another, and indulge daily in the bitterest hate toward one another, so that each man's faith is known more easily from the latter [i.e., his hate] than from the former [i.e., his love, etc.]. For long ago things reached the point where you can hardly know what anyone is, whether Christian, Turk, Jew or Pagan, except by the external grooming and dress of his body, or because he frequents this or that place of worship, or because he is attached to this or that opinion, or because he is accustomed to swear by the words of some teacher. All lead the same kind of life.

[15] What, then, is the cause of this evil? Doubtless that to ordinary people religion has consisted in regarding the ministry of a church as a position worthy of respect, its offices as sources of income, and its clergy as deserving the highest honor. For as soon as this abuse began in the church, the worst men acquired a great desire to administer the sacred offices; the love of propagating divine religion degenerated into sordid greed and ambition, and the house of worship itself into a theater, where one hears not learned ecclesiastics, but orators, each possessed by a longing, not to teach the people, but to carry them away with admiration for himself, to censure publicly those who disagree, and to teach only those new and unfamiliar doctrines which the people most admire. From this, of course, there had to come great quarrels, envy, and hate, whose violence no passage of time could lessen.

[16] It is no wonder, then, that nothing has remained of the religion that used to be, beyond its external ceremony, by which the people seem more to flatter God than to worship him, no wonder that faith is nothing now but credulity and prejudices. And what prejudices! They turn men from rational beings into beasts, since they completely prevent everyone from using his free judgment and from distinguishing the true from the false, and seem deliberately designed to put out the light of the intellect entirely.

[17] Piety—good heavens!—and religion consist in absurd mysteries, and those who scorn reason completely, and reject the intellect as corrupt by nature, they are the ones who are most undeservedly thought to have the divine light. Of course if they only had even the least spark of divine light, they would not rave so proudly, but would learn to worship God more wisely, and would surpass others in love, not, as now, in hate. Instead of persecuting with such a hostile spirit those who disagree with them, they would pity them—if, indeed, they feared for the salvation of the others, and not for their own position.

[18] Moreover, if they had any divine light, it would at least be manifest from their teaching. I confess that they could never have wondered sufficiently at the most profound mysteries of Scripture. Nevertheless, I do not see that they have taught anything but Aristotelian and Platonic speculations. Not to seem to constantly follow Pagans, they have accommodated Scripture to these speculations.

[19] It was not enough for them to be insane with the Greeks; they wanted the Prophets to rave with them. This clearly shows, of course, that they do not see the divinity of Scripture even through a dream. The more immoderately they wonder at these mysteries, the more they show that they do not so much believe Scripture as give [merely verbal] assent to it. This is also evident from the fact that most of them suppose, as a foundation for understanding Scripture and unearthing its true meaning, that it is, in every passage, true and divine. So what one ought to establish by understanding Scripture, and subjecting it to a strict examination, and what we would be far better taught by Scripture itself, which needs no human inventions, they maintain at the outset as a rule for the interpretation of Scripture.

[20] When I weighed these matters in my mind—when I considered that the natural light is not only scorned, but condemned by many as a source of impiety,

that human inventions are treated as divine teachings, that credulity is considered faith, that the controversies of the Philosophers are debated with the utmost passion in the Church and in the State, and that in consequence the most savage hatreds and disagreements arise, by which men are easily turned to rebellions—when I considered these and a great many other things, which it would take too long to tell here, I resolved earnestly to examine Scripture afresh, with an unimpaired and free spirit, to affirm nothing concerning it, and to admit nothing as its teaching, which it did not very clearly teach me.

CHAPTER 1

[13] In the opinion of certain Jews, the words of the Decalogue were not pronounced by God. They think, rather, that the Israelites only heard a sound, which did not pronounce any words, and while it lasted, they perceived the laws of the Decalogue with a pure mind. I too have sometimes conjectured this, because I saw that the words of the Decalogue in Exodus are not the same as those of the Decalogue in Deuteronomy. Since God spoke only once, it seems to follow from this [variation] that the Decalogue does not claim to teach the very words of God, but only their meaning.

[14] But unless we wish to do violence to Scripture, we absolutely must grant that the Israelites heard a true voice. For Scripture says expressly, in Deuteronomy 5:4, that *face to face God spoke to you and so on*, that is, as two men usually communicate their concepts to one another, by means of their two bodies. So it seems more compatible with Scripture [to suppose] that God truly created some voice, by which he revealed the Decalogue...

[15] But not every difficulty is removed in this way. For it seems quite foreign to reason to maintain that a created thing, dependent on God in the same way as any other, could express, in reality or in words, or explain through his own person, the essence or existence of God, by saying in the first person, "I am your God, Yehowah, and so on." Of course, when someone says orally "I have understood," no one thinks that the mouth of the man saying this has understood, but only that his mind has. Nevertheless, because the mouth is related to the nature of the man saying this, and also because he to whom it is said had perceived the nature of the intellect, he easily understands the mind of the man speaking by comparison with his own.

[16] But if people knew nothing of God beyond his name—and desired to speak to him, in order to become certain of his Existence—I do not see how their request would be satisfied by a creature (who was no more related to God than any other creature and who did not pertain to God's nature) who said, "I am God." What if God had twisted Moses' lips to pronounce and say the same words, "I am God"? Would they have understood from that that God exists? What if they were the lips, not of Moses, but of some beast?

MOSHE HALBERTAL and AVISHAI MARGALIT

## "Imagination as a Source of Error," from *Idolatry* (1992)

Imagination is both the power of creating mental images, and as such a precondition of knowledge and thought, and a power unconstrained by logic and reality, and as such an obstacle to true knowledge and a source of illusions. Attempts to reconcile these two senses have resulted in an ambivalence toward imagination dating as far back as Aristotle. The traditional assumptions behind this ambivalent attitude are taken from the psychology of mental faculties, which claims that the mind is divided into separate faculties such as memory, learning, perception, intelligence, and imagination. As the faculty of creating mental images, the imagination is divided into two parts: the faculty of creating copies of what has already been perceived by the senses, which is required primarily for memory, and the faculty of creating images that are new combinations of copies of familiar elements. The constituent elements are always taken from reality, but the combinations may not be. In Aristotelian psychology the first type of imagination is the imitative imagination, while the second type is the creative imagination. It is the second type of imagination that is a cause of illusions.

Today we do not see an essential connection between the imagination and images. We judge acts and people as imaginative without any connection with images. A football player may be considered an "imaginative and inspired passer" not because any image appeared in his or our mind's eye but because he passed the ball in an unexpected way, while his teammate who received the ball may be judged unimaginative not because there was no image that appeared in his or our mind's eye but because he caught the ball as might have been expected. However, this dissociation between the imagination and images is relatively new. Philosophers have traditionally perceived an internal relation between the imagination and images, and the assumption that such a relation exists was common to the rationalists and the empiricists. In addition, both of these schools considered the imagination to be a source of errors and biases. For example, Hume believed that there is nothing more dangerous to reason than flights of the imagination, and that nothing has given rise to more opportunities for error on the part of philosophers (*A Treatise on Human Nature*, book 1, part 4). On the other side, the rationalist Spinoza said something very similar in a famous theorem in the *Ethics* (book 2, prop. 41). Spinoza claimed that cognition based upon images and imagination is a source of falsehood. The images, however, no matter how strange they may be, cannot be errors by themselves: they may become errors only when they are accompanied by a judgment (which is a matter of the will). But the images seduce us into the judging one way rather than another, and thus they contribute to error.

Not every thought, according to the rationalists, is based on images. We have no trouble imagining a triangle, but we are unable to imagine a thousand-sided figure in such a way that it would be distinct in our imagination from a figure with ten thousand sides. It is precisely because we are able to stop thinking in images and think conceptually instead that we are capable of creating an abstract concept of the divinity that is nevertheless not an empty concept. But those people whose thoughts are dependent upon images fall victim to severe corporealizing illusions and errors with respect to the nature of the divinity.

Both rationalists and empiricists believe that the faculty of imagination is a misleading and deceptive cognitive faculty. They differ in their views as to whether people need to use this faculty in their thinking to create visual images. On the issue of the contribution of the imagination to the falsehood of our beliefs about God, however, the contrast is not between the empiricists and the rationalists but between Enlightenment thinkers and Romantics. The Romantics accorded the creative imagination the supreme place in their hierarchy of cognitive faculties, definitely above knowledge acquired through the use of reason. Imagination grants us religious insight, while reason gives us an abstract God rather than a living God. We mention this contrast between Romanticism and the Enlightenment in order to dissociate ourselves from the identification of the Enlightenment with rationalism, while nevertheless attributing to the Enlightenment the criticism of the faculty of the imagination.

We have inherited from the Eleatics an enigma about the possibility of error, which is essentially the following: in order for a sentence to be meaningful it has to be about reality, that is, some fact has to fit the sentence. If this is so, then what is a false sentence about? If, on the one hand, the sentence is about a fact, then this fact exists and the sentence is not false. If, on the other hand, there is no fact that fits the false sentence, then it is not false but meaningless. Therefore it is impossible for a sentence to be false, and so there is no possibility of error.

Plato's thoughts on error are relevant to our discussions. In his view error and falsehood are based on wrong combinations. A wrong combination can occur in a sentence, as in the combination of words "Theaetetus flies": both Theaetetus and flying are elements of reality, but their combination is not an element of reality. An erroneous combination can also occur within a word, as in the case of "Pegasus," which is a combination of two ideas that do not go together—a horse and wings. The paradigm, according to Plato, is that of a misspelling. Such an error is based on the fact that the elements of the word (the letters) exist but the combination does not go together. Similarly, the components of Pegasus—a horse and wings— are elements of reality, but the combination of the winged horse is fictional. The creative imagination is responsible for these fictional combinations and is thus the source of illusion. It is true that a fictional combination in and of itself does not compel anyone to believe in it, but it provides the fictional objects for belief.

This argument is a fairly trivial one. It states that the imagination has the power to represent what does not exist, and if error is the belief in what does not exist, then the imagination is what provides us with objects for error. It is still necessary to explain what factor causes us to believe in the creatures of our imagination: is there something in the imagination itself that leads us to believe in its creations? Hume has an answer, which is certainly not trivial but is doubtfully true, that the degree of our belief is determined by the degree of vivacity of the images in our mind's eye. It is the vividness of the image that determines the strength of the belief. Someone whose mechanism for registering vividness is distorted, such as an insane person, sees with great vividness images that no one else will see in this way, and so he is subject to hallucinatory illusions. But this is not only true of insane people and hallucinators. All of us know from our own experience that during a dream we "believe" in the sights of the dream, and the only explanation for this according to Hume is the sights' great vividness. It is the power of the imagination that creates beliefs in us. The explanation for error must be found in the power of the imagination, as it is both the faculty that provides the images and the one that determines their vividness. The vividness of images in ordinary cases is determined not by the creative imagination but by the imitative imagination. The farther we are from the source in reality that creates the image, the more blurred the image will be. But there are people whose creative imagination succeeds in creating within them images that are like the vivid images that a normal person has from a primary impression of something in reality. When this occurs the person is susceptible to illusion, and in the worst case to deceptive hallucinations of the insane.

Hume's discussion, like Aristotle's, is based on the idea that the imagination is dependent upon the formation of images. Although we reject this idea, it remains crucial for understanding the Enlightenment enterprise of criticizing the faculty of the imagination as a separate faculty. It is especially important for our discussion of the imagination as a source of one specific illusion—the idolatrous illusion. The imagination as the ability to form images, and as a continuation of perception, is dependent upon the material. In other words, the source of the imagination, like the source of perception, is in the way material objects act upon us. This "material" character of the imagination has two "idolatrous" effects. One is the tendency to corporealize—to imagine in corporeal terms even those things that are not naturally such. Another is the tendency to multiplicity, since matter is the basis of particularity, and so thought mediated by the imagination is particularized thought. The imagination thus by its very nature leads to the two main elements of idolatrous thought about God: corporeality and multiplicity.

The critique of the imagination as a source of religious illusion does not stop here. It is not dependent upon the problematic assumption of a connection between the imagination and its source in the material world. The question we are asking within the context of the Enlightenment critique of the faculty of the imagination is: what is actually wrong with living according to the imaginative faculty?

### *Living According to the Imaginative Faculty*

Maimonides (*Guide of the Perplexed,* 3:29, 36, 37, 44) and Spinoza (preface to *Tractatus Theologico-Politicus*) are useful guides to constructing a worldview on the faculty of imagination. The imagination, according to both of them, is the mental faculty that motivates the masses. Idolatry is the manipulation of the imagination for controlling the masses by means of an image of the world built upon meaningless promises and threats. These promises and threats, in the name of gods and demons that are products of the imagination, constitute a dangerous substitute for a causal understanding of the world.

The faculty of the imagination is activated in an existential situation in which human beings, as finite and limited creatures, live in conditions of uncertainty accompanied by anxieties and fears for the future. An outstanding example of this is the climatic uncertainty confronting farmers—an uncertainty that undermines their basic existential security. Maimonides had good reason to believe that farmers are especially vulnerable to manipulation by means of the imagination, as this faculty is meant to provide solutions for their anxieties. This is the source of the association between agriculture and idolatry perceived by Maimonides, as by Augustine before him.

The order of things, according to this view, is as follows: the uncertainty in our world as human beings is a constant source of fear and anxiety. Increasing or decreasing this fear constitutes an outstanding means of control in the hands of an idolatrous leader. The fear itself increases both the tendency to imagine and the strength of the imagination. The masses are dependent upon their imagination because they lack the critical intellectual faculty required to harness the imagination and attain appropriate causal knowledge.

An immediate counterargument to Maimonides' view is that promises and threats as means of political direction relying on the imagination are not limited to idolatry. Promises of heaven and threats of hell are among the instruments of religious instruction used by the monotheistic religions as well. What differentiates them, in this respect, from idolatry? According to this argument the critique of the imagination should not be confined to the idolatrous religions, but should apply to religion in general.

Maimonides was not unaware of this possibility. His general conception of the Torah commandments provides a possible retort. Maimonides argues again and again (see, for example, 3:29) that "the first intention of the Law as a whole is to put an end to idolatry," where "idolatry" refers to a whole way of life including beliefs, rituals, and magic. If a central idolatrous custom was the placation of the gods by means of sacrifices, consisting mainly of private rituals, then the Torah adopts this means but limits its use (it permits sacrifices only in one temple) and also narrows the categories of the rituals and the reasons for bringing sacrifices. The Torah thus uses the "germs" of idolatry to fight against the "disease" of idolatry.

This immunization model is also appropriate for the description given by Maimonides of the way monotheistic religion uses the faculty of the imagination. The people who make use of the imaginative faculty for religious instruction in monotheistic religion are the prophets. The moral and spiritual virtues required of them in their role as prophets serve as guarantees that their use of the imaginative faculty will not involve gross manipulation of the masses' imagination.

Maimonides' critique of the imaginative faculty, as well as Spinoza's wider critique of it, are replete with inner tension. On the one hand, the imaginative faculty is the source of illusions with respect to the acquisition of the knowledge of causes. On the other hand, it is impossible to avoid making use of it in religious instruction directed at the masses.

### Projection and Errors in Idolatry and Religion

Psychologists, as well as people with common wisdom, see projection as a device for self-defense, for protection from beliefs that are difficult to bear. Thus, for example, it is difficult for a miser to believe that he is one, and so he "projects" his stinginess onto other people: misers tend to see more misers in their surroundings than do spendthrifts. In projection we discover the traits of the projecting person in what he imagines about others. Sometimes projection appears in reverse. If the mechanism of direct projection is the false attribution of one's own characteristics to others, then in reverse projection the person attributes to others characteristics which are opposite to the ones that he should have attributed to himself. Thus, for example, a weak person may use reverse projection to attribute omnipotence to some external force.

Xenophanes regarded the generation of religious concepts, or at least those of folk religion, as the result of direct projection, although he obviously did not use the word "projection" to denote this process. In principle he believed, as mentioned above, that man creates God in his own image. Aristotle (*Politics* 1252b, 24–7) adds to Xenophanes' argument, claiming that people project onto the gods not only their form but also their ways of functioning. Thus they say, for example, that the gods have a king. They imagine that the gods conduct their lives like people. Direct projection is a transparent device, whereas reverse projection is a sophisticated mechanism. We are speaking here, of course, of self-illusion: these are not devices for deceiving others but mechanisms of self-deception.

We must note that this discussion of projection is subject to ambiguity between projection in the sense of the individual who projects his own particular traits onto someone else, and projection in the sense of human beings who generally project human characteristics, or those that the human race is capable of, onto the divinity, whether directly or in reverse. This at any rate is the view of modern religious critics, including Feuerbach, Marx, Nietzsche, and Freud.

Freud stresses the motivational character of reverse projection, whereas Feuerbach stresses the fact that it is an outstanding product of the human faculty of imagination. According to Feuerbach, the imagination is a cognitive mechanism that serves the desires of the heart. Every thought involves abstraction, but the tendency to enliven abstract objects and to reify them as having independent existence is an outstanding activity of the imaginative faculty, which is applied to those abstractions that we are personally interested in. This tendency is central to the strategy of reverse projection according to Feuerbach, but the complexity of the projection mechanism prevents us from recognizing the phenomenon. This complexity is connected with the fact that religious projection, in Feuerbach's view, is a generic type of projection rather than the projection of the individual traits of a particular person.

The religious Enlightenment, which we regard as being represented by thinkers as different as Xenophanes and Maimonides, attributed to the mass of believers anthropomorphic projections from themselves onto the divinity. In the view of these thinkers, a pure belief that has been refined of the dross of anthropomorphism is nevertheless possible. The thinkers of the secular Enlightenment, among whom we include its later disciples, such as Marx and Freud, considered this move of the religious Enlightenment as even more deceptive than the transparent beliefs of the idolatry of the masses. In cases where projection is gross and direct it is easy to uncover its illusionary character. A person who prays anthropomorphically to his idol is relatively easy to convince that he is really praying to himself. It is much more difficult to convince someone whose belief is cloaked in the abstraction of an omnipotent, omniscient, absolutely simple force that he is praying to himself. By praying to himself Feuerbach means that the person is praying to the human essence of man, not that the individual person is unconsciously worshipping his own individual personality.

The peak of monotheistic abstraction is the theory of negative attributes. This is, in Feuerbach's view, also the peak of religious illusion. It expresses the believer's terror of existence, since every existence is limited and bounded, and uses reverse projection in the form of negative attributes to attribute to God a kind of existence without any limits or bounds.

## YITZHAK MELAMED

### "Idolatry and its Premature Rabbinic Obituary"

> Holy is the Memory of this Flag
> (Rabbi Avraham Yitzhak Kook)[1]

> And were you to say: 'We are a Nation! We have a land of our own! We have a state. We have soldiers. We have the IDF: we are strong!' – I would ask you: 'Were not your fathers and grandfathers – who lived before these idolatries – Jews?'
> (Rabbi Eliezer Menachem Shach)[2]

### *Introduction*

The Babylonian Talmud narrates the following story regarding Ezra and the Judean exiles who returned to Jerusalem, after seventy years of captivity in Babylon. Upon their return to Jerusalem the exiles cried: "Woe, woe it is he who destroyed the Sanctuary, burnt the Temple, killed all the righteous, driven all Israel into exile, and is still dancing among us!"[3] The entity responsible for all these miseries was the evil inclination toward idolatry. Anticipating the common Rabbinic theodicy which explains the creation of this evil inclination as aiming to bring reward to the righteous who are able to resist it, the exiles cried: "We want neither him, nor reward through him!" "Thereupon" – continues the Talmud – "a tablet fell down from heaven for them, whereupon the word 'truth' was inscribed … They ordered a fast of three days and three nights, whereupon [the evil inclination toward idolatry] was surrendered to them. He came forth from the Holy of Holies like a young fiery lion. Thereupon the Prophet said to Israel: This is the evil desire of idolatry."[4]

There are several extraordinary elements in this Talmudic account of the historical moment at which the inclination toward idolatry had been eliminated by the "Men of the Great Assembly" (e.g., why did the fiery lion come from the Holy of Holies, the most sacred place in the Temple?). Yet, it is crucial that we not miss its significance as designating a radical break between Biblical and Rabbinic Judaism. While the Bible is replete with injunctions against, and condemnations of, idolatry (thus attesting to the frequency of this practice among contemporary Israelites), the Talmudists often seem to be at loss in trying to understand how the Biblical Israelites could engage in such an egregious cult. Thus, we read in another Talmudic tale of Rav Ashi (352–427 CE), a Babylonian talmudist who used to deliver sermons mocking the three Israelite kings that practiced idolatry: The night before Rav Ashi was about to deliver his sermon, Menashe, one of the three idolatrous kings, appeared in his dream, and asked him a simple question of rabbinic law (which required some modest reasoning). Embarrassed that he was unable to answer the question, Rav Ashi asked Menashe to resolve it, and Menashe did so with ease. "Since thou art so wise, why didst thou worship idols?" asked Rav Ashi. "Wert thou there, thou wouldst have caught up the skirt of thy garment and sped after me," Menashe replied.[5] The Talmudic narrator of this tale is keenly aware of the fact that he is living in a completely different epoch than the Biblical Israelites. Indeed, the main point of the last tale seems to be emphasizing the rupture between the two periods.

The topic of the current paper – idolatry – may be defined in various ways. In order to avoid prejudging this notion, I suggest the following, non-partisan, working definition: *having an attitude (or attitudes) toward an entity other than God which is (are) otherwise typical and unique to one's attitude toward God.*[6] People have various views as to the proper attitude a religious person has, or should have, toward God; whatever that attitude is, having *this* attitude towards anything other than God is idolatry.[7]

The current paper aims at merely charting a brief outline of Jewish philosophical attitudes toward idolatry. In its first part, I discuss some chief trends in the Rabbinic approach toward idolatry.[8] In the second part, I examine the role of idolatry in the philosophy of religion of Moses Maimonides and Benedict de Spinoza, two towering figures of medieval and early modern Jewish philosophy. In the third and last part, I address the relevance of the notion of idolatry to contemporary Jewish life, and argue that the early rabbinic announcement on the perishing of the inclination toward idolatry might have been premature.

### Rabbinic Attitudes towards Idolatry

The Rabbinic Hebrew term for idolatry, *Avoda Zarah*, means literally, "a foreign worship." The Talmud designates *Avoda Zarah* as one of the three most severe prohibitions which a person is not allowed to transgress even at the price of one's own life.[9] The severity of the issue of idolatry is reflected in a Midrash which relates the conversation between God and Moses before his death. According to this Midrash, God explains to Moses that if Moses would not die, the Children of Israel "will err, confuse you for a God, and engage in your cult."[10]

While the intricate details prohibiting idolatry were expounded in great specificity in post-Biblical, rabbinic, literature, it was quite rare for (post-Biblical) Jews to suspect other Jews of committing idolatry. Thus, when, David Nieto (1654–1728), an early eighteenth century rabbinic scholar, was suspected of pantheism due to his repeated announcements that God and Nature are one and the same, the senior rabbinic authority that was asked to arbitrate the issue insisted that it makes no sense to ascribe to an intelligent person a cult of inanimate objects. The arbitrator, Rabbi Tzvi Hirsch Ashkenazi (1656–1718) – commonly known as the "*Hakham Tzvi*" – writes: "If the accusers [of Nieto] sought to decipher his claim as insinuating that the heating or humid thing is divine, this is something one cannot suspect of even the most dumb and foolish heretic in the world."[11]

For medieval rabbinic figures, the issue of idolatry was primarily present in the context of discussions of the status of Christianity. While there has been a wide rabbinic consensus on the monotheistic nature of Islam,[12] the crucial Christian doctrine of the trinity pushed the scales toward conceiving Christianity as full-fledged idolatry. Thus, Maimonides explicitly rules that Christianity is idolatry.[13] A crucial question in this context was the status of the belief in "communality" [*shituf*], i.e., a belief that recognizes other deities, *in addition* to the genuine God. The doctrine of the trinity has been commonly thought of as an instance of the belief in "communality." There has been a rabbinic consensus that *for Jews* the prohibition on idolatry pertains also to the cult of "communality" and thus Jews who practiced Christianity were considered full-fledged idolaters. According to rabbinic teaching, gentiles too were prohibited to engage in idolatry as part of the seven universal commandments given to Noah and his descendants. However, it was not clear whether the cult of "communality" fell within this prohibition. Some medieval rabbinic authorities argued that the descendants of Noah (i.e., gentiles) were not warned to avoid the cult of "communality," and thus a gentile who took part in Christian cult should not be considered an idolater.[14]

The charge of belief in "communality" has also been raised in internal Jewish contexts. Medieval critics of the Spanish Kabbalah argued that the belief in the ten *Sefirot* (divine emanations) is even worse than Christianity, since Christians believe merely in *three* divine beings while the Kabbalists believe in *ten*.[15] Similar charges of engaging in a variant of the worship of "communality" were brought by Ezekiel Landau (1713–1793) – the Chief Rabbi of Prague and one of the major rabbinic figures of early modernity – against certain Kabbalistic practices (primarily, against theurgic prayer), in a sermon that has been published only recently.[16]

So far we have very briefly surveyed some aspects of the rabbinic attitude toward idolatry. In the following section we will turn to philosophical inquiries about the nature of idolatry by Maimonides and Spinoza. It is noteworthy that in his legal code Maimonides begins his discussion of the prohibitions on idolatry with a lengthy genealogy of this practice. We will begin by studying carefully the first two paragraphs of Maimonides' extraordinary theory about the origin of idolatry.

## Maimonides and Spinoza on the Nature and Origins of Idolatry

> In the days of Enosh the children of mankind erred grievously... Their mistake
> was to say 'because God made the stars and planets to rule the universe and
> placed them on high to share honor with them, for they are ministers who
> render service in His presence, they are worthy of praise, glory and honor.'
> They also said that, 'It is the will of God – blessed be He – to exalt and
> honor what He exalted and honored, just as a king desires to honor those who
> stand before him: such is the prerogative of the king.' When this idea arose in
> their hearts, they began to build temples, to offer sacrifices, and to praise and
> glorify them in words. Because of a wrong belief they bowed down before
> the stars in order to reach the will of the Creator. *This is the basis of idolatry
> and was the verbal tradition of the worshipers who knew its origin.* They did
> not say there was no God except one special star.[17]

Why does Maimonides commence his discussion of the laws of idolatry with this
genealogical explanation of the origin of idolatry? What is the point in including
such a theory in a *legal* code? I suspect that the answer to both questions lies in
the estrangement that many rabbinic figures felt from the practice of idolatry.
We have seen that the talmudists stressed the existence of a rupture between
their world and the epoch of the Israelites who frequently engaged in idolatry.
Presumably, by providing this genealogy of idolatry, Maimonides attempts to
explain how intelligent and mostly decent people could engage in the gross cult
of idolatry. The key element in this explanation is that the deterioration of the
original and natural *true* religion of humanity into idolatry happened through a
*very long process*. Maimonides attempts to reconstruct the crucial stages of this
process in order to show that apparently minor deviations from true religion are
likely to lead later to the coarsest forms of idolatry.

If we look closely at the passage above we could see that *Maimonides is doing
his best to diminish our feeling of estrangement from idolatry.* The people of the
age of Enosh did not intend to engage in an idolatrous cult, but merely adored
God's servants – the stars and the planets – and shared God's own appreciation
for these servants; by serving God's most powerful servants, they just intended *to
serve God*, through his most powerful and visible creatures.

Cult and culture frequently become a second nature. Indeed, after a few
generations the original reason for the cult of the planets and stars was forgotten,
and the practice of the cult of stars became an end for itself.

> After a long time [*ahar she-arkhu ha-yamim*] there arose among the children
> of men false prophets who said that God has commanded them to serve such
> and such a star, or all the stars. They brought offerings and libations to drink
> in certain quantities, built a temple and made an image for all the people,
> men, women, and children to bow down before it ... Then other deceivers
> arose who said that the star itself, or the planet or messenger had spoken
> with them and told them to serve the idol and to worship it by doing one

thing and not another. The service of images by different ceremonies with sacrifice and bowing down before them spread throughout the world. After a long time [*ve-keivan she-arkhu ha-yamim*] the great and awesome Name was forgotten, and the people, men, women, and children, only recognized an image of wood or stone which they had been brought up from infancy to serve by bowing down, and by swearing by its name. The wise men among them, the priests and such like, thought that there was no god except the stars and planets whose images were made in their likenesses.[18]

It seems that the penultimate stage in this process was the cult of "communality": the people engaged in a cult of both God and the stars. Only in the final stage of this very long process the name of the true God was forgotten, and that cult was dedicated squarely to the stars and planets.

Before we turn to examine the crucial role of idolatry in Maimonides' explanation of the Commandments of the Torah, let me stress two more points about the genealogy constructed by Maimonides. First, we should note that at some point the new cult of the stars became a full-blown religion with its own commandments and prohibitions ("and told them to serve the idol and to worship it by doing one thing and not another"). Secondly, notice how each link in this process leads to another in an almost deterministic chain. This might have been a mirror image of the rabbinic justification for the injunction against social contact with idolaters: "[The rabbis] decreed against [consuming the idolaters'] bread and oil on account of their wine, and against their wine on account of their daughters, and against their daughters on account of idolatry."[19]

Chapters 35 to 49 of the third part of Maimonides' *Guide of the Perplexed* are dedicated to the issue of the reasons for the commandments. In this context Maimonides argues: "the first purpose of the law is to remove idolatry and to wipe out its traces and all that belongs to it, even its memory, and everything that leads to carrying out some action connected with it."[20] Maimonides notes that he gained a genuine insight into the reasons of many of the commandment by studying ancient books describing the cult of the Sabians, an ancient pagan religion, associated mostly with the geographic area of Haran (Syria).

> I say that the meaning and the causes of many laws became fully clear to me only when I studied the beliefs, views, actions, and methods of worship of the Sabians, as you will see when I come to explain the motives of those commandments which are wrongly assumed to have no reason.[21]

I will not address here the question of the historicity of this alleged cult; it is clear that Maimonides, many of his Arab contemporaries, and quite a few modern scholars took the Sabians as a genuine, specific, historical religion.[22] The Sabians, according to Maimonides, engaged in the cult of the stars as deities, and considered the sun as the supreme god.[23] Maimonides explains many of the commandments of the Torah as intending to eradicate specific common practices of the Sabian religion.[24] Probably the boldest of these explanations is Maimonides' claim that it was God's cunningness [*talattuf*] that stood behind the Torah commandments to bring sacrifices and the intricate laws of the temple rituals.

> At the time the generally accepted custom all the world over, and the common method of worship ... was to offer sacrifices of various animals in those temples in which the statues has been placed, to prostrate oneself before them, and to burn incense before them ... This being so, God's wisdom and subtlety, evident in all his creatures, did not decree that He should proclaim in His law a complete ban on all these kinds of worship, and their abolition. It would in those days have been quite inconceivable that such a thing should have been accepted ... For this reason God permitted those methods of worship to continue, but instead of their being directed at created beings and figments of the imagination devoid of any reality, He caused them to be directed to Himself and enjoined us to carry them on in His name.[25]

According to Maimonides the intricate laws of the service in the temple had one aim: to gradually educate the Hebrews by severely restricting and transforming the practice of sacrifices.[26] This divine plot, says Maimonides, was so successful that "the very memory of idolatry was in course of time wiped off the earth. The essential and real principle of our faith, the existence and Unity of God, was thus established without people being shocked and dismayed."[27] It is thus not a historical accident that the Talmudist could not fathom how their ancestors could engage in the cult of idolatry. The decisive anti-Pagan consciousness of the Talmudists was the result of a lengthy educational process devised by a cunning God.[28]

Whether or not it was God's aim in decreeing the commandment, it is clear that the eradication of idolatry and the practices which lead to idolatry was one of the chief aims of Maimonides' writing. The *Guide* opens with the elucidation of the Biblical verse that asserts that man was created in God's image (Gen 1:27), a verse that may provide crucial support for an anthropomorphic conception of God. For Maimonides, there is a clear path from anthropomorphic religion to full-fledged idolatry. Therefore, the refutation of anthropomorphic religion has a crucial religious significance in Maimonides' philosophy.

Like Maimonides, Spinoza considered anthropomorphism (and anthropocentrism) as one of the greatest errors and impediments for true knowledge of God.[29] Spinoza dedicates a considerable share of his *Theological Political Treatise* (1670. Henceforth: *TTP*) to the issue of superstition [*superstitio*]. While this issue has some affinity to idolatry – both address erroneous forms of religion – the two are distinct, since Spinoza clearly allows for a superstitious worship of the true God.[30] Like many of his medieval predecessors, Spinoza reserved the notion of idolatry to *the conception of a created being as divine*. The discussion of idolatry in the *TTP* is far more specific and punctual. The context of this discussion is the question of the nature of God's revelation on Mt. Sinai. Spinoza rejects the view that at Sinai the Hebrews heard merely an inarticulate noise,[31] and insists that we should not digress from the testimony of scripture according to which God spoke with the Hebrews "face to face" (Deut. 5:4), that is, in the manner in which two people normally communicate their thoughts through the mediation of speech. Then, Spinoza notes:

> However, this does not remove every difficulty. For it seems quite unreasonable to maintain that a created thing, dependent on God in the same way as any other, could express, in reality or in words, or explain through his own person, the essence or existence of God, by saying in the first person, "I am the Lord your God, etc." Of course, when someone says orally "I have understood," no one thinks that the mouth of the man saying this has understood, but only that his mind has. Nevertheless, because the mouth is related to the nature of the man saying this, and also because he to whom it is said has previously perceived the nature of the intellect, he easily understands the thought of the man speaking by comparison with his own. But since these people knew nothing of God but his name, and wanted to speak to him to become certain of his Existence, I do not see how their request would be fulfilled by a creature who was no more related to God than any other creature, and who did not pertain to God's nature, saying "I am God." What if God had twisted Moses' lips to pronounce and say the same words, "I am God"? Would they have understood from that that God exists? What if they were the lips, not of Moses, but of some beast [*alicuius bestiae*]?[32]

The danger of idolizing a creature as a result of divine revelation by means of a creature was not merely speculative, since shortly after the revelation in Sinai the Hebrews engaged in the cult of the golden calf. Spinoza might have been alluding to this possibility in the very last sentence of the quote above. Indeed, one of the major medieval rabbinic commentators on the Bible suggested that the golden calf spoke.[33]

Why then was God revealed to the Hebrews through speech? As if answering this question, Spinoza adopts the style of Ibn Ezra and notes: "I do not doubt that there is some mystery concealed here" (III/19).

The threat of idolatry is employed by Spinoza for polemical purposes later in the *TTP* when he criticizes his adversaries that refuse to entertain the possibility of any corruption in the biblical text. Spinoza accuses these adversaries of excessive zeal that leads them to "begin to worship [*adorare incipiant*] likenesses and images, i.e., paper and ink, in place of the Word of God."[34] By ascribing to a created entity – the text of the Bible – infallibility which properly belongs only to God, Spinoza's (Calvinist) opponents engage in an idolatrous cult. This striking charge seems to be a radical, if not absurd, culmination of the rather common understanding of idolatry in Jewish literature as the cult of a created being.

### *Idolatry and the Modern Jew*

Modernity is commonly conceived as the age of secularization, and as such one could expect that the issue of idolatry would simply disappear from the discourse of the period. The very opposite, however, seemed to be the case.

In 1938, on the verge of the Second World War, Rabbi Elhanan Wasserman (1874–1941), one of the prominent rabbinic figures of the inter-war period, published a collection of essays titled, *"Ikveta de-Meshikha"* [*In the Footsteps of the Messiah*]. The collection is imbued with the feeling of an approaching catastrophe and messianic times. One of Wasserman's most striking claims in the book is his description of nationalism, including Jewish nationalism, as genuine idolatry, i.e., cult of the Jewish nation as idol.[35] Wasserman stresses that this grave charge is not pressed merely against the secular Zionists; even religious Zionist Jews who take part in the cult of the nation commit the severe sin of idolatry insofar as they practice "communality," an adoration of both God and the Jewish nation.[36] Wasserman was not alone in making such charges,[37] and in order to better understand them it would be useful to look briefly at the connection between modern secularism and cult.

Whatever account of the emergence of modernity one may adopt, the French Revolution is one of its major landmarks. Anti-clericalism was an integral part of the ideology of the revolution, but the revolutionaries were not satisfied with the mere de-Christianization of France, and attempted to cultivate instead a variety of *civil* religions. Of such a kind was the *Culte de la Raison* of the early 1790s, which developed its own ceremonies, rituals and festivals.[38] Thomas Carlyle quotes Anacharsis Cloots – a Prussian nobleman who became one of the Jacobin disseminators of the new religion – as openly proclaiming: "There is one God only: *the people.*"[39] Forty years later, Jules Michelet, the great historian of the French Revolution would write retrospectively: "My noble country, you must take the place of God who escapes us, that you may fill within us the immeasurable abyss which extinct Christianity left over."[40]

In various ways, modern nationalism at once continued and replaced Christianity as the cult of modern Europe.[41] Jewish nationalism followed a similar path. The adoration of pagan culture was a vital topos in early Zionist literature.[42] More importantly, the cultural mainstream of Zionism aimed at a "transvaluation of values" in which the nation, the homeland, and the national hero, took the place of the old Jewish God. One striking example of this process is the still widely popular Hanukkah children's song, *"Mi Yemalel Gvurot Israel"* [*Who can verbalize the Glory of Israel*]. The title of the song is a paraphrase of a stanza from the famous liturgy of *"Shir ha-Kavod"* [*Song of Glory*] – "Who can verbalize the Glory of the Lord" – which, in its turn, refers to Psalms 106:2. Just as the above verse in the Song of Glory refers to God as *ineffable*, so does the Zionist Hanukkah song turn *the nation into an ineffable Being*, one whose sublimity transcends the capacities of language. The result is a negative theology whose cult-object is the Jewish nation. Every single stanza in this common Hanukkah song engages systematically in transferring divine qualities to the nation and the national hero.

To this striking example one can adduce innumerable other key texts of Zionist culture and literature that engage in the transformation of Judaism from the cult of the Jewish God to the cult of the Jewish Nation.[43]

Let me conclude by briefly discussing a *halakhic* question which was brought before Rabbi Moishe Feinstein (1895–1986), the towering rabbinic authority of the second half of the twentieth century. Rabbi Feinstein was asked whether one is allowed to pray in a synagogue in which national flags are staged next to the Holy Ark. In his typical, mild-mannered, response Rabbi Feinstein notes that though it is plainly improper to put flags, which are "objects of vanity" [*inyan shel hevel ve-shtut*] in a synagogue, it is not clear what kind of prohibition could be at stake. The most relevant injunction, says Rabbi Feinstein, is the prohibition against idolatry. But since those who employ the flag as their symbol did not consider it a *sacred* object, he does not think there is a genuine prohibition at stake. Therefore he advised the inquirer to try to peacefully convince the members of the synagogue to remove the flags, but not to engage in sectarian fight over this issue.[44] Rabbi Feinstein's responsum seems to imply that if the national flag *is* considered as a sacred object, the severe injunctions against idolatry may well be pertinent.

## Notes

1 Levin 2000, 58. I would like to thank Clare Carlisle, Sam Fleischacker, Yoni Garb, Michah Gottlieb, Zev Harvey, Aaron Segal and Jason Yonover for their most helpful comments and criticisms of earlier drafts of this paper.
2 Shach 1988, 30.
3 *BT Yoma* 69b.
4 *BT Yoma* 69b. Cf. *Shir ha-Shirim Rabbah*, VII 8.
5 *BT Sanhedrin* 102b.
6 Cf. Maimonides, *Mishneh Torah, Hilkhot Avodat Kokhavim*, 2:1. It is an interesting question whether the mere performance of a worshipping *act* toward an idol without considering the idol as divinity (for example, when one is forced by threats to bow before an idol) constitutes a bona fide idolatry. For the Talmudic debate about this issue, see *BT Sanhedrin* 61b–62a. I am indebted to Aaron Segal for drawing my attention to this issue.
7 Thus, for example, the early modern French philosopher, Nicole Malebranche argued that ascribing genuine causal powers to finite things is idolatry, since God is the only genuine cause of all things; see Malebranche 1997, 682–5. Notice that the definition above excludes from the scope of idolatry improper religious practice toward God. Indeed, within rabbinic law, improper cult of God (e.g., bringing sacrifices outside of the temple, or any other violation of the laws of sacrifices) is a severe transgression, yet it is not considered idolatrous.
8 Though the focus of this volume is Jewish *philosophy*, a proper understanding of the rabbinic attitude toward idolatry is essential since throughout the vast majority of Jewish history, its most important, if not sole, literary, normative, corpus has been rabbinic literature.
9 *BT Sanhedrin* 74a. The other two prohibitions are on murder and incest (which includes adultery).
10 Eisenstein 1915, II:363.

11 Ashkenazi 1981, Question 18. On Nieto and the controversy, see Petuchowski 1970 and Melamed n.d.. The Nieto affair is one of the very rare cases in which pantheism was suspected as heresy in the Jewish context.

12 See, for example, Maimonides *Epistles*, 42. See, however, Fenton 1983, 89, for discussion of RADBAZ's of Islam as "tantamount to Idolatry" in spite of its monotheistic nature.

13 *Mishneh Torah, Hilkhot Avodat Kokhavim*, 9:4, *Hilkhot Ma'akhalot Asurot*, 11:7, and *Commentary on the Mishnah, Avodah Zarah*, 1:3. In spite of his unequivocal classification of Christianity as idolatry, Maimonides considers it a step forward from paganism toward genuine monotheism. See *Hilkhot Melakhim*, 11:4–5 (notice that this passage has been censored in many editions due to its explicit denunciation of Jesus).

14 See the claims of Rabbeinu Tam (1100–1171) in the Tosafot's commentary on *Sanhedrin* 63b. Rabbeinu Tam's view was accepted by many rabbinic authorities. See, for example, Rabbi Moshe Isserlis's (1530–1572) gloss on *Shulhan Arukh Orah Hayim*, 156:1, and Rabbi Shabbtai Kohen's (1622–1663) commentary on *Shulhan Arukh Yoreh Deah*, 151:7. For recent endorsement of that view, see Rabbi Yoel Teitelbaum 1982, 110. For a scholarly study of this issue, see Katz 1961, 35, 164–8.

15 See the claims of "one of the philosophers" in *Shut ha-Ribash* [The responsa of Rabbi Yitzhak ben Sheshet (1326–1408)], 157. The same critique also appears in an epistle by Avraham Abulafia (1240–1291?). See Idel 1993, 109.

16 See Kahana and Silver 2010, 358–359. Notice that Landau does not reject the kabbalah *tout court*, but rather the practices he considers to be bordering on communality.

17 *Mishneh Torah, Hilkhot Avodat Kokhavim*, 1:1. Italics added. Unless otherwise marked, I use here the translation of Russell and Weinberg (1983).

18 *Mishneh Torah, Hilkhot Avodat Kokhavim*, 1:2.

19 *BT Shabbat* 17b.

20 *Guide*, 3:29; 1995, 178 (cf. p. 180). See also Halbertal and Margalit 1992, 128.

21 *Guide*, ibid.; 179. Cf. Stroumsa 2009, 101.

22 See *Guide*, ibid. For a fascinating discussion of perception of the Sabians in the early Islamic world and of the "modern Sabian myth" of twentieth century scholarship, see Stroumsa ibid., 84–102.

23 *Guide*, ibid.; 175.

24 See Stroumsa 2009, 101–2, notes 88–89 for a (partial) list of such explanations.

25 *Guide*, 3:32; 1995, 181–2.

26 "All those laws concerning sacrifices and pilgrimages to the Temple were merely in order to achieve that principle. For its sake I have transferred those acts of worship to Myself, until the traces of idolatry should be extinguished and the principle of My unity established." *Guide*, ibid.; 183–4.

27 *Guide*, ibid.; 182.

28 Maimonides was sharply criticized for his views on the issue of temple sacrifices. For Nachmanides' vigorous attack on these views, see Nachmanides' *Commentary on the Pentateuch*, Leviticus 1:9.

29 See Melamed 2010. For Spinoza too there is a clear path leading from anthropomorphism to idolatry. Paraphrasing Xenophanes, Spinoza writes: "a triangle, if it could speak, would likewise say that God is eminently triangular, and a circle that God is eminently circular. In this way each would ascribe to God its own attributes, *assuming itself to be like God* and regarding all else as ill-formed" (Letter 56; Spinoza 2002, 904, italics added).

30 See, for example, Spinoza's ascription of superstition to "the Pharisees" whom he never charges with idolatry (*TTP*, Ch. 3; III/53).

31 See *Guide*, 3:32–33.

32 Spinoza, *TTP*, Ch. 1; III/18–19. I am indebted to Edwin Curley for granting me permission to use his forthcoming translation of *TTP*, from which all quotes in this

paper are cited. Cf. Spinoza, *Short Treatise on God, Man, and His Well Being*, II 24 (I/107/13): "To make himself known to man, God *neither can, nor need, use words, miracles, or any other created thing, but only himself.*" (Spinoza 1985, 145, italics added).

33  See Rashbam (Rabbi Shmuel ben Meir, ~1080– ~1160) on Exodus 32:4.

34  Spinoza, *TTP*, Ch. 12 (III/159).

35  Wasserman 2002, 43 and 141–2.

36  Wasserman 2002, 43 and 141–2. Indeed, it is customary in current Israeli official ceremonies to speak about "the Holiness of God, the Nation, and the Land" [*Kedushat ha-Shem, ha-Am ve-Ha'aretz*]. I am indebted to Zev Harvey for pointing this out to me. For the very same critique of "religious nationalism" as idolatrous 'communality', see Rabbi Eliezer Menachem Shach 1988, 45–46.

37  The group of twentieth century Jewish thinkers who considered nationalism as idolatry is rather wide and includes figures from very different backgrounds and ideologies. Some notable figures in this group are Rabbi Aharon Shmuel Tamres (1920, 15–16), Yesha'ayau Leibowitz (1984), Franz Rosenzweig (1927, 185), Rabbi Yoel Teitelbaum (1982, 119), and Rabbi Eliezer Menachem Shach (1988, 30–2, 37, 45–6).

38  Citing the work of Mona Ozouf, David Bell (2001, 167) writes: "The formal content of the festivals overwhelmingly referred not to Christianity, but to pagan antiquity … The festivals amounted to an attempt to 'transfer sacrality' to the human world, the Revolution itself, and the *patrie*."

39  Carlyle 1903, 225.

40  Michelet 1959, I:83. Quoted in O'Brien 1988, 17.

41  See Bell 2001, Ch. 1, for a nuanced discussion of the issue.

42  See, for example, Tschernichovsky's important 1899 poem, "*Lenokhah Pessel Apollo*" [*Before Apollo's Statue*], and Avraham Shlonsky's 1924 essay "*Zelem*" [*Idol*]. For a discerning discussion of these texts, see Stahl (forthcoming), Ch. 1–2.

43  Consider, for example, Naomi Shemer's popular song from the early 1970s, "*Shivhei Maoz*" in which the reference of the phrase "*Maoz zur Yeshuati*" is transferred from God, to the IDF bunkers [*maozim*] on the Suez Canal. Yoni Garb helpfully pointed to a stanza from another famous Israeli Hanukkah song ("*Yemei ha-Hanukkah*" [*The Day of Hanukkah*] which asserts that these were the Maccabees, rather than God, who made miracles ("*al ha-nisim ve-al haniflaot asher holelu ha-makabbim*").

44  Feinstein 1982, 105–6.

## Further Reading on Idolatry

Batnitzky, L. *Idolatry and Representation: The Philosophy of Franz Rosenzweig Reconsidered* (Princeton, NJ: Princeton University Press, 2000).

Cohen, H. *Religion of Reason Out of the Sources of Judaism*, trans. S. Kaplan (Atlanta, SA: Scholars Press, 1995), 53–69.

Frank, D. "Divine Law and Human Practices," in *The Cambridge History of Jewish Philosophy: From Antiquity through the Seventeenth Century*, eds. S. Nadler and T. M. Rudavsky (Cambridge: Cambridge University Press, 2009), 790–807.

Frank, D. "The Politics of Fear: Idolatry and Superstition in Maimonides and Spinoza," in *Judaic Sources and Western Thought: Jerusalem's Enduring Presence*, ed. J. Jacobs (New York: Oxford University Press, 2011), 177–189.

Freudenthal, G. *No Religion Without Idolatry: Mendelssohn's Jewish Enlightenment* (Notre Dame, IN: University of Notre Dame Press, 2012).

Halbertal, M. and A. Margalit. *Idolatry* (Cambridge, MA: Harvard University Press, 1992).

Johnston, M. *Saving God: Religion After Idolatry* (Princeton, NJ: Princeton University Press, 2009).

Kaplan, L. "Maimonides and Mendelssohn on the Origins of Idolatry," in *Perspectives on Jewish Thought and Mysticism*, eds. A. Ivry, E. Wolfson, and A. Arkush (Amsterdam: Harwood Academic Publishers, 1998), 423–456.

Kreisel, H. *Maimonides' Political Thought: Studies in Ethics, Law, and the Human Ideal* (Albany, NY: SUNY Press, 1999), 29–35.

Seeskin, K. *No Other Gods: The Modern Struggle Against Idolatry* (West Orange, NJ: Behrman House, 1995).

Trakakis, N. "Does Univocity Entail Idolatry?" *Sophia* 49 (2010), 535–555.

Wolterstorff, N. "Would You Stomp On a Picture of Your Mother? Would You Kiss an Icon?" *Faith and Philosophy* 32 (2015), 3–24.

# 6 Human Ontology and Personal Immortality

Classical Jewish texts and later Jewish thinkers offer a wide variety of views on the ultimate destiny of individual human beings. The views range from the denial that anything at all lies beyond the grave to the embrace of an elaborate combination of purgatory, heaven, reincarnation, and eventual resurrection to eternal life. This section focuses on two medieval Jewish positions, both of which ostensibly embrace the possibility of an eternal afterlife but differ considerably over the details: What does the eternal afterlife consist of? How does one attain it? And what sort of thing are we, metaphysically speaking, that we are able to survive the decomposition of our bodies?

**Steven Nadler** presents the view of Gersonides. On the matter of what we are, metaphysically speaking: we are literally constituted by the truths we know. One survives death if one has already come to know some eternal (necessarily existing) truth, and thus to have it as a constituent. Finally, the afterlife consists exclusively in constant contemplation of eternal truths. Nadler argues, however, that Gersonides failed to pursue his position to its logical conclusion. According to Nadler, Gersonides' premises lead inexorably to the denial of personal immortality (and afterlife).

Some of Nadler's arguments echo earlier objections leveled by **Hasdai Crescas**. Crescas attacks Gersonides' position both for its poor fit with traditional sources and for its intrinsic implausibility. Intellectual achievement, traditional sources suggest, is not necessary for the ultimate blessing of eternal life, and eternal life won't be spent exercising the intellect. It is implausible, and perhaps absurd, to suggest that we are constituted by the truths that we know. Crescas, therefore, holds a very different opinion on these matters. We are simple substances. One attains the afterlife not by cultivating one's intellect but by following God's way. Finally, the afterlife consists in loving devotion to God.

**Aaron Segal** evaluates the debate between Crescas and Gersonides. He finds Gersonides' position on human ontology untenable and his position on the "entrance criteria" morally and religiously problematic *in excelsis*. With the collapse of Gersonides' position on these matters, the chances for a naturalistically acceptable path to eternal life are slim at best. Eternal life will require divine intervention of some sort. On the character of the afterlife, however, Segal declares no clear victor. That aspect of the debate raises axiological questions about the ultimate good for human beings, and, more specifically, about what value or disvalue there might be in an *eternal* life of any sort. Segal concludes his discussion of the axiological questions, and with them his essay, by tentatively suggesting that an eternal afterlife is for God's sake, not for the one who lives it.


## STEVEN NADLER

*Spinoza's Heresy: Immortality and the Jewish Mind* (2001)

*[excerpt from Chapter 4: The Philosophers]*

In the *Guide* Maimonides distinguishes between four varieties of human perfection. At the bottom of the ranking there is the perfection of possessions, where an individual has acquired a great deal of material and social wealth: money, clothing, land, slaves, and even power. Then there is physical perfection, 'the perfection of the bodily constitution and shape'. Both of these 'lower' types of perfection are fleeting and mutable. Wealth and health are easily subject to change and usually due to circumstances beyond our control. More significantly, they do not represent the improvement of a human being *as* a human being. More desirable is the perfection of the moral virtues. These are the character traits that, on Maimonides' view, dispose us to be useful to other human beings: generosity, courage, temperance, and so on. While also useful to its possessor, this 'excellence in moral habits' is not really an intrinsic perfection of the person himself. It is more a matter of relative perfection and a kind of social good. 'For if you suppose a human individual is alone, acting on no one, you will find that all his moral virtues are in vain and without employment and unneeded, and that they do not perfect the individual in anything; for he only needs them and they again become useful to him in regard to someone else.' Practical virtue is thus not an end in itself and not our ultimate goal. Rather, it is of merely instrumental value, 'good as a means toward' something higher.

'True human perfection', on the other hand, consists—as in the halachic writings—in intellectual perfection, or what Maimonides now calls 'the acquisition of rational virtues'. 'I refer to the conception of intelligibles, which teach true opinions concerning the divine things. This is in true reality the ultimate end; this is what gives the individual true perfection, a perfection belonging to him alone; and it gives him permanent perdurance; through it man is man.' Through knowledge and wisdom, the soul can achieve a non-relational perfection within itself; it may perfect itself intrinsically as an intellect. Important to this perfection, of course, is a rational understanding of the natures of things in the world, of the laws and order of Nature itself, and of the nature and ordering of the celestial realm. All of this belongs to natural science. But this is only a preliminary stage on the way to the greater and more important divine science, that is, to an understanding of the highest possible object of apprehension: God. Through an intellectual grasp of the essence of God—'the apprehension of His being [*metziyut*] as He, may He be exalted, is in truth'—and of his actions, we enter into a state of worshipful union with God. And this, according to Maimonides, is what we should all strive for. The practical virtues are useful and good, especially in our relations with others. But the perfection of the intellect is the true and highest good, the *summum bonum* of human existence.

Now when the intellect ordinarily comes to know a thing, what happens is that the form of the object—but not its matter—enters the soul of the knower. When a person knows a horse, the human intellect assumes the form of 'horse'. The intellect does not literally become a horse, of course, since the appropriate matter is lacking. It does, however, become 'informed' by the essence of horse, and so in a very literal sense becomes one with its object: the same form that, in the matter, makes a horse a horse now exists cognitively in the knower's soul and makes him a horse-knower. In knowledge, the mind thus becomes identical in character with its object (the mind of the horse-knower is, in an important sense, truly horselike). To know a thing is to move from a state of potentiality (that is, from being merely 'receptive' to the forms of things) to a state of actualization (that is, actually assuming the form of one known object or another). Here is how Maimonides puts it:

> Know that before a man intellectually cognizes a thing, he is potentially the intellectually cognizing subject. Now if he has intellectually cognized a thing (it is as if you said that if a man has intellectually cognized this piece of wood to which one can point, has stripped its form from its matter, and has represented to himself the pure form—this being the action of the intellect), at that time the man would become one who has intellectual cognition in actualization. Intellect realized in actualization is the pure abstract form, which is in his mind, of the piece of wood. For intellect is nothing but the thing that is intellectually cognized.
>
> (*Guide* I: 68; 1963, 163–164)

The intellect so actualized, Maimonides concludes, just *is* its content or object, the form of the thing. Before knowing, the intellect is mere potential or capacity, that is, nothing actual. In a state of knowing, on the other hand, what is actual is the form that now constitutes the mind.

> Accordingly, it has become clear to you that the thing that is intellectually cognized is the abstract form of the piece of wood, that this form is identical with the intellect realized in actualization, and that these are not two things —intellect and the intellectually cognized form of the piece of wood. For the intellect in actualization is nothing but that which has been intellectually cognized.
>
> (ibid.)

The actualized intellect, the intellect that is in a state of knowing, is not distinct from *what* it knows. On the contrary, the former is reduced to the latter; they are 'always one and the same thing'. 'That which has been assumed to be an intellect in actualization has nothing belonging to it except the form of the piece of wood. Accordingly, it is evident that whenever intellect exists in actualization, it is identical with the intellectually cognized thing.'

It now becomes clear what it is that is immortal for Maimonides. In the halachic writings he spoke of the intellect—*nefesh*, as distinct from the *neshamah*—as the 'form' of the soul, and as that which, when perfected, remains after a person's death. When we thus strive for our specific perfection—the perfection of the intellect—and seek to acquire knowledge of the highest kind, what we are really striving for is the greatest actualization of our intellects. In his philosophical writings he explains that the intellect is, when actualized, nothing but the forms of the things known. Or, in other words, the actualized intellect—also called the 'acquired intellect'—is nothing but the contents of the knowing mind, or the objects known *as* they are known. Thus, it is this knowledge alone that will remain after the death of the body. If a person is righteous, it is this that will be granted entry into the world to come.

> The souls that remain after death are not the soul [*neshamah*] that comes into being in man at the time he is generated. For that which comes into being at the time a man is generated is merely a faculty consisting in preparedness, whereas the thing that after death is separate from matter is the thing that has become actual and not the soul that also comes into being; the latter is identical with the spirit that comes into being.
>
> (ibid. I:70; 173–174)

And if a person has followed the path of true intellectual perfection, the actualized intellect that will remain after death just is the knowledge of God. The halachic writings themselves say as much: 'There is nothing which remains eternally except the knowledge of the creator of the world' (*MT Hilkhot Mezuza* 6:13). As God is the highest of all possible objects of knowledge, the knowledge of God is the supreme good of the rational intellect; and it is a knowledge that partakes of the character of its object. The pursuit of intellectual perfection—the pursuit of the knowledge of God—thus leads to immortality, but only because the knowledge thus acquired is itself (like its object) eternal. 'The soul . . . refers to the form of the soul, the knowledge of the Creator which it has comprehended according to its potential . . . This is the form that we described in chapter four of *Hilchot Yesodei haTorah* [of the *Mishneh Torah*]. This life, because it will not be accompanied by death . . . is called "the bond of life".' Now it seems very difficult to find much here that could, in any interesting sense, be viewed as an individual and *personal* kind of immortality. To what extent can a body of knowledge—which is all that the perfected intellect consists in—be seen as my *self*? Can memory and consciousness belong to it once it is separated from the body and the other, mortal faculties of the soul? How, in fact, can one perfected intellect, outside of the body and the space-time parameters that define existence in this life, be distinguished from another? What, in other words, is personal and individual about the perfected intellect?

It is this question—one that is raised by the accounts of immortality in both the halachic works and the *Guide*—that puzzled Maimonides' contemporary critics, as well as later scholars. It also gave at least one of his intellectual disciples the opportunity he was looking for to move carefully but (I believe) deliberately even closer to depersonalizing the immortal soul.

Unlike Maimonides, whose views on the immortality of the soul need to be gleaned from a variety of his halachic and philosophical writings, Gersonides devoted an entire book of his philosophical *magnum opus* explicitly to this issue. The opening fourteen chapters of his *Sefer Milchamot haShem* (*The Wars of the Lord*) are entitled *behasha'arut hanefesh* ('On the Immortality of the Soul'). His, too, is a thoroughly Aristotelian conception of the human soul and of its capacity for immortality. But it also stands in stark contrast to the views of earlier Aristotelians, such as Alexander of Aphrodisias (a second-century Greek commentator on Aristotle's works) and Averroes, or Ibn Rushd, the great but highly controversial twelfth-century Arabic philosopher and the author of several important commentaries on Aristotle. The topic of the immortality of the soul is of supreme importance for Gersonides, for upon it depends not just the metaphysical fate of the soul, but also our happiness and well-being—and not only in the afterlife, but in this life as well.

Gersonides begins his discussion by singling out that part of the soul that is the prime candidate for immortality.

> Since the intellect [*hasekhel*] is the most fitting of all the parts of the soul [*nefesh*] for immortality—the other parts are obviously perishable together with the corruption of the body because they use a bodily organ in the exercise of their functions—it is necessary that we inquire into the essence of the human intellect before we investigate whether it is immortal or not, and whether if it is immortal, in what way it is immortal.
>
> (*Wars* I.1; 1984, 109)

Although Gersonides uses *nefesh* to refer to the soul as a whole, the echoes of Maimonides' distinction between *neshamah*, or the part of the soul that governs and depends upon the body and thus perishes with it, and *nefesh* or *ruach*, the rational part of the soul, are unmistakable here. The soul, for Gersonides, is likewise composed both of parts that use the body in their functioning (such as sensibility and imagination) and of pure intellect, *hasekhel*.

That part of the soul that does depend on the body—and, in particular, on the senses and the imaginative faculty—for its operations is called the 'material intellect' (*hasekhel ha-hayulani*). The material intellect is pure potentiality, the bare capacity for thought. ...

And this brings us, finally, to immortality. What is immortal in a human being is, for Gersonides, nothing beyond the acquired intellect. Despite the fact that the acquired intellect is generated *in us*, it does not follow that it is corruptible;

Gersonides rejects Aristotle's claim that 'everything generated is corruptible' (ibid. I:11; 212). Because the rational order of the world in the Agent Intellect is eternal and incorruptible, our knowledge of that order (once it is acquired) must likewise be eternal and incorruptible, since knowledge (being identical with what is known) takes its character from the object known. Moreover, he argues, the acquired intellect (unlike the material intellect) is both immaterial and separable from the body, and thus not subject to the forces that destroy the body. 'The acquired intellect is immaterial, and an immaterial substance does not have the conditions requisite for corruption' (ibid.). Hence, he concludes, 'the acquired intellect is immortal'. When a person dies, the soul understood as the material intellect ceases along with the body. As a result, all further acquisition of knowledge necessarily comes to an end as well. But the acquired intellect remains. The immortality available to any human being consists only in this persistence, after the death of the body, of the knowledge that he or she has acquired in this lifetime.

To his contemporaries, Gersonides must have seemed to be treading perilously close to—if not right into the eye of—the Averroist storm. Averroes' writings, especially his commentaries on Aristotle, were the subject of several virulent condemnations in the thirteenth century. His views were regarded as inconsistent with a number of Christian dogmas, indeed, with the whole notion of there being a single, Christian truth. In fact, Averroes saw himself as simply laying out the proper understanding of Aristotle's views, and philosophers and theologians in the Latin West who were committed to the Aristotelian system had to drive a wedge between the master and his important but heretical commentator.

Among the Arabic Aristotelian's greatest sins, at least in the eyes of his Christian critics, was the denial of an individual, personal immortality. Averroes had argued that the material intellect in a human being is not a particular product of the union of a body (matter) and an individual soul (form), but rather simply the manifestation in that person of the single, all-embracing Agent Intellect. Thus, a person's 'soul'—the form animating his body—is nothing but the Agent Intellect itself; and his cognitive powers and achievements are simply the direct activity in him of that higher intellect, which actualizes certain potentialities in his body. All human beings, that is, literally share the same form—the Agent Intellect is common to them all. And a person 'thinks' only because of his union or 'conjunction' with the Agent Intellect and the intelligibles it contains.

Although in itself general, the Agent Intellect undergoes a temporary process of 'individuation' when it is attached to and embodied in an individual human being in a lifetime. But since the Agent Intellect is, in truth, *one*, and thus the same in and for all individuals, when a person dies all such individuation acquired through the body disappears and his 'soul' reverts back to its transcendent, separate, impersonal existence as the pure Agent Intellect. There is no *personal* immortality for Averroes.

Gersonides is aware of the philosophical problems here. For example, if all human beings literally share the same intellect, he argues, then how can we account for the different intellectual attainments of different people? But of even greater importance, it seems, are the religious and theological objections he has in mind. As Gersonides goes to great lengths to distinguish his own view of the soul from that of Averroes, he concentrates especially on the issue of personal immortality. If the human intellect is really nothing but the Agent Intellect, then immortality is of no practical value or moral consequence. For, he suggests, it would follow that *all* human beings, whatever their character or virtue—'be he fool or sage', good or evil—will, because they literally share the same eternal soul, obtain this alleged immortality. Moreover, if immortality is indeed a totally impersonal affair, as Averroes claims, then it can have no relevance for our very personal and particular lives. If it is not *I* who survive postmortem, then that eternal existence can be of no interest to me and have no connection to (and play no motivating role in) what I do in *this* lifetime. 'It has no utility at all', Gersonides says of Averroes' view; in it 'theoretical knowledge plays no role in the attainment of human perfection' (ibid. I:4; 131).

But does Gersonides himself have a doctrine of *personal* immortality? After a person's death, can the body of knowledge that constitutes his acquired intellect be distinguished from that of another person? More importantly, since it is presumably one's *self* that is rewarded with immortality, can that person's acquired intellect, postmortem, be linked up with his life and identified as his self? Gersonides apparently thinks so. Each person's acquired intellect is, he argues, a 'unity' (*echad*), 'numerically one', and thus can be distinguished—without any reference to the body at all—from other acquired intellects, even if those intellects have some knowledge in common. 'One piece of knowledge can be common to Reuben and Simon yet differ in them insofar as the kind of unity differs in them; so that, for example, the unity in the acquired intellect of Reuben differs from the unity in the acquired intellect of Simon' (ibid. I:13; 224). What gives each acquired intellect its unity and identity is both the amount of knowledge it involves and the content or character of that knowledge—not just its items, but also the way they are connected or synthesized.

> These differences [between the acquired intellects of Reuben and Simon] are attributable to the differences in the acquisition of this knowledge with respect to quantity and quality. For when someone acquires more knowledge within a particular science, the unity of his knowledge in [his acquired intellect] differs from the unity of knowledge who has acquired less knowledge in that science. Similarly, he who has acquired knowledge in a science different from the science in which another has acquired knowledge, his acquired intellect differs from the acquired intellect of the other. In this way, the levels of intellectual perfection are considerably differentiated.
>
> (ibid.)

Different people acquire different, and different amounts of, intellectual knowledge. This will presumably allow one disembodied acquired intellect to be distinguished from another. And Gersonides seems to think that a sense of selfhood will accompany this unity. He speaks of the happiness and pleasure that the immortal soul will feel when, having been released from the body, it will contemplate the knowledge it acquired during its temporal, embodied existence. But what Gersonides offers seems like both a rather thin kind of unity and an accidental kind of individuality for the acquired intellect to possess. It is not a unity that accrues to a collection of bits of knowledge because of the substantial unity of the knower or consciousness (or 'soul') to which they belong, much in the way a bunch of grapes has a unity because of the stem to which the grapes are connected. There is nothing to the acquired intellect beyond the knowledge itself; the content does not literally *belong to* something. Nor is there anything here similar to the 'internal' phenomenological unity—the unity that we *perceive* and are conscious of—that memory provides for our states of consciousness. Gersonides' acquired intellect is not a consciousness, nor even a true substance; it is a body of knowledge. And it would seem to be theoretically possible for two persons, in their lifetimes, to acquire exactly the same amount and kind of knowledge about exactly the same things. To use Gersonides' own words, two minds might 'approximate the unity of knowledge in the Agent Intellect' in precisely the same way and to the same degree, in which case each possessor of that knowledge has attained the same 'level of perfection'. Would not the acquired intellects of two such people be indiscernible from each other, particularly after the death of their bodies? If the quantity and content of their intellectual attainments are the same, then how could the acquired intellect of the one be distinguished from the acquired intellect of the other? And if the acquired intellects cannot be at least qualitatively distinguished, how can they be personalized, that is, identified with one human life rather than another? Moreover, whence does this alleged sense of self derive? What explains the consciousness and memory that Gersonides seems to attribute to the immortal acquired intellect?

Gersonides does not appear to be worried by such questions. In his mind, the philosophical and theological advantages of his own account of immortality over the Averroist doctrine are obvious. And the consequences for our happiness and well-being—certainly in this life, and more importantly in the world to come—are immense. True human happiness consists in the intellectual achievement represented by the perfecting of the mind, by the attainments of the acquired intellect.

> The true reward and punishment [for righteousness and sin] do not consist of these [material] benefits and evils that we observe [in this life]. For the reward and punishment that accrue to man insofar as he is a man have to be good and evil that are truly human, not good and evil that are not human. Now human good consists of the acquisition of spiritual happiness, for this good concerns man as man, and not of the pursuit of good food and of other sensual objects.
>
> (*Wars* IV:6; 1987: 182–183)

In this lifetime we can enjoy some measure of this perfection. The knowledge it affords us will grant us a degree of protection from the vicissitudes of this world. It is good and useful for navigating life in this world to possess a knowledge of nature that approximates that of nature's maker. But the demands of the body and the force of worldly circumstances often stand in the way of the enjoyment of true perfection. Thus, even virtuous people—those who have devoted their lives to the search for true knowledge—are subject to the elements, to the disturbances and imperfections of the world. It is only when they die that they are capable of enjoying their highest happiness to the highest degree.

> It is important to realize that each man who has attained this perfection enjoys the happiness resulting from his knowledge after death. We have some idea of this pleasure from the pleasure we derive from the little knowledge we now possess which subdues the animal part of our soul [so that] the intellect is isolated in its activity. This pleasure is not comparable to the other pleasures and has no relation to them at all. All the more so will this pleasure be greater after death; for then all the knowledge that we have acquired in this life will be continuously contemplated and all the things in our minds will be apprehended simultaneously, since after death the obstacle that prevents this kind of cognition, i.e., matter, will have disappeared . . . After death, [the intellect] will apprehend all the knowledge it has acquired during life simultaneously.
>
> (*Wars* I:13; 1984, 224–225)

The true reward for virtue, for pursuing the life of knowledge and intellectual achievement, will, Gersonides believes, be in the world to come.

> The view of our rabbis (of blessed memory) is that true reward and punishment occur in the world to come and that there is no necessity for reward and punishment in this world to be such that the righteous and the sinner receive material benefits and evils, respectively.
>
> (*Wars* IV:6; 1987, 197)

The immortality of the soul understood as the eternity of a body of knowledge—this is surely a far cry from what the rabbis of the Talmud and the *midrashim* had in mind. Both Maimonides and, perhaps to a greater extent, Gersonides offer a highly intellectualized conception of immortality, one that seems to threaten the personal character of this, the ultimate reward. This may even have been their intention. To Maimonides, reducing immortality to the persistence of abstract knowledge may have appeared to be the most effective means of discouraging metaphysical speculation about the world to come, and especially the overly simplistic and materialistic pictures of that realm being offered by his contemporaries. But neither philosopher, however rationalistic his commitments, was willing to dispense altogether—at least openly and explicitly—with the broad Jewish conception of immortality and the world to come, especially its moral dimension as the domain of ultimate reward for virtue. It would take a bold thinker indeed to do so.

HASDAI CRESCAS (1340–1410/11)

## The Light of the Lord (1410)

### Book 2, Part 6, Chapter 1 (tr. W. Z. Harvey)

*Does Man's Happiness Require Intellectual Perfection?*

We must dwell on this question [namely, whether man's ultimate happiness requires intellectual perfection], for from what we have seen, the feet of some of the savants of our nation have stumbled upon it. We, however, shall rectify ourselves upon it to understand the true end of this Law.

We say that it is agreed among [those savants] that the intellect becomes constituted as a substance from what it apprehends of the intelligibles; that from them is originated an acquired intellect which is not commingled with the hylic [material] intellect; and that owing to its being separate from the hyle, even though it was generated and originated, the acquired intellect survives eternally, for it has no cause of corruption, since matter is the cause of corruption and evil, as was demonstrated in the *Metaphysics*. Accordingly, eternal happiness consists of the apprehension of the acquired intelligibles; and the more concepts one apprehends, the greater in quality the happiness, all the more so when the concepts are valuable in their own right. And it is also agreed among them that each of those who attain happiness will rejoice and delight after death in that which he has apprehended. Now they speculate this by [extrapolating from] the pleasure we experience in our lifetime when we apprehend the intelligibles, which will be even greater after death, when we shall intellectually cognize them together in perpetuity. It also follows from this that there is no proportion between the pleasure which will come from the lesser intelligibles and that from the nobler intelligibles; for the pleasure in our lifetime differs exceedingly in this respect. This is the entirety of what they commonly affirm and upon which they agree.

However, we have found a difference among them. For one of them holds that this happiness will be greater when many existents are apprehended, whether they be material or incorporeal. For he holds that, inasmuch as the order of all things is in the soul of the Agent Intellect, the more its degree of apprehending the intelligibles approaches that of the Agent Intellect, the higher its rank. And there is one who holds that what survives is what the human intellect truly apprehends of the existence of God (may He be blessed), and His angels; and that the more it apprehends the higher its rank. The meaning of this, apparently, is that the intellect becomes constituted as a substance through its cognition of the incorporeal substances alone, and that is what survives eternally. The more it apprehends of them, the more immense the happiness.

And these two opinions, while they destroy the Law and extract the roots of the Tradition, are demonstrably untenable from the point of view of philosophic speculation. That they destroy the principles of the Law and the tradition will be seen for the following reasons:

First, it is one of the principles of the Law and the Tradition that by the performance of the commandments a man attains eternal life, as is stated explicitly in the Mishnah: 'Upon all who perform one commandment, goodness is bestown.' And its explanation appears in the Gemara that what is referred to 'is the goodness reserved for the righteous' [i.e., the world-to-come]. However, according to these opinions the practical commandments are only preparatory for the intelligibles, and since the intellect becomes constituted as a substance out of the latter, there is no advantage in the performance of the commandment.

Second, from the Law and the Tradition we learn of matters concerning reward and punishment that are contained in the practical commandments and prohibitions, and that could not possibly be the case according to these opinions. Thus regarding reward there is the matter of those who give their life in sanctification of the name, as in the Rabbis' statement: 'There is no creature who can stand in the rank of the martyrs of Lydda.' Now, the Rabbis did not specify the condition that the martyrs had become constituted as substances through the intelligibles. And if they had become constituted as substances, what advantages would there have been in the death of their bodies? Regarding punishment one finds cases like informers, traitors and he who shames his fellow in public of whom it is stated in the Tradition that 'they have no portion in the world-to-come.' Yet if their intellect had become substantiated through the intelligibles, it would be impossible for it not to survive eternally, unless God were to work a miracle and punish that acquired intellect, whose nature is to survive eternally, and annihilate it!

Moreover, the sectarians are included in this category [i.e., of those who have no portion in the world-to-come] if they deny one principle of the principles of the Tradition; e.g., he who says that the resurrection of the dead is not attested to in the Law. Now, if his intellect has become constituted as a substance through other intelligibles, even though the intelligible which he denies, and in virtue of which he is called a heretic, does not survive, why should the remaining intelligibles not survive? Nevertheless, according to the true Tradition, he has no portion in the world-to-come.

Third, it has assuredly become well known and accepted among the [Jewish] nation, that the delight and misery of the souls [after death] shall be according to the number of merits and sins. Thus, there are many homilies concerning the Garden of Eden and Gehinnom. Yet according to these opinions, reward and punishment consist in nought whatsoever but the survival or loss of the acquired intellect. Now, the proposition that the intellect delights in its intelligibles after death is demonstrably false, as will be shown later, God willing. But even if it should be granted that it is capable of delight, still there is no way to account for misery, even should one wish to contrive some contrivance!

Fourth, from the dicta of our Rabbis (of blessed memory) it appears that the practical part [of observance] is that which is the final cause. For some of them said, 'Practice is greater [than Study]', and in the end they voted and concluded that 'Study is greater, in that Study brings one to Practice.' Thus, they considered the practical part to be the final cause of the speculative part.

For all these reasons, it is manifest that these [two] opinions go against the roots and principles of the Law. That they are also untenable from the point of view of philosophic speculation will be seen from the following reasons:

First, if these opinions were true, the goal of the Law would be something other for man than what it is for his species. For according to these opinions, the surviving acquired intellect is incorporeal and not commingled with him; and therefore it is not his form. Nor is it an accident conjoined to him, since it has been posited as incorporeal and as becoming constituted as a substance out of the intelligible.

Moreover, the corruption of a man may be conceived without the acquired intellect's corruption, as, in fact, is posited in regard to its survival after death. And that whose corruption is possible without the corruption of a certain thing, and which is not commingled with it, is necessarily a different individual from that thing. And whatever is a different individual from a thing, and is disjoined from it, is not its form.

Moreover, the passing away of the incorporeal substance (sc. the acquired intellect) may surely be conceived without the passing away of the man. Now, once it has been demonstrated that [the acquired intellect] is not his form, it is ipso facto demonstrated that the end of the Law for man – i.e., to bring about the survival of this intellect – is for something other than him! That it is for something other than his species, is easily demonstrated from the nature of each. For man by his nature moves towards corruption, and the eternal existence of an individual man is impossible. But the acquired intellect is qua individual, posited to be eternal by nature, and impossible of corruption, owing to its very essence. Whatever has such characteristics differs in species [from man].

Second, it is remote with regard to divine justice that man's true reward and punishment should accrue to something other than to him who serves or him who rebels.

Third, the proposition that the intellect becomes constituted as a substance out of its objects of apprehension, and that it is originated separate from the hylic intellect, is demonstrably untenable for several reasons:

One of them is that since [the acquired intellect] has been posited to be non-hylic, it has no matter which could be its substrate and from which it could come into being. And since it is posited to be originated, it follows that it must come into being ex nihilo. But this proposition is notoriously false, for coming into being ex nihilo is among the impossible things that have a stable nature; unless it is by a miracle from the Absolute Power, may He be blessed!

Moreover, this proposition contradicts itself. For when it is posited that the intellect becomes constituted as a substance out of its objects of apprehension, what is meant is not the hylic intellect. This is because the intellect which has become constituted as a substance has already been posited separate from the hylic one. And should we mean by it the acquired intellect, then, indeed, since we have said that it 'becomes constituted as a substance out of its objects of cognition', we will be positing it to exist before its coming into being! By God!

It is as if we are saying that the thing brings its own self into existence! This is obviously ridiculous and false!

Moreover, that the intellect should be constituted as a substance out of its objects of cognition is demonstrably absurd. This is because a disjunction is unavoidable: either the intellectual cognition, which is the act of apprehending the intelligible, is the intelligible itself (as is the agreement of the philosophers, [i.e.] that the intellect, the intellectually cognizing subject, and the intelligible are one and the same thing) or it is not. If the intellectual cognition is the intelligible itself, one of the two absurdities necessarily follows: Either one intelligible must be the same as the other, and all the intelligibles are likewise one intelligible, provided that the intellectual cognition is one and unvarying for all intelligibles. But this is clearly absurd, for there would be no advantage or pre-eminence of him who apprehends many intelligibles over him who apprehends one intelligible! Or one intelligible is different from the other intelligible; and the act of the intellectual cognition of one intelligible is not the act of the intellectual cognition of the other intelligible. But it follows that when the intellect has become constituted as a substance through one intelligible, and afterwards apprehends another intelligible, it will have as many substances as it has intelligibles! Or else it will undergo change, and one intelligible will become constituted as a substance through the other, and it will take on another essence different in species from the previous! But this is perfectly absurd.

Moreover, since according to this [hypothesis] the essential form of man is continuously originated, it follows that the individual man will change and vary from essence to essence. This is perfectly absurd and ridiculous.

Fourth, this acquired intellect, which was constituted as a substance through its intelligibles, cannot avoid being either living, or dead, or not predicable by life and death. Now it is false that it is not predicable by them, for that sort of thing is an inanimate body or a certain accident. And it is false that it is dead, for then it would have no advantage and pre-eminence in its eternality. Thus it necessarily is alive. And since it is self-evident that life is different from intellectual cognition, it must be, therefore, that this intellect is compounded of life and intellectual cognition. Thus, there unavoidably is a substrate. But it has already been posited separate. This is a contradiction!

For these reasons, the untenability of these [two] opinions is proved manifest. But the first opinion is more reprehensible in one respect, and the second in another respect. With regard to the first, because it follows necessarily from it that survival depends upon the apprehending of the intelligibles which are in philosophy, the principles of the Law would therefore be derivatives of philosophy! And it would follow that he who intellectually cognizes one of the intelligibles of geometry, inasmuch as they all exist in the soul of the Agent Intellect, will live eternally! But this is a fantasy and a contrivance, wholly without merit.

With regard to the second, because the intellectual cognition of the essences of the separate beings is not through affirmation but through negation, as the Master of the *Guide* has expounded at length; and thus the cognition will be imperfect, and, surely [the intelligible] will not be in the intellect as it is extramentally.

And so I wish I knew how this deficient intelligible, which does not exist so extramentally, becomes constituted as a substance!

But the philosophers contrived these opinions, as if the nature of the truth had obliged them to believe in the survival of souls, and they thought up thoughts and increased words that increase vanity. Some of the savants of our nation were seduced to follow them, and they did not perceive, nor did it enter their minds, how thereby they were razing the wall of the edifice of the Law and breaching its hedges, even as the theory itself is groundless!

Now, inasmuch as it has been demonstrated concerning the perfection of opinions that this end [viz., the eternal happiness of the soul] is not consequent upon it, in the way that [those savants] had supposed, and since it has also been established concerning the other perfections [viz., the happiness of the body and the perfection of moral qualities] that they are only a preliminary to the intelligibles, it follows from this that this end [viz., the eternal happiness of the soul] is primarily and essentially consequent neither upon opinions nor upon actions. And inasmuch as this end necessarily belongs to the Law, in accordance with what is found concerning it in the Tradition, it necessarily follows that it is primarily and essentially consequent upon a part of [the Law] which is neither of opinions without qualification nor of actions without qualification. Now when we examined [the Law] and its parts, we found in it a part small of quantity but large of quality, which is neither of opinions without qualification nor of actions without qualification, namely, the love for God, may He be blessed, and the true fear of Him. I say that it is upon it that this end [viz., the eternal happiness of the soul] is consequent, by every analysis, according to the Law and the Tradition, and according to philosophic speculation itself ...

## AARON SEGAL

## "Immortality: Two Models"

### *Some Questions and Some Answers*

There are many questions one might ask about the immortality of human beings. Here is a partial list: Will some human beings survive their deaths? If so, under what circumstances? In particular, will they require a miracle? And in what condition will they be afterwards? What are we human beings like, metaphysically speaking (are we material or immaterial? substances or bundles of perceptions), and do the answers to any of the previous questions depend on the answer to this question? Supposing some human beings do in fact survive their deaths, does each of them ultimately perish, as Cebes suggested to Socrates, or do at least some go on existing forever? And if some do, in what condition?

By the beginning of the Rabbinic period (at the latest), canonical Jewish texts and standard Jewish practice had answered some of these questions fairly unequivocally. Thus, the second blessing of the *Amidah* prayer refers to God no fewer than six times as the One who resurrects the dead. If God will one day resurrect the dead, then it is clear that at least some human beings will indeed survive their deaths. One of the central Biblical verses upon which that blessing is based, Daniel 12:2, goes further still, in stating that the resurrected will enjoy *hayei olam*, that is, *everlasting* life. And although that verse is certainly the most explicit on this score, there are other Biblical "intimations of immortality," including the promise recorded in Isaiah 25:8 that God will "destroy death forever" and the description in Psalms 125:1 of those who trust in God as being "like Mount Zion that cannot be moved, enduring forever."[1] In any case, and despite standing in some tension with other Biblical verses, the positions that some human beings will survive their deaths and live forever quickly became authoritative and exerted a heavy influence on normative Jewish liturgy.[2] As such, they have since then gone virtually unchallenged (at least explicitly) by self-consciously Jewish philosophers.[3]

While this settled some of the questions we posed, others remained, and remain, unsettled. The character of the everlasting afterlife, its consistency with a thoroughgoing naturalism, the conditions for its attainment, and the metaphysical nature of human beings were battlegrounds for later Jewish philosophers. Our two selections, one primarily representing the view of Gersonides and the other authored by Hasdai Crescas, defend very different packages of views on these other issues. We might summarize the two packages as follows:

*Intellectualism*

(IN-1) A human being, whenever she exists, has as parts whatever eternally existing facts she then knows (such as facts of metaphysics, mathematics, and physics); when, and only when she is "embodied," she also has a human organism as a part (which, together with the facts she knows, compose her then);

(IN-2) Whether one survives death and endures forever in a conscious state entirely depends on whether one has come to know some such fact,[4] and

(IN-3) the eternal afterlife of one who does survive death consists in a steady, continuous, and perfect cognition of those truths the person knew only dimly when she died, since she is finally unencumbered by bodily needs and desires (a circumstance often referred to by the Talmudic rabbis as *Olam Haba*, "The World-to-Come.")

(IN-4) The fact that a person survives death and endures forever, and the character of her eternal life, is wholly due to the natural course of things, without the need for any special divine action; indeed, it is not clear God could prevent such a person from attaining the sort of eternal life she does even if God wanted to.

(Incidentally, some human beings who die will one day be embodied again – this is the resurrection of which Daniel spoke and for which traditional Jews pray thrice daily – but they will die yet again and return to their more perfect state of constant cognition.[5])

*Devotionalism*

(DV-1) A human being is a substance with no relevant ontological structure;

(DV-2) Whether one survives death and endures forever in a conscious state entirely depends on whether, and to what extent, one has devoted oneself emotionally, cognitively, and behaviorally to God, and

(DV-3) the eternal afterlife of one who survives death consists in an increasingly intense devotion to God and reciprocally loving relationship with Him while in the embodied state that she attains upon resurrection (a circumstance referred to by the Talmudic rabbis as *Olam Haba*, "The World-to-Come").

(DV-4) The character of a person's eternal life is determined at least in part by special Divine action.

(Incidentally, those who will be resurrected exist in the period of time between death and resurrection. The character of their existence in that intervening period is much like the character of their existence post-resurrection, except that they do not then enjoy the full panoply of benefits that attend an embodied religious devotion.)

In a nutshell, that is what Gersonides and Crescas, respectively, believed about our immortality. Their positions or variations thereof dominated the "immortality landscape" of medieval Jewish philosophy.[6] We might ask which position, if either, is right. Relatedly, we might wonder what view on these matters strikes the best balance between a fidelity to Jewish texts and practices, on the one hand, and overall plausibility and defensibility, on the other hand. It seems to me that with regard to the issues of human ontology and the conditions under which one survives death – issues (1) and (2) – Crescas's withering critique of Intellectualism was decisive. Moreover, the prospects for a view about those issues that is consistent with the sort of naturalism advanced by Intellectualism are not good: (IN-4) is thus not in good shape. However, on issue (3) the Intellectualist seems to me to have something of an advantage; but not an unanswerable one. Let me elaborate.

### Human Ontology

The first thing to say about (IN-1) is that it is not entirely clear what it is a view *of*. Adherents of Intellectualism frequently speak of a person's intellect – or his *nefesh* – being constituted by what the person knows, but it is not entirely clear what the relationship is supposed to be between a person and his intellect. Consequently, it is not entirely clear whether their view is supposed to be a view about the ontology of human persons at all. I have (I hope charitably) assumed that theirs is indeed a view with implications for what human persons, and not just their intellects, are at least partly made of. For otherwise their claims about immortality would be either non sequiturs or much less important than they take them to be. If their claims about immortality are about the immortality of human persons, then they would not follow (without further premises) from facts about the ontology of intellects. If their claims about immortality are instead about the immortality of human intellects, then they would lack the existential importance that they attribute to them. It would be like learning that my favorite bicycle will be preserved forever. Interesting, I suppose, but not particularly comforting. (Crescas makes this very point. He assumes that their ontological view is only about what human intellects are made of and that their claims about immortality are consequently only about the immortality of human intellects.) The second thing to say about the view is what a contemporary philosopher has said about a strikingly similar view: it sounds "like the sort of thing that comes to one in a dream after eating too many oysters."[7] Less colorfully, it is simply incredible. Could I really be made up even in part by such things as *the fact that 2 + 3 = 5* and *the fact that it is wrong to kill babies for no reason*?

More specific difficulties abound when we look at the conjunction of (IN-1) and (IN-2). That conjunction rules out the possibility of two people knowing exactly the same facts, in exactly the same way, when they die – at least if no two things can be composed of exactly the same facts and two things cannot become one thing.[8] But that scenario is surely possible.[9] (Gersonides seems to be aware of the difficulty (Feldman 1984, p. 224), but relies in his reply on the implausible assumption that while it is possible for two people to know the same facts, it is not possible for them to know those facts "in the very same way" – a matter of seeing the explanatory relations between facts, which, for some reason, do not constitute facts to be known.) Likewise, that conjunction rules out the possibility of a human being who dies knowing just one eternally existing fact – assuming, again, that two things cannot become one thing.[10] But that scenario is surely possible. And that problem is only exacerbated, *greatly* exacerbated, if every set of eternally existing facts composes something. For then an analogous argument shows that if (IN-1) and (IN-2) are true, it is not possible for anyone to die knowing *any* eternally existing facts. And that is a devastating blow to Intellectualism. For at least these reasons, (IN-1), and certainly the conjunction of (IN-1) and (IN-2), fails the test of overall plausibility and defensibility.[11]

### *Conditions for Eternal Life*

The same can be said about (IN-2) all by itself. It fails the test of overall plausibility and defensibility, as I shall argue. But, as Crescas argues, it also fails the test of fidelity to Jewish texts and practices. Crescas cites several Rabbinic texts, which, taken together, clearly imply that pious devotion to God and his commandments is both necessary and sufficient for attaining *Olam Haba*; he thus takes himself to have established (DV-2). He infers that (IN-2) is false, and twice over. Cognitive achievement is not necessary for attaining *Olam Haba*, since pious devotion suffices, and cognitive achievement is not sufficient for attaining *Olam Haba*, since pious devotion is necessary.

In making this inference, Crescas is assuming both (a) that (the relevant sort of) pious devotion does not suffice for (the relevant sort of) cognitive achievement – otherwise the fact that pious devotion suffices for attaining *Olam Haba* would fail to show that cognitive achievement is not necessary for attaining *Olam Haba*; and (b) that (the relevant sort of) cognitive achievement does not suffice for (the relevant sort of) pious devotion – otherwise the fact that pious devotion is necessary for attaining *Olam Haba* would fail to show that cognitive achievement is not sufficient for attaining *Olam Haba*. And each of these can be challenged by adherents of Intellectualism. Indeed, each one has. Gersonides took issue with (a): in the penultimate chapter of his treatise on immortality, he interprets the Mishna's statement that "All Israel has a portion in the World-to-Come" to mean "that since the Torah has directed Israel toward the acquisition of this knowledge in the marvelous way that is found in it, it is impossible that many should not acquire some knowledge, much or little."[12] And Maimonides took issue with (b): in his commentary on the continuation of that Mishna, which excludes certain individuals from the World-to-Come ostensibly on the grounds that they were religiously wicked, he writes that "none of these activities could come about – even though they are thought to be insignificant – except from a deficient *nefesh* that was not perfected and [hence] was unfit for the World-to-Come." Given his views on the conditions for attaining *Olam Haba*, the deficiency to which he refers is presumably cognitive.

However, Crescas seems to have the better of this argument. While Gersonides's claim is plausible – it is hard not to acquire a *little* knowledge of eternal truths – Maimonides's defense is much less so. Is it not clear that one can be a very fine metaphysician, mathematician, or physicist and yet be religiously wicked? Indeed, it is not just religious wickedness that seems compatible with such significant cognitive achievements, but moral wickedness as well. And therein lies the overall implausibility of (IN-2), even setting aside Jewish texts and practices. Any view according to which a permanently unreformed moral reprobate can enjoy a blessed eternal life is one that we should believe only on the basis of the strongest of evidence. And if we are evaluating that view against a background that includes the assumption that there is a perfectly just God, then I am not sure any amount of evidence would suffice to have us reasonably accept the view.[13]

### A Role for God?

The difficulties that confront (IN-1) and (IN-2) infect (IN-4), the naturalistic component of Intellectualism. It is not quite the case that (IN-4) implies (IN-1) or (IN-2); though something near enough is the case. The Intellectualist's naturalism, coupled with the assumption that some human beings are in fact immortal, is consistent with only a very narrow range of positions on both human ontology and the conditions under which a human being manages to be immortal. The Intellectualist position on these issues – (IN-1) and (IN-2) – was probably the best bet for a marriage of their naturalism with the *hayei olam* of which traditional Jewish texts speak. Barring their position, even just surviving death in a conscious state, let alone enduring in such a state forever, will require either divine intervention or some highly specific conditions, conditions that do not align particularly well with devotional or moral ones. After all, if you are a biological organism that endures from moment to moment (i.e., you do not persist by having a so-called temporal part at each moment that you exist), and God does nothing particularly special for you when you die, then your prospects for survival are worse than dim.[14] Your organs and cells will quickly disintegrate, you will be recycled for parts, and there is not much you can do about it. And even if you (and everyone else) are interestingly constituted – maybe you are constituted by but distinct from an organism, or maybe you persist by virtue of having temporal parts, or maybe you are an immaterial substance – but God does not step in to help you survive death, then either you will survive as a conscious being only if you have made some very special arrangements, such as arranging to have your psychological makeup imposed "in the right sort of way" on an unsuspecting cobbler,[15] or you will survive as a conscious being no matter what you do or how you lived your life, à la Plato. Neither of those views on the conditions under which you survive death comports particularly well with traditional Jewish texts. And neither fares better morally than (IN-2).[16] Worse still, it is not clear there are any arrangements you could reasonably make which are special enough to ensure an *eternal* life. Any hope for an eternal life whose existence and character is determined by our religious devotion and moral rectitude will have to be a hope for God to shape our ultimate individual destiny.

### *Character of Eternal Life*

Intellectualism has not made out very well so far. But on the issue of the character of one's eternal life, of what it will be like to live forever, Intellectualism has a prima facie advantage, I think, over Devotionalism. Their dispute about this issue is itself multi-faceted. For one, and true to my labels, they differ over whether one's eternal life will be primarily of the mind or primarily of the heart, of arresting intellectual vision or growing devotion.[17] (It should be noted that when this facet is taken all by itself, the positions of the two sides are not mutually exclusive.) On this question, both sides can claim the authority of tradition, for there are rabbinic texts that support each position.[18] And the test of overall plausibility is equally inconclusive. The question of what the *summum bonum* is cuts so deep that it is unlikely to be settled conclusively by any argument. It is also far from obvious whether there is a single ultimate good, given that people have such varied temperaments. Perhaps some will see the Intellectualist *Olam Haba* as Gersonides did, while others will see it as akin to endless *shiur* (Talmud class) without recess or lunch.[19]

For another, they differ over whether one will spend eternity embodied or disembodied. Here, while the bulk of Biblical and rabbinic material that speaks of or intimates immortality seems to assume as a matter of course that immortality will be corporeal – as many have pointed out, the Greek idea of an incorporeal immortality is foreign to the Bible – there are nonetheless rabbinic sources that can easily be read as suggesting the opposite. As Maimonides queries, what sort of bodies would it make sense for one to have in *Olam Haba* if, as Rav (third century) contends, one will not eat or drink or procreate?[20] As to be expected, Devotionalists have a ready retort: Why would Rav bother telling us that that there is no eating or drinking in *Olam Haba* if no one there had any mouth with which to eat or drink? And how would they wear the crowns of which Rav spoke if they had no heads?[21] But this exegetical dispute just demonstrates that Rav's statement can reasonably be construed either way. And here too, the test of overall plausibility is hardly conclusive. The question of whether our corporeal existence is something preferably escaped or preferably embraced is not something I could hope to settle here.

Nevertheless, although taken singly each of the two facets – intellect/devotion and corporeal/incorporeal – provides no dialectical advantage to either side, taken together they do. Intellectualism has a distinct *structural* advantage, in the following sense. The eternal afterlife, according to Intellectualism, is radically unlike the life we live now; or at least it is sufficiently different to provide its beneficiaries with a great good that is simply *unattainable* in our present state. This is because the intellectual goods promised by Intellectualism are, according to Intellectualism itself, unavailable to a person while she is covered by the epistemic veil that is her body.[22] On the other hand, Devotionalism, at least as articulated by Crescas, offers nothing to the eternal "afterlifer" that is not in principle available to her in this life.[23] And this structural difference confers an advantage upon Intellectualism. Devotionalism, but not Intellectualism, stands in a rather uncomfortable tension with some of the earlier Biblical teaching on death. As others have noted, death often seems in the Bible to be nothing to lament – and not only in cases where it cuts off an otherwise tormented life, but also in cases where the life that it ends was complete as it was. Thus, Abraham is said to have died "in a good old age ... and full of years" (Genesis 25:8); while there is no hint in this and other verses of the Epicurean view that *no* experience can be made better by being longer, there is a strong suggestion that more life of roughly the sort they already had would not have added one bit to Abraham's or others' already complete life. What good then would an eternity of such a life be? And yet that is precisely what Devotionalism appears to offer. Even regarding those whose pre-resurrection life was less blessed than Abraham's, couldn't many of them come to have such blessing by living a mere additional 175 years, like Abraham? Why have them live forever? Intellectualism avoids this tension, ironically enough, by promising something that is in many ways foreign to the world of the Bible.

### Defending Devotionalism

We could of course bring this to a close now, declaring "victory" to the Devotionalist on points (2) and (4) and to the Intellectualist on point (3). (The Intellectualist "lost" on point (1), but as far as we argued, the Devotionalist might "lose" on that point as well.) As far as I can tell, there is nothing inconsistent with adopting such a mixed package ourselves. But there is something awkward and mismatched about it. So I will instead close with two suggestions for denying Intellectualism its alleged advantage on point (3).

The first suggestion is to deny the datum on which the alleged advantage is based. In some versions of Devotionalism, the character of one's eternal afterlife, though embodied, is indeed radically different from the character of one's life now. The suggested differences are agential (we are no longer able to turn against God), motivational (we no longer desire evil), and even epistemic (we have a qualitatively different sort of knowledge of God).[24] According to these versions of Devotionalism, Intellectualism is robbed of its alleged advantage. But Devotionalists need to tread carefully here. Such radical differences threaten to undermine some of the central motivations for a Devotionalist characterization of the afterlife. Supposing such radical differences, it is not obvious that we would be embodied, strictly speaking, or that our pious devotion – with no desire or ability to do otherwise – would be of much value.

The second suggestion, to which I incline, is to accept the datum on which the alleged advantage is based, but to deny a presupposition of the objections we raised. In objecting to (DV-3), we presupposed that God's purpose in granting eternal life was to make the afterlifer's life better than it would otherwise be. Medieval adherents of Devotionalism, including Crescas, explicitly assumed as much.[25] And the assumption is certainly implicit in much of rabbinic literature on *Olam Haba*.[26]

Perhaps, though, that is not the only way to see things; perhaps even a finitely long life suffused with devotion to God and intimacy with Him can be as good as a human life can get. Even so, a world in which those who were once intimately related to God nevertheless perish and will never again live is a world in which *God's own interests* – His eternally abiding interest in the lives of those whom He loved and cared for – have been thwarted by death. Indeed, the great Jewish mystical work, the *Zohar*, consistently applies to the age of the resurrection a verse in Psalms (104:31) that speaks exclusively of God's glory and joy: "May the glory of the LORD endure forever; let the LORD rejoice in His works!"[27] God's own interests thus provide purpose enough for the resurrection, and purpose enough for granting the resurrected everlasting life.[28] On this way of seeing things, there is no tension between the fact that Abraham already lived as full a life as one can live and the fact that we can expect God to one day resurrect him. God will resurrect Abraham, not necessarily because it will make his life better, but because the God of life cannot abide Abraham's absence and will always rejoice in his presence.[29]

## Notes

1   For these and other related sources, see Levenson 2008, chapters 5 and 12.
2   Some verses that seem to suggest that death is the final word for each and every human being include Genesis 3:19; 3:22; Psalms 49:10; Psalms 89:49, Ecclesiastes 9:2. See Maimonides' *Essay on Resurrection* (Halkin and Hartman 1994, 225–6) for a more comprehensive list.

3 There were some exceptions, such as the fourteenth-century philosopher, Moses Narboni, who followed Averroes in denying individual immortality. See Bland 1982. Narboni attributes to Maimonides as well a denial of individual immortality, an attribution endorsed by some contemporary scholars (see Pines 1963, cii–cii, Sirat 1985, 170 and Rudavsky 2010, 102–107); Pines 1979 goes further still and claims that Maimonides denied the possibility of an afterlife altogether. Cf. Davidson 1992–93.

4 This is the view of Gersonides (see Feldman 1984, chapters XI and XIII). Several of the interpreters of Maimonides cited in the previous note attributed to Maimonides the view that a person survives death if and only if he has come to know fully the Agent Intellect (or God) – a condition whose attainability by human beings is dubious. (Crescas mentions roughly this distinction in the selection above. For a discussion of Crescas on this point, and which variation he found more objectionable, see Harvey 1977.)

5 See, inter alia, Halkin and Hartman 1994, 232.

6 Maimonides, of course, and Joseph ibn Kaspi stand out as devotees of some version or other of Intellectualism, while Nachmanides and R. Meir Abulafia (Ramah) were prominent defenders of some version or other of Devotionalism.

7 Olson 2007, 143. In deference to the Jewish tradition, we might replace 'oysters' with 'gefilte fish balls.'

8 On the question whether two things can become one thing, see Gallois 1998.

9 See Olson, ibid. Steven Nadler, in the selection printed above, effectively argues that for this reason Gersonides could not really have accepted (IN-1) and (IN-2), strictly speaking. Gersonides is ultimately committed, according to Nadler, to a denial of personal survival.

10 The conjunction implies that such a person would, after death, be identical with the fact he knows. The trouble is, that fact existed before the person died, and the person wasn't then identical with the fact. After all, one, but not the other, had a material part. Such a scenario would thus involve two things becoming one thing.

11 To be fair, I should note that one can perhaps parry some of the foregoing objections if one adopts the view that human beings (among other beings) persist by having temporal parts. See Olson 2007, 144–45. But (IN-1) is still incredible.

12 Feldman 1984, 225.

13 To be fair to Maimonides, he might have been defending a different view with a *much* higher cognitive standard, one that entails intimate knowledge of, and behavior in accordance with, all moral truths. See *Guide for the Perplexed* 3:54 and nt. 4. In that case, his view does not imply that a moral reprobate can enjoy blessed eternal life. However, that just makes (a) unassailable. If the relevant sort of cognitive achievement is so nearly unattainable, then it is very unlikely that every moral-religious exemplar will achieve such cognitive heights. In effect the Intellectualist faces a dilemma, one already posed by Judah Halevi in his *Kuzari* 5:14. (Thanks to David Shatz for discussion on this point.)

14 For some of the particularly special things God might do to help save an enduring organism, see van Inwagen 1978, Zimmerman 1999, and Zimmerman 2012.

15 Less drastically, if you are indeed interestingly constituted, your survival might just depend on your attitude! See Johnston 2010 and Zimmerman 2012.

16 Though Johnston 2010 is at least an *attempt* to develop a naturalistically acceptable and morally adequate view according to which some of us survive death.

17 A similar tension exists in the Christian theological tradition. See Hick 1994, 202–7.

18 A favorite prooftext for the Intellectualist camp is the Talmudic description (*BT Berakhot 17a*) of *Olam Haba* as a situation in which the righteous sit with their crowns on their heads feasting on the brightness of the divine presence; the Devotionalists could cite the passage in *BT Sanhedrin* 92a that portrays the righteous in *Olam Haba* as engaging in the very same righteous activities in which they engaged before death.

19  The remark about recess was made by a classmate of the historian of medieval Judaism, David Berger.
20  See, inter alia, Halkin and Hartman 1994, 214.
21  Abulafia, commentary to *BT Sanhedrin* 90a.
22  See, inter alia, Maimonides, *Mishneh Torah, Laws of Repentance,* 8:2 and *Guide* 3:9. For an excellent account of the multifarious nature of this veil, see Stern 2013, especially chapters 4 and 5. For discussion of whether Maimonides, at least, might have acknowledged exceptional cases, such as Moses, in which embodied people are able to overcome that veil, see Stern ibid. and Shatz 1990.
23  Indeed, R. Isaac Abarbanel understood R. Nissim of Gerona (Crescas's teacher) to be making precisely this point in the latter's explanation of the Torah's omission of *Olam Haba.* See Abarbanel's commentary to Leviticus 26:1 (sixth answer). See also *Kuzari* 1:104–17 and Kogan 2004.
24  See Nachmanides's commentary to Deuteronomy 30:6 for the agential and motivational metamorphoses (although there he dates them to the Messianic Age, which, by his account, precedes the resurrection of the dead) and his *Torat ha-Adam* (Chavel 1964, 303–6) for the epistemic ones. See also Levenson 2008, 189.
25  See Crescas' *Or Hashem* (Fisher 1990, 231 and 250–1).
26  Consider, e.g., the statement of R. Ya'akov in *BT Kidushin* 39b, which interprets the verse (Deuteronomy 5: 15), "that it may be good for you," as a reference to "the day that is entirely good," i.e., the age ushered in by the resurrection.
27  *Zohar* I 119a, 182a, and II 57b. See also R. Moshe Hayim Luzzatto's *Da'at Tevunot,* sections 128–30. Luzzatto maintains that the final purpose of creation, which will be realized only in *Olam Haba,* is for God to rejoice in His creatures (2012, 181–3). In this connection he cites the verse from Psalms 104, a verse with tellingly serves as a closing epigraph for both *Da'at Tevunot* and *Mesilat Yesharim.*
28  See also Levenson 2008, 200: "… it would seem that death … is one of the enemies, or even the ultimate enemy, of the people of God, and no victory of that God can be complete until this lethal foe is finally eliminated."
29  Many thanks to David Shatz and Tyron Goldschmidt for invaluable comments and criticisms of an earlier draft. Work on this paper was supported by a generous grant from the Immortality Project at UC-Riverside, sponsored by the John Templeton Foundation.

## Further Reading on Human Ontology and Personal Immortality

Batnitzky, L. "From Resurrection to Immortality: Theological and Political Implications in Modern Jewish Thought," *Harvard Theological Review* 102 (2009), 279–296.
Brody, B. "Jewish Reflections on the Resurrection of the Dead," *The Torah u-Madda Journal* (forthcoming).
Corcoran, K. *Soul, Body, and Survival: Essays on the Metaphysics of Human Persons* (Ithaca, NY: Cornell University Press, 2001).
Edwards, P. (ed.), *Immortality* (Amherst, NY: Prometheus Books, 1997).
Fischer, J. M. "Immortality," in *The Oxford Handbook of Philosophy of Death*, eds. B. Bradley, F. Feldman, and J. Johansson (New York: Oxford University Press, 2013), 336–354.
Goldschmidt, T. and A. Segal. "The Afterlife in Judaism," in *The Palgrave Handbook on the Afterlife*, eds. B. Matheson and Y. Nagasawa (New York: Palgrave Macmillan, forthcoming).

Goodman, L. E. *On Justice: An Essay in Jewish Philosophy* (New Haven: Yale University Press, 1991; 2nd ed. Oxford and Portland, MA: Littman Library of Jewish Civilization, 2008), 195–234.

Hasker, W. *The Emergent Self* (Ithaca, NY: Cornell University Press, 1999).

Hudson, H. *A Materialist Metaphysics of the Human Person* (Ithaca, NY: Cornell University Press, 2001), 167–192.

Kogan, B. "Who Has Implanted Within Us Eternal Life: Judah Halevi on Immortality and the Afterlife," in *Judaism and Modernity: The Religious Philosophy of David Hartman*, ed. J. W. Malino (Aldershot: Ashgate, 2004), 445–463.

Mittleman, A. *Human Nature & Jewish Thought: Judaism's Case for Why Persons Matter* (Princeton, NY: Princeton University Press, 2015).

van Inwagen, P. and D. Zimmerman (eds.), *Persons: Human and Divine* (Oxford: Clarendon Press, 2007).

# Part III
# Philosophical Theology

# 7 Divine Justice

In this general section on *Philosophical Theology* we focus on three issues: God's justice in a world that includes the suffering of so many innocents, God's election of the Jewish people from among all others, and God's redemption, both past and future.

The problem of evil in its classic form can be put rather succinctly: if God is all-powerful and perfectly good, whence evil? The problem is posed a bit differently in classical Jewish sources, but can also be put rather succinctly: if God is all-powerful and perfectly just, why do the righteous suffer?

The most sustained biblical treatment of that problem is, of course, the book of Job. And yet, the book's solution, or even whether it offers one, is far from clear. On **Kenneth Seeskin's** reading, the book "rejects any theory that views suffering as a good, even a qualified good needed to achieve a higher purpose." Indeed, Seeskin contends that no such theory could be true or should be proffered. Throughout the book, Job rightly remains indignant at God; he asserts his standing as an end-in-himself, and thereby exposes the fundamental flaw in his friends' theodicies. What Job learns by the end of the book is that we can know nothing at all about God, other than His being a moral agent "who guarantees the possibility that the world can be perfected." We are completely in the dark, however, about what God's intentions are and how the morality of those intentions might be reconciled with what we observe.

**Maimonides**, on the other hand, believes Job to be culpably ignorant about what is of value and consequently to be the author of his own suffering. Job's suffering is a function of thinking that "health, possessions, and children were the true aim of life," and only by revising this view, with God's intervention, does he overcome his plight. As Daniel Frank explains, Maimonides' exegesis is "an implied critique of Aristotle's moral paradigm."[1] Aristotle maintains that there are conditions necessary for the good life that lie beyond the control of the one who lives it, such as health, possessions, children, and even moral goodness. Prioritizing these conditions renders us vulnerable. Maimonides, on the other hand, believes that the sole condition for the good life is knowledge of God, a condition that lies squarely within each individual's control. Thus, Job's real suffering, due to his ignorance of God and what truly matters, is of his own making. The rest of his misfortunes are beyond his control, but they play no constitutive role in his happiness. When Job comes to understand this, he *ipso facto* no longer suffers.

**Edward Halper** generalizes the Maimonidean approach. He begins not with Job, but with the verses in Exodus that prescribe "an eye for an eye" as restitution for tortious damage. Halper finds in these verses the "Torah's only principle of justice": what the Rabbis called *midda k'neged midda,* or "measure for measure." Whoever does what is truly good gets more of that sort of good; and likewise for what is bad. But the scope of this principle depends on what is truly good (and bad). If the performance of God's commandments (*mizvot*) is truly good, then it will give rise to more opportunities to perform *mizvot*: the currency of justice will be *mizvot*. If knowledge of God and His providence is truly good, then such knowledge will give rise to further such knowledge, through either natural means or special divine action: the currency of justice will be knowledge. Each of these accounts can be employed to understand Job, along with other biblical texts that present the suffering of innocents. There are of course differences between the accounts. But common to all of them is the idea that "justice is ultimately about what an individual does for himself or another, rather than what he suffers. It is primarily about one's *own action*, and the reward lies in the action itself."

## KENNETH SEESKIN

### "Job and the Problem of Evil," in *Jewish Philosophy in a Secular Age* (1990)

#### *The Scandal of Theodicy*

Kant once argued that traditional theodicy is a case where the defense is worse than the charge. (Despland 1973, 283–297) He concluded that it is certain to be detested by anyone with the slightest spark of morality. Nowhere is this clearer than in the book of Job. Called upon to comfort a sick and bereaved friend, Eliphaz, Bildad, and Zophar do exactly the opposite. Suffering is the consequence of sin. Therefore if Job is in pain, he must have transgressed – if not openly, then secretly. In the mouths of the comforters, this explanation is nothing but a cliche which Job disposes of in short order. But it is a cliche whose consequences are decidedly inhumane. Their "comfort" is little more than an indictment: "Know that God exacts from you less than your sin deserves" (11.6). As the book develops, the indictment becomes more and more severe. Job's cries for pity are ignored and by chapter 22, Eliphaz accuses him of everything from stripping clothes from the needy to assaulting widows and orphans: "Your depravity knows no bounds" (22.5).

The fact that neither Eliphaz nor anyone else has ever witnessed this depravity is irrelevant: it is required by the view that suffering is the consequence of sin. So Kant is right; traditional theology has gotten in the way of Eliphaz's natural feelings of compassion. Earlier Job had told him that if their situations were reversed, "the solace of my lips would assuage your pain" (16.5). It is not that Eliphaz or the others are stupid. They simply think that acknowledging innocent suffering is detrimental to belief in God. The atheist assumes the same thing. The atheist holds, however, that because innocent suffering is undeniable, belief in God is groundless. For the traditional theologian, it is just the opposite: because God is undeniable, innocent suffering cannot occur.

Faced with living proof that innocent suffering does occur, the comforters try out a number of diversions: suffering brings one closer to God (5.17), no one is truly innocent (25.4–6), God is such a mystery to us that we cannot do or know anything (11.6–8). The effect of these claims is to belittle Job's pain. Either there is a simple explanation for it or else the world is too vast for us to explain anything. What is missing in all of this is a sense of indignation. None of them seem troubled by Job's plight or anxious to plead on his behalf. Job's insistence that "the upright are appalled at this" (17.8) falls on deaf ears. We have seen that Abraham, Moses, and Jeremiah spoke out when they thought they saw injustice. The comforters resort to theodicy.

Not only do the comforters not sympathize with their friend, they never really come to grips with the question he has posed. Job never denies that God exists. And while he questions God's justice several times (9.22–24, 12.5–6, 221.7–8), he never makes what could be considered an outright denial. On the contrary, it is because God exists and is just that Job cannot make sense of his situation. The poignancy of his question owes everything to the fact that he has not given up his belief in cosmic justice. Without a just God, there would be no court in which to argue his case (9.15–16, 13.20–23, 23.1–6), no avenger (*goel*, 19.25) to right his wrong. As Paul Ricoeur put it in a recent essay: "Suffering is only a scandal for the person who understands God to be the source of everything that is good in creation, including our indignation against evil, our courage to bear it, and our feeling of sympathy toward victims" (Ricoeur 1985).

That is why Job insists repeatedly that all he needs is a fair hearing. It is true that God has laid His hands on Job and treated him like an enemy (13.21–42). But in addition to a slayer, God is described as Job's avenger, his witness (16.19, 19.26), his judge. The notion that God is adversary, advocate, and judge is more than a confused picture given by a tormented man. Job is, in effect, citing God against Himself. In so doing, he repeats Abraham's question: Shall not the judge of all earth do what is just? It is as if God's unfailing sense of justice will correct the wrong He Himself has done or is about to do. For the metaphysician convinced of God's radical unity, this literary division is a nightmare. What it shows is that Job does not think acknowledging innocent suffering is detrimental to belief in God. For Job the problem is never that God might not exist but that He has temporarily hidden Himself: "Oh, that I knew where I might find Him" (23.3).

When Job does find God in the whirlwind, he does not receive a direct answer to his question. In fact, his question is met by still more questions. The lack of any explicit theodicy in God's speech has caused some scholars to proclaim it irrelevant and others to doubt its authenticity. We must ask, however, what would be gained if God had answered with a treatise on natural theology. Suppose, for example, that He had answered Job with the principle of plenitude, arguing that "localized privations" such as Job's pain are needed to achieve the greatest amount of perfection overall. Or suppose He had claimed that Job's misfortune is a necessary evil that must be endured in order to achieve a greater good. Would Job's or anyone else's plight be more bearable?

I suggest it would not. All it would do is allow another generation of "comforters" to look human misery in the face and take refuge in platitudes. My contention is that the book of Job implicitly rejects any theory that views suffering as a good, even a qualified good needed to achieve a higher purpose. That is, it rejects such theories insofar as God does not avail Himself of them and expresses anger at those who do (42.7). There is no reference in God's speech to "chastisement of love," no attempt to show that suffering is necessary or to generalize from Job's suffering to others'. God simply refuses to say anything from which a theodicy could be derived. According to Robert Gordis, God does not deny there is innocent suffering, and in some passages, such as 40.9–14, comes close to admitting it (Gordis 1965, 87–89). If a solution to the problem of evil means we must convince ourselves that Job's pain serves a religious purpose and is good when viewed from the long run, then, I submit, *a solution cannot and should not be found*. Anyone who justifies suffering, or attempts to view it with equanimity by adopting a "long-run" perspective, is, as Kant claimed, making a defense worse than the charge.

It is sometimes argued that the Book of Job is powerless to solve the problem of evil because it lacks a sufficiently developed notion of the afterlife. Some scholars have seen in Job's remarks at 19.26 a veiled reference to the doctrine of resurrection, but the line is obscure and quite possibly corrupt. According to the normal interpretation, *sheol* is a place where people go whether they have led a just life or not (3.17–19). Like Hades, it does not offer any prospect of reward or atonement. Job describes it as a land of gloom and chaos (10.21–22), and while he prefers it to his current condition, he does not contemplate anything like salvation (cf. Psalms 6.6, 88.11–31).

It is important to see, however, that even if a fully developed notion of the afterlife were known to him, Job would be no closer to a resolution of his problem. The prospect of finding happiness in the world to come might make Job feel less despondent, but it would do nothing to assuage the indignation he feels right now. He is suffering unjustifiably. Though he does not claim to be perfect, he protests that his pain is far out of proportion to his guilt (13.23–26; cf. Isaiah 40.2). What he wants is recognition of this fact, not compensation at a future date. Whatever happens to innocent souls in the world to come, the upright will be appalled at the misery they must experience now. This point is made in a forceful way in *The Brothers Karamazov*. (Dostoevsky 1950, 286–7) After going into intricate detail about the torture of a young child by her parents, Ivan protests that nothing, not the rewards of heaven or the punishments of hell, nor the greater, more comprehensive good for which the child's suffering is supposedly necessary, can overcome the injustice done to her. There are no grounds for saying that the world is "better off" because a human being was subjected to torture. Even if the victim is compensated in a future life, the outrage persists.

Note, however, that if the author wants us to sympathize with Job and feel indignant at his plight, the book seems to lead us into a dilemma. On the one hand, we are shown the inhumane consequences of theodicy. God Himself does not attempt to justify innocent suffering when given a perfect opportunity to do so. Nor does He offer an explanation of Job's plight. On the other hand, we are encouraged to regard Job's plight as outrageous. We, too, want to know why a righteous man has been reduced to an ash heap. We want someone to be held to account. But when we put the two together, we find ourselves in a situation where we are indignant at something that can neither be justified nor explained. How does the book resolve this tension? Does it point to a reconciliation between Job and God or does it leave us with nothing but a futile protest over something we cannot possibly understand?

There is no question that Job is comforted by God's speech. The man who raised the finger of protest to heaven and demanded to confront his accuser claims in chapter 42 that he has spoken of things too great for him to know and repents in dust and ashes. Is he, at this late stage, denying his innocence? Has he been frightened by the thunder and bluster of God's voice? A standard interpretation of the book is that God has the right to shroud Himself in mystery. But if this is true, what becomes of the moral indignation we feel on Job's behalf? Does it get submerged in a theological skepticism according to which we have no choice but to resign ourselves to the will of God? It is to these questions that we must now turn.

### *Morality and the Limits of Human Knowledge*

In addition to theodicy, the book raises a number of questions about the scope of human knowledge. To his friends who have come with "maxims and proverbs of ashes," Job replies with scorn: "What you know, I also know; in no way am I inferior to you" (13.2). To God he protests: "Make me know my transgression and my sin" (13.23). To everyone he proclaims that he knows his avenger lives (19.25). When their theodicies begin to crumble, the comforters resort to an extreme form of skepticism. Bildad maintains that we are but of yesterday and "know nothing" (8.9). He even foreshadows the final speech of God (11.7–8):

> Can you find out the deep things of God?
> Can you find out the ultimate purpose of the Almighty?
> It is as high as heaven; what can you do?
> Deeper than sheol, what can you know?

So, too, Elihu (37.14–16):

> Do you know how God commands them?
> And causes the lightning of His cloud to shine?
> Do you know the balancings of the clouds?
> The marvelous works of Him who is perfect in knowledge?

Maimonides (*Guide* 3.23) interprets the speeches of Elihu as further evidence of the truth of negative theology. We have seen that the inability of humans to penetrate the unfathomable wisdom of God is also put in the mouth of Job in the disputed speech of chapter 28. This speech ends with the famous claim that fear of the Lord is wisdom.

Strictly speaking, this sort of skepticism is incompatible with theodicy. For theodicy to work, it must be the case that this world is the best possible, that suffering serves a higher purpose, and that God's intentions can be discerned from a consideration of earthly events. But if human wisdom is as limited as the comforters say, if, when it comes to God's ultimate purpose, we know nothing at all, how can we make the judgments theodicy requires? This inconsistency is most apparent in the speech of Eliphaz in chapter 15. He repeats Job's scorn: "What do you know that we do not know?" (15.9). But in the next dozen lines, he takes it upon himself to speak for God. If man has nothing but "windy knowledge," by what authority can Eliphaz discover a divine purpose in the misery of his friend?

When God speaks for Himself, the limits of human knowledge are very much at issue: "Who is this that darkens counsel by words without knowledge?" (32.2). In fact, God is not above sarcasm in responding to Job's protest. At several places (38.5, 18, 21, 33), He asks Job a question and follows it with a taunt: "for surely you know." The picture which emerges from God's speech is that of a universe where forces of good and evil far beyond the scope of human understanding are controlled by a ruler who insists on His kingly prerogatives: "Will you condemn Me that you may be justified?" (40.8). It is true, as Charles Hartshorne points out, that despite the thunderous tone of God's oration, Job is never in physical danger. (Hartshorne 1967, 116–120). At no time does God threaten him with violence. But the point of these taunts is not lost. In his final speech of the book, Job humbles himself before divine perfection: "I have uttered what I did not understand, things too marvelous for me, which I did not know" (42.3). So while God does not violate human reason in the manner suggested by Kierkegaard, He certainly points out its limits.

The lesson to be drawn from Job's humility seems obvious. We have no comprehension of what it is like to create entire galaxies or to control natural forces on a cosmic scale. We therefore have no basis on which to protest divine rule. The moral concepts we live by are limited to the actions we are capable of understanding. Hence there is no reason that God should justify Himself in our eyes. As Isaiah (55.8) says about God: "My thoughts are not Your thoughts."

This is an easy lesson to draw but not one which preserves the integrity of the book. The humble Job who repents in dust and ashes may replace the angry, impatient Job who demands an explanation of his plight, but simple humility is not the end of the story. Both are replaced in the epilogue by a new Job who prays for his friends – Job the prophet. The tradition for regarding Job as a prophet is established as early as Ezekiel (14.12–14), where a righteous man named Job is mentioned alongside Noah and David. In any case, the editors of The New Oxford Annotated Bible are right to point out that Job's restoration follows not his repentance but his willingness to intercede on behalf of others. (May and

Metzger 1962, 655). In view of the precedent established by Abraham, Moses, and Jeremiah, intercession involves trust in God's saving power but falls short of what is normally meant by submission. The prophet is someone who pleads with God, even argues with Him, not someone who accepts divine decrees without question. As Abraham J. Heschel put it, the soul of the prophet exhibits an extreme sensitivity to human suffering: when he is with the people, he takes the side of God; but when he is with God, he takes the side of the people. (Heschel 1959, 121). So the prophet does not necessarily think that once one has heard God, everything is right with the world. Nor is he a lonely knight of faith. The stormy relationship between God and Moses is enough to refute both suggestions. The prophet never relinquishes his status as a freethinking, moral agent.

Job may not know the dimensions of the heavens or the ordinances which govern the Pleiades; yet by the end of the book, he does have the proper standing to argue a case before the heavenly court. What, then, of his own case? Here is the one place where skepticism is never an issue. In the midst of his torment, he is told by his three closest friends to stop proclaiming his innocence and repent of the heinous crimes he has committed. Confused, betrayed, and racked by pain, a lesser character would have followed his friends' advice, thinking that he must be mistaken about his innocence and that even if he is not, a little servility never hurts. In short, he would throw himself in the dirt and grovel for forgiveness. Job, however, will have none of it. He will not allow his friends to proclaim moral superiority and will not confess a crime he did not commit. In defiance of everything he has heard, he stands up like a hero and affirms his innocence (27.3–6):

> All the while my breath is in me,
> And the spirit of God is in my nostrils,
> Surely my lips shall not speak unrighteousness,
> Neither shall my tongue utter deceit;
> Far be it from me that I should justify you;
> Till I die I will not put away my integrity from me.
> My righteousness I hold fast, and will not let it go;
> My heart shall not reproach me so long as I live.

If this character were to become totally submissive, even in the face of God, the book would lose whatever claim it has to being a unified whole. The hero's most important speech would amount to a lie and his elevation to the status of prophet, a gratuitous addition to an unbelievable story. Note, for example, that while God rebukes Job for speaking about things he does not understand, He never rebukes him for proclaiming his innocence. The challenge, then, is to see how Job can retain his moral integrity at the same time he admits his intellectual limits.

Kant has a ready-made answer. When Job repents before God, he is confessing not that he has spoken sacrilegiously but that he has spoken unwisely about things beyond his comprehension (Despland 1973, 283–297). We have seen that for Kant, there is no inference by which we can move from experience of the world to knowledge of its Creator. In particular, we cannot infer the intentions of the Creator by looking at the objects of His creation. That is why theodicy is impossible. The ultimate purpose served by things in the physical world is hidden from us. Even more hidden is the connection between the physical order and the moral. God's ways are known only to Him. In this scheme, the comforters represent the attempt of speculative reason to understand God on the basis of principles extrapolated from experience. Hence the charge that Job is a sinner. Kant takes this as a dogmatic assertion that presupposes that experience must be in harmony with our conception of divinity. Job represents the attempt to make morality rather than speculative reason the basis of faith. Citing the speech quoted above (27.3–6), Kant claims that Job's faith was founded on the uprightness of his heart rather than a metaphysical understanding of God.

Although it presupposes philosophical sophistication beyond anything available to the author of the text, Kant's interpretation is right to this extent: the world is not a book from which we can infer the intentions of the author. Every time God says to Job "for surely you know," he underscores this point. Kant is also right in saying that Job's confession is not a retraction of his earlier claim of innocence. The inability of our minds to fathom the will of God does not imply inability to insist on our own moral worth. It is still true, after the confession, that Job is a righteous man who was falsely accused by his friends.

In the last analysis, though, Kant's Job is yet another version of the patient hero who endures pain with stoic resolution. Put otherwise, Kant maintains that Job's primary virtue is honesty. Unlike the comforters, Job does not try to flatter God by concocting a dogmatic theodicy: he is sincere about what he knows and what he does not. Since he cannot know the reason for his suffering, he has little choice but to bear it. On the reading I have suggested, it is honesty coupled with indignation. It is true that this indignation is tempered by awe in the face of God's infinite wisdom and strength, but it is never extinguished; if it were, Job could not assume the role of prophet. It may be said, therefore, that the prophet is both a servant and an adversary. Like Jeremiah, the prophet admits God's superiority but argues his case all the same.

We can understand this duality by returning to the question of analogy. I have argued that in one respect, there is an analogy between human beings and God, in other respects not. When it comes to knowledge of the origins of the universe, or power in controlling it, the analogy is impossible. Maimonides writes (*Guide* 3.13):

> Be not misled in your soul to think that the spheres and the angels have been brought into existence for our sake. For it has explained to us what we are worth: Behold, the nations are as a drop of a bucket. Consider accordingly your substance and that of the spheres, the stars, and the separate intellects; then the truth will become manifest to you, and you will know that man and nothing else is the most perfect and the most noble thing that has been generated from this [inferior] matter; but that if his being is compared to that of the spheres and all the more to that of the separate beings, it is very, very contemptible.

All we can say about God is that He is not limited in the way we are. This does not mean that He has greater knowledge and power if "knowledge" and "power" are understood in a conventional way; it means, that His knowledge and power bear no relation to ours. But knowledge and power are not the whole story. We can agree with David Hartman when he says that for all Maimonides' insistence on the insignificance of human beings before God, the great philosopher also insists on God's adherence to the Sinai covenant and the rationality of its terms (Hartman 1985, 126). The fact that we are insignificant from a physical standpoint does not mean that God can treat us in an arbitrary fashion when it comes to morality. Both God and humans are rational agents capable of willing the moral law. And the law is the same for both no matter how different the details of their respective situations. So the moral judgment that recoils at the sight of innocent suffering has application beyond the small part of the universe we occupy. It is this duality on which the movement of the book rests. Job confesses ignorance of creation but still has the right to plead a case before the Almighty. From a philosophic perspective, the duality resolves itself in the following claims: (1) We cannot conceive God except as a moral agent who guarantees the possibility that the world can be perfected; (2) in regard to empirical facts, we cannot tell when perfection has been realized; we have no way of telling whether God wills a specific event as an end, a means, or a third possibility.

In the last analysis, then, Jeremiah is right. As moral agents, we have no choice but to protest when we see innocent people afflicted. Since every human being is an end in him- or herself, innocent suffering is *always* outrageous. But as beings of limited knowledge and power, we have no hope of understanding the fine points of God's creation. The result is that we cannot allow the physical circumstances of a person's life to determine our estimate of his or her worth and are wont to cry out in anguish when the two seem out of joint. According to Cohen (*Religion of Reason*, 22), the fact that they can be out of joint implies one thing: "that all measuring and comparing of the inner *dignity* of man with the outward appearance of his earthly lot is futile and meaningless, short sighted and deluded." If this is right, we do not please God by failing to recognize human dignity either in others or in ourselves. In its own way, failing to recognize human dignity is as serious an error as asserting a resemblance between God and humans with respect to knowledge or power. The depth and sensitivity of Job's character derive from the fact that he refuses to do either.

**MOSES MAIMONIDES (1138–1204)**

*The Guide of the Perplexed* **(1190)**

**Book 3, Chapters 17–18, 23 (tr. Rabin)**

*Providence and Suffering*

CHAPTER 18

...This means that divine providence does not extend to all individuals of the human race in the same way, but to a degree varying in proportion to their share of human perfection. From this consideration it necessarily results that God's providence for the prophets is particularly intensive, graded again according to their prophetic rank. His providence for the men of virtue and the pious will also correspond to the degree of virtue and piety they possess, since it is that quantity of divine emanation which makes the prophets speak, and produces the good deeds of the pious, and perfects the knowledge of the men of virtue. As for the ignorant and impious, the less they possess of this emanation, the less attention will they enjoy and the more they will approach the order of individuals of animal species: *he is like the beasts that perish* (Psalm 49, 12). For this reason killing them is considered a small matter; if it is to the public benefit it is even commanded.

This rule constitutes one of the basic principles of the Law. Indeed the Law can be said to be founded on this concept, that different human individuals enjoy the benefits of providence to a varying degree.

CHAPTER 17 (FIN)

...This [just mentioned] then, in my opinion, is the view which agrees both with reason and with the express statements of Scripture. The other views discussed before say either too much or too little: either they exaggerate so much as to produce utter lunacy, estrangement from reason and obstinate denial of the evidence of the senses; or they fall into immense underestimation which leads to evil beliefs about God, corruption of the proper order of human existence, and effacement of the moral and intellectual superiority of man. I refer here, of course, to the theory of those who deny individual providence to man and place him upon one level with the animals.

CHAPTER 23

Job's view about the fact that the most perfect and upright man is afflicted with the greatest and most acute pain was that this is proof that the just and the wicked are equal in the eyes of God, owing to His contempt for, and lack of interest in, the human race. This is expressed in His utterance: *And I say, it is all one thing; therefore I say, the innocent and the wicked both he can bring to their end. Be it by a torrent that slays unawares, he will mock at the trial of the guiltless* (Job 9, 22–23). He says that if the torrent comes suddenly and kills and carries off everyone it meets in its way, God mocks at the trial of the guiltless. He reinforces the argument by saying: *This one dieth in the fullness of his health, all his life being restful and safe; his veins are full of milk, and his bones bathed in marrow. And another dieth with an embittered soul, and has never partaken of anything good. Yet together they must lie upon the dust, and decay shall cover them* (21, 23–6). He attempts to draw similar inferences from the prosperity of the wicked and their success in life. He speaks about this at great length, and says: *And yet when I think of it I am terrified, and shuddering takes hold of my body. Wherefore do the wicked live, become stout, yea, are mighty in wealth? Their posterity is established in their sight with them, and their progeny in their presence* (21, 6–8). Having described this complete success, he turns to his two interlocutors and says: If it is as you assert, that the children of that prosperous sinner will perish after his death and their traces be effaced – what does it matter to this man, in the midst of his own prosperity, what will befall his family after his death; *for what care hath he of his household after him, when the number of his months is all accomplished to him?* (21, 21). He proceeds to explain that there is nothing to hope for after death. The only possible conclusion is that all this is due to neglect. Now, however, he expresses astonishment that God did not neglect the original work of bringing man into being and fashioning him, yet neglects to govern him: *Hast thou not poured me out as milk and curdled me like cheese?* etc. (10, 10).

All this is in effect the same as one of the (above-mentioned) beliefs and theories about divine providence. You know well that the Rabbis pronounced these opinions of Job's heretical in the extreme and said: 'Dust into the mouth of Job! – Job wished to turn the bowl upside down – Job was one of those who disbelieve in the resurrection of the dead – Job began to curse and blaspheme' (Baba Bathra 16a). Yet God said to Eliphaz: *for ye have not spoken before me the thing that is right concerning my servant Job* (42, 7). The Rabbis, however, justify this by saying that 'no man is punishable for things done in grief' (Baba Bathra 16b), i.e., he was excused because of his intense pains.

This kind of talk, however, has no real bearing upon this parable. The reason for those words (of God) is another one, which I shall now explain, namely that Job subsequently gave up this opinion, which is indeed erroneous in the extreme, and adduced logical proofs to dispose of his error. After all, this is the idea that most readily at first suggests itself to one's mind, especially to one who has been affected by misfortunes, though he knows of himself that he is guiltless. This is a fact which no one will dispute. This is why this opinion is attributed to Job. However, he only said these things as long as he was not in possession of true knowledge, but knew of God by hearsay, as most adherents of revealed religions do. As soon as he obtained reliable knowledge of God he realized that true happiness, which consists in knowing God, is in store for all those who know Him, and none of all those afflictions can dull it. Job had imagined that those imaginary kinds of happiness such as health, possessions, and children were the true aim of life, as long as he knew of God only by report, not by his own thinking. This is why he fell into all those perplexities and said such things. That is what he means when he says: *I had heard of thee by the hearing of the ear, but now mine eye hath seen thee. Therefore I abhor and repent upon the dust and ashes* (Job 42, 5–6). Completed according to the meaning this should read: 'I abhor all that I desired before and repent for having been in dust and ashes', as his state allegedly was *while he was sitting down among the ashes* (2, 8). Because of this last utterance, which indicates that he had grasped the truth, it is subsequently said of him 'for ye have not spoken before me the thing that is right concerning my servant Job'.


## EDWARD HALPER

## "The Currency of Justice: Divine Justice and Human Suffering"

In a just world, the good should be rewarded and the bad punished. Although Judaism assumes that God governs the world and is just (Deut. 32:4; Ps. 145:17, 119:137), the goods and evils of the world scarcely seem to be justly distributed. How can God permit such injustice? Why do the righteous suffer?

It is natural to turn to Tanakh to answer this question, but so far from finding an answer—or consolation—we find passages that make the issue more acute. At the covenant of the parts, Abraham, who had been singled out by God and told that his descendants would be more numerous than the stars in heaven, is now told that these descendants will be slaves in Egypt for 400 years (Gen. 15:1–21). Job was a famously righteous man, but God nonetheless took his children and his property, and afflicted him with an excruciating skin disease. Abraham and Job seem to be innocent victims of injustice. Indeed, the history of the Jewish people is a lengthy chronicle of undeserved suffering. On the other hand, when the Torah speaks of punishments and rewards, these are often meted out collectively. Thus, Israel is enjoined to obey the commandments and promised that, when they do so, the rains will fall at the right time and their crops will grow (Deut. 11:13–21). Later, they are warned in graphic terms that if they fail to fulfill the commandments, they will be expelled from the land (Deut. 28). Why is living or not living in Israel an appropriate reward or punishment? Is it just to reward those few who do not fulfill the commandments along with the many who do, or to punish those who continue to fulfill them?

The question of why the righteous suffer is extremely difficult if not unanswerable. One problem is that we are never in a position to know whether anyone is or is not truly righteous, not even ourselves. Consequently, we cannot know whether someone's suffering is unjust. Nor can we know whether the balance sheet is somehow righted in the world to come (as per *Mishna Avot* 2:21).[2] So we lack the proper perspective to determine whether or not some particular case violates divine justice. A more theoretical obstacle to considering whether the righteous suffer and why is determining what counts as justice. This determination requires answering at least three questions: (1) What makes a person righteous? (2) What is suffering? (3) What counts as an appropriate reward or punishment?

As a preliminary gauge of the issue, consider the extremely rigorous training regimen of an Olympic athlete. Someone forcibly subjected to such a routine could plausibly claim to be a torture victim. Yet, the athlete willingly undertakes the regimen and believes he has profited from it. Is human suffering sometimes a means to improve the soul, just as the training regimen can improve the body? Is suffering a punishment or a beneficial opportunity for development or, perhaps, even a kind of reward?

## *I*

Any treatment of our topic should begin with what is surely the Torah's canonical text on justice:

> And a man—if he strike mortally any human life, he shall be put to death. And a man who strikes mortally an animal shall make restitution, a life for a life. And if a man inflicts a wound on his fellow, as he did, so shall be done to him: a break for a break, an eye for an eye, a tooth for a tooth; just as he will have inflicted a wound on a person, so shall be done to him. One who strikes an animal shall make restitution, and one who strikes a person shall be put to death.
>
> (Lev. 24: 17–21, Scherman trans.)

This passage is often taken to propound the simple, primitive code of Hammurabi according to which the perpetrator suffers *in his own person* the same type of pain that he inflicts on the victim. However, Jewish commentators have always understood the passage to speak of the monetary compensation exacted from the perpetrator on behalf of the victim (see *BT Baba Kamma* 83b). It is easy to see why. First, the second sentence mentions the monetary compensation owed to an animal's *owner* by someone who strikes the animal dead, and the Torah justifies this restitution by explaining "a life for a life." Obviously, the perpetrator does not pay with his own life. Rather, the perpetrator owes the *value* of the animal to its owner as compensation for the animal's life. Analogously, we can infer that had his blow blinded his fellow, the perpetrator would be obliged not to lose his own eye—that is of no value to anyone—but to compensate the victim the value of the eye. The taking of a human life is the limiting case because the victim cannot be compensated. In this case, the perpetrator pays with his own life.[3] In short, the victim's physical loss is compensated him with the perpetrator's monetary loss; but when the loss is not merely physical, the compensation cannot be physical. The passage is *limiting* the perpetrator's punishment to the compensation he owes the victim.

There is another reason that the passage cannot be taken literally. The context of the discussion is the problem of the man who blasphemed God. The quoted passage aims to explain why this man is put to death. "An eye for an eye" is the general principle of compensatory punishment for physical losses. As I said, because the murder victim cannot be compensated, the perpetrator is put to death. But blasphemy is not murder, nor can God be harmed. It is because it is unclear how to apply the principle that Moses must be instructed about appropriate punishment. It should be death, he learns, because an eye for an eye, etc. That is to say, the overall point of the passage is to draw an equivalency between blasphemy and murder. Because the former is tantamount to the latter, it receives the same punishment. Were the "eye for an eye" concept taken strictly literally, the Torah could not punish the blasphemer with death.

There is another dimension to the "eye for an eye" principle: the punishment must exactly fit the crime not just quantitatively in its severity, but qualitatively *in kind*. Since the loss of an eye makes someone less productive, monetary compensation for the victim makes up for his loss. Since the perpetrator, on the other hand, has acted from a defect in his character, he is forced to compensate his victim, and the pain—not the financial loss—he experiences in doing should be exactly suited to his character and, thus, intended to reform it. A punishment that was only physical would not do for a transgression that was not physical. By the same token, the idea that heavenly bliss (whatever that might mean) rewards virtuous action violates this "in kind" qualification, for this principle of equivalence holds not only for punishment, but also for reward. Its Talmudic formulation is: *midda k'neged midda*. As Shakespeare renders this phrase: "measure for measure." In accordance with the sort of crime committed, so the sort of punishment inflicted; as the merit, so the reward. The punishment and the reward must specifically fit the defective or virtuous trait. In this way each person gets exactly what he deserves. So understood, justice is self-certifying: someone with a character that is defective in one area receives an antidote in that area; someone whose character is exemplary in some area receives a precisely fitting reward.

So far as I can see, measure for measure is the Torah's only principle of justice. In contrast, Aristotle has two principles: rectificatory justice and distributive justice. A judge uses the former to restore stolen property; a ruler uses the latter to distribute offices and other goods according to a person's abilities (*Nicomachean Ethics* 5.2–3). The Torah has little need of the latter because priestly offices are hereditary, because kings and other administrative offices of the state are necessary evils rather than goods, and because, except for the Levites, the land is distributed and redistributed equally. When it comes to other goods—e.g., length of days, living in Israel, and peace—an unlimited supply makes apportionment unnecessary. Hence, a court can administer rectificatory punishment, whereas rewards are given by God, on the same principle.

## II

At the end of his *Guide of the Perplexed* Maimonides has a brief, but extraordinary discussion of justice that both supports and extends the analysis here. He distinguishes two types: (1) granting to each person what he has a right to, and (2) giving every being that which corresponds to his merits. Sense (1) includes paying "a hired man his wages" and paying debts. This is not what the prophets refer to as justice. Referring to (2), he goes on to say:

The fulfilling of duties with regard to others imposed on you on account of moral virtue, such as remedying the injuries of all those who are injured, is called "justice." Therefore, it says with reference to the returning of a pledge: "And it shall be justice unto you."[4]

What is the difference between (1) paying debts and (2) returning a pledge? Do not both grant to someone what he is owed? The injunction is to return a pledged garment to the poor person who needs it for the night and who will, it is assumed, provide another pledge in its place. The creditor gains nothing by this exchange; however, Maimonides explains: "For when you walk in the way of the moral virtues, you do justice unto your soul, giving her the due that is her right." This suggests that the difference between the two senses lies in where justice is located. A person who receives that to which he has a right *receives* justice from others, but the person who returns a pledge or remedies a wrong, *acts* with justice and thereby has justice in his own soul. The recipient of justice benefits materially, but the agent of justice gives his own soul *its* due, moral virtue. Hence, (2) is most properly called justice. There are, as it were, two actions here: one is physical, the returning of the money to the person to whom it is owed; the other is the agent's moral action. The creditor gets the money he is owed: *midda k'neged midda*. The agent gets the act of justice that is his soul's right: *midda k'neged midda*. There is a perfect correspondence. As Maimonides says, there are two types of justice. There is, as it were, a different currency for each type: the currency of the first type is material; the currency of the second is virtue in the soul.[5]

Material is often necessary for an act of justice type 2, but its real value, the justice that the prophets speak about, is giving the *soul* its due. What is its due? Although Maimonides' example is an act of justice to others, he thinks that the intellect is the soul's essence and that it is a *mizva* for us to develop it.[6] Saadia, on the other hand, emphasizes the moral *mizvot*. In any case, what is particularly interesting about the justice that is due to the soul is that, although it may require a transfer of material, it is not a zero-sum enterprise: all souls can give themselves the justice that is their due through their own actions. We might wonder how this could be an instance of *midda k'neged midda* when there is nothing exchanged. The answer must be that the just soul gets as its reward the opportunity to exercise justice. This is a long-winded way of saying that justice is its own reward.

If virtue is its own reward, there would seem to be no need to reward it in any other way. Nonetheless, the Rabbis speak of attaining the reward for virtue in the world to come (*Mishna Avot* 2:21; *B. T. Sanhedrin* 90a–b). Interestingly, the justification for an afterlife is the same principle of justice that figures into all discussions, *midda k'neged midda*. The claim is that those who deny the doctrine of the resurrection of the dead (*t'hiyat hametim*) will not be resurrected (*Sanhedrin* 90a–b). Moreover, the justification for resurrection rests on various claims in the Torah that particular people will perform *mizvot* requiring a body in the future. Only if the dead are resurrected can these *mizvot* be performed by the very people who the Torah said would perform them. As I understand this discussion, the performance of additional *mizvot* after resurrection is the reward that a person receives. The doing of still more *mizvot* is the *midda k'neged midda* of a worthy soul. Ironically, it is just because the exercise of virtue is intrinsically good that there must be an opportunity for worthy souls to exercise it. A premature death deprives a person of sufficient opportunities to perform those *mizvot* that require a body; hence, she is rewarded with more opportunities after resurrection.[7] Thus, the notion of a general resurrection evens the game as it were: those deprived of performing *mizvot* in this world will have another opportunity. We might quibble that those who die young do not get fully compensated if resurrection is widespread, but they are also spared the suffering intrinsic to a full life. They resemble athletes who win without training.

What consequence is precisely appropriate for the person who performs or violates a *mizva*? Performing another *mizva* or being deprived of opportunity to do so, I have been suggesting. What is clearly not *midda k'neged midda* is wealth or poverty or any trapping of material success or failure; for, as Maimonides and Saadia see, a material loss is due a material restitution, but a merit of soul is due another merit of soul. And the merit of the soul received in reward must be precisely appropriate to the merit that is being rewarded. That is why the reward for performing a *mizva* either lies within the act or consists of performing another such *mizva*. Someone who performs the *mizvot* should be happy, but it is a *mizva*, not happiness, that is *midda k'neged midda*. The idea here is that the currency of justice is all the *mizvot*. Let us call this position "moralism." Although Maimonides sometimes seems to endorse it, it is Saadia's view, not his.

Even though moralism is cast in terms of *mizvot*, more traditional rewards come in as accessories, as it were. Since performing a *mizva* requires suitable circumstances, moralism requires that the righteous be granted such circumstances and, likewise, that the wicked be denied them. In particular, performing most *mizvot* requires a body, and some *mizvot* can only be performed in Israel. Hence, Divine justice dictates a bodily resurrection and a redemption in which the people return to Israel. Even that does not suffice because life in this world is not without troubles. Thus, Saadia argues that Divine justice also dictates that the righteous dwell in another world, still physical but different, in which they may live in eternal physical ease and in which the wicked be eternally punished.[8]

Contrast moralism with what we can call "intellectualism." According to Maimonides, performing the *mizvot* stills the passions and imagination and, thereby, conditions the soul toward intellectual pursuits.[9] That is to say, the *mizvot* (except for the *mizva* to love God, that is, to know his works) have instrumental value. They contribute to the study of Torah as well as the acquisition of other knowledge, for its own sake. What is the reward that a person who achieves this knowledge deserves? Obviously, since *midda k'neged midda*, he deserves more knowledge. Hence, Maimonides speaks of a person receiving an intellectual overflow from God. When someone's intellect has reached human perfection, an overflow makes it surpass normal human limits, engendering prophecy. Conversely, someone whose desire and imagination impede knowledge is punished with his own ignorance. In both cases, an individual's intellectual attainments correspond somehow to his intellectual reward or punishment. Here, the currency of justice is not all *mizvot*, but a single one, knowledge.

We might suppose that this is the end of the story, but, again, the exercise of knowledge requires that other conditions be met. A person whose life is cut off prematurely is deprived of opportunities to acquire and exercise knowledge. This is why, I suggest, Maimonides considers whether someone with knowledge would fare the same as others on a ship in a storm or when thrown into a lion pit.[10] He claims that in respect of and to the degree of his knowledge, he is granted a special protection from misfortunes.[11] As I understand him, the eternity of knowledge corresponds to the eternity of the possessor of knowledge (*midda k'neged midda*). It is, thus, knowledge that preserves its possessor.

In ascribing justice to God in this way, Maimonides does not violate his contention that we cannot ascribe attributes to God because he considers justice solely in terms of God's action: God grants each person the trait that fits his own character. One advantage of his account is that a person may attain knowledge in an afterlife without retaining a body.

We saw, however, that the Torah speaks of rewards and punishments for justice that obtain in this world. A third position is what we can call "naturalism." The natural processes of the physical world are generally beneficial: the rains fall at a time that is propitious for the crops, the temperature on earth is in a range within which human beings can live and the plants and animals that sustain us thrive, there is an abundance of air, water, and the other elements necessary for human life, and so forth. However, just as all mechanisms occasionally go awry, the processes that usually sustain life are sometimes thrown off balance and cause destruction. The rains can be excessive and cause flooding or deficient and cause drought. Analogously, the biological organism that constitutes the human body is sometimes undone by the very mechanisms that normally sustain it. Understanding the structure of the cosmos and of our bodies enables us to appreciate the wonderful way in which the world generally meets our needs. Knowledge is proof against despair: any mechanical system must be imperfect. We notice the imperfections because they are rare.

Like the other two positions, naturalism has some basis in Maimonides.[12] Gersonides thinks it is Maimonides' position, but it is more clearly his own.[13] Both philosophers emphasize the centrality of knowledge for fulfilling and preserving human nature. But Gersonides differs from Maimonides in removing the idea of a special Divine protection for the wise person. Instead, it is the latter's own knowledge that enables him to predict the course of nature and so to mitigate its ill effects.

Whereas moralism and intellectualism assume that perfect justice exists for each individual over the span of her existence in this world and the next, naturalism denies the possibility of perfect justice in this world—no mechanical system can function perfectly—but offers the prospect of acquiring the knowledge that could bring more justice for its possessor and, indeed, for the world. There is a fourth possible position: one could simply deny any sort of Divine governance of the world and, likewise, any justice. However, in this case suffering from natural causes becomes a matter of chance and has no meaning, and one must forsake the possibility of moral or intellectual improvements in response to it as well as Divine consolation.[14] This is not Gersonides' naturalism.

## *III*

How do the three main accounts sketched here deal with the three problematic cases from Tanakh that introduced this paper, namely, Abraham, Job, and collective reward and punishment?

For a moralist like Saadia, Abraham and Job were being tested. The trials they endure make them more worthy of future reward. Abraham is rewarded through his descendants, whereas Job's reward must be granted in a world to come because his (first set of) children died. The hardships of slavery help the Jewish people acknowledge and serve the God who liberated them. Likewise, a moralist can explain the Torah's promise to the Jewish people that if they observe God's commandments, the rains will come, the grain will grow, they will eat, be satisfied, and praise God by noticing the cycle in this passage: *mizva*, rain, crops, eating, *mizva*. The reward for a *mizva* is another *mizva*. As long as they continue to perform *mizvot*, they will stay in the land where they can continue to perform them. As Ben Azzai said, "a *mizva* begets a *mizva*" (*Mishna Avot* 4:2). Since those who observe the commandments have a responsibility to rebuke and encourage others, they bear some responsibility for others' not following the commandments; hence, their punishment with the others is not unjust.

For the intellectualist, Abraham stands as a unique figure because he came to grasp God through his own intellect. In a world where nothing is stable, he realized that there must be an eternal first cause. Fitting, then, to reward him with a type of eternity *in this world*, that is, with numerous descendants who remember him. But to remember him properly is to recall his intellectual connection with God, and one cannot properly do so without himself having an intellectual connection. The slavery of Abraham's descendants leads to the giving of the commandments and these, we saw, are instrumental for attaining knowledge. As such, slavery is akin to the athlete's strenuous exercise for the sake of victory.

Maimonides devotes two chapters of the *Guide* (3.22–23) to Job. As I read them, he understands Job to have moral virtue but not intellectual virtue. Job's punishment induces him to examine himself and eventually to see his defect and to pursue intellectual virtue. Hence, he ultimately reaps rewards. It is not right to punish the morally virtuous and, anyway, Job's punishment is not in kind, nor is his ultimate reward. These are, I suggest, the reasons that Maimonides insists Job is a parable.

As for the problem of collective punishment and reward, Maimonides thinks that the rains that fall are the result of a Divine overflow whose purpose is to sustain the wise but which must, because of the nature of physical processes, fall on a wide area and, thereby, sustain all. Understanding the physical mechanisms involved, e.g., how the heavens, especially the moon, cause the rain to fall, how the separate intellects move the heavens, and so forth, helps us to understand the *mizvot*.[15] In causing rain, these separate intellects are responding not so much to the morality of those who observe the *mizvot* as to the level of human intellect that observing the *mizvot* makes possible.

According to the third approach, naturalism, Abraham has come to see the inevitable consequence of a predictable widespread drought that would bring his descendants to the one place that was not dependent on rain but on the flooding of the Nile. It is up to Abraham to prepare his family, as it is later up to Joseph to steel Egypt, against misfortune. Likewise, though Job is prosperous and righteous, he is not immune from natural disasters. It is his faith in God's justice that consoles him and allows him to persevere. Finally, droughts affect an entire community, the righteous and wicked alike, but when people have knowledge they can work together to mitigate their effects; when they have turned away from knowledge, they are less able to do so. Justice is a goal of human governance, not a feature of nature.[16]

In short, all three approaches can accommodate the problematic texts. Indeed, they were designed to do so.

## IV

At this point, I should argue for one of them or for some other solution. Instead, I want to mention still another approach. Whereas the three we have seen consider why some individual suffers, modern thinkers shift the focus of the issue to the suffering of others. Hermann Cohen set the terms of subsequent discussions. His *Religion of Reason* argues that the suffering of certain individuals is valuable insofar as it provides other individuals opportunities to come to their aid. In doing so, the others must regard these sufferers not only as moral agents worthy of respect (as Kantian morality dictates), but as fellow humans worthy of happiness. To sacrifice their own happiness to relieve the suffering of others is to do justice. On this reasoning the existence of suffering in the world allows the Jewish people to take up the mantle of divine justice.[17]

So far as I can see, this approach cannot explain the problematic passages in the Torah because there sufferers are not aided by others. Nonetheless, it does help to bring out the central aspect common to all the positions, a principle we might have missed because of their differences: justice is ultimately a matter of what an individual *does* for himself or another, rather than what he *suffers*. It is primarily about one's *own action*, and the reward lies in the action itself. This idea is suggested in the first passage cited from Maimonides. We would like to think that there is some sort of protection for the righteous as well as some compensation, an appropriate *midda* that follows and corresponds to what is done or what is known. There may well be, but it is clear that we cannot count on it in this life. Human suffering is unavoidable. Still, it is up to us to do what we can to achieve justice, and in doing moral and intellectual acts of justice, we do justice *to and for ourselves*. One principal way in which we do justice to ourselves is to pursue knowledge, which is itself commanded. Ironically, in the very process of striving to do what God commands, we come to possess what we can of Divine justice.

## Notes

1  Frank 2000.
2  Saadia 1976, 210.
3  Saadia 1976, 185–6, feels the need to justify this punishment by referring to the murder's threat to others.
4  *Guide* 3:53 (1963, 631) is quoting Deut. 24:13. My essay is indebted to the discussion of this Maimonides passage in Goodman 2008, 2ff.
5  Cf. Plato, *Phaedo* 69a–b.
6  *Guide* 1:1, 3:54 (1963, 23, 635–7).
7  See Saadia 1976, 277–83.
8  Saadia 1976, 323–6, 340. He discusses resurrection and redemption in Treatises 7 and 8.
9  See Halper 2011, 199–204.
10  *Guide* 3:17 (1963, 466). He must have Jonah and Daniel in mind.
11  Ibid. 3:17–18 (474).
12  Ibid. 3:12 (442–4).
13  Gersonides 1999, 208–9, argues that Maimonides cannot suppose that God has the knowledge of particulars that would protect the righteous.
14  Seeskin 1990, 175.
15  See *Guide* 2:2 (1963, 253–4).
16  Goodman 2008, 123.
17  Cohen 1972, 433–35, 11–23, 113–43.

## Further Reading on Divine Justice

Berkovitz, E. *Faith After the Holocaust* (New York: Ktav Publishing House, 1973).
Carmy, S. "Tell Them I've Had a Good Enough Life," *The Torah u-Madda Journal* 8 (1998–1999), 59–96.
Citron, G. "Dreams, Nightmares, and a Defense Against Arguments from Evil," *Faith and Philosophy* (forthcoming).
Fackenheim, E. *To Mend the World: Foundations of Post-Holocaust Jewish Thought* (New York: Schocken Books, 1982).
Frank, D. "Prophecy and Invulnerability," in *The Jewish Philosophy Reader*, eds. D. Frank, O. Leaman, and C. Manekin (London: Routledge, 2000), 79–83.
Goldschmidt, T. "Jewish Responses to the Problem of Evil: Traditional Texts in Contemporary Categories," *Philosophy Compass* 9 (2014), 894–905.
Goldschmidt, T. and B. Seacord. "Judaism, Reincarnation, and Theodicy," *Faith and Philosophy* 30 (2013), 393–417.
Goodman, L. E. *On Justice: An Essay in Jewish Philosophy* (New Haven, CT: Yale University Press, 1991; 2nd ed. Oxford and Portland: Littman Library of Jewish Civilization, 2008).
Leaman, O. *Evil and Suffering in Jewish Philosophy* (Cambridge: Cambridge University Press, 1995).
McBrayer, J. and D. Howard-Snyder (eds.), *The Blackwell Companion to the Problem of Evil* (Oxford: Wiley-Blackwell, 2013).
Nadler, S. "Theodicy and Providence," in *The Cambridge History of Jewish Philosophy: From Antiquity through the Seventeenth Century*, eds. S. Nadler and T. M. Rudavsky (Cambridge: Cambridge University Press, 2009), 619–658.
Nadler, S. "Virtue, Reason, and Moral Luck: Maimonides, Gersonides, Spinoza," in *Spinoza and Medieval Jewish Philosophy*, ed. S. Nadler (Cambridge: Cambridge University Press, 2014), 152–176.

Rudavsky, T. "A Brief History of Skeptical Responses to Evil," in *The Blackwell Companion to the Problem of Evil*, eds. J. McBrayer and D. Howard-Snyder (Oxford: Wiley-Blackwell, 2013), 379–395.

Schlesinger, G. *New Perspectives on Old-Time Religion* (Oxford: Clarendon Press, 1988), 165–191.

Shatz, D. "From Anthropology to Metaphysics," in *Judaism and Modernity: The Religious Philosophy of David Hartman*, ed. J. W. Malino (Aldershot: Ashgate, 2004), 104–120.

Shatz, D. "Does Jewish Law Express Jewish Philosophy? The Curious Case of Theodicies," in *Jewish Thought in Dialogue* (Brighton, MA: Academic Studies Press, 2009), 291–304.

Shatz, D. "On Constructing a Jewish Theodicy," in *The Blackwell Companion to the Problem of Evil*, eds. J. McBrayer and D. Howard-Snyder (Oxford: Wiley-Blackwell, 2013), 309–25.

Soloveitchik, J. B. *Out of the Whirlwind: Essays on Mourning, Suffering and the Human Condition*, ed. D. Shatz, J. Wolowelski, and R. Ziegler (Jersey City, NJ: Ktav, 2003).

Stump, E. "Saadia Gaon on the Problem of Evil," *Faith and Philosophy* 14 (1997), 523–549.

Stump, E. *Wandering in Darkness* (Oxford: Oxford University Press, 2010).

Wettstein, H. "God's Struggles," in *Divine Evil? The Moral Character of the God of Abraham*, eds. M. Bergmann, M. J. Murray, and M. C. Rea (Oxford: Oxford University Press, 2011), 321–334.

Wettstein, H. "Against Theodicy," *Philosophia* 30 (2003), 131–42, reprt. in Wettstein, *The Significance of Religious Experience* (New York: Oxford University Press, 2012), 151–161.

# 8    Chosenness

The idea that God chose the Jewish people from among all others lies at the foundation of traditional Jewish thought and practice. It stretches back to God's covenant with Abraham and pervades the traditional liturgy. But it immediately raises certain questions: What is chosenness, exactly? What is its relationship to love? Why does God choose a people, and why, specifically, the Jewish people? Beyond these straightforward philosophical questions, there are theological difficulties with the idea of chosenness: If God chooses just one people, is He playing favorites? Is God's choosing one people consistent with His being just? Is it consistent with His loving all of humanity?

The first reading in this section comes from **Judah Halevi's** work, *The Kuzari*, written in defense of the 'despised faith' and the Jews who cling to it. He claims that in fact the Jews are "a most select group." While the "divine order"—something like a preparedness for divine inspiration—is found among individual non-Jews, it is found, even if sometimes only latently, in the entirety of the Jewish people. While Halevi doesn't explicitly account for chosenness in these terms, it would be quite natural to do so: God's choice of the Jews either consists in or is to be explained by their being eminently choiceworthy. Given Halevi's premise, chosenness is intelligible and not obviously theologically objectionable. But his premise is not borne out by experience.

For **Michael Wyschogrod**, God's choice of the Jews is to be understood as His exclusive love for them. And He loves them because in them He sees the face of His beloved Abraham. But His love of Abraham has no further explanation in terms of how Abraham is. In this way it is no different from any other love, Wyschogrod argues. Love, by its nature, is of a concrete particular, not an abstract universal. If one loves another because the beloved is smart or good-looking, then the lover really loves smarts or good looks, both abstract universals. But, by the same token, it is exclusive. Any given love will have an individual, not a class, as its object. Thus, there is no room for a single love to encompass all of humanity. Wyschogrod provides us with an analysis of chosenness, an explanation of the exclusivity of God's love, and an explicit disavowal of any rationale for God's love of Abraham and the Jewish people.

**Jerome Gellman** reconstructs several of Wyschogrod's arguments and finds them wanting. He suggests that at least in the contemporary climate it is morally odious to espouse Halevi's view. His alternative account, in broad outlines, is as follows: God has always loved all humans equally. He wanted everyone to come to him freely but knew that if we were given no indication of His overwhelming love, we would mistakenly think Him indifferent. So He *showered* His love upon exactly one nation, thereby demonstrating to the rest of humanity that He sincerely wants them to come to Him, without coercing them to do so. Gellman thus analyzes chosenness not as love but as a coercive demonstration of love, and he provides a rationale for God to choose just one people, but none for God's choosing the Jews specifically.

## JUDAH HALEVI (1075–1141)

### The Book of Refutation and Proof on Behalf of the Despised Faith (The Kuzari) (c. 1140)

#### Book 1, Section 95 (tr. Kogan and Berman)

*The Israelites and the Divine Order*

The sage said: Give me a little [more time] so that I may establish the nobility of the people in your eyes. It is sufficient evidence for me that God took them [for Himself, both] as a group and as a nation from among [all] the religious communities of the world, and that the divine order (*al-amr al-ilāhī*) dwelled with the multitude of them so that all of them reached [the level of] being addressed [by God]. Moreover, the matter [also] extended to their women so that some of them became prophetesses after [a period during which] the order (*amr*) used to dwell only with unique [male] individuals among the people from *Adam* on down.

Now *Adam* was altogether perfect because there [can be] no fault in the perfection of an artifact that derives from a wise [and] capable Artisan, [and] consists of matter that He chose for the form He wished [to give it]. No obstacle interfered [in his case] because of the father's sperm mingling with the mother's blood, nor because of diet and regimen during the years of [early] education and childhood, nor because of the influence of [different kinds of] air, water and soil, since [God] created him, rather, as someone at the very peak of youth, who was perfect in regard to both his physical constitution and his character traits. Accordingly, it is he who [simultaneously] received the soul in its most perfect state, the intellect at the highest degree [of development] possible for human nature, and also the divine capacity [that comes] after the intellect, I mean, the level at which one may have contact with God and the spiritual beings and also know truths without their being taught, but rather with [only] the slightest thought. Among us, he was called 'a son of God'. He and all those like him among his offspring are [also called] 'sons of God'. He begat many children (Gen. 5:4), but none of them was fit to be *Adam's* successor except *Abel*, because he [alone] was like him. When his brother *Cain* killed him out of jealousy over this status, [*Abel*] was replaced by *Seth*, who was also like *Adam*, for he was [*Adam's*] choicest [offspring] and the best part of him, while others were like husks and dates of poor quality. ... The choicest [offspring] of *Seth* was *Enosh*. In a similar way, the order (*al-amr*) reached *Noah* through individuals who were the best part [of their predecessors], like *Adam*, and they were also called 'sons of God'. They [too] were perfectly endowed in regard to [their] physical constitution, character traits, longevity, [knowledge of] the sciences, and strength. The length of their [combined] lifetimes is identical with the chronology from *Adam* to *Noah*, and [it is] likewise from *Noah* to Abraham.

Now at times there were those among them to whom the divine order (*al-amr al-ilāhī*) did not attach itself, such as *Terah*, but Abraham, his son, was the *disciple* of his grandfather, *Eber*. Yes, and he also knew *Noah* himself. Thus, the divine order (*al-amr al-ilāhī*) ended up establishing a continuous chain from ancestors to descendants, for Abraham was the choicest [offspring] of *Eber* as well as his disciple. That is why he was called a Hebrew (Gen. 14:13). *Eber* was the choicest offspring of *Shem* and *Shem* was the choicest offspring of *Noah* because he was the heir of the temperate climes, whose central and most distinguished part is Syro-Palestine, the land of prophecy, while *Yefet* departed for the North and *Ham* for the South. Now the choicest [offspring] of Abraham from among all his sons was Isaac, and [Abraham] sent all of his [other] children far away from this special land so that it might become the exclusive possession of Isaac. The choicest [offspring] of Isaac was Jacob. His brother Esau was rejected because Jacob was entitled to that land [by right]. Now all of the children of Jacob were the choicest [offspring of their father] and fit for the divine order (*al-amr al-ilāhī*). Accordingly, that place which is specially set aside for the divine order (*al-amr al-ilāhī*) came to be theirs. This was the beginning of the divine order's dwelling with a [whole] community after having been found only among particular individuals [beforehand].

Then God undertook to preserve them, cultivate them, and care for them in Egypt, just as a tree, which has good roots, is cultivated until it has borne perfect fruit like the original fruit from which it was planted, I mean, [of course,] Abraham, Isaac, Jacob, Joseph and his brothers. The fruit produced Moses, peace be upon him, and also Aaron and *Miriam*, peace be upon them, as well as [others] like *Bezalel*, *Oholiab*, (Exod. 35:30–35), the heads of the tribes, and those like the seventy elders, who were fit for continuous prophecy (Num. 11:24–5), Joshua, Caleb (Num. 13:30; 14:6ff.) and Hur (Exod. 17:10; 24:14), and many others besides them. At that time, they were [all] worthy of the light [of God] manifesting itself to them as well as that [aforementioned] divine providence, even though there were rebellious and loathsome individuals among them. But they are undoubtedly a most select group in the sense that, because of their innate character as well as their natures, they belonged to the choicest [part of humanity]. Moreover, they begat those who would become [the] choicest. Accordingly, the father who was rebellious would be preserved for the sake of that which is mingled within him of what is choicest, which would [later] appear in his child or in his grandchild, insofar as the semen was pure, as we have said with regard to *Terah* and others besides him, to whom the divine order (*al-amr al-ilāhī*) did not attach itself. However, it was in their innate character to bring forth choice offspring, [while] there was nothing comparable to that in the innate character of anyone descended from *Ham* and *Yefet*. We see something like this in things that are natural. [Consider] how many men do not resemble their fathers at all, but do resemble their grandfathers! There is no doubt that that nature and that resemblance were latent within the father, even though they were not evident to the senses, just as the nature of *Eber* was latent within his children until it became manifest in Abraham.

## MICHAEL WYSCHOGROD

## "A Chosen Nation" (section 4), from *The Body of Faith: Judaism as Corporeal Election* (1983)

### 4. Love and Election

Why does God proceed by means of election, the choosing of one people among the nations as his people? Why is he not the father of all nations, calling them to his obedience and offering his love to man, whom he created in his image? More fundamentally, why must the concept of nation intrude itself into the relation between God and man? Does not God address each individual human being as he stands alone before God? Because those questions are so fundamental, we must answer them with caution.

We must avoid an answer that does too much. Any answer that would demonstrate that what God did was the only thing he could have done or that it was the right thing to do would be too much of an answer. God must not be subject to necessity or to a good not of his own making. He is sovereign and his own master, and must not be judged by standards external to him. Much of religious apology misunderstands this fundamental point and therefore defeats itself just as it succeeds because it limits God's sovereignty as it proves that he could not have done anything other than what he did or, more usually, that what he did measures up to the highest standards of morality. Having thus succeeded in providing the best possible reasons for God's actions, the apologist does not realize that he has subjected God to judgment by criteria other than his free and sovereign will and that, however much he has justified God's actions, he has infringed his sovereignty and is therefore no longer talking of the biblical God. We must avoid this sort of justification at all cost and therefore begin our answer to the questions posed by noting that God chose the route of election, and of the election of a biological instead of an ideological people, because this was his free choice. He could have acted otherwise. He could have dispensed completely with election or he could have constituted the elected group in some other way, and had he done so, we would have praised those choices as we now praise these. Rarely has any theology come to grips with the contingency that follows from God's freedom. Christian theology has rarely conceded that God could have decided to save all men without the need for an incarnation, crucifixion, and resurrection. The vast preponderance of Christian thought makes it seem that given man's fall, only the sacrifice of God's only begotten son could have served as atonement for man's sin. The Christian faith ought to contend that the way of the incarnation was the way chosen by God, though he could have chosen another. Correspondingly, we will assert the same of the election of Israel, dispensing with all claims of necessity or that this was the best possible course for God to take.

Having said this much, we must also permit the praise of God. There is hardly any literary activity more prevalent in the Bible than the praise of God. The Bible is first and foremost the word of God, in which man is told what God wants him to know. But the Bible is also the word of man as man responds to the word of God. This response takes a number of forms. There is the direct response of those, like Abraham, Moses, and others, whom the Bible reports as being addressed by God and whose responses are reported as part of the dialogue. There is the biblical Wisdom literature most prominent in Proverbs, which, in a sense, is the form that most closely resembles philosophy because it seems to consist of the insights of human experience distilled over the centuries. There is also the praise of God that we find in Psalms as well as many other places in the Bible. The human encounter with God that is expressed in praise is the one response most difficult for modern man, and particularly for the contemporary Jew, to understand. For post-Auschwitz Jewry it is the voice of Abraham contesting the justice of the divine decree against the corrupt cities of man that speaks most recognizably of the human condition. There has crept into our consciousness a profound anger at God, and this anger is shared by all Jews, even those who will not permit this anger to become conscious. Yet we must recognize that there was a time when men in general and Jews in particular were overwhelmed by a deep emotion of gratitude for the wonderful favors bestowed by God. In Psalms this is rooted in David's unshakable faith in his election and the divine protection that insured triumph over those wishing God's anointed ill. Praise of God is thus rooted in gratitude and wonder at the complexities and beauty of creation. Most important for our purpose is the recognition that praise does not involve measuring God's creation and conduct by external standards and declaring them good because they live up to those standards. Praise is an act of gratitude that is totally focused on God to whom we are grateful. Gratitude rises in the human soul when an act of love is bestowed that is felt not to be deserved. It is difficult to be grateful for what is owed one. When, however, man is dealt with kindly without deserving it, it is natural for him to be grateful. In gratitude there is a feeling of loving dependence on the other because gratitude makes it necessary for man to feel his vulnerability, in the absence of which he would not need the favor that has been bestowed on him. Israel must therefore praise God. This will not justify God's election of Israel, but it will enable us to express our wonder and gratitude for the election of Israel.

All this has been preliminary to our discussion of election, which we will not justify but which we might come to understand somewhat from the standpoint of praise. The question we asked was, Why does God proceed by election rather than by being the impartial father of all peoples? Behind these questions lurks the pain of exclusion. If God elects one individual or group, there is someone else whom he does not elect and that other is left to suffer his exclusion. With exclusion comes envy of the one elected and anger, perhaps even hatred, of the one who has done the exclusion. David's love for God reaches great peaks because he is so deeply grateful for his election, but the modern reader finds it difficult not to have some sympathy for his enemies, whose downfall is so certain because they have not been chosen and have dared to conspire against the elect of God. We begin to feel the pain of exclusion and ask why it was necessary for pain to be caused by love. Would it not have been better for God not to have favored Israel, so as not to hurt the other peoples of the world?

This leads us to think about the wonder of love. Western man has, as we have seen, distinguished between *eros* and *agape*. *Eros* is sensual love, the love of man for woman, where jealousy is a possibility. In *eros* the other is a means toward the pleasure of the self, so that *eros* is really self-love. *Agape* is the love of parent for child. Sometimes this love is distorted where children are made into appendages of the parents and used for self-gratification. True *agape* demands nothing in return because it is a love truly directed to the other, to his welfare and prosperity, to what is good for him rather than the pleasure of the one who loves. *Agape* is thus charity in the purest sense but without condescension and any sense of superiority. The love of the Greek world, it has further been said, is *eros*, while that of the Judeo-Christian, *agape*. The question we have posed is thus a question about *agape*. God's love for man is surely *agape* rather than *eros*. How, then, can it exclude? Does a parent who loves one child exclude another? Is not equal love of all children the essence of parental love?

There is something wrong about the distinction between *eros* and *agape*. It resembles the distinction between body and soul. *Eros* seems to be a bodily love and *agape* love of and by the soul. Such a distinction would be valid if the distinction between body and soul were. But in the biblical view, body and soul are aspects of the one being that God created in his image. Human love, correspondingly, must not be bifurcated into the *agape-eros* mold or any similar scheme. There is no doubt that there are imperfect examples of human love, as there are imperfect human beings. But it is simply not true that love as charity applies equally to all and makes no distinctions as to person. This would be conceivable if charitable love were primarily an emotion within the person who loves, with the recipient of the love being a dim image at the periphery of consciousness serving as an occasion for the activation of love. If this were the case, we would be dealing with an I-It relationship in Buber's sense, hardly the model of true love in charity. Love that is in the realm of the I-Thou is directed toward the other who is encountered in his being and on whom we do not impose our preconceptions. Undifferentiated love, love that is dispensed equally to all must be love that does not meet the individual in his individuality but sees him as a member of a species, whether that species be the working class, the poor, those created in the image of God, or what not. History abounds with example, such fantastic loves directed at abstract creations of the imagination. In the names of these abstractions men have committed the most heinous crime against real, concrete, existing human beings who were not encountered in their reality but seen as members of a demonic species to be destroyed. Both the object of love and that of hate were abstract and unreal, restricted to the imagination of the lonely dreamer who would not turn to the concretely real persons all around him. Unlike such fantasies, the divine love is concrete. It is a genuine encounter with man in his individuality and must therefore be exclusive. Any real love encounter, if it is more than an example of the love of a class or collectivity, is exclusive because it is genuinely directed to the uniqueness of the other and it therefore follows that each such relationship is different from all others. But difference is exclusivity because each relationship is different, and I am not included in the relationship of others.

And it also follows that there must be a primacy of relationship. The authentic person is open to all. When he is with a particular individual, he devotes himself to that person completely, listening with all of his being to the presence of the other. Such listening cannot be a technique that succeeds equally in all cases at all times. The counterfeit of such listening could presumably be standardized and applied with regularity to person after person. But it would then clearly not be a real encounter but a clever imitation of real relationship. In any true I-Thou encounter, nothing can be controlled, no certainty of result can be preordained. It is for this reason that those who live with the possibility of meeting find that it happens with some and not with others. Instead of lamenting this fact, they pray for the continuing possibility of meeting, while recognizing the inherent exclusivity of those meetings that have happened. There is no denying a dimension of guilt in the knowledge that the primacy of relationship with a few cannot be repeated with many others who thus remain strangers. Even among the small circle of persons with whom there is an ongoing relationship, some are loved more than others because each is who he is and because I am who I am. The only alternative is a remote, inhuman love, directed at universals and abstractions rather than real persons.

Our praise of God expresses our gratitude that he loves man in a human way, directing his love to each one of us individually, and that by so loving he has chosen to share the human fate such love involves. The election of Israel is thus a sign of the humanity of God. Had he so willed it, he could have played a more godly role, refusing favorites and loving all his creatures impartially. His love would then have been a far less vulnerable one because impartiality signifies a certain remoteness, the absence of that consuming passion that is a sign of need of the other. Herein resides the inhumanity of *agape* and the humanity of *eros*. Agape demands nothing in return. It asks only to give, never to receive. However noble this sounds at first hearing, it must quickly be realized that it also implies an incredible position of strength. To be able only to give, never to need, never to ask for anything in return for what we give, is a position that truly befits a God. And to need something from the other, to need the body of the other for my satisfaction, is the misery of human being. Human being is need, the state of incompleteness within myself and therefore the longing for what the other can give. The *eros* of Don Juan is therefore a more human condition than the agape of the saint who needs nothing and no one and distributes his gifts from the height of his Olympian self-sufficiency. The truth is that human love is neither *eros* nor *agape*.

Both are caricatures because reality is a combination of the two, which are not different kinds of love but aspects of human love with a constantly changing composition of elements. No human love is totally indifferent to the reaction of the other. If the relationship is a human one, if the person loved is not perceived as an object to which things are done but a person to whom one speaks and whose answer one awaits, then the response received must be an important element in the direction of the developing relationship. This does not mean that a rebuff necessarily results in the termination of concern or even love. It is possible to love—and here is the truth of *agape*—in spite of rebuff or absence of response. But such absence is never a matter of indifference and plays an important role in the relationship because response is always sought, needed, and hoped for. Similarly, there is no erotic relationship without an element of concern. The sexual, even in its most exploiting and objectifying form, reveals a glimmer of gratitude and affection. If totalitarian states find it necessary to repress the sexual, it is because they are dimly aware that the person to whom the sexual is a reality is a person whose humanity has not been totally deposited with the state and who is therefore untrustworthy for the purposes of a system whose presupposition is dehumanization. All this is not to deny that there are loves in which *agape* predominates and those in which *eros* does. But none is exclusively one or the other because man is created in the image of God as a being constituted by need who gives and also asks to be given in return.

The love with which God has chosen to love man is a love understandable to man. It is therefore a love very much aware of human response. God has thereby made himself vulnerable: he asks for man's response and is hurt when it is not forthcoming. For the same reason, God's love is not undifferentiated, having the same quality toward all his children. God's love is directed toward who we are. We are confirmed as who we are in our relationship to God. And because God is so deeply directed toward us, because his love is not self-love (in spite of Plato, Neoplatonism, and the tradition flowing from these) but true meeting of the other (and there is an other for God; this is the mystery of creation), there are those whom God loves especially, with whom he has fallen in love, as with Abraham. There is no other way of expressing this mystery except in these terms. God's relationship to Abraham is truly a falling in love. The biblical text tells us this when it fails to explain the reason for the election of Abraham. The rabbis, of course, were aware of this omission and perplexed by it. They supplied reasons, making of Abraham the first natural philosopher who saw through the foolishness of the idol worship of his time and reasoned his way to the one God. In the Bible, it is not Abraham who moves toward God but God who turns to Abraham with an election that is not explained because it is an act of love that requires no explanation. If God continues to love the people of Israel—and it is the faith of Israel that he does—it is because he sees the face of his beloved Abraham in each and every one of his children as a man sees the face of his beloved in the children of his union with his beloved. God's anger when Israel is disobedient is the anger of a rejected lover. It is above all jealousy, the jealousy of one deeply in love who is consumed with torment at the knowledge that his beloved seeks the affection of others. To much of philosophical theology, such talk has been an embarrassment in urgent need of demythologization. But theologians must not be more protective of God's dignity than he is of his own because God's true dignity is the sovereignty of his choice for genuine relation with man.

What, now, of those not elected? Those not elected cannot be expected not to be hurt by not being of the seed of Abraham, whom God loves above all others. The Bible depicts clearly the suffering of Esau. The Bible is, after all, the history of Israel and could therefore be expected to be partial to the Jewish cause. And yet, in recounting the blessing of Jacob and the exclusion of Esau, no careful reader can fail to notice that the sympathy shown Esau is greater than that for Jacob. God shows Esau compassion even if Jacob does not. The consolation of the gentiles is the knowledge that God also stands in relationship with them in the recognition and affirmation of their uniqueness. The choice, after all, is between a lofty divine love equally distributed to all without recognition of uniqueness and real encounter, which necessarily involves favorites but in which each is unique and addressed as such. If Abraham was especially loved by God, it is because God is a father who does not stand in a legal relationship to his children, which by its nature requires impartiality and objectivity. As a father, God loves his children and knows each one as who he is with his strengths and weaknesses, his virtues and vices. Because a father is not an impartial judge but a loving parent and because a human father is a human being with his own personality, it is inevitable that he will find himself more compatible with some of his children than others and, to speak very plainly, that he love some more than others. There is usually great reluctance on the part of parents to admit this, but it is a truth that must not be avoided. And it is also true that a father loves all his children, so that they all know of and feel the love they receive, recognizing that to substitute an impartial judge for a loving father would eliminate the preference for the specially favored but would also deprive all of them of a father. The mystery of Israel's election thus turns out to be the guarantee of the fatherhood of God toward all peoples, elect and nonelect, Jew and gentile. We must, at the same time, reiterate that none of this amounts to some sort of demonstration of the "necessity" of election in any sense. It can be understood only from the point of view of man's gratitude for the fatherhood of God, since only the invocation of the category of "father" and the divine permission we have to apply this category to God enable us to begin to fathom the mystery of election. When we grasp that the election of Israel flows from the fatherhood that extends to all created in God's image, we find ourselves tied to all men in brotherhood, as Joseph, favored by his human father, ultimately found himself tied to his brothers. And when man contemplates this mystery, that the Eternal One, the creator of heaven and earth, chose to become the father of his creatures instead of remaining self-sufficient unto himself, as is the Absolute of the philosophers, there wells up in man that praise that has become so rare yet remains so natural.

JEROME GELLMAN

## "Halevi, Wyschogrod, and the Chosen People"

### 1. Michael Wyschogrod

Wyschogrod's view on Jewish election has a negative and a positive argument. The negative argument seems to go as follows:

(1) If in choosing the Jews God could have done only what was morally right, then God was bound by a morality external to God.
(2) If God was bound by a morality external to God, then something limited God.
(3) If something limited God, then God is not sovereign.
(4) But, God *is* sovereign.
(5) Therefore, when God chose the Jews, it was not the case that God could have done only what was morally right.

It is clear that Wyschogrod means to infer from (5) that

(6) We cannot employ moral standards when trying to explain why God chose the Jews.

(1) is false on a reputable view of God and morality. This says that God does what is good and right by God's very nature. It is built-in to God's character that God does no wrong. We are, therefore, not to see God having to consult God's moral obligations before God acts. God is self-motivated to do the right and the good independently of any moral *obligations*.[1] So when God acts, God is not limited by any *external* morality. But then, the antecedent of (1), "God could have done only what was a morally right thing to do," is true, since by *nature* God can do only the right thing, but the consequent of (1), "God was bound by a morality external to God" will be false. So, the first premise of the negative argument is not secure.

Another respectable view would challenge the inference from (5) to (6). It says that God has sovereignly *decreed* the moral standards there are, and has freely decided to act in self-limitation in accordance with those standards. This can be found in *Leviticus Rabbah* 35, where God is unlike a human king who makes decrees and does not observe them himself. God makes decrees and observes them as well. The Jerusalem Talmud (Rosh Hashanah 3:1) applies this as well to a *moral* decree, that of respecting an older person.

Now, if God *chooses* to conform to the morality God decreed, then we could agree that no *external* moral standards *obligate* God and still think that in choosing the Jews there *was* a moral standard according to which God acted. We need only believe that the valid moral standard in question is of God's own making and that God had decided to act in accordance with it. (6), then would not follow from (5). I conclude that Wyschogrod's negative argument is not persuasive.

Wyschogrod now argues for why God might well have chosen Abraham exclusively, among all others, with the exclusive choice of the Jews then following from their being Abraham's children. Here is my reconstruction of the core of the second argument. (Implicit to the argument is that God knows the truth of all the premises in the argument.)

(1)   God wanted to give true love to whomever God chose.
(2)   Love is true love if and only if given I-Thouly to the individuality of the recipient.
(3)   Love for everyone equally is remote and abstract.
(4)   So, love for everyone equally is not given I-Thouly to the individuality of the recipient (From 3).
(5)   So, love for everyone equally is not true love (From 2 and 4).
(6)   Therefore, God did not want to give love to everyone equally (From 1 and 5).
(7)   On the other hand, exclusive love *can take the form* of love given I-Thouly to the individuality of the recipient.
(8)   So, exclusive love *can take the form* of true love.
(9)   So, God wanted to give an exclusive love that indeed *takes the form* of true love (From 8 and 1).
(10) So, when God chose Abraham only, God was able to fulfill God's desire to give true love.

This argument is invalid. As formulated, (9) does not follow formally from (8) and (1). It follows, formally at least, only if (8) were: "*Only* exclusive love *can take the form* of true love." This was not shown by simply showing that love of *everyone* is not true love, for that leaves open the possibility that one might be able to give true love to, say, a few people. This would be neither love for everyone nor exclusive love. The reason to think (3) true comes from our inability to have personal contact with just everyone, and from our limited resources of attention, time, and capacity for love. Our love for "everyone" would remain distant, more akin to love of species, as Wyschogrod says, rather than to the individuals in the species. So love for everyone must remain remote and abstract. This does nothing to show that a person could not have sufficient resources for true love for *more* than just one person, yet not for everyone. This seems obviously the case. So, that a person wishes to grant true love and that exclusive love *can* take the form of true love, it does not follow that exclusive love is what the person will give, as long as there is another way to give true love.

A deeper problem, perhaps, is that (3) might be acceptable when considering the limited capacities of *humans*. Yet, this has no implications for the unlimited capacity of *God* to be in concrete contact with every person, to love them equally, and for the love to be given I-Thouly to the individuality of every recipient of that love. And it has no implications for God's love to be so deep and sincere as to be perceived by each person as an intimate love than which there can be no greater. And it has no implications for God's abilities, as opposed to humans', for that love to be undiminished in its individual glory by the recipients knowing that God loves everybody else to the same extent. God can love every single person there is without that love being remote and abstract in the least. Since (3) and consequently (5) are acceptable for only human love, (6), concerning God, does not follow from (5).

I conclude that Wyschogrod's first argument fails to prohibit employing moral considerations in explaining why God chose the Jews, and that his second argument, fails to provide viability to exclusivist election.

So, what should be the situation regarding our moral standards when thinking about the reasons God had when choosing the Jews? There is a clear place in the religious life to defer to God's sovereignty, and to be still before God's inscrutable actions. However, that can be expected of a person only if she is either a thorough fideist believer, whose devotion floats free from any justificatory considerations, or of a believer who already has some reason to believe in and trust a sovereign God in the first place. Many of us will practice deference to God's sovereign inscrutability only when we believe that *at the core* God is morally good and does not act capriciously or worse. Only then will we trust God in those situations in which God appears to act in ways mysterious and beyond our moral understanding. Then we do so because we have faith in God's goodness to carry us beyond what we can know or understand.

God's having chosen the Jews is a fundamental, lasting act of God's, determining the course of Jewish history, and having serious influence on world history. If we cannot give a morally acceptable account of such a central tenet of Judaism, then our faith in God's goodness should suffer serious doubt. In applying our moral intuitions here we are not trying to make God comply with our rules, but are trying to ground for ourselves trust in God's goodness, this trust serving us elsewhere where we cannot fathom God's goodness.

## 2. Yehuda Halevi

By "Yehuda Halevi" I shall mean the position put forth by the Wise Man in the *Kuzari*. I ignore the question of what was the real view of the historical person who was Yehuda Halevi, as might be argued from a dialectical reading of the book.[2] Yehuda Halevi puts forward two claims. Claim One is a genetic account of what is distinctive about the Jewish people. Claim Two is that this distinctiveness makes the Jews' "nobility" and "the choicest" among the nations. In Claim One, what is distinctive about the Jews is the special "divine faculty" ("divine order") that was in Adam and passed on genetically and selectively to Abraham, in individuals, until eventually it passed into an entire community of Abraham's descendants, the Jewish people. The divine faculty is a latent character of a person that makes that person especially apt, roughly, for the attachment to him or her of divine manifestation in the world.[3] Halevi thought of the divine faculty as belonging exclusively to the biological descendants of the early Israelites.

The second Halevi-claim is that the divine faculty makes the Jews superior to other human beings. The divine faculty creates inequality between those who are the "core" and the others who are the "husks." Jews are superior because the divine faculty resides in them and in them alone. One could not come to possess the divine faculty by becoming a "spiritual descendent" of Abraham. In *Kuzari*

1:27, Halevi says that, "Anyone who joins us from the nations as an individual, receives from our goods, but is not equal to us." Halevi allows a degree of spiritual perfection obtainable by a convert, but lower than that possible in principle for a born Jew.[4]

Claim One, that the Jews have *something* distinctive about them, does not imply the Jews are superior to other nations. Even if that *something* Jews have does imply superiority of Jews over others in some trait or ability, it still does not follow that the Jews are superior *in toto*, are superior as *human beings*. In a sense relevant here, that the Jews have a distinctive trait or traits (T) implies their being *superior human beings* only if (1) T confers so much value on the Jews as human beings that no trait or traits of anyone else confers (or: could confer) such value on others even close to the value T confers on Jews, and (2) that the Jews have no trait or traits that diminish the superiority they have in virtue of T. Halevi believes that the divine faculty is of such value that having it exclusively, makes the Jews superior to anybody else, with the implicit assumption, I gather, that there is nothing about the Jews that cancels out that superiority.

Now, let us say that, strictly speaking:

> A person, P, holds a *racist* position when P maintains a morally reprehensible belief, regarding people *whom P takes to be* a race (or races), that (1) they are superior/inferior, qua human beings, to other people *whom P takes to be* a race (or races), solely in virtue of (*what P takes to be* racial) characteristics that P believes the former to possess or lack, and (2) the superior/inferior warrant treatment appropriate to their rank, relative to the inferior/superior, in virtue of the judgment in (1).

Notice a few things about this definition. (A) One can be a racist on this definition only if the position taken up is morally reprehensible. In this way the definition recognizes that "racism" is a term of moral condemnation. (B) It would be too narrow to tie the definition to actual races and racial characteristics, rather than to what P considers such. That would not conform to common usage. (C) We might widen the definition by including whatever P regards as an *ethnic group* and *ethnic* characteristics, or even identifiable social or national groupings. This might be closer to how present usage has burst the boundaries of the term "racism." In that case, we can read "racial" as including those others. For simplicity, I stick with the definition as stated. (D) I leave it open whether to include in the definition that P is judging a race other than the one P identifies with. If P thinks her race is the worst on earth and should be treated badly on that account, is P to be called a "racist"? Finally, (E) A racist need believe only that a race warrants distinct treatment but need not take any steps in that direction. This accounts for closet racists.

I have said this is a strict definition of a racist view. However, increasingly, according to contemporary western moral sensibilities, it is "racist" to endorse just the first clause of the definition, that is, to make any judgment that any race is superior/inferior to others, without knowing whether or not the second clause, about treatment, is also being endorsed.[5] So, for example, if someone were to recognize the inferiority of a race and dedicate his entire life, from love and self-sacrifice, to helping them, with their enthusiastic support, with genetic self-modification, he might very well be charged with holding a racist belief, in any case. In our societies, it has become morally reprehensible to make any judgment that one group or another is innately better or worse than others. We have become highly sensitized to the enormous potential for such judgments to create untold human suffering. We have become extremely sensitive to people picking up views from others for sinister and destructive purposes, whether or not the source intended such results. The twentieth century with its horrendous genocides and racial wars has taught us to be on the alert to any endorsement of the first clause of our definition of a racist point of view.

So, whether or not we want to call Halevi's position itself "racist," strictly speaking, we have come to appreciate the dangers of proclaiming any group to be superior or inferior human beings.[6] It has become morally reprehensible to do so, at least on pragmatic grounds.[7] For this reason, the chosenness of the Jews has become a stumbling block to belief in Judaism and identity with the Jewish people. Chosenness seems to imply, and has been assumed to do so in our history, the racial superiority of the Jews, and at times has sanctioned Jews to subjugate others, if only they have the power to do so. It is important to counter this conception, to foster respect for the Jewish people and to remove a stumbling block toward Jewish religious belief. Adopting a morally acceptable understanding of chosenness by contemporary standards can help toward removing a barrier that need not exist. At the same time, we must be modest about what *we* think is morally correct, remaining open to the possibility of our being wrong. However, we have no choice but to employ our own moral sensibilities if we are to gain confidence in God for those situations in which God's behavior is morally unfathomable.

I do not offer any idea why God would choose specifically the Jews, rather than anybody else. I am willing to attribute that exact choice to divine inscrutability. In my view, the crucial moral issue is not why God chose the Jews, rather than another people, but how God could justifiably choose *any* nation to be God's chosen people. What we need is a theology for why God would choose *any* nation, the Jews or the Hittites, a theology that maintains contemporary moral good taste.

Elsewhere, I have provided a proposal for a contemporary theology of the Jews as the chosen people that addresses this new sensitivity. (Gellman 2013) I do not mean a theology for understanding what went before in history, but a new theology for the future, irrespective of the past. In putting forward a new theology of Jewish chosenness, uppermost to me was that it negate Jewish superiority and not imply degradation of non-Jews. It was also important to advance a respectful and appreciative attitude, *in principle*, toward other world religions.[8] The a priori discrediting of religions other than Judaism is but the other side of the coin of a priori discrediting of non-Jews.

I conclude with a brief skeleton of this new theology of Jewish election. I begin with a definition useful for what comes afterward. Let us say that the Jews are "*God's chosen people*" means:

(1) God has a permanent, non-revocable, loving relationship with the Jews that God neither has created nor will create with any other nation.

And:

(2) This relationship is of supreme value relative to any type of relationship God may have created or will create with any other *specific* nation.

The key to this definition is that God having the loving relationship with the Jews that God has with no other *specific* nation, is to be consistent with God coming to have that same quality of a loving relationship with *all* of humanity at large, including all nations. It is just that no other nation *qua* specific nation had, has, or will have, that relationship to God.[9] Indeed, I propose a theology in which the love God has for the Jews is the same love God has for all of humanity.

The loving relationship God wishes to have with all of humanity is that all come to God in freedom and joy. God cannot overwhelm people with God's sheer presence or with God's transparent works, for that would have such force that a person could not help but believe in and be devoted to God. In such circumstances a person would not be free to come to God from her own initiative. Perhaps there could be some joy in that, but not the fullness of blessedness when responding to God from within one's existential freedom.

God must recede to the edges of human consciousness so as to leave space for freedom. This is what happens in in the opening chapter of Genesis. For six days, God creates, pouring God's creative energy into the world, the world impacted by God's overbearing presence. On the seventh day, God rests. For God to "rest" is for God to withdraw God's overwhelming presence so as to create the conditions for humanity to come to God in freedom. That God rests is the precondition for Eve, and then Adam, to be free to choose to eat from the forbidden tree. What it means, in Genesis 1, for the seventh day to be holy, is for it to provide the conditions for coming to God in freedom.

At the same time, God wishes humanity to know of God's love for them and of God's desire that they come to God in freedom, all this contra-indicated by God retreating into the shadows and peeking out at them with only hints of God's presence. For this purpose, God's manifest love of the Jews is to be a figure, a picture, of the love of God for all. So, God chooses the Jews in a thunderous theophany at Sinai, which so seared God's presence into their consciousness that they had no freedom to choose to serve God. Rabbi Hanina (Numbers Rabbah 2:16) has God declaring to the Israelites "Against your will shall you be my people!" And Rabbi Dimi (Avodah Zarah 2:2) said: "[At Mt. Sinai] God turned the mountain over above them like a bowl and said to them: 'If you accept the Torah, fine. But if not, there you will be buried.'" On this latter, I quote the Hasidic Master, Rabbi Shneur Zalman of Liady (1745–1812):

God's love for us is greater than our love [for God]. The Rabbis said, "God turned the mountain over above them like a bowl." This means that because of the intensity of God's love for us [the Jewish people] He acts to arouse in us love of Him, so that we should not want to separate ourselves from Him. It is like a person who hugs a person [from behind] and turns him around face to face and won't let him go, because the love of the hugger is greater than that of the hugged, and so that the hugged will not forget the love of the hugger.[10]

On this interpretation, God overwhelms the Israelites with God's love to spur them to respond to God in kind. God hugs them tightly (the "bowl"), so that the feeling of God's love will stay with them forever after. God was making resistance a perverse response to His manifest love.

The Jews serve as God's servants, enduring curtailing of *their* own freedom, for the sake of making God's immense love for humanity tangible, while not violating the freedom of humanity at large.[11] (The Jews will in future have to freely accept what they had already had been made to observe earlier.) The election of the Jews involves no undertakings that they would be better at than anybody else. The election begins and ends with what God does. The election of the Jews involves no superiority of the Jews over anybody else. The Jews are God's instrument. "Why the Jews?" remains inscrutable. The election of the Jews does not involve God's greater love for them than for anybody else.

In the new theology of chosenness, the nations of the world will not have to guess why God chose the Jews, possibly misunderstanding it. This focus will be how the Jews perceive their being chosen by God.

It is my hope that this skeleton will motivate the reader to read my full exposition of this theology, to seek answers to questions that come to mind, but which I cannot address here.[12]

## Notes

1  See Morris 1991.
2  See Goodman 2012.
3  For a discussion of the divine faculty in Halevi, see Silman 1995.
4  For more on the issue of Halevi and conversion to Judaism, see Kreisel 2001.
5  I believe that divine providence stands behind moral developments over the ages, and so believe that contemporary moral stances deserve to be considered seriously, although not slavishly.
6  For good discussions of whether Halevi was a racist, see Bodoff 1989 and Jospe 1997.
7  This can be carried too far, as when it becomes suspect to judge that any race has any characteristic superior or inferior to others, without thereby judging them to be superior or inferior human beings.
8  I say "in principle," because any religion might have unacceptable components.
9  Due to a lack of clarity when I presented this definition in my book, Shalom Carmy, in a review, unfortunately missed this nuance in the definition, and, mistakenly, took this definition to clearly imply superiority of the Jews. See Carmy 2013.
10  2006, 195–196 (my translation). I am indebted to Yehuda Zirkind for leading me to this text.
11  Rabbinic literature has texts opposed to this line, when referring to the willingness of the Jews to agree to fulfill the Torah before they "hear." However, those texts have several dissenting texts, and do not figure in the present theology.
12  I am indebted to Aaron Segal for several comments that helped improve this essay.

## Further Reading on Chosenness

Frank, D. (ed.), *A People Apart: Chosenness and Ritual in Jewish Philosophical Thought* (Albany, NY: SUNY Press, 1995), 9–106 [articles by D. Novak, M. Kellner, and Z. Levy].

Frankfurt, H. *The Reasons of Love* (Princeton, NJ: Princeton University Press, 2006).

Jospe, R. "Teaching Judah Ha-Levi: Defining and Shattering Myths in Jewish Philosophy," in *Paradigms in Jewish Philosophy*, ed. R. Jospe (Cranbury, NJ: Associated University Presses, 1997), 112–128.

Kaminsky, J. *Yet I Loved Jacob: Reclaiming the Biblical Concept of Election* (Nashville, KY: Abingdon Press, 2007).

Kaplan, L. "Maimonides on the Singularity of the Jewish People," *Daat* 15 (1985), v–xxvii.

Kellner, M. *Maimonides on Judaism and the Jewish People* (Albany, NY: SUNY Press, 1991).

Kolodny, N. "Love as Valuing a Relationship," *Philosophical Review* 112 (2003), 135–189.

Novak, D. *The Election of Israel: The Idea of the Chosen People* (New York: Cambridge University Press, 1995/2007).

Rosenberg, S. *In the Footsteps of the Kuzari,* ed. J. A. Linsider, trans. G. Weinberg (New York: Yashar Books, 2008), 128–139.

Stump, E. *Wandering in Darkness* (Oxford: Oxford University Press, 2010), 85–107.

# 9 Redemption and Messianism

The previous part examined competing accounts of God's unique relationship with the Jewish people, a relationship whose foundations were laid, according to the biblical narrative, with God's redemption of the Israelites from Egyptian bondage. While the redemption from Egypt was indeed of a single nation, the prophetic and rabbinic tradition saw in that redemption a precursor to a much more sweeping, future redemption. The future redemption is to usher in the "messianic era," an era of universal peace, justice, and divine service.

Messianism—the doctrine that there will be such a redemption—immediately raises metaphysical, moral, and epistemological questions: What does the world have to be like—in moral and non-moral respects—for messianism to be true, and what other aspects of a religious worldview entail it? How will we know that the redemption has come?

In our first selection, **Hermann Cohen** maintains that messianism is no more and no less than the claim that good will ultimately have dominion on earth. We will know redemption has come when we see it, in others and in ourselves. Messianism entails that evil is not a fundamental, ineliminable aspect of reality. It is in turn entailed by monotheism: the one God, who stands equally with the oppressed and downtrodden, cannot abide injustice forever.

But how will the redemption come about? And what is God's role in it? A good proxy for the latter question, is whether the messianic era requires a literal messiah, an individual, flesh-and-blood human being. **Lenn Goodman** argues that it does not. The Messiah "is not a person" and the redemption "depends not on a literal Davidic restoration but on the rule of justice established through the changing of human hearts." And those hearts are changed, Goodman argues, by fulfilling the *mizvot* (Torah laws) and absorbing their significance. That the *mizvot* have the capacity to perfect humanity is "a central premise of the Law" and embodied in the covenant God made with the Jewish people. Thus, messianism is not necessarily entailed by monotheism as such. It is entailed by the goodness and rationality of the Torah, a law that leads without any further divine intervention to the redemption of humanity.

**Joseph Soloveitchik**, on the other hand, looks to the redemption from Egypt—which preceded the giving of the Torah—as a model for redemption in general. God desired to redeem the Israelites, but would not do so until Moses acquiesced to act on God's behalf. The principle that emerges is this: "God waits for man, for a single person, to accept responsibility and initiate the process of *ge'ulah*, of redemption." But that human person acts only as an agent of God; and only in God's presence, not in God's absence. When all is said and done, God and not Moses is acknowledged as 'the redeemer of Israel.' And so it will be regarding the future redemption. God will redeem, but in concert with a human agent. Messianism, in broad strokes and in some of its fine details, is entailed by a "paradoxical idea in Judaism: God longs for man." No matter where we find ourselves, God ultimately desires to bring us close, and He desires the help of a human being in doing so.

**Kenneth Seeskin** delineates five approaches to messianism, and, in particular, to the danger in holding it: it leads to dashed hopes, failed rebellions, and rival religions. Seeskin's preferred approach, which echoes that of Maimonides and Goodman, is 'deflation,' i.e., lowering the bar so that redemption requires no super-human effort or divine intervention. If we set our sights lower, then the dangers in setting our sights at all are reduced. And if redemption has not come, we have no one to blame but ourselves.

## HERMANN COHEN (1842–1918)

### *Religion of Reason Out of the Sources of Judaism* (1919)

#### *Introduction/B, sections 13–17* (tr. Kaplan)

13. Religion opposes this kind of "rotten reasoning," and thereby establishes its own worth. The God of whom religion teaches means nothing else but the repeal of this prejudice of ethical rigor. Plato once says in passing, in the *Theaetetus,* that evil can never cease, for it has to remain in opposition to the good. This idea separates Judaism from paganism, even from the paganism in Platonism. If the prophet, in opposition to Parsiism, makes God also the creator of evil, *this evil is rather the ill,* which men usually identify with evil. The prophet, however, intends to teach that God can be the creator only of perfection, which is expressed and signified by *peace.*

Hence, it is understandable that monotheism reaches its summit in Messianism. *Messianism,* however, means the dominion of the good on earth. One daily encounters the opinion that the Messiah could come only when injustice ceases. However, this is exactly the meaning of the Messiah: that injustice will cease. This view, which even Plato did not have, is the new teaching that the one God brings to messianic humanity. Morality will be established in the human world. Against this confidence, no skepticism, no pessimism, no mysticism, no metaphysics, no experience of the world, no knowledge of men, no tragedy, and no comedy can prevail. The distinction between ideal and actuality must not be transferred to the realm of the shadows and receive this kind of eternalization; it will be buried by the Messiah. The virtue of men will still have to tread new ways of unsuspected steepness, but a level of morality will be attained, which will secure the course of human morality.

14. We have depicted the messianic God as the God of ethics, but in the interest of historical clarification we must add that in our *Ethics of Pure Will* this messianic God appears only as the God of ethics. Just as scientific ethics must use all its literary sources correctly, so have we transplanted this God from the religion of monotheism into ethics. And yet this God, derived from religion, is an ethical God merely in virtue of the connection that exists between monotheism and morality; he is not yet the God of religion proper. The apex of monotheism is Messianism, but its center of gravity lies in the relation between God and the individual. At this point Ezekiel deviates from the mainstream of Messianism, insofar as he ceases to look at the world and turns to an inward look into the individual.

*Ezekiel transmitted to religion the God of the individual man.* Now the question of the Thou and the I can be raised anew. If it at first appeared dangerous to morality that the Thou be under the sign of sin, then the real image of sin, the mirror as a means of self-knowledge, has now been formed. In myself, I have to study sin, and through sin I must learn to know myself. Whether other men sin has to be of less interest to me than that I learn to realize how I myself in my innermost being am afflicted by sin, and instead of all sentimentality about my suffering, I should rather become sensitive to my moral frailty.

15. *The connection between sin and suffering,* which mythology discovers as its deepest mystery, may now become in some way intelligible to me. Now it does not do any harm when I detect moral deficiency in the tragic suffering of men, in the hero on the stage or in man on the world stage; for now I myself have become the true archetype of human frailty. Now I would not slip into the unfortunate idea, which would dull my compassion irreparably, that the Thou suffers for his sins; now I am permeated by the thought that I do not know any man's wickedness as deeply, as clearly, as my own. And if suffering is a payment for sin, I would wish to test this only in myself.

However, the God of religion is never a theoretical concept only, never a concept which merely should enlarge and enlighten man's knowledge and understanding. Hence, also, the knowledge of one's own sin and, through it, of oneself is for the sake of improvement, of paving the way to God. *God is not a concept of fate;* he does not have to reveal where suffering comes from. And as little has he to reveal where sin comes from. The legend of the Fall originated in Persia. The one God, therefore, cannot be responsible for the relation between life and guilt, let alone for a parity between them as measured by human standards. We shall have to recognize the depth of the monotheistic teaching of God in this high point of its view that all measuring and comparing of the inner *dignity* of man with the outward appearance of his earthly lot is futile and meaningless, shortsighted and deluded. The old question of why it goes badly for the good and well for the bad will receive an answer, of which even the Platonic wisdom had no inkling.

16. The prophets were not philosophers, but they were politicians, and in politics they were more consistent idealists than Plato himself. In politics, they were, with all their patriotism, messianic world citizens. Their own state was for them merely a stepping-stone to the federation of mankind.

They recognized another problem in the state besides the international one; they recognized that the distinction between poor and rich presented the greatest danger to the equilibrium of the state. *The poor became for them the symbol of human suffering.* If their messianic God is to annul suffering by establishing morality on earth, he has therefore to become lord over poverty, the root of human suffering. Thus, their God becomes the God of the poor. The social insight of the prophets recognizes in the poor the symptomatic sign of the sickness of the state. *Thus, their practical view is diverted from any eschatology of the mysteries.* They do not view death as suffering; death can offer no magic mysticism to them. Their view is concerned with men in the economic stream of the state and with its seemingly deep-rooted poverty, which manifests for the prophets the root of social suffering, the only one that can be redressed and therefore the only one worthy of notice.

17. If, then, it is the case that it is the prophetic religion which, just as it discovered man in the suffering of poverty, also discovered the unique God as the unique advocate of the poor, as the unique helper of all ranks of men, then through this peculiar realization of morality, *religion itself becomes a peculiar branch within the moral teaching.* Furthermore, it will have to be examined whether this peculiarity is due only to historical contingency or whether the concept of religion, the concept of monotheism, attests itself in this discovery, so that it has to be acknowledged as a necessary consequence of the concept of religion. The religion of the unique God had to let this ray of hope rise up for men out of the tribulations of social misery, out of the innermost contradictions of political justice. Ethics remains unchanged in its basic theoretical value, according to which its method has to guide the determination of human worth; but religion has discovered objective insights and derived them from its own principles of the concept of God and the concept of man, which remained closed to the method of ethics. These objective insights establish the peculiarity of religion, which is the more undisputed as the application of these religious concepts adapts itself to the general method of ethics.


## LENN GOODMAN

## "Demythologizing the Messiah," from *On Justice: An Essay in Jewish Philosophy* (1991)

The epic is not tragedy; but epic celebration of the heroic leads to tragedy as surely as the poetic elaboration of heroic virtues leads to dramatization of their clash. Biblically there is no epic. There are champions, of course, *gibborim*, and again *shoftim*, but no focus on the man, the woman—no hero worship. We are given no description of the person or personality of Deborah, no details of the upbringing of Samuel or Samson, no *Bildungsroman*, no cinematic visualization of the battles of David or Saul. The focus is always at a plane just beyond that where fictive personalities are resolved, a plane of moral virtuality by whose normative appeal *real* personalities and societies emerge. This is the reason, I suspect, that a cult of personal messiahship never did succeed among Israelites—still less any belief in avatars or *hulûlî* imams. Messiahship is a function, not a personality, and at bottom Jews always knew this—hence the radical insistence of the Passover *Hagaddah* on the immediacy of God's act in Egypt: "Not by the hands of an angel, not by the hands of a seraph, not by the hands of an emissary ..." Rashi argues that R. Hillel's denial of a messiah for Israel serves only to underscore the dependence of our redemption upon God alone.

There was no divine kingship in ancient Israel. The first hints at the idea of monarchy voice its radical critique; its acceptance is *faute de mieux*. The identities, appetites, and weaknesses of even the most celebrated monarchs, David and Solomon, are never confounded with the work for whose sake such kings (but never their failings) are tolerated or admired. And, as Mendelssohn explained, the very act that established a monarchy in ancient Israel, by creating a state distinguishable from the Law of God, whose standards it was to uphold, but whose standards did not alone determine its existence or dictate its form, drove a deep wedge, ultimately not removable, between the idea of God's will and the demands of any merely human government.

In Jeremiah (33: 14–15) we read God's promise that the restored scion of David will "execute justice and right in the land." This is the task of legitimate government and the criterion of its recognition. The longing for a Davidic restoration, then, is the longing to regain national autonomy and self-respect, restoration of Israel to Zion and of Zion to itself—less to its past than to its potential. The achievement of that goal cannot be identified with the advent of any single individual or mechanism of administration. The foundation of a messianism that does not quail at the facts of history or place responsibility for enhancing human destiny outside the realm of humanly acquired deserts is in the recognition that the righting of the world (*tikkun 'olam*) depends not on a literal Davidic restoration but on the rule of justice established through the changing of human hearts.

### Who is the Messiah?

It has been argued that the secular messianism of the founders of modern Zionism expresses a revulsion against the cult of personality, a reaction to the trauma of Shabtai Zvi. But the case can be generalized. The early Zionists, like the rest of the world, were in reaction against Napoleon; the later ones, against Hitler. Jewish messianism was never a personalistic concept; its modern forms do not depart from but continue the ancient conception of messiahship as a role rather than an identity. The secularism of Zionist leaders was a reaction specifically against the use of religion as a surrogate for action—against the passivity of awaiting the messiah. But Judah Halevi, whose poetry attuned him to the yearnings of his people, expressed in their sacred songs, reacted equally strongly—not with secular sentiments but with activist intentions, long before. What stirred him was not the thought of a man but the vision of a life. Even with Shabtai Zvi, the Jews like Glückel's father-in-law who sold their goods and packed provisions for imminent removal to the land of Israel were awaiting historical redemption, not a particular personality. The question in their minds was one of time—would redemption come now, next week, next year? They were confident of what redemption meant, regardless of its vehicle. Shabtai's personality was of consequence only to the close circuit of his devotees and sponsors—until his political and then his moral failure ruined his cause and made clear the vanity of the hopes that had been pinned to him. Then all but the most committed of his adherents discarded him and put their hopes once more in abeyance.

In recognizing the criteria of messiahship we must confront a question of temporal scale. If the messianic ideal of society, of history and the world, can be the achievement only of a generation or of a lengthy series of generations progressively working out their destiny and defining that destiny as they work, then the tasks of the messiah can never be achieved by a single pair of hands. Thus Rabbi Tarfon: "It is not your responsibility to complete the work, but you are not free to desist from it" (*Avot* 2:21). If we ask the question of the prophets who or what the messiah is, we discover that the messiah, properly called the hope of Israel, is not a person at all. The function of governance vested in a king is the natural paradigm and symbol of an epoch. The generations and their age must be the object to which the symbol points. The messiah is a person in the poetry of political imagination, the paradigm of an age.

A similar personification in the ancient Confucian texts is instructive. Shun, we read, a sage king of antiquity, ruled if any monarch did, by indirection; he had only to take his place reverently facing due south, and all things were done as was proper (*Analects* XV 5). As Confucius said, "He who rules by moral force is like the pole star, which remains in place while all the lesser stars pay it obeisance" (II 1). The anointed king of the canonical Jewish sources is not, of course, a figurehead, a symbol representing nothing but the image of authority. He is seen as a ruler; indeed, the founder of a regime. His role is dynamic. There is much to be built and accomplished before his reign as such can begin. As a symbol he represents the causal agency by which what must be done shall be done to set right the world and to maintain and augment its peace and justice even after they are established. Still, the messiah does not invent but only implements and reforms the Law; and even the Law does not fulfill its own requirements. Only its subjects can do that. Just as Shun's rule was typified by the propriety internalized in the minds of all his courtiers and administrators so that none so much as required a command, messianic rule is typified by the internalization in human hearts of all the obligations of love of God and regard for another which are central objects of the Torah's legislation. The messianic rule is one of moral force; and the order the messiah ushers in is not the project of his fiat but the outcome of our reformation. As Ibn Verga argued a century before Hobbes published the Leviathan: "The king in essence is the people."

Nowhere is conscious personification more evident in imaging the theme of historic redemption than in the book of Isaiah: "How lovely on the mountains— the feet of the messenger who bringeth the news of peace, good news, of victory, telling Zion, 'Thy God is King.' The voice of thy lookouts! They raise up their voices together, joyously, as each eye seeth the return of God to Zion." Our transformation will be decisive as the news of a battle won and a war ended, visible on all sides—"Look how my servant shall prosper. He shall be lifted up, exalted, raised most high. Just as many were appalled at thee—so marred was his appearance, unlike that of a man, his form beyond the human semblance—so shall many nations be astounded at him and kings shut their mouths. For they shall see what has not been told them and recognize for themselves what they have never heard tell of" (Isaiah 52:7–8, 13–15; cf. Rashi and Ibn Ezra ad loc.).

The prophet's slipping into the second person—"appalled at thee"—reveals the identity of the servant. It is Israel, explicitly identified (in 49:25–26), whose historic revival is at once the vindication of her faithfulness and the proof of God's faithfulness to her. The gaping kings admit their fault (53:5). Israel, so lately shunned and despised, seeming mad in clutching her ideals with no apparent purchase on reality (53:1–3) triumphs, like a gnarled, all-but-dead root in the desert that bursts forth as a sapling with the first rain. The servant is not a person but a nation of people who refuse to relinquish the vital insight embodied in their covenant: that justice rewards and evil destroys itself. The coming of the messiah confirms that truth, by the redemption of humanity in rightful living; its means is neither force nor fraud but the example of Israel living her law (42:1–4, 49:6–7).

### The Messianic Role

Maimonides resolves into prose the hopes that the prophets entrusted to imagery and recaptures conceptually the tinctures their images leave in rabbinic homily— their yearning and sense of immediacy, the contingency of the world's destiny upon the intimate turn of our moral choices. His summary has a value beyond the sway of his name, because it is conceptual. No mere figment of imagination joined to hope, alternating naturally with despair, could win a comparable authority. I divide his statement from the final pages of his *Code* into its theses:

> The King Messiah will arise and restore the kingdom of David to its former state and original autonomy.
>
> (*Hilkhot Melakhim* 11.1)

The criterion of messiahship, then, as the ancient rabbis held, is functional, critically political. As Samuel's distillation requires, it means reconstituting Israel as an autonomous state governed under the principles of the Torah.

In a restored Israel, Maimonides argues, prophecy will be recovered. For prophecy is philosophic insight given wings by imagination, and so translated into norms and symbols—the beliefs and practices by which we may live and visualize our place in nature and history. Self-confidence is the only requisite of prophecy lacking to a subjugated or exiled Israel, so prophecy will return with the restoration of Israel to sovereignty in her homeland. In such circumstances the insights will not be lacking to restore and reform the ancient practices of Israel. Even if the cult of animal sacrifices has been outgrown, prophetic authority will be at hand to adjust our worship to the spiritual modes of the matured nation, just as the ancient worship was adjusted to the conditions of our spiritual infancy:

He will rebuild the sanctuary and gather the dispersed of Israel. All the ancient laws will be reinstituted in his days. Sacrifices will be offered once again [even if not the very animal sacrifices of antiquity, whose details Maimonides sees as restrictions on the time, place, manner, and object of sacrifice so as to perfect the ethos and spirituality of the people]. The Sabbatical and Jubilee years will be observed as commanded in the Torah.

*(Hilkhot Melakhim* 11.1)

The restoration of Zion will mean an ingathering, an end to unnatural and unhealthful dispersion. The laws will be amplified, as in ancient times, by interpretation grounded in the insights of the prophets and sustained by a populace who derive guidance from the symbolisms of the ancestral religion and the governance of its principles—not only in personal and family matters but in agriculture, industry, stewardship of nature—as in the practices of *yovel* and *shemittah.* Central here is the moral thematic. For it is not mere performance of the laws unelaborated or elaborated only as rituals that constitutes the messianic fulfillment of history, but their moral implementation—the establishment of a society founded on their principles.

He who does not believe in a restoration or expect the coming of the messiah denies not only the teachings of the Prophets but also those of the Law and of Moses our teacher. For the text affirms the rehabilitation of Israel: "Then the lord thy God will reverse thy captivity and have pity on thee and return and gather thee. ... Even if you are scattered to the furthest reaches of the heavens. ... the Lord thy God will bring thee into the land which thy fathers possessed. ..." (Deuteronomy 30:3–5). These words explicit in the Torah comprehend all that the Prophets said on the subject.

*(Hilkhot Melakhim* 11.1)

Sandwiched between the seeming severity of a dogma and the authority of his proof-text, the Rambam makes two radical but textually anchored claims here: (1) The messianic idea is embedded in the Mosaic Torah, since, as he argues a few lines further on, no commandment was given without a view to its fulfillment. This means that the Torah is given with a view to instituting the entire socio-legal system it projects. (2) Nothing more is intended by our messianism than is implied in the biblical expectation of a world reformed through the fulfillment of the Law. Symbolic and projective visions of a supernatural end to history are mere surrogates of the moral changes by which alone the transhistoric goal is brought about and made lasting. Without moral transformation, cosmic cataclysms would be mere pyrotechnics.

The Rambam expresses his thesis negatively, as though excoriating incredulity— for much the same reasons, I suspect, that Plato couches his radical reconstitution of the idea of divinity in an excoriation of "the poets" for suggesting that the divine is venal: The blow falls not on the poets but on the vulgar notion that the venal can be divine. Similarly, when Maimonides defends belief in the messiah, his target is not an audience who have no taste for messianism but rather one inclined to believe too well, or to interpret such beliefs in primitive terms, as a prelude to bracketing them. He muffles the radicalism of his view, sidestepping his adversaries who reject the very idea that a divine law might address human needs and purposes and who prefer to regard each commandment (even in isolation from the system that gives them life) as though it were an end in itself rather than a means to God's end, the perfection of humanity through the commandments. Yet Maimonides' radicalism is of a piece with prophetic and rabbinic radicalism. Messianism is not merely a bundle of isolated promises but a central premise of the Law, made explicit in the proof-text (as so many Mosaic principles are in Deuteronomy), but implicit, as we have argued, in the very fabric of the Mosaic legislation. That was my first point.

As for the proof-text itself, my second point emerges from the comprehensiveness and exclusivity of Maimonides' reading of it. Beyond the expectation of Israel's return to live as God's people under God's law; there is no further content to our messianism. Anything more is poetical expansion or spurious, possibly unwholesome invention. Maimonides argues that the themes found in the prophets of Israel are broached in the prophecy of Balaam—a momentous remark, since Balaam's prophecy and its exigency insist that Israel's ultimate vindication, like her general well-being, rest upon allegiance to the precepts of the Law. What rendered Balaam incapable of cursing Israel was that she was already blessed; and what made her blessed was her way of life—its order and goodliness, outcomes of the moral and social appropriation of justice and tact, inspired by the commands of Perfection. The duality of Balaam's vision suggested in the words "I see him but not now; I behold him but not nigh" (Numbers 24:17), is glossed by Maimonides as alluding to two historic phrases: the monarchy of David and the ultimate national restoration, with its attendant international order. Both are outcomes of Israel's allegiance to her laws. Supernatural readings miss the force of the inference from the peace and order Balaam beholds, first to the immediate future—in his blessing—and then to the remote future (where the observed tendencies are consummated)—in his prophecy. ...

## JOSEPH SOLOVEITCHIK (1903–1993)

## "Moses and the Redemption," in *Festival of Freedom* (2006)

### *Come unto Pharaoh*

If we examine the semantics of God's command to Moses, *"Bo el Par'oh*, Come unto Pharaoh" (Ex. 10:1), we find that it contains an important message. The term *bo* implies that the being commanded is far from the speaker and comes closer. If Moses were near the Almighty and commanded to go to Pharaoh, the verse should have read *"Lekh el Par'oh*, Go to Pharaoh." Why does God express this command in such a strange form?

When God chose him, Moses was very reluctant to accept the mission. He argued with the Almighty, according to our tradition (Ex. Rabbah 3:14), for seven full days. He considered himself unqualified to be the leader of the people and to confront Pharaoh; he was too modest, too humble. "Moses said to God: Who am I, that I should go to Pharaoh, and that I should take the children of Israel out of Egypt?" (Ex. 3:11)—who am I, that I am worthy of becoming the redeemer? God answered him: "*Ki eheyeh imakh*, I shall accompany you" (Ex. 3:12). God promised Moses that He would never desert him; He would participate in the implementation of the mission, and together they would enter Pharaoh's chambers. Therefore, when God instructed Moses to appear before Pharaoh, He used the imperative *bo* instead of *lekh*. When Moses addresses Pharaoh, God will be present; when he raises the staff, God will be with him. In effect, God says, "*Bo imadi el Par'oh*, Come along with Me to Pharaoh."

There is a halakhic principle involved here. The Halakhah knows of two kinds of *shelihut*, two kinds of power of attorney, of acting as a plenipotentiary, of acting by proxy. One type of *shelihut* is a purely formal-juridic assignment given to a person. The other type of *shelihut* is personalistic and experiential. The former is a purely practical institution, designed simply to perform legal transactions by proxy. Quite often, one cannot attend to business personally, and therefore the Halakhah provides the opportunity to act through a proxy, to ask someone else to finalize or sanction certain obligations or certain deeds or agreements. This kind of acting through a proxy is always associated with the absence of the real owner; for example, Abraham's authorizing his servant to travel to Haran and choose a bride for Isaac. Once the authority is granted, whatever the agent does is valid.

The second kind of *shelihut* is personalistic; it is a relationship between two people who are united by a bond of friendship, two people committed to the same destiny, two people sharing in each other's travails and joys, two people working for the same cause and confiding in each other, two people living an open, frank existence. These two people achieve a common identity from the viewpoint of the Halakhah. Each one of them may act in certain areas on the behalf of the other, even though the latter is right there and is capable of performing the same deeds by himself. Basically, the *shelihut* is a merger of identity. One acts on behalf of the other in the other's presence.

For example, we know that when a *kohen*, a priest in the Temple, offered a sacrifice, he acted as an agent of the person who brought the sacrifice. If the *kohen* is my agent, why do I have to travel from Upper Galilee to Jerusalem in order to be present at the offering of the sacrifice? It is because this kind of *shelihut* is not merely a formal relationship between the sender and his proxy, but rather a personalistic, experiential *shelihut*. Similarly, the high priest on Yom Kippur was the representative of the people. However, the people did not leave him alone; they did not say, "Now that you are appointed our representative; you may confess on our behalf and do whatever is necessary in order to obtain atonement, but we will sleep on Yom Kippur." Rather, the Temple courtyard was filled with the priests and the people (Mishnah *Yoma* 6:2). All Jerusalem did not sleep the night of Yom Kippur because the high priest was awake. This is because personalistic *shelihut* is performed only when the sender is present; in his absence, there is no *shelihut*.

Similarly, the Mishnah informs us that the principle of *shelihut* is applicable to congregational prayer: "*Sheluho shel adam kemoto*, One's emissary is tantamount to oneself" (*Berakhot* 5:5). The *hazzan* is the *shali'ah*, the representative, the plenipotentiary, the agent of the people. But the congregation must be present. This is a peculiar kind of *shelihut*, which is optimally performed in the presence and with the participation and direct involvement of the *meshale'ah*, the sender. The *shelihut* is nurtured not by transfer of authority but by common identity, by common awareness, by a personalistic union. Therefore, the *sheli'ah tzibbur* recites the prayer on behalf of the whole congregation—not in their absence, but in their presence. The *hazzan* is united with the congregation, and through him the whole congregation prays.

This idea is a halakhic principle, not mysticism. Maimonides (*Hilkhot Tefillah* 11:4) held that the *sheli'ah tzibbur* should not stand near the *aron kodesh*, the holy ark, because then he would be removed from the congregation; rather, he should stand in the center and the congregation should surround him. This principle is also stated explicitly in the prayer *Heyei im pifiyot sheluhei amekha* recited on Rosh haShanah and Yom Kippur, which entreats God to accept the *hazan's* supplications as a representative of the community: "They bring Your people before You, and they pass in their midst. The eyes of Your people are cast upon them … and Your people surround them like a wall." The congregation surrounds the *sheli'ah tzibbur* just as a fortress surrounds a city, and the moment he is separated from the congregation, no authority under the sun can make him their representative. He is a spokesman as long as he is one with the congregation.

The *shelihut* entrusted to a prophet belongs to the second category of personalistic *shelihut*. Man unites with God, cleaves to God, and loves God with a great passion. He feels the hot breath of eternity upon his cold face. He feels the Almighty; he experiences the great sweetness and exaltedness engendered by the touch of infinity. That is why God says *Bo el Par'oh*. It is not the formal *shelihut* wherein I absent myself and you do whatever I told you to do. It is the personalistic *shelihut*, where there is union between Me and you. My thoughts will become your thoughts, My speech will break through you; therefore, Moses, you are qualified because I am qualified. *Bo el Par'oh*—Come with me, I will walk with you, I will be there when you enter the palace, and I will not leave you on your own. You are the *sheli'ah tzibbur*; I am the *tzibbur*. I am united with you; we will walk together arm in arm, so to speak. Man can come so close to the Almighty that he and the Almighty are united—one voice, one feeling, one experience, finitude somehow embraced by infinity and yet not disappearing.

### The Human Role

Let us analyze a little further this union of man and God, in order to gain insight into the role the Torah has assigned to the individual leader in history. History, Judaism says, cannot move or progress without the individual. God waits for man if there is something to be done. He does nothing until man initiates action. God waits for man, for a single person, to accept responsibility and initiate the process of *ge'ulah*, of redemption. It is strange. On the one hand, God is the *Go'el Yisrael*, our redeemer and liberator; however, God wills man to become His *shali'ah* in the drama of *ge'ulah*, the personalistic *shali'ah* with whom will God walk. God will not desert him, but God alone does not want to take the initiative. The Jewish people have been waiting a long time for the *Mashi'ah*—a human being like us who will initiate the process of *ge'ulah*.

The Gemara (*Sanhedrin* 98b) tells us that Rabbi Hillel—not Hillel the Elder—said, "*Ein Mashi'ah le-Yisrael*, Israel has no messiah." Instead, God Himself will liberate Israel; He will not use an agent. Indeed, why should we wait for a human being to liberate the Jewish people, redeem the land, and reconstruct the Temple? Why should the fulfillment of all the glorious prophetic promises depend upon a human being, who had a father and a mother, and not upon God Himself? Yet the Talmud considers this statement heretical. "Rav Yosef said: May the Almighty forgive Rabbi Hillel for this." Rabbi Hillel did not deny the future redemption; he denied man's role in it. According to *Hazal*, to deny the role of man in the future redemption is heresy: "May the Almighty forgive Rabbi Hillel."

God wants an individual great in knowledge, in morality, in prophecy, to be a participant in the drama of *ge'ulah*. God wills man to emerge as a great being through his acceptance of the *shelihut*. Not the collective, but the individual, seizes the initiative. "It came to pass in the course of those many days, that the king of Egypt died, and the children of Israel sighed by reason of the bondage and their cry rose up to God ... and God saw their affliction, and God knew" (Ex. 2:23–25). God was ready, the people were ready, the time had passed, *ge'ulah* was possible, and God could have taken them out in a split second. But God had to wait for someone. Immediately, in the next verse, Moses is mentioned: "Now Moses kept the flock of Jethro" (Ex. 3:1).

In every generation, there is a *shali'ah* who is qualified to become the *Ish E-lokim*, the person with whom God walks, who speaks on God's behalf, through whom God speaks. In that generation, it was Moses. Had God not succeeded in persuading Moses to accept the assignment, there would have been no exodus! Yet even though nothing happens in the absence of the *shali'ah*, nevertheless, the *shali'ah* is not recognized after he performs his mission.

Let me qualify this statement. The individual deserves no praise as long as his contribution consists of, or is translated into, political, economic, or military victory. However, if the share he contributes to the history of the people is of an intellectual nature, if he teaches the people and elevates them to new spiritual heights, if he is their mentor and teacher—then his contribution is not only recorded but is glorified, as if he were the origin of all that spiritual greatness, as if he deserved the gratitude of the people forever.

God is the warrior; man is not. "God is a man of war" (Ex. 15:3). When it comes to teaching, however, man claims credit, and credit is given to him. Man cannot act as the plenipotentiary of the Almighty as far as military, political, or economic power is concerned. *Bo el Par'oh*—God accompanies Moses and joins him. The warnings and stern words were announced by the Almighty; the plagues were performed by the Almighty; He did everything. God acted, and brought along Moses as a companion and friend. Here we come across a paradoxical idea in Judaism: God longs for man. He does not need man, but He longs for him. This is the love story later told so beautifully in the Song of Songs—infinity longs for finitude. We should not say this, but we have no way to express ourselves other than in anthropomorphic terms.

Once Moses was present, God did everything. The Haggadah states clearly and unequivocally that "'The Lord brought us forth out of Egypt' (Deut. 26:8)—not through a *malakh*, not through a seraph, and not through a messenger, but by the Holy One, blessed be He, alone and in His glory." How can the Haggadah say "not through a messenger" when the Almighty Himself said to Moses, "Therefore, I shall send you to Pharaoh" (Ex. 3:10)? Moses, in his epistle to Edom at the end of the forty years, stated clearly that God "sent a *malakh* and brought us out of Egypt" (Num. 20:16). (*Malakh* in this verse does not mean an angel but a plenipotentiary.) How, then, is it possible for the Haggadah to say "not through a *malakh*"?

Of course, the answer is simple. There was a *shali'ah*, but he belonged to the second category, not the first. Had the *shali'ah* belonged to the first category, he would have deserved credit, he did it all by himself. He was authorized by the Almighty, but the deeds were his own. Moses, however, was a *shali'ah* who served only as a companion for the Almighty. Such a *shali'ah* does not deserve credit, so his name is not mentioned. Every miracle executed by Moses was performed by the Almighty; the Almighty "looks in at the windows, peers through the lattices" (Song 2:9).

Note the paradox. On the one hand, without Moses there would have been no *ge'ulah*. Moses is the individual; he is the hero of Jewish history. He fulfilled his assignment beautifully. On the other hand, when his assignment on the historical stage was done, the lights dimmed and he walked off in darkness. On Pesah night, when we celebrate the exodus, Moses is not the hero. The *ge'ulah* is credited to one account only—that of God. *Bo el Par'oh*: Come with Me; I cannot go without you—yet you will not get any credit. Moses himself proclaims, in an act of self-effacement, "I will sing to the Lord, for He has triumphed gloriously; the horse and his rider has He thrown into the sea" (Ex. 15:1). Moses claims no credit.

What, then, is Moses' role in Jewish history? Is he completely forgotten and erased? To the contrary, from the time his birth is recounted in *parashat Shemot*, he is mentioned in every *sedrah* but one. He was not immortalized as a political hero or a strategist. Moses was immortalized as a teacher. We do not say *Moshe Go'alenu*, or *Moshe Moshi'enu*, or *Moshe Meshi'henu;* we say *Moshe Rabbenu*. Calling him *Moshe Go'alenu*, Moses our Redeemer, would be blasphemy. Man cannot usurp God's attributes of power. A man who calls himself powerful is nothing but an idiot. A malignant little cell kills the most powerful man, and nothing can stop it. It is ridiculous to speak of man as powerful.

Moses was not the political architect of the Jewish people, but he was the architect of our spiritual history. Why is it permissible to say that Moses is our teacher, and wrong to say that he is our liberator and redeemer? The teacher of mankind, and particularly of the Jewish community, is the Almighty. Behind every teacher, every *melammed*, every *rosh yeshivah*, stands God. The attributes of wisdom, knowledge, kindness, and grace belong exclusively to God, but man has a right—even a duty—to usurp them, to take something of God's attributes for himself. He is duty-bound to imitate God—not regarding power, but regarding teaching.

Here we encounter something very strange. Although Moses' name is not recorded in the story of exodus in the Haggadah, God nonetheless permitted His Torah to be called *Torat Moshe* (e.g., Mal. 3:22). True, the Torah is *Torat Hashem*—"The Torah of the Lord is perfect, restoring the soul" (Ps. 19:8)—but God delivered it to Moses, and said: Moses, you act. You will never be called a man of power, because man cannot be powerful. But you will be called a great teacher and the greatest of all scholars in the history of your people. According to *Hazal* (Ex. Rabbah 47:3), the second tablets were given exclusively to Moses. Had he wanted, he could have retained the *luhot*, the tablets, for himself and his descendants. There was no need for Moses to turn over the *luhot* to the people, but he was generous. Moreover, the Torah became a part of Moses, and he was free to give it to others. He took pride in it; he was the master and the owner of the Torah. People have no idea how much freedom we have in interpreting the Torah. They speak about the Halakhah as fossilized, but people who say so simply do not know what Halakhah is; they have never studied Halakhah. If there is an area in which human ingenuity, freedom of research, sweep, and depth play a role, it is in the area of Halakhah.

The extent to which man's role is almost unlimited in the research and application of the Torah is reflected in the following story. The Gemara (*Bava Metzi'a* 59b) tells us that there was a very heated controversy between Rabbi Eliezer ha-Gadol and the rest of the academy. Rabbi Eliezer said that a certain item was ritually pure, while the vast majority said it was impure. Of course, the decision was accepted in accordance with the majority. Rabbi Eliezer then summoned supernatural support for his position, including a voice from heaven announcing that the Almighty was in agreement with Rabbi Eliezer against the majority. Then Rabbi Yehoshua stood up on his feet and said: We do not listen to heavenly voices. You have already decreed in Your own Torah that the opinion of the majority should prevail (Ex. 23:2). We have the majority, and we voted against You.

In the area of Torah and morality, man is the victor. When the victory is not one of power but of finitude encountering infinity, not of the warrior but of the teacher, not of political authority but of a kind and contrite heart—here the Almighty lets man share in His own attribute.

Moses' name was eliminated from the pages of the Haggadah as if he had never existed. But we are a grateful people; we feel very sorry for him on Pesah night. I remember that when I was a small child, I asked why Moses is not mentioned in the Haggadah, and all the answers my father gave me—which were similar to the explanation I have given here—were futile. Simply, I cried. Finally, my father, in order to placate to me, found the name of Moses in the Haggadah. It is not in the Haggadah proper but in a proof-text: "They believed in the Lord, and in His servant Moses" (Ex. 14:31). This calmed my mind somewhat, but I still felt that we were committing an injustice against Moses.

Apparently, this is not only the feeling of a kind and compassionate little boy, but of *Knesset Yisrael*, of the congregation as a whole. It looks for Moses on Passover night but will never find him.

> "On my bed at night"—this refers to the night of Egypt; "I sought him whom my heart loves"—this refers to Moses; "I sought him, but I found him not".
>
> (Song Rabbah 3:1)

Similarly, when, with God's help, the Haggadah of our final redemption is written, the name of the *Mashiah* will not be mentioned either.

> "'Give thanks unto the Lord, for He is good, for His mercy endures forever'— so let the redeemed of the Lord say" (Ps. 107:1–2). ... Why does it say "the redeemed of the Lord" and not [simply] "Israel"? It is as Isaiah (35:10) explains, "The redeemed of the Lord shall return"—[they are] not [called] "the redeemed of Elijah," nor "the redeemed of the Messiah," but "the redeemed of the Lord." Therefore, here too it says, "the redeemed of the Lord".
>
> (*Midrash Tehillim*, 107)

Where can we find Moses? Where is Moses rewarded and glorified as the leader? It is at Sinai on Shavu'ot. There he is the great teacher of the people, *Moshe Rabbenu*.

> "Scarce had I passed from them, when I found him whom my soul loves"— this refers to Moses; "I held him and would not let him go, until I had brought him into my mother's house"—this refers to Sinai; "and into the chamber of her that conceived me"—this refers to the Tent of Meeting.
>
> (Song Rabbah 3:4)

He is called *Moshe Rabbenu* only in reference to Sinai, not in reference to *ge'ulat Mitzrayim*. "I stood before the Lord and you ... to show you the word of the Lord" (Deut. 5:5)—I am the mediator between God and the congregation, and I told you the word of God, so I deserve credit. This is the philosophy of *Bo el Par'oh*.

## KENNETH SEESKIN

## "Speedily In Our Time"

Although it is often said that monotheism is Judaism's greatest contribution to world culture, one could make an equally powerful case for messianism: the belief that however bad the past was or the present is, the future holds unrealized possibilities that point to a new and better age.[1] The groundwork for such a belief is laid right from the opening line of Genesis: "In the beginning..." If there is a beginning of history, then it is reasonable to ask about the middle and the end.

Along the same lines, it is noteworthy that few of the characters in the Torah live stable or settled lives. Abraham is asked to leave the home of his father and go to a land that God will show him. Jacob is constantly fleeing his adversaries and spends much of his life in distress until he is finally united with Joseph in Egypt. Moses flees Egypt and is asked to lead an entire nation into the Promised Land. These stories are significant not only because the characters go from one place to another, but because the places to which they are going hold out the promise of a new and better life. Unlike Odysseus, who returns to Ithaca to reestablish existing conditions, biblical characters are typically asked to go somewhere they have never been before.

Rarely is the journey they undertake smooth. Throughout the narrative of the Exodus, the people rail against Moses and provoke God. Thus Numbers 14:11: "How long will this people treat me with contempt?" By the end of the journey, as the people are finally ready to enter the Promised Land, this is how God asks Moses to prepare for death:

> Behold, you are about to sleep with your fathers; then this people will rise up and play the harlot after the strange gods of the land, where they go to be among them, and they will forsake me and break my covenant which I have made with them. Then my anger will be kindled against them in that day, and I will forsake them and hide my face from them, and they will be devoured; and many evils and troubles will come upon them, so that they will say in that day, "Have not these evils come upon us because our God is not among us?" And I will surely hide my face in that day on account of all the evil which they have done, because they have turned to other gods.
>
> (Deut. 31: 16–18)

Is this really what is going to happen? Are the people going to repeat all their past mistakes and continue to show contempt for God?

The answer of the great literary prophets is no. While it is true that the people are going to show contempt for God, this cannot be how the story ends. Though it may take something as dramatic as a cosmic upheaval to set things straight, eventually the people will turn from their evil ways, justice will prevail, and God and Israel will be reunited in a bond of genuine partnership. If the situation looks bleak at present, that is only because the story is still unfolding. It is a small step from this sentiment to formation of the concept of a messiah: literally the anointed one of God. At first, the term referred to a king or priest set apart from the rest of the people. But eventually it came to mean a future king or redeemer from the House of David who will restore political sovereignty to Israel and put an end to oppression. According to Jeremiah 23:5: "The days are surely coming, says the Lord, when I will raise up for David a righteous branch, and he shall reign as a king and deal wisely, and shall execute justice and righteousness in the land."

From our standpoint, such pronouncements may seem naïve. But before rejecting them, we should ask what lies behind them. Simply stated, it is the view that no tragic necessity dooms the human race to repeat its past mistakes. The way things are now is not the way they have to be or the way they are necessarily going to be. If so, then despair is never the right response to misfortune. As Maimonides once put it: the eyes of mankind are set to look forward, not backward. In time, hope for a better future would become so much a part of our worldview that the philosopher Immanuel Kant could say that without it, people would have no motivation to work for the common good.[2]

Any idea this far-reaching inevitably brings with it a host of problems. "There is something grand about living in hope," wrote Gershom Scholem, "but at the same time there is something profoundly unreal about it."[3] Needless to say, the history of Judaism is littered with false hopes, false messiahs, and wild speculation about the circumstances in which the true one will appear. Christianity faces the same problem in connection with the second coming of Christ. Though hope is needed when things get difficult, it is precisely when things get difficult that people are most susceptible to folly. Such folly normally expresses itself in either of two ways.

The first way is a vision of apocalypse, which carries with it an "us versus them" mentality and a promise of divine vengeance against "them." For many of the prophets, the current situation is so awful that justice cannot be done until every sin is exposed and every sinner punished. Thus Amos (8–9) claims that the day of the Lord will not be a joyous time but a bitter, awful one when no light will shine and famine will destroy the land. Jesus, too, foretells a time when the sun will be darkened, the stars will fall from heaven, the heavens will shake, and all the tribes of the earth will mourn (Matthew 24:29–34). Although these passages are excessive, the thinking behind them is clear. Religion directs one's attention to the absolute. The more one is focused on the absolute, the more human behavior will appear wanting. The more human behavior appears wanting, the more devastating corrective measures will have to be.

The second way is the vision of what will follow the apocalypse: a world totally unlike this one, where peace will reign, death will be overcome, haughtiness and pride eliminated, and idolatry give way to worship of the true God. In Judaism this vision was extended to include the restoration of a divinely appointed King, political sovereignty for Israel, the ingathering of the exiles, the rebuilding of the Temple in Jerusalem, and, following Daniel, resurrection of the dead. The problem is that false hopes not only leave people disappointed, in many cases, they can make a bad situation worse.

During the Roman occupation of Judea, two attempts at revolution failed, leading to the imposition of two periods of death and destruction. In regard to the first, the historian Josephus writes:[4]

> Their chief inducement to go to war was an equivocal oracle also found in their sacred writings, announcing that at that time a man from their own country would become Monarch of the world. This they took to mean the triumph of their own race, and many of their own scholars were wildly out in their interpretations.

Here, then, is a case where hope for a better future was misguided and led to catastrophe. In the second attempt, the Jews put their fate in the hands of Bar Kochba (Son of the Star), a man proclaimed the Messiah by no less an authority than Rabbi Akiba. Unfortunately the "messiah" was defeated by a scorched earth policy meant to teach the Jews a lesson for all time.

We can now understand why early rabbinic leaders approached messianic longings with ambivalence. Given exile and the ever-present reality of political oppression, they were not in a position to squelch a belief that gave the people hope. At the same time, they could not be completely comfortable with a doctrine that had led to two disastrous wars, spawned a rival religion, and, on some interpretations, puts more emphasis on military prowess than on study of the Torah or observance of the commandments. In this respect, they were neither the first nor the last people to realize that messianic fervor can be dangerous. We have seen, however, that while dangerous, messianic fervor can also be inspiring. As the historian Heinrich Graetz put it, messianism is both Pandora's box and the elixir of life.[5]

Not surprisingly, the rabbinic response was to articulate not one but several answers to the question of when the Messiah will come.[6] The Messiah will come when human behavior reaches its zenith. The Messiah will come when human behavior reaches its nadir. The Messiah has already come so that all we can do is commit ourselves to improved behavior. The Messiah will usher in an apocalypse. The Messiah is already here in the person of a leper bandaging his wounds outside the gates of Rome. With such variety, it is a misnomer to speak of *the* rabbinic position on the coming of the Messiah or on what the Messiah will do.

How does one deal with such ambivalence? For the most part, responses to this question take one of five forms: (1) inflate the idea of the Messiah, (2) deflate it, (3) marginalize it, (4) internalize it, or (5) defer it. One point to keep in mind as we consider these alternatives is that they are not mutually exclusive. In some cases, a thinker might subscribe to more than one, in others the line separating one alternative from another may be hard and fast.

*Inflation* involves raising the bar of acceptance for the Messiah so high that for all intents and purposes, it can never be crossed. If Elijah has not come to herald the Messiah's arrival, if the exiles have not returned to Zion, if the Temple has not been restored, if there has not been a groundswell of repentance, if there has not been an apocalypse similar to those described by the prophets, and if the dead have not been resurrected, then the Messiah has not come, and we will just have to wait until he does. According to some, waiting for the Messiah is a virtue even if the prospect of his coming is remote. There is no question inflation has one major advantage: it makes it all but impossible for pretenders to the title of Messiah to make a case. The problem is that without a realistic hope for redemption in the future, life becomes frozen in the present. If this is true, then we have no choice but to live our lives as if the present state of things is all we have and all we are likely to have.

*Deflation* is the opposite: lower the bar of acceptance so that the expectations we have for the Messiah become more realistic. The most famous proponent of deflation is Maimonides, who argued that when the Messiah comes, the normal course of nature will remain the same.[7] There will still be rich and poor, healthy and sick, gifted and challenged. Put otherwise, the Days of the Messiah will not be an earthly paradise. People will still have to work for a living and deal with floods and droughts. The only difference between what we have now and what we will have then is that Israel will regain political sovereignty and live in peace with the other nations of the world. In this way, any reference to cosmic upheavals, new revelations, or radical changes in human nature are eliminated. But deflation too comes with a cost: to the degree that the bar of acceptance is lowered, it becomes easier for pretenders to claim they have crossed it.

*Marginalization* means arguing that the main challenge we face has always been remaining faithful to God and that everything else is a distant second. One can do this either by saying that the Messiah has already come or by downplaying the importance of his arrival.[8] A good way to understand this response is to say with Jacob Neusner that the purpose of religious life is not salvation, understood as a future event, but sanctification, understood as an ever-present possibility.[9]

*Internalization* involves claiming that the Messiah should not be understood as a historical figure but rather as an allegory for the transformation of an individual from a life of sin to a life of holiness. Accordingly each of us has the ability to bring about – or even to *be* – the Messiah by undergoing a change of heart and setting ourselves on the path of justice. In the words of Emmanuel Levinas: "The Messiah is Myself [*Moi*]; to be Myself is to be the Messiah."[10] Simply put, to be myself is to live up to the moral standards that I hold out for myself.

This position has always appealed to philosophers in the internalist tradition, which is to say those who measure the worth of an action by looking at the intention or sincerity of the agent who performs it rather than its outward manifestation. We can see such a view expressed in the writings of the prophets when they say that God is fed up with hymns and sacrificial offerings that the people have made because such things have not led to improvement in the moral quality of their actions. Are those who bring the sacrificial offerings really concerned about the poor and the sick or only with courting favor with an all-powerful deity in the interest of furthering their own ends? This motivates Hosea (6:6) to say in God's name: "I desire mercy, not sacrifice." The problem with internalization is that it severs any connection between messianism and the larger question of historical redemption. Important as it is, a change of one heart is not enough. The prophets longed for a day when the hearts of an entire nation would be changed and the results visible in the public arena.

Finally *deferral* means putting off the coming of the Messiah so that his arrival will come either in the distant future or, by some accounts, at infinity. This alternative is usually associated with Kant and culminates in the view that the Messiah should not be understood as a specific person who will come at an appointed time but rather as a moral ideal that history approaches asymptotically as the graph of a function approaches but never touches its axis. *Deferral* is a misleading description of this position if we take it to mean that the coming of the Messiah is an event that keeps getting put off in the way that one puts off going on a diet. Rather it is a way of describing humanity's quest for moral perfection. Although perfection is the goal, surely it is unrealistic to think – or presumptuous to claim – that perfection has or will ever be achieved.

According to Hermann Cohen, the most prominent Jewish representative of this position expressed it this way: "his [the Messiah's] coming is not an actual end, but means merely the infinity of his coming, which in turn means the infinity of development."[11] This is another way of saying that the messianic age is always ahead of us. As Steven Schwarzschild put it, "the Messiah not only has not come but also will never have come . . . [rather] he will always be coming."[12]

To understand Cohen's contribution to this discussion, we need to see that he changed the nature of the debate in several respects. First, where traditional Judaism envisioned the emergence of an extraordinary individual who would usher in and preside over a new age, Cohen focused his attention on the age itself.[13] For him any reference to a particular person would be tantamount to a return to mythology, where heroes engaged in super-human feats. According to Lenn Goodman, the shift from a personal Messiah to a messianic age is not as dramatic as it may appear because the cult of personal messiahship never really succeeded among the Jewish people.[14] While this may be true if we are talking about the people as a whole, we should not forget that false messiahs with personal cults were able to attract thousands, in some cases even millions, of followers and to wreak untold suffering. Even Maimonides looked forward to the day when a king would arise from the house of David.

Second, where traditional Judaism saw the restoration of political sovereignty to Israel as an essential feature of messianism, Cohen argues that messianism is by its very nature universal so that any hint of nationalistic pride is illegitimate. In his words: "Israel, as a nation, is nothing other than the mere symbol for the desired unity of mankind."[15] Finally, as we have seen, Cohen views the messianic age not as something that will be realized in future time but as an ideal toward which humanity must strive but always fall short.[16]

The problem with deferral as a solution to the problems posed by messianism was formulated by Franz Rosenzweig: if the Messiah is not coming for all eternity, then for all intents and purposes, he is not coming – to which we can add: if he is not coming, then there are no serious alternatives to what we currently have.[17] Again further explanation is required. The dispute between Cohen and Rosenzweig hangs on the question of whether humanity will ever be able to achieve everything that morality requires of it. For Cohen, as for Kant, there will always be something in human behavior that falls short of the ideal so that any person or group of people who claim to have achieved it are immediately suspect. Simply put: sin is inevitable.[18] If this is so, then the messianic age as Cohen understands it will always be out of reach.

Messianism began as a religious doctrine, a way of asking people to look beyond the misfortunes of the present and focus on what could be realized in the future. Up till now, I have discussed it in largely religious terms. It is noteworthy, however, that in the twentieth century, messianism took on a secular dimension. In one form, it played a crucial role in political movements like communism and fascism, both of which offered dire assessments of the current state of things and argued that nothing short of a fight to the finish could rectify them. In another form, it expressed itself as skepticism toward the progress that was supposed to take place as humanity liberated itself from superstition and adopted the rational ideals of the Enlightenment.

In the Jewish world, such skepticism can be seen in thinkers like Ernst Bloch, and Walter Benjamin.[19] Like the ancient prophets, both saw oppression and injustice everywhere. In their view, to suggest that we can correct them by making steady progress toward a better society in the manner suggested by Kant and Hegel is to cooperate with the very people one is trying to overthrow – the forces of appeasement. The only hope we have is for a force beyond history to burst onto the scene and free us from the tedium of living through an endless series of days each like the one before it. In this way, hope for a Messiah makes life worth living. To be sure, the nature of such a "Messiah" was largely undetermined and meant only a radical disruption of the present order in the form of either revolutionary socialism or some as yet unknown event.

Graetz is right to say that messianism is both Pandora's box and the elixir of life. Few ideas have had such a devastating impact on human history and yet few ideas are harder to do without. What then? To return to the five alternatives mentioned above, you can inflate the idea of a better future to the point where it becomes so unrealistic that the only sensible alternative is to live with what we have and try to make steady improvements. You can deflate it so that the mythological overtones disappear and the goal of realizing a messianic vision seems closer than one might think. You can internalize it or marginalize it. Finally you can follow Cohen by making it an ideal that history approaches but never fully attains.

The advantages of Cohen's view are easy to see: (1) Because we are talking about an infinite process, we will never be in the position of having to decide which claimants to the title of Messiah are genuine, and (2) we will never be guilty of the false conceit that comes with thinking that we have achieved the ultimate in human moral striving. The disadvantage is that this position is at odds with a principle that Kant himself insists on numerous times: "ought" implies "can." To say that I ought to do something is to say that I am capable of doing it. By contrast, if there is something I am not capable of doing, e.g., running a four minute mile, then one can hardly say that it is something I am obliged to do. As Cohen himself admits: "God can assign no task that would be a labor of Sisyphus."[20]

In Judaism, the "ought implies can" principle is asserted at the end of Deuteronomy (30:11–14), when Moses tells the people:

> What I am commanding you today is not too difficult for you or beyond your reach. It is not up in heaven, so that you have to ask: "Who will ascend into heaven to get it and proclaim it to us so we may obey it?" Nor is it beyond the sea, so that you have to ask: "Who will cross the sea to get it and proclaim it to us so we may obey it?" No, the word is very near you; it is in your mouth and in your heart so you may do it.

I take this to mean that the Torah was never meant to impose superhuman standards or to set a goal beyond the reach of human effort to achieve.

This presents us with a dilemma. One can reject the idea of a messianic future, but the costs of doing so are steep. Not only is it at odds with the whole Judeo-Christian tradition, it leaves us with no significant reply to the question: "What can I hope for?" Do we really want to say: "Not much more than what we already have?" I think not. On the other hand, if we accept the idea of a messianic future, we face the question of how to interpret it without succumbing to wishful thinking or apocalyptic visions.

My preference is to accept some form of deflation. While a serious alternative to the conditions we now have is possible, it will not require super-human effort, divine intervention, or a fight to the finish. Like Maimonides, I am suggesting that the end of history lies within the reach of history. By the end of history, I do not mean that every day will be perfect, that science will find answers to all its questions, that sickness and poverty will be eradicated, that the state will whither away, or that conflicts will no longer arise. To stay with Maimonides, I mean that peace will prevail, that the needy will be cared for, and that people will see that material comforts are not the be all and end all of human existence. Rather than constant preparation for war, humanity will devote itself to study, worship, artistic expression, and other ennobling ends.

Whether this age will be brought about by a single individual, an institution, or a host of institutions, no one can know. Nor can anyone know when it will occur and how long it will last. It is possible that having been achieved, it will eventually deteriorate so that historical progress will have to begin anew. All of these things are beyond our ability to predict.

My only claim is that belief in the coming of a messianic age is justified, if not on historical grounds, then at least on moral ones. It is not a matter of saying that if we continue on our current path, we will reach a new and better age because our current path seems to be going in the wrong direction. It is rather to say that it is within our power to change that path and fulfill our nature as human beings. If we do not succeed, then the problem is not that fate has intervened to stop us, that God has turned his back on us, or that the project was too difficult to begin with. As Joseph Soloveitchik put it: "God waits for man if there is something to be done. He does nothing until man initiates action."[21] The problem, then, will be that we did not try hard enough to live up to the expectations we set for ourselves.

## Notes

1  For a fuller treatment of this issue, see Seeskin 2012, especially chapter one.
2  Kant 1974.
3  Scholem 1971.
4  Josephus 1959. As Josephus goes on to say, the oracle was actually about Vespasian.
5  Graetz 1975.
6  For the variety of rabbinic views on the Messiah, see *BT Sanhedrin* 91b, 97a–b, 98a, 99a.
7  *Laws of Kings and Wars*, chapters 11–12 (trans. in Hershman 1959).

8　Note, as both Soloveitchik 2006, 153 and Goodman 2008, 164 do, that the suggestion that the Messiah has already come is met with rebuke.

9　Neusner 1984.

10　Levinas 1990.

11　Cohen 1972, 314–15.

12　Schwarzschild 1990.

13　Cohen 1972, 249.

14　Goodman 2008, 166.

15　Cohen 1972, 253.

16　Cf. Goodman 2008, 165: "Just as human strivings inform our vision of the messianic future, so the conception of that future gives orientation to those strivings and imparts a meaning to them even when they fail of their proximate goals."

17　Rosenzweig 1979.

18　Cohen 1972, 211–13.

19　Bloch 2000; Benjamin 2003.

20　Cohen 1972, 207.

21　Cf. Soloveitchik 2006, 152–3.

## Further Reading on Redemption and Messianism

Carmy, S. "Don't Stop Hoping For Redemption: Religious Optimism and the Meaning of Life," *Tradition* 39 (2006), 1–6.

Leibowitz, Y. *Judaism, Human Values, and the Jewish State*, trans. E. Goldman (Cambridge, MA: Harvard University Press, 1992), 106–27. [Chapters 10 and 11, on messianism].

Morgan, M. and S. Weitzman (eds.), *Rethinking the Messianic Idea in Judaism* (Bloomington, IN: Indiana University Press, 2015). [Introduction and chapters by M. Kellner, M. Morgan, B. Pollock, K. Seeskin, and D. Shatz].

Ravitzky, A. "'To the Utmost of Human Capacity': Maimonides on the Days of the Messiah," in *Perspectives on Maimonides: Philosophical and Historical Studies* ed. J. Kraemer (Oxford: Oxford University Press, 1991), 221–256.

Ravitzky, A. *Messianism, Zionism, and Jewish Religious Radicalism*, trans. M. Swirsky and J. Chipman (Chicago: University of Chicago Press, 1996).

Saadia Gaon. *The Book of Beliefs and Opinions*, trans. S. Rosenblatt (New Haven, CT: Yale Judaica Series, 1948/1976), 290–322 [Treatise VIII, concerning the redemption].

Scholem, G. *The Messianic Idea in Judaism and Other Essays on Jewish Spirituality* (New York: Schocken Books, 1971; 2nd ed., 1995), 1–77.

Seeskin, K. *Jewish Messianic Thoughts in an Age of Despair* (Cambridge: Cambridge University Press, 2012).

Soloveitchik, J. *Kol Dodi Dofek: Listen, My Beloved Knocks*, trans. D. Gordon and ed. J. Woolf (Jersey City, NJ: Ktav, 2006).

Spero, S. "Does Traditional Jewish Messianism Imply Inevitability? Is There a Political Role for Messianists in Israel Today?" *Modern Judaism* 8 (1988), 271–285.

# Part IV
# Practical Philosophy

# 10 Ritual and Rationality

In this general part on *Practical Philosophy* the focus is on legal, moral, and social and political philosophy. The reasons or explanations for the divine Law and for obedience to it, a problem in moral responsibility and agency that arises in Exodus when God 'hardens' Pharaoh's heart, the nature of repentance and forgiveness in Judaism, and finally the grounds for religious pluralism and toleration—all of these are issues discussed with subtlety by Jewish philosophers.

**Maimonides** was by no means the first to engage in the foundational project of *ta'amei ha-mitzvot*, ascertaining the reasons and purposes of the commandments. In the Jewish philosophical tradition, Saadia pre-empted him by more than two centuries. But no one surpassed Maimonides in his insistence that *all* the commandments, both *mishpatim* (judgments) and *hukkim* (statutes), are rational, at least in a general way. A product of divine wisdom, the commandments all serve a useful purpose, indeed they were instituted for a two-fold purpose, "the welfare of the soul" and "the welfare of the body." The commandments (the Law) serve both political and supra-political functions. They establish and harmonize a community and ultimately ground that community in the knowledge and service of God. As in any legal system, the devil is in the details, and Maimonides does not disappoint. But he is keen to point out "that wisdom rendered it necessary … that there should be particulars [of any law] for which no cause can be found." It is madness to ask why seven or eight lambs are prescribed for sacrifice. The project of *ta'amei ha-mitzvot* entails knowing the reasons for the commandments *and* that such inquiries are perforce limited in scope.

**Daniel Rynhold** focuses upon some of the minutiae of the Law in the Maimonidean scheme, and highlights the historical nature of the explanations that Maimonides offers to rationalize the *hukkim* (statutes). To understand the Talmudic laws of sacrifice (*korbanot*)—indeed *why* sacrifices, reminders of idolatrous worship, were retained and brought under legal jurisdiction— Maimonides refers to the ancient, polytheistic Sabians and their sacrificial cult, and he does so to underscore the importance of taking history and human nature into account in understanding the reasons for the Law and its ultimate goal of extirpating idolatrous worship. Given the social and psychological realities of the time, a wholesale revision of sacrificial worship would have been overwhelming and "would have seemed … tantamount to abandoning the only possible form of worship." As a result, an accommodation (a divine trick, in fact) was effected in the form of the *korbanot*: sacrificial worship was retained but shorn of all its idolatrous content. As Rynhold puts it: "If He is to achieve the governing first intention of the Law [knowledge of God and the extirpation of idolatry], God has to work with the social and psychological realities of the time and adapt the Law in accordance with them."

But a worry arises just here. If history and ancient idolatrous worship is offered as an explanation for the Law, then what *enduring* value does the Law have for us today? We are not Sabians, so why are the *korbanot* applicable to us? And if the sacrificial laws may be viewed as a relic, then what about other Laws? Antinomian concerns cannot easily be dismissed.

**Jed Lewinsohn** offers a close reading of the sixth chapter of Maimonides' *Shemonah Perakim* (*Eight Chapters*), the introduction to his commentary on Avot. As often with Maimonides, the issue on the table arises from a prima facie dilemma between philosophical and rabbinic sources. In this particular instance there is apparent disagreement between the philosophers and the rabbinic sages over the rank-ordering of the virtuous ("wholehearted") individual and the continent individual. The latter lacks the psychological integrity (the "wholeness") of his virtuous counterpart, and as a result the philosophers (read, Aristotle) rank-order virtue over continence, while the sages rank-order continence and psychological struggle over virtue. In a way it looks like a debate between Aristotle and Kant, and the relative value of virtue and moral struggle. For his part, Maimonides brings about "a wonderful reconciliation" of the two views by carefully demarcating "generally accepted laws" and "traditional laws"—in effect, *mishpatim* ('rational' laws such as those prohibiting murder and theft) and *hukkim* (ritual laws such as those prohibiting mixing meat with milk and wearing mixed fabric)—and arguing that the rank-ordering of virtue and continence must be relativized to the very distinction between rational and ritual laws. In particular, when the sages rank-order continence over wholeheartedness, it is (only) with reference to the *hukkim*, which "if it were not for the [divine] Law, they would not be bad at all." This discussion immediately raises a more general issue of moral motivation, and as Lewinsohn puts it, "of whether and how the subject of the divine command ought to engage with the extra-halakhic values ... in the course of the fulfillment of his legal requirements."

**MOSES MAIMONIDES (1138–1204)**

*The Guide of the Perplexed* **(1190)**

*Book 3, Chapters 26–8* **(tr. Pines)**

*The Reasons and Purpose of the Law*

CHAPTER 26

Just as there is disagreement among the men of speculation among the adherents of Law whether His works, may He be exalted, are consequent upon wisdom or upon the will alone without being intended toward any end at all, there is also the same disagreement among them regarding our Laws, which He has given to us. Thus, there are people who do not seek for them any cause at all, saying that all Laws are consequent upon the will alone. There are also people who say that every commandment and prohibition in these Laws is consequent upon wisdom and aims at some end, and that all Laws have causes and were given in view of some utility. It is, however, the doctrine of all of us—both of the multitude and of the elite—that all the Laws have a cause, though we ignore the causes for some of them and we do not know the manner in which they conform to wisdom. With regard to this the texts of the Bible are clear: "righteous statutes and judgments" (Deut. 4:8); "the judgments of the Lord are true, they are righteous altogether" (Ps. 19:10).

About the statutes designated as *hukkim*—for instance those concerning the "mingled stuff, meat in milk," and "the sending of the goat"—[the sages] make literally the following statement: "Things which I have prescribed for you, about which you have not the permission to think, which are criticized by Satan and refuted by the Gentiles" (Yoma 67b). They are not believed by the multitude of the sages to be things for which there is no cause at all and for which one must not seek an end. For this would lead, according to what we have explained, to their being considered as frivolous actions. On the contrary, the multitude of the sages believe that there indubitably is a cause for them—I mean to say a useful end—but that it is hidden from us either because of the incapacity of our intellects or the deficiency of our knowledge. Consequently there is, in their opinion, a cause for all the commandments; I mean to say that any particular commandment or prohibition has a useful end. In the case of some of them, it is clear to us in what way they are useful—as in the case of the prohibition of killing and stealing. In the case of others, their utility is not clear—as in the case of the interdiction of the "first products" (Lev. 19:23) (of trees) and of (sowing) "the vineyard with diverse seeds" (Deut. 22:9). Those commandments whose utility is clear to the multitude are called *mishpatim* (judgments), and those whose utility is not clear to the multitude are called *hukkim* (statutes). The sages always say with regard to the verse: "For it is no vain thing" (ibid. 32:47)—"And if it is vain, it is because of you"; meaning that this legislation is not a vain matter without a useful end and that if it seems to you that this is the case with regard to some of the commandments, the deficiency resides in your apprehension. You already know the tradition that is widespread among us according to which the causes for all the commandments, with the exception of that concerning the red heifer, were known to Solomon; and also their dictum that God hid the causes for the commandments in order that they should not be held in little esteem, as happened to Solomon with regard to the three commandments whose causes are made clear.

All their dicta proceed according to this principle, and the texts of the (Scriptural) books indicate it. However, I found in *Bereishit Rabbah* (ch. 44) a text of the sages from which it appears when one first reflects on it that some of the commandments have no other cause than merely to prescribe a law, without there having been in view in them any other end or any real utility. This is their dictum in that passage: "What does it matter to the Holy One, blessed be He, that animals are slaughtered by cutting their neck in front or in the back? Say therefore that the commandments were only given in order to purify the people. For it is said: 'The word of the Lord is purified' (Ps. 18:31)." Though this dictum is very strange and has no parallel in other dicta, I have interpreted it, as you will hear, in such a matter that we shall not abandon the views of all their dicta and we shall not disagree with a universally agreed upon principle, namely, that one should seek in all the Laws an end that is useful in regard to being: "For it is no vain thing" (Deut. 32:47). He says: "I said not to the seed of Jacob: Seek Me for nothing; I, the Lord, speak righteousness, I declare things that are right" (Is. 45:19).

What everyone endowed with a sound intellect ought to believe on this subject is what I shall set forth to you: The generalities of the commandments necessarily have a cause and have been given because of a certain utility; their details are that in regard to which it was said of the commandments that they were given merely for the sake of commanding something. For instance the killing of animals because of the necessity of having good food is manifestly useful, as we shall make clear (III, ch. 48). But the prescription that they should be killed through having the upper and not the lower part of their throat cut, and having their esophagus and windpipe severed at one particular place is, like other prescriptions of the same kind, imposed with a view to purifying the people. The same thing is made clear to you through their example: "Slaughtered by cutting their neck in front or in the back" (Gen. Rabbah, ch. 44). I have mentioned this example to you merely because one finds in their text: "Slaughtered by cutting their neck in front or in the back." However, if one studies the truth of the matter, one finds it to be as follows: As necessity occasions the eating of animals, the commandment was intended to bring about the easiest death in an easy manner. For beheading would only be possible with the help of a sword or something similar, whereas a throat can be cut with anything. In order that death should come about more easily, the condition was imposed that the knife should be sharp. The true reality of particulars of commandments is illustrated by the sacrifices. The offering of sacrifices has in itself a great and manifest utility, as I shall make clear. But no cause will ever be found for the fact that one particular sacrifice consists in a lamb and another in a ram and that the number of the victims should be one particular number. Accordingly, in my opinion, all those who occupy themselves with finding causes for something of these particulars are stricken with a prolonged madness in the course of which they do not put an end to an incongruity, but rather increase the number of incongruities. Those who imagine that a cause may be found for suchlike things are as far from truth as those who imagine that the generalities of a commandment are not designed with a view to some real utility.

Know that wisdom rendered it necessary—or, if you will, say that necessity occasioned—that there should be particulars for which no cause can be found; it was, as it were, impossible in regard to the Law that there should be nothing of this class in it. In such a case the impossibility is due to the circumstances that when you ask why a lamb should be prescribed and not a ram, the same question would have to be asked if a ram had been prescribed instead of a lamb. But one particular species had necessarily to be chosen. The same holds for your asking why seven lambs and not eight have been prescribed. For a similar question would have been put if eight or ten or twenty had been prescribed. However, one particular number had necessarily to be chosen. This resembles the nature of the possible, for it is certain that one of the possibilities will come to pass. And no question should be put why one particular possibility and not another comes to pass, for a similar question would become necessary if another possibility instead of this particular one had come to pass. Know this notion and grasp it. The constant statements of (the sages) to the effect that there are causes for all the commandments, as well as the opinion that the causes were known to Solomon, have in view the utility of a given commandment in a general way, not an examination of its particulars ...

CHAPTER 27

The Law as a whole aims at two things: the welfare of the soul and the welfare of the body. As for the welfare of the soul, it consists in the multitude's acquiring correct opinions corresponding to their respective capacity. Therefore some of them (namely, the opinions) are set forth explicitly and some of them are set forth in parables. For it is not within the nature of the common multitude that its capacity should suffice for apprehending that subject matter as it is. As for the welfare of the body, it comes about by the improvement of their ways of living one with another. This is achieved through two things. One of them is the abolition of their wronging each other. This is tantamount to every individual among the people not being permitted to act according to his will and up to the limits of his power, but being forced to do that which is useful to the whole. The second thing consists in the acquisition by every human individual of moral qualities that are useful for life in society so that the affairs of the city may be ordered. Know that as between these two aims, one is indubitably greater in nobility, namely, the welfare of the soul—I mean the procuring of correct opinions—while the second aim—I mean the welfare of the body—is prior in nature and time. The latter aim consists in the governance of the city and the well-being of the states of all its people according to their capacity. This second aim is the more certain one, and it is the one regarding which every effort has been made precisely to expound it and all its particulars. For the first aim can only be achieved after achieving this second one. For it has already been demonstrated that man has two perfections:

a first perfection, which is the perfection of the body, and an ultimate perfection, which is the perfection of the soul. The first perfection consists in being healthy and in the very best bodily state, and this is only possible through his finding the things necessary for him whenever he seeks them. These are his food and all the other things needed for the governance of his body, such as a shelter, bathing, and so forth. This cannot be achieved in any way by one isolated individual. For an individual can only attain all this through a political association, it being already known that man is political by nature. His ultimate perfection is to become rational *in actu*, I mean to have an intellect *in actu*; this would consist in his knowing everything concerning all the beings that it is within the capacity of man to know in accordance with his ultimate perfection. It is clear that to this ultimate perfection there do not belong either actions or moral qualities and that it consists only of opinions toward which speculation has led and that investigation has rendered compulsory. It is also clear that this noble and ultimate perfection can only be achieved after the first perfection has been achieved. For a man cannot represent to himself an intelligible even when taught to understand it and all the more cannot become aware of it of his own accord, if he is in pain or is very hungry or is thirsty or is hot or is very cold. But once the first perfection has been achieved it is possible to achieve the ultimate, which is indubitably more noble and is the only cause of permanent preservation.

The true Law then, which as we have already made clear (II, ch. 39) is unique—namely, the Law of Moses our Teacher—has come to bring us both perfections, I mean the welfare of the states of people in their relations with one another through the abolition of reciprocal wrongdoing and through the acquisition of a noble and excellent character. In this way the preservation of the population of the country and their permanent existence in the same order become possible, so that every one of them achieves his first perfection; I mean also the soundness of the beliefs and the giving of correct opinions through which ultimate perfection is achieved. The letter of the Torah speaks of both perfections and informs us that the end of this Law in its entirety is the achievement of these two perfections. For He, may He be exalted, says: "And the Lord commanded us to do all these statutes, to fear the Lord our God, for our good always, that He might preserve us alive, as it is at this day" (Deut. 6:24). Here He puts the ultimate perfection first because of its nobility; for, as we have explained, it is the ultimate end. It is referred to in the dictum: "For our good always." You know already what [the sages] have said interpreting His dictum: "That it may be well with you, and that you may prolong your days" (ibid. 22:7). They said: "That it may be well with you in a world in which everything is well and that you may prolong your days in a world the whole of which is long" (Kiddushin 39b; Hullin 142a). Similarly the intention of His dictum here, "For our good always," is this same notion: I mean the attainment of "a world in which everything is well and (the whole of which is) long." And this is perpetual preservation. On the other hand, His dictum, "That He might preserve us alive, as it is at this day," refers to the first and corporeal preservation, which lasts for a certain duration and which can only be well ordered through political association, as we have explained.

## CHAPTER 28

...[W]henever a commandment, be it a prescription or a prohibition, requires abolishing reciprocal wrongdoing, or urging to a noble moral quality leading to a good social relationship, or communicating a correct opinion that ought to be believed either on account of itself or because it is necessary for the abolition of reciprocal wrongdoing or for the acquisition of a noble moral quality, such a commandment has a clear cause and is of a manifest utility. No question concerning the end need be posed with regard to such commandments. For no one was ever so perplexed for a day as to ask why we were commanded by the Law that God is one, or why we were forbidden to kill and to steal, or why we were forbidden to exercise vengeance and retaliation, or why we were ordered to love each other. The matters about which people are perplexed and opinions disagree—so that some say that there is no utility in them at all except the fact of mere command, whereas others say that there is a utility in them that is hidden from us—are the commandments from whose external meaning it does not appear that they are useful according to one of the three notions we have mentioned: I mean to say that they neither communicate an opinion nor inculcate a noble quality nor abolish reciprocal wrongdoing. Apparently these commandments are not related to the welfare of the soul, as they do not communicate a belief, or to the welfare of the body, as they do not communicate rules useful for the governance of the city or for the governance of the household. Such, for instance, are the prohibitions of the "mingled stuff," of the "mingling" (of diverse species), and of "meat in milk," and the commandment "concerning the covering of blood, the heifer whose neck was broken," and the "firstling of an ass," and others of the same kind. However, you will hear my explanation for all of them and my exposition of the correct and demonstrated causes for them all with the sole exception—as I have mentioned to you—of details and particular commandments. I shall explain that all these and others of the same kind are indubitably related to one of the three notions referred to—either to the welfare of a belief or to the welfare of the conditions of the city, which is achieved through two things: abolition of reciprocal wrongdoing and acquisition of excellent characters.

Sum up what we have said concerning beliefs as follows: In some cases a commandment communicates a correct belief, which is the one and only thing aimed at—as, for instance, the belief in the unity and eternity of the Deity and in His not being a body. In other cases the belief is necessary for the abolition of reciprocal wrongdoing or for the acquisition of a noble moral quality—as, for instance, the belief that He, may He be exalted, has a violent anger against those who do injustice, according to what is said: "And My wrath shall wax hot, and I will kill" (Ex. 22:23), and so on, and as the belief that He, may He be exalted, responds instantaneously to the prayer of someone wronged or deceived: "And it shall come to pass, when he cries out to me, that I will hear; for I am gracious" (ibid. 22:26).

DANIEL RYNHOLD

## "Rationalizing the Commandments: The Maimonidean Method", from *Two Models of Jewish Philosophy: Justifying One's Practices* (2005)

### *Maimonides' Intellectualism*

According to Maimonides, there are those who do not believe that reasons should be given for any law, believing that if there were any utility in the laws for humans this would lessen their divinity. Inscrutability is somehow supposed to be a mark of the divine. Of course the question of whether or not God's commandments are merely dependent on His will or have some independent form of rationality that stems from their content is a question with a long history, given its best known formulation in Plato's *Euthyphro*. Within Judaism, the question of the *ta'am* (usually translated as 'reason') for the commandments had been discussed since Talmudic times, but more often than not the request for a *ta'am* was a request for the scriptural basis and subsequent derivation of a commandment, not its philosophical justification. In a philosophical context Philo had devoted much space to the question of the rationality of the commandments, though it was Saadia Gaon who brought the topic to the fore in medieval times with his introduction of the specific category of rational commandments. Saadia was much influenced by the Mu'tazilite school of Kalam theologians for whom God was subject to an objective standard of justice, a view opposed by the Ash'arite school, according to which God must be the only source of value. Against a background in which this Ash'arite view, with al-Ghazali as its most influential proponent, had become the theological orthodoxy in the Islamic world, Maimonides comes down unequivocally on the side of extreme intellectualism ...

### *Maimonides' Teleological Rationalization of the Commandments*

... Maimonides thinks it obvious that the commandments were given in order to bring about the perfection of man, and this would be the realization of his form. What he attempts to do therefore is draw out the causal connections between the commandments and the form of man. Thus, at *Guide* III: 27, where he initially discusses the purpose of the 'Law as a whole' he writes:

> The Law as a whole aims at two things: the welfare of the soul and the welfare of the body. As for the welfare of the soul, it consists in the multitude's acquiring correct opinions corresponding to their respective capacity ... As for the welfare of the body, it comes about by the improvement of their ways of living one with another.
>
> (*Guide* III: 27, 510)

With these notions of the welfare of the body and soul in play, Maimonides then goes on to discuss two corresponding perfections:

For it has already been demonstrated that man has two perfections: a first perfection, which is the perfection of the body, and an ultimate perfection, which is the perfection of the soul. The first perfection consists in being healthy and in the very best bodily state ... His ultimate perfection is to become rational *in actu*, I mean to have an intellect *in actu*; ... It is clear that to this ultimate perfection there do not belong either actions or moral qualities and that it consists only of opinions toward which speculation has led and that investigation has rendered compulsory.

*(Guide* III: 27, 510–11)

It appears as if the welfare of the body is a function of social order and a necessary prerequisite for the welfare of the soul, which consists in the multitude gaining correct opinions in speculative matters. The perfections of body and soul on the other hand consist respectively of the physical health of the individual and the acquisition of correct opinions 'that investigation has rendered compulsory'... [W]e can readily understand this as referring to opinions that have actually been demonstrated rather than simply accepted on some other basis such as the authority of tradition.

The commandments, we are told, aim at the two perfections and generally do so via the establishment of the two types of welfare.

The True Law then ... has come to bring us both perfections, I mean the welfare of the states of people in their relations with one another through the abolition of reciprocal wrongdoing and through the acquisition of a noble and excellent character. In this way the preservation of the population of the country and their permanent existence in the same order become possible, so that every one of them achieves his first perfection; I mean also the soundness of the beliefs and the giving of correct opinions through which the ultimate perfection is achieved.

*(Guide* III: 27, 511)

The commandments therefore regulate society (welfare of the body) so as to allow for the health of the individual (perfection of the body), or teach correct opinions (welfare of the soul) as a precursor to further investigation in which these opinions and others that are not explicitly taught can be demonstrated (leading to the perfection of the soul). The commandments are rational inasmuch as they fulfil these aims and the Torah is seen as a means to achieving these ends to the extent that is possible for all society.

However, as indicated in this paragraph by his use of the term 'ultimate perfection', for Maimonides both the two perfections and the two aims of the Law are arranged in a hierarchical order just as they are in Book X of Aristotle's *Nicomachean Ethics*: 'know that between these two aims one is indubitably greater in nobility, namely the welfare of the soul' *(Guide* III: 27, 510).

While the precise nature of this ultimate perfection is a hotly disputed topic in Maimonidean scholarship, the final end for man appears to be theoretical rather than practical for Maimonides, as he states quite unequivocally in a number of places in the *Guide*:

> The fourth species is the true human perfection; it consists in the acquisition of the rational virtues—I refer to the conception of intelligibles, which teach true opinions concerning the divine things. This is in true reality the ultimate end; this is what gives the individual true perfection, a perfection belonging to him alone; and it gives him permanent perdurance; through it man is man.
>
> (*Guide* III: 54, 635)

This theoretical perfection, which is gained by knowledge of God and 'divine things', is, of course, the form of man and as such is the fundamental explanatory concept in rationalizing the commandments. But since man's form is the starting point Maimonides can therefore give a scientific explanation of the rationality of the commandments by finding the teleological causal connection between them and man's form. Beginning from the form of man, we are able to deduce the commandments from starting points that fulfil the various conditions of truth, necessity, 'primitiveness', etc.

This leads us to conclude that Maimonides rationalizes the commandments by showing how they fit into an overall theory that begins from minimal (by Maimonidean standards) universal and necessary assumptions about the form of humanity. As such, we appear to have found a foundation on the basis of which we might demonstrate the entire system of commandments. As Twersky writes, the rationalization of the commandments is an entirely deductive enterprise for Maimonides that 'at least in part, is as precise and objective as any scientific discipline' (Twersky 1980, 402).

The intellectual religious task that remains for Maimonides, therefore, is to reconstruct this knowledge so as to come to know the commandments in their relationship to the ultimate end for man. Such a reconstruction is no easy task and Maimonides himself does not actually believe that he can construct such a system. Though all of the laws do have reasons, 'we ignore the causes for some of them and we do not know the manner in which they conform to wisdom' (*Guide* III: 26, 507). As Stern [1998] puts it, we must separate the ontological claim that the commandments have causes from the epistemological point that we may not always be able to discover them, and Maimonides gives specific reasons for our inability to understand certain commandments as being either because of 'the incapacity of our intellects or the deficiency of our knowledge' (*Guide* ibid.).

There are, as we shall see, some rather more far-reaching reasons why we might be incapable of producing the strictly demonstrative Aristotelian model for the system of the commandments. But before turning to these we must first complete our exposition of the Maimonidean method by considering his famously problematic explanations of the *huqqim*.

*Rationalizing Huqqim and Historical Explanations*

Maimonides believed that all the Laws have a cause: 'It is, however, the doctrine of all of us—both of the multitude and of the elite—that all the Laws have a cause, though we ignore the causes for some of them and we do not know the manner in which they conform to wisdom' (*Guide* III: 26, 507).

Such a thoroughgoing intellectualism was a new departure, for whilst traditionally the *mishpatim* (judgements) were accepted as rational in some sense, the commandments known as *huqqim* (statutes) were believed to be dependent entirely upon the will of God for their validity, lacking any such rational back-up. Moreover, though the list of *huqqim* was very limited in rabbinic tradition, Maimonides extended it to cover entire categories of law that had not previously been subsumed under that heading. Most notably, in the *Mishneh Torah* he identifies all the sacrificial laws and all the laws regarding purity and impurity as *huqqim*.

The problem with extending the category in this way is that whilst the form of explanation that we have been discussing might seem viable for the moral laws, it is more problematic for these *huqqim*, which according to Maimonides' categorization constitute far more than a few anomalies. How do the sacrificial laws, for example, contribute to human perfection?

The first thing that Maimonides does is recast the distinction between *mishpatim* and *huqqim* by saying that the only difference between them is the transparency of their utility to the multitude; the utility of the *mishpatim* is clear to the multitude, whilst that of the *huqqim* requires more research. Both though admit of rational explanation, and such a thoroughgoing intellectualism is licensed by Deuteronomy 4:6: 'Keep them therefore and do them; for this is your wisdom and your understanding in the sight of the nations, who shall hear all these statutes, and say, Surely, this great nation is a wise and understanding people.'

How, the argument goes, could the nations of the world appreciate the wisdom and understanding of the Jewish people through their statutes if they are unintelligible in principle? Rather, there must be universal criteria of truth that we all share and that can be used to rationalize these laws. How though can this rationality be demonstrated? Essentially, Maimonides does not deviate from the teleological model of explanation that we have been discussing but supplements it with historical/genetic explanations. Taking his rationalization of sacrifices as an example, he begins by subsuming them under the general category of laws of worship, which as a group contribute to the final intellectual perfection by realizing God's 'first intention of the Law' (*Guide* III: 29, 517). This first intention we are told is 'the apprehension of Him, may He be exalted, and the rejection of *idolatry*' (*Guide* III: 32, 527), a rejection that is so total that it has 'to wipe out its traces and all that is bound up with it, even its memory as well as all that leads to any of its works' (*Guide* III: 29, 517). Commandments that direct our attention towards God and away from such false opinions are therefore said to be of great utility and the sacrificial laws are seen as instrumental in achieving this end, thus giving us a teleological explanation for them akin to those given for the *mishpatim*.

However, this explanation as it stands is extremely problematic since there does not seem to be any reason to assume that the sacrificial laws should communicate these correct opinions. In fact the sacrificial cult is a prominent part of the Sabian culture, the ancient polytheistic civilization discussed at some length by Maimonides at *Guide* III: 29, and used as a subsequent point of reference throughout his discussion of *ta'amei ha-mitzvot*. This idolatrous culture, with its belief in astrology and utilization of myth and magic in order to serve the stars, was precisely what, according to Maimonides, the Torah laws were supposed to be effacing. How, then, could laws that incorporate idolatrous practices serve to produce correct opinions?

In order to give a full rationalization of these commandments Maimonides has to appeal to 'the second intention' of the law, whereby in order to realize its first intention, the law must take historical circumstance and human psychology into account. This necessitates supplementing the teleological structure by adding an historical explanation that uses historical information together with certain general assumptions about the causal relevance of this information to explain the evolution of a system out of an earlier system.

Maimonides' first example of the use of this second intention is found at *Guide* III: 30, where he tells how the priests of idolatry would preach the close link between star worship and agricultural success. Worship of the planets leads to agricultural plenty, whereas neglect of such worship leads to drought and calamity. In order to efface such idolatrous ideas, God had to reverse this mindset for the people of Israel. However, God could not do so by denying the link between worship and material gain. If He is to achieve the governing first intention of the Law, God has to work with the social and psychological realities of the time and adapt the Law in accordance with them. The Torah therefore speaks of how the worship of the stars would lead to drought and calamity whilst the worship of God would lead to material plenty, since this is the scheme that the people understood. Given people's inability to comprehend the ultimate intellectual reward that is the true purpose of worship, the use of such language is a necessity. It is only through the holding out of such promises that people will be weaned away from idolatrous belief and practice onto belief in and practice of the Torah. But of course, in truth Maimonides is no great advocate of the idea of material reward and punishment for the observance of the Law. At best, material gains (or losses) are seen as instrumental in providing (or hindering) the conditions under which one can gain the ultimate intellectual perfection. They are certainly not the ultimate rewards or punishments.

It is just this gradualism, that takes account of human nature in the attempt to realize the first intention of the Law, that we find in Maimonides' rationalization of the *huqqim* generally. Thus, in his explanation of sacrifices, Maimonides similarly gives us a description of the Sabian modes of worship and explains how they were relevant to the evolution of the Judaic sacrificial cult. The fundamental psychological fact again is that people who become accustomed to certain ideas are unable to adopt a wholesale revision of them. Had God commanded the abolition of sacrifices during that historical period it would have seemed to the people to be tantamount to abandoning the only possible form of worship. Taking this into account, God prescribed a modified version of the sacrificial cult, thereby safeguarding the people's trust in the law and purifying the sacrificial cult of all its idolatrous elements, transforming it into a more legitimate form of worship. So Maimonides combines certain psychological generalizations about human nature with historical information about the Sabian culture in order to show that the system of sacrifices was a kind of divine trick (termed 'wily graciousness' by Maimonides). The trick consisted of God using modified idolatrous practices in order to wean the people off idolatrous worship altogether.

> If you consider the divine actions—I mean to say the natural actions—the deity's wily graciousness and wisdom, as shown in the creation of living beings, in the gradation of the motions of the limbs, and the proximity of some of the latter to others, will through them become clear to you ... Many things in our Law are due to something similar to this very governance on the part of Him who governs ... For a sudden transition from one opposite to another is impossible. And therefore man, according to his nature, is not capable of abandoning suddenly all to which he was accustomed ... For just as it is not in the nature of man that, after having been brought up in a slavish service occupied with clay, bricks, and similar things, he should all of a sudden wash off from his hands the dirt deriving from them and proceed immediately to fight against the children of Anak, so it is also not in his nature that, after having been brought up upon very many modes of worship and of customary practices, which the souls find so agreeable that they become as it were a primary notion, he should abandon them all of a sudden.
>
> (*Guide* III: 32, 525–8)

Effectively therefore, while some laws such as those pertaining to prayer 'come close', though notably are not identified with the direct realization of the first intention of the Law described above, the sacrificial laws 'pertain to a second intention' (*Guide* III: 32, 529). What we see here when faced with the *huqqim* is a clash between the ideal of what worship of God should be like and the demands of human nature given the historical circumstances of the legislation. In the final analysis, sacrifices are rational because given the exigencies of human nature, they were necessary as a means to the final end of intellectual perfection. They belong, however, to the second intention of the Law in not requiring the abolition of all modes of worship that might originally have had idolatrous associations, but rather accommodating some such practices as a concession to human nature.

Certainly, not all of the *huqqim* were accommodatory in this fashion. Many were more directly opposed to Sabian practices. Thus, *sha'atnez* [wearing mixed fabric] was prohibited precisely because of its use in the garments of the Sabian priests (*Guide* III: 37, 544); or, contrariwise, the positive use of sheep, goat, and oxen in the sacrificial cult was dictated by the prohibition on killing such animals amongst different Sabian sects (*Guide* III: 46, 581–2). The particular type of *hoq* presumably depended on the psychological needs of the people regarding each of the particular Sabian practices that a commandment was addressing. But again the pattern of explanation for such *mitzvot* remains historical and this approach is extremely characteristic of the section of the *Guide* under discussion. Though we have focused primarily on this general explanation of sacrifices ..., one could choose any number of *huqqim* in order to make the same point. But while we needn't get into the details of these explanations, what we need to stress is that in general we still end up with a teleological method of explanation for all of these commandments. The historical supplements are there to show how the *huqqim* are directed towards man's *telos* by God's wisdom. Ultimately, the history is a servant to the teleology.

### Critique of the Maimonidean Method: History and Antinomianism

The most famous criticisms of Maimonides' rationalization are usually directed at his use of historical explanations and can be well illustrated by reference to his use of idolatrous practices in order to explain the *huqqim*. Such associations in themselves might be problematic in the eyes of many and lead them to doubt the validity of commandments that have such associations. However, the problem that has exercised Maimonides' critics in this regard is that the historical explanations imply that commandments like those connected to sacrifices have outlived their usefulness. If the sacrificial laws were understood to be means to the specified end, but only due to the historical circumstances, the fact that these circumstances no longer apply would appear to make it rational to choose more efficient means to the end, means that are more amenable to the modern religious consciousness for example. According to Maimonides' reasoning one could argue that since we are no longer held in thrall by idolatry and understand that one can communicate with God in other ways, by praying for instance, why not pray rather than sacrifice? Indeed, according to Stern, it is the very risk of antinomianism that defines Maimonides' reconceptualization of the notion of a *hoq*. Maimonides redefines *huqqim* as problematic commandments whose utility is not made manifest to the multitude for this very reason. The *huqqim* are not commandments without reasons, but rather commandments whose reasons would, if revealed to the multitude, cause problems for their faith given their idolatrous associations and historicity (Stern 1998, chapter 2).

The problems raised here for the authority of the Law are many and varied. Can the Law adapt in order to take historical changes into account? And if not, what obligates a person to continue to adhere to the laws in question? Is there any reason now to perform these commandments given that the historical approach does not furnish us with any sort of reason that we can use? One can in fact find answers, at times explicit, at times less so, to some of these questions in the *Guide* ...

...[I]t is possible that [such] criticism is not entirely fair to Maimonides, who might not have been attempting to do anything other than give reasons that would have been valid in biblical times. Indeed, he states explicitly during the discussion of *ta'amei ha-mitzvot* that 'at present my purpose is to give reasons for the [biblical] texts and not for the pronouncements of the legal science' (*Guide* III: 41, 558). Our argument here, though, is that at a purely philosophical level the eternity of these laws and the reason one ought to perform them cannot be directly derived from Maimonides' rationalization, at least not as we have presented it.

But again, what is of interest here is that it is not in fact the historical explanations that would lead to the heterodox conclusions. If we were to criticize the commandments purely in terms of these historical considerations, we would indeed be committing the genetic fallacy of judging the validity of the commandments in terms of their causal origins. But the real problem is the teleological structure to which these historical explanations are subordinated. The reason we believe that the commandments are no longer rational is because they no longer serve the ends that Maimonides believes once rationalized them. The historical explanations merely serve to make this clear, showing that the ritual commandments no longer stand in any instrumental relationship to these ends. But it is the teleological structure into which they are then inserted that causes the problems of heterodoxy, for the commandments no longer lead to the end posited by Maimonides as the reason for their existence. The problem therefore is that Maimonides rationalizes the commandments in terms of a means–end relationship and the historical explanations make it clear that this relationship no longer holds. But the historical explanations are only relevant to our recognition of the rationality or validity of the commandments. They are not relevant to the substantive rationality of the commandments themselves.

Thus, whilst the historical part of Maimonides' rationalization has traditionally come in for the most criticism, it is only when combined with the teleological approach that the central problems arise. And this of course means that the problem pervades Maimonides' entire approach. It is not simply a problem for the historical explanations of the *huqqim*. It is a problem for any teleological approach to the commandments ...


### JED LEWINSOHN

### "Reasons for Keeping the Commandments: Maimonides and the Motive of Obedience"

The investigations that are pursued or classified under the heading of *taamei ha-mitzvot* ("reasons for the commandments") purport to specify the values realized by specific laws in the halakhic corpus. Although the immediate aim of such investigations is to identify the considerations that might have led a divine lawmaker to issue particular commands, the values that are identified as reasons for the commandments may also be marshaled as reasons for acting in conformity with the law. Conversely, the specter of antinomianism is raised by the possibility that compliance would not serve the values on account of which the law was first promulgated; a possibility that might arise, for example, if the values in question would not be promoted by compliance in a particular historical context, or if the values could be promoted just as well (or even better) without compliance in a given case.[1] In order to counter such a challenge, a defender of the law would need to either point to the existence of other reasons that could supplement the reasons that were deemed insufficient on a particular occasion, or else offer a theory of authority that would apply even when there is daylight between the lawmaker's reasons and a subject's particular circumstances – that is, a theory that would explain why there is a duty to obey the law even when the lawmaker's reasons for issuing the command related to values or interests that would not be undermined by disobedience on a particular occasion.

The problem of antinomianism rears its head in the context of *taamei ha-mitzvot* because the latter project throws into sharp relief the existence of an axiological domain that is in some fairly robust sense independent of the halakha. After all, it is only if a given value does not owe its appeal or validity entirely to the existence of a particular law that it can be used to *explain* why that law might have been brought into existence by a rational lawmaker. Once such an independent evaluative domain has been acknowledged, however, the question arises as to why it should not be appealed to directly as sole polestar of our practical lives, and it is this possibility of discarding the legal intermediary that, at the most basic level, underwrites the aforementioned antinomian challenge. However, antinomianism is by no means the only problem that arises for the halakhically-oriented Jew when confronted by the reality of an independent domain of value that serves to rationalize the halakha. Less hostile from the point of view of halakha, though no less vexing, is the question of whether and how the subject of the divine command ought to engage with the extra-halakhic values – as opposed to the command alone – in the course of the fulfillment of his legal requirements, and it is this question of motivation that I would like to consider.

No treatment of the relation between reasons for the commandment, on the one hand, and the motivation for compliance with the commandments, on the other hand, has been more influential than that offered by Maimonides in the sixth of his *Eight Chapters* ("EC6"), and in the present essay I will do no more than subject his account to scrutiny.[2] In EC6, Maimonides purports to resolve an apparent conflict between "the philosophers" and the "sages" regarding the relative merits of wholehearted and continent individuals. The continent individual, according to Maimonides, "performs virtuous actions, he does good things ... while strongly desiring to perform bad actions." By contrast, the wholehearted individual, free from such internal conflict, "does good things ... while strongly desiring them" (78). Having drawn this contrast, Maimonides goes on to observe that "there is agreement among the philosophers that the virtuous man is ... more perfect than the continent man." According to the sages, by contrast, "someone who craves and strongly desires transgressions is more ... perfect than someone who does not crave them and suffers no pain in abstaining from them" (79). In rehearsing the rabbinic view, Maimonides does not merely attribute to them the understanding that the continent individual, on account of overcoming her conflicting impulses, deserves more reward or praise than her wholehearted counterpart. More significantly, he reads them as prescribing how we are to exercise the control we have over our own psychological constitutions.

Even more significant is their *commanding* a man to be continent and their *forbidding* him to say: 'I would not naturally yearn to commit this transgression, even if it were not prohibited by the Law.' This is what they say: Rabban Shimon ben Gamliel says: 'Let a man not say, "I do not want to eat meat with milk, I do not want to wear mixed fabric [*shaatnez*], I do want to have illicit sexual relations," but [rather let him say] "I want to, but what shall I do? – my Father in heaven has forbidden me."'

(79, emphasis added)

Note that on Maimonides' interpretation, the norm promulgated by R. Shimon ben Gamliel[3] does not merely enjoin one from *saying* that one does not desire to transgress; additionally, one must actually take care to retain the desire to transgress, for it is only by so doing that one could fulfill the commandment "to *be* continent." And later in the same chapter, Maimonides clarifies that the sages "said that a man *needs* to let his soul remain attracted to them and *not place* any obstacle before them other than the law" (80, emphasis added). The normative thrust of Maimonides' interpretation is significant, since there are certainly occasions in rabbinic literature – and also in Maimonides' own corpus – where a ranking of relative merits is devoid of such implications. For instance, to use two related examples, when the sages say that "he who is commanded and performs is greater than he who is not commanded and performs" (*Gadol ha-metzuveh ve-osseh*), this cannot be understood as imposing a requirement to join the class of the commanded, not least because it is so often out of an individual's control whether or not he or she is commanded to perform some act.[4] Even more clearly, Maimonides' statement that "repentant individuals are greater than those who never sinned at all" cannot be understood as a license, let alone an imperative, for transgression.[5]

Maimonides resolves the apparent conflict between the philosophers and the sages by restricting the scope of the rabbinic holding to the class of ritual commandments. More specifically, he invokes the rabbinic distinction between two classes of halakhic commandment, *hukkim* and *mishpatim*, and limits the rabbinic endorsement of continence only to the *hukkim*. Quite clearly, in considering this resolution much turns on how the categories *hukkim* and *mishpatim* are understood.

### Mishpatim and Hukkim

Maimonides offers three closely related, but non-identical, characterizations of each of the categories. He begins by quoting, approvingly, the primary tannaitic characterization of *mishpatim* that appears in the form of a gloss on a verse in Leviticus, "Mine ordinances (*mishpatim*) shall ye do, and My statutes (*hukkim*) shall ye keep, to walk therein: I am the LORD your God" (18:4). On the tannaitic construal, the *mishpatim* refer to those laws, which, "if it were not for the law, it would be proper (*din*) to write them".[6] This is to say that were the *mishpatim* not commanded, there would have been decisive reason, perhaps amounting to a rational requirement, for a human community to impose them.[7] Since the categories of *hukkim* and *mishpatim* are mutually exclusive and jointly exhaustive of all the commandments, this implies a corresponding characterization of *hukkim* as those commandments which, had they not been written, are not such that it would have been proper (*din*) to write them. However, instead of spelling out this implied characterization of the *hukkim*, Maimonides says that they enjoin acts that, "if it were not for the Law, would not be bad at all" (80). Assuming that this is intended as a sufficient condition of *hukkim* (and not merely as something that is true of all *hukkim*, but possibly of some *mishpatim* as well), the characterization implies that *mishpatim* forbid actions that would have been wrong even if they had not been prohibited by the Divine Law. On one reading of this formulation, the actions would be wrong *in virtue of* the "logical" legislation that human communities would, presumably, impose. On another reading, the actions would be wrong whether or not forbidden by positive or customary law, human or divine. This latter reading presupposes a non-conventional conception of morality, according to which an act can be wrong even if not acknowledged as such by human practices or divine decrees. The third, and final element of Maimonides' characterization of the distinction is that the laws that are "called commandments [*mishpatim*] in the explanation of the sages" forbid acts and omissions "*generally accepted by all the people as bad*, such as murder, theft, robbery, fraud, harming an innocent man, repaying a benefactor with evil, degrading parents, and things like these" (79, emphasis added). The significance of this general acceptance for Maimonides is not altogether obvious: perhaps the fact that all of humanity actually does accept the *mishpatim* is good reason for thinking that the community *would* have accepted the norms even if they had not been halakhically mandated. Alternatively, more in line with a non-conventionalist approach, perhaps the fact that specific norms are generally accepted constitutes evidence that these norms are valid, and valid for reasons independent of their inclusion in the halakhic corpus.

EC6 is often read as implying that *hukkim* "have no reason for their legislation independent of the fact that they are commanded by God" (Stern 1998, 53). Although this interpretation is widely held, it is, I believe, based on a misreading.[8] Maimonides does not, in fact, state in that chapter that the *hukkim* were legislated for no reason. Rather, as we have seen, he excludes the *hukkim* from the class of halakhic norms that every community would have decisive reason to impose in the absence of halakhic recognition. In order to see why this does not entail that God legislated for no reason, we need to understand why God's reasons need not provide human communities with decisive reason to impose the *hukkim* on their own initiative, and to do so we need look no further than the reasons Maimonides himself offers for the *hukkim* in his later works.

In his *Guide of the Perplexed*, Maimonides maintains that the first intention of Jewish law is the eradication of idolatrous beliefs and practices (3.29). Since the idolatrous Sabian cult exercised significant sway over the early Israelites, a portion of the divine laws – the *hukkim*, in general, and the laws governing sacrifices and purity, in particular – were designed to influence those caught in the grip of Sabian practices, and can only be explained by reference to those practices.[9] Since, according to this view, the *hukkim* are explained by the specific historical situation of the early Israelites, the reasons to impose them would not apply to human communities operating in relevantly different times and places.[10]

The reasons for the commandments sporadically offered in Maimonides' legal code, *Mishneh Torah*, in contrast with those given systematically in the *Guide*, rarely make reference to the historical situation of the early Israelites and instead depict the commandments, in the words of a leading commentator, as "primarily concerned with bringing to the surface those underlying motives and goals which discipline the human faculties, quell evil impulses, subdue inclination to vices, discipline the moral disposition and advance the individual toward ethical-intellectual perfection."[11] For example, "as long as phylacteries are on a man's head and arm, he is humble and God-fearing, is not drawn into frivolity and idle talk, does not dwell on evil thoughts but occupies his mind with thoughts of truth and righteousness" (*Laws of Tefillin*, 4:25). Even in the case of immersion rites prescribed for the ritually impure, Maimonides suggests "a moral basis" for the "divine decree": "[The immersion ritual teaches or reminds us that] just as one who sets his heart on becoming clean becomes clean as soon as he has immersed himself, although nothing new has befallen his body, so, too, one who sets his heart on cleansing himself from the uncleanness that beset men's souls – namely, wrongful thoughts and false convictions – becomes clean as soon as he consents in his heart to shun those counsels and brings his soul into the waters of pure reason" (*Laws of Mikvaot* 11:12).

In contrast with the historical reasons offered in the *Guide* – where, "if we knew the particulars of those practices and heard details concerning those opinions, we would become clear regarding the wisdom manifested in the details of the practices prescribed in the commandments" (3.49) – these more generally applicable reasons radically *underdetermine* the *hukkim* in the sense that there is an indefinite number of rituals that could have served the same purposes. Accordingly, there is no reason why even a community committed to these ends – that is, to encouraging its members to shun lives of frivolity, and to inculcating a vivid sense of the possibility of atonement – should be, in the absence of divine mandate, under any rational pressure to institute rituals involving *tefillin* or *mikvah*.[12]

To be sure, the issue of underdetermination must be handled with some delicacy if the distinction between *hukkim* and *mishpatim* is to be preserved. After all, surely there are aspects of the halakha's treatment of robbery, for example, that are not so narrowly tailored to the guiding values of the law of property as to preclude reasonable divergence by other legal regimes. In the absence of halakhic guidance, should a community be faulted for not imposing a fine on a robber (but not a burglar) in the amount of exactly double the value of the stolen object, with exceptions for cases involving stolen sheep or ox, where the fine rises to four or five times the value of the slaughtered animal, respectively? Nevertheless, even if one is unwilling to insist on the status of proper "*din*" at this level of detail, one may characterize the Jewish laws related to robbery at a sufficiently abstract level – for example, by invoking the notions of compensation and penalties and not the particular amounts owed – such that the characterization applies not only to halakha's treatment of the subject matter but to that of any reasonable regime of private property. By contrast, in the case of *tefillin* and *mikvah*, there is arguably no statement of the rule at any level of generality that reaches the level of *din* for all human communities.

There is another reason, apart from their underdetermination of the laws, that the rationales offered in the *Mishneh Torah* would not give human communities decisive reason to legislate on their own. Many of the ends attributed to the ritual law in that work are only advanced if the law is perceived by its subjects as emanating from a divine source. In such cases, human communities could not plausibly appeal to the same ends in an effort to justify imposing the norm on their own, much less be subjected to criticism for failing to do so.

### Duty vs. Inclination

Equipped with the foregoing account of the *hukkim-mishpatim* distinction, we may turn to consider the bearing of the distinction on the rabbinic endorsement of continent observance of the law. Notwithstanding the influence of Maimonides' interpretation, and its air of plausibility, it is by no means obvious why norms governing our desires and impulses should be sensitive to the distinction between *hukkim* and *mishpatim*. For even if it is true that some kinds of behavior would not be bad were it not for a law that human communities would have no decisive reason to impose on their own, the fact remains that, on Maimonides' understanding, the *hukkim were* in fact laid down, by no less an authority than God, in the service of important ends. Moreover, presumably there are myriad counterfactual scenarios that would dislodge the "logical" status of many of the *mishpatim* as well, and so it cannot be the logical contingency of the *hukkim* alone (i.e., their sensitivity to counterfactuals) that justifies their differential treatment. For example, in a world where resources were not scarce and where humans were marked by boundless altruism, it is doubtful that there would be decisive reasons for communities to prohibit stealing.

Several explanations of the rabbinic endorsement of continent observance must be briefly considered only to be set aside. While the sheer effort and determination needed to overcome wayward desires presumably contributes to the greater praise owed to the continent individual according to the Rabbis (for whom, as Maimonides quotes, "the reward is in accordance with the pain"), the struggle to resist temptation cannot explain the normative thrust of Maimonides' construal of Rabbi Shimon's teaching (80). As we have seen, as a general matter a relative ranking of types of individuals does not entail a prescription to join the higher rank, and surely a life of halakhic observance is sufficiently challenging as to render implausible a putative requirement to manufacture further obstacles solely to make observance more difficult. Likewise, the normative thrust of the teaching rules out the interpretation that "[i]n the discussion in [*Eight Chapters*], the only question is whether having ongoing inner impulses and desires toward evil, although they are controlled at the behavioral level, is in itself bad" (Spero 1983, 343 n. 37). This interpretation, like the previous one, is not altogether beside the point: it is presumably true that the Rabbis would not have recommended the acquisition or preservation of impulses and appetites that they regarded as intrinsically bad, and would have adopted a different position if they held that reasons not to *perform* forbidden acts are equally reasons not to *desire* to perform them. However, it does not follow, from the fact that it is not intrinsically bad to have certain desires and impulses, that one ought to acquire or preserve such desires and impulses. To reach the latter, prescriptive conclusion on the basis of views about the intrinsic value of the desires and impulses in question, the Rabbis would have needed to hold that such desires and impulses are not only *not* intrinsically bad, but also intrinsically *good* or *desirable*. But it is difficult to take such a position seriously, and Spero, to his credit, does not attribute it to them. However, by the same token he fails to explain the prescriptive dimension of the rabbinic teaching.

This leads us to a third explanation, based on the value of acting from the motive of obedience to God's command. Recall that R. Shimon, as understood by Maimonides, held not only that we should preserve our desire for the forbidden objects, but also that we obey out of recognition of the divine command ("because our Father in heaven has forbidden it"), and the present suggestion is that the reason for the former directive is to enable compliance with the latter. A glaring problem with this suggestion is that it is by no means obvious *why* acting from the motive of obedience requires that one maintain an inclination to transgress. It is commonplace for individuals to act for multiple reasons, and it would be uncharitable to interpret the Rabbis as denying this mundane phenomenon, that is, as denying that a motive of obedience can be operative alongside other motives. And even if one were to deny this commonplace, and insist that no more than one motive can be operative in the production of a given act, it would hardly follow that the presence of an appetite or inclination for the performance of an act should preclude one from acting from the motive of obedience – after all, why couldn't someone act from the motive of obedience without regard for the satisfaction that the act might bring him in virtue of his other desires? Moreover, charity aside, it is not plausible to attribute to the Rabbis the view that acting from the motive of obedience is incompatible with having desires or inclinations, unrelated to the act's halakhic consequences, that would be satisfied by performance. Although it is a matter of controversy among the rabbis of the Talmud, the generally authoritative position conditions fulfillment of ritual obligations on the presence of an intention to fulfill that accompanies the performance ("*mitzvot tzerikhot kavanna*"). For example, according to this view, if my only motive for blowing a *shofar* is to create pleasing music, then I have not discharged my duty since I have not acted with the aim of so doing. Now, if acting from the motive of obedience were incompatible with the presence of a desire or inclination for the performance unrelated to the discharge of a legal duty, then the position under discussion would have to insist that one could not be attracted to features of the blowing other than its halakhic consequences. Even the slightest inclination or appeal owing to the aesthetic dimensions of the ritual, or to one's childhood memories, or to an interest in pleasing other parties would serve as an insuperable obstacle to fulfillment. Yet such strictures are no part of the position that requires an intention to discharge the obligation. On the contrary, the requirement of *hiddur mitzvah* (beautification/enhancement of the *mitzvah*) instructs individuals to invest resources into making the experience of performance as beautiful and pleasing as possible.[13] Thus, even though identifying the operative motive of an act may be difficult when the act would serve more than one of an individual's interests – and even though the presence of an independent appetite or inclination can create opportunities for insincerity and self-deception in the self-ascription of a religious motive – we cannot attribute to R. Shimon the view that acting from the motive of obedience is inconsistent with the presence of desires for aspects of the performance unrelated to the immediate halakhic consequences. Why, then, does he direct us to preserve desires for forbidden objects in the interest of acting from the motive of obedience?

We may make headway by observing that each of R. Shimon's three examples involves a "negative commandment," that is, one that requires us to refrain from acting in some manner (e.g., mixing milk and meat, wearing fabric of wool and linen, and engaging in illicit sexual relations), as opposed to a "positive commandment" that requires an affirmative act. There is a noteworthy asymmetry between negative commandments and positive commandments with respect to the conditions of complying from a motive of obedience. In the case of positive obligations, as I have mentioned, one can act from the motive of duty regardless of whether one also has other motives for complying. I donate blood, let us imagine, out of a sense of obligation but also in order to receive a free glass of orange juice and a sticker announcing my good deed – each motive may be strong enough to produce the act in the absence of any of the others, but as it happens the motives join forces and over-determine my act – whereas you donate blood solely out of a dutiful motive. By considering such cases we see that *acting* from a motive of obedience requires neither the presence of motives for noncompliance nor the absence of additional motives for compliance. By contrast, one cannot be said to refrain from doing X for any reason, including the motive of obedience, unless one sees something desirable in X-ing, something that casts X-ing in a favorable light, something that would render it a contender in the course of one's deliberations.[14] If one does not satisfy this condition, then one cannot refrain from X-ing *out of obedience*, or for any motive at all, regardless of whether one recognizes a halakhic prohibition.[15] If you were to ask me why I did not break out into dance while delivering a lecture to a distinguished university faculty, it would not be correct to say that I refrained out of respect for the venue or for the audience, given that I dislike dancing in general, did not see how it would advance any of my ends, and was not overcome by any momentary impulses of a Dionysian nature. This is so, even though, having been raised well, I would have refrained out of respect even if I had felt an urge. Accordingly, when it comes to forbidden foods or fabrics or sexual relations, if one does not have any appetite for these things, then, barring special cases when one has reason to perform the forbidden act even without any appetite to do so (e.g., if food is scarce), one would not be able to abstain from a motive of duty. Since R. Shimon (and the rabbinic worldview more generally) finds value in acting from the motive of obedience to

God, he naturally instructs us to preserve the desires that serve as preconditions for such omissions to be made out of duty.

These considerations not only help us make sense of the motive-of-obedience interpretation of R. Shimon's teaching, but serve as a powerful argument in its favor. For, as a general matter, it is implausible to extend R. Shimon's teaching beyond the realm of the thou-shalt-nots. Extending his teaching to the realm of affirmative commandments would require that we develop an aversion to ritual performance (be it blowing the *shofar*, eating *matzah*, etc.) that we would then overcome by our sense of duty. However, as I have already noted, this is altogether inconsistent with the rabbinic approach to *mitzvah* performance. Accordingly, any viable interpretation of R. Shimon's teaching will need to explain on principled grounds why the teaching he is advancing is sensitive to the distinction between positive and negative commandments. And, as I have purported to show, the explanation that appeals to the value of acting from the motive of obedience does just that, since it is only with respect to the negative commandments that an independent desire for the transgressive state of affairs is, in general, needed to comply from the motive of obedience.

### *Duties to God and to Humanity*

This brings us to the final stage of our analysis. Given the rationale of R. Shimon's teaching – enabling compliance from the motive of obedience – what principled basis is there to restrict it, following Maimonides, to the class of *hukkim*? There are, it would seem, two natural places to look: On the one hand, to the problematic nature of desires to transgress the *mishpatim*, the badness of which would perhaps outweigh whatever value would otherwise inhere in complying from a dutiful motive, and, on the other hand, to the value of the dutiful motive itself, which is perhaps attenuated in the specific context of the *mishpatim*.

It can be inferred, both from Maimonides' examples of *mishpatim* ("murder, theft, robbery, fraud, harming an innocent man, repaying a benefactor with evil, degrading parents, and things like these") and from his claim that they are "generally accepted by all the people as bad", that, at least in the context of EC6, *mishpatim* include all and only "commandments between man and his fellow" (*mitzvot bein adam l'chaveiro*) and none of the "commandments between man and God" (*mitzvot bein adam l'makom*). Whereas an infraction of either kind of commandment constitutes a wrong against God, violations of the former class also constitute a wrong against one's fellow human being. A proponent of the first approach might appeal to this and observe that, in the cases of *mitzvot bein adam l'chaveiro*, the relevant desire or impulse would generally be a desire to wrong a fellow human being (e.g., a desire to kill or to deceive) and that, even when they are not acted upon, such malicious desires impair our relations with other humans, relations that are partially constituted by the attitudes and feelings we harbor toward one another. Although this solution can perhaps go some of the distance toward supplying an explanation, it cannot take us all of the way, in part because, even in the case of *mitzvot bein adam l'chaveiro*, many of the relevant desires to transgress do not constitute desires to harm *as such*, as when I desire to drink from the bottle of scotch in the cabinet and the bottle happens to belong to you. In such a case, the wish to drink from the bottle is not malicious, and is consistent with the most harmonious relationship, provided that the desire does not morph into the more insidious feeling of envy, an attitude that encompasses one's fellow man and not merely his possessions.

According to the second approach, we must focus our analysis on the motive of obedience itself within the context of the *mishpatim*. A straightforward suggestion along these lines is that the reasons for God's commands in the case of *mitzvot bein adam l'chaveiro*, as opposed to *bein adam l'makom*, are not sensitive to whether we comply from the motive of obedience to God or any other motive. When one thinks of norms that protect the bodily integrity or promote the well-being of human beings, for example, the reasons for these norms are arguably served by compliance even in the absence of a religious motive. However, even if this were true regarding particular commandments, we may ask why there is not independent basis for encouraging a motive of dutiful obedience to each of God's commands – if not as a condition for their fulfillment, then as a distinct requirement, or at least aspiration, that would apply to *hukkim* and *mishpatim* alike. Such an aspiration would be rooted in the value of subordinating one's will to that of a divine commander, a value the centrality of which to halakhic Judaism it would be difficult to overstate, and that can only be fully realized by conforming with the deliberate aim of heeding God's command. As Aharon Lichtenstein explains: "The concept of mitzvah, our stance vis-à-vis the [master of the universe] as commanded beings, as sons and servants both, lies at the epicenter of Jewish existence. Not only do we glorify servile fealty to divine orders but following [the Rabbis], and in the face of intuited common morality we revel in the contention that action in response to the halakhic call is superior to the same act voluntarily undertaken. *Gadol ha-metzuveh ve-osseh* ['Greater is he who is commanded and performs than he who performs voluntarily']. And this, presumably, not or, not only because … it assures a more conscientious implementation, but because, over and above the practical result, the halakhic charge renders the act intrinsically and qualitatively superior, inasmuch as it engages the agent in a dialogic encounter with his Master" (Lichtenstein 2006, 20). In light of the centrality of this value, and the fact that *mishpatim* as much as *hukkim* reflect the will of God, why differentiate between the two, at least at the level of aspiration, merely because God's reasons for commanding the *mishpatim* would arguably be satisfied by mere conformity?[16]

It is, we have seen, a hallmark feature of *mishpatim* that we are in some sense *independently* obligated to comply with them, either because of a binding, non-conventional moral rule corresponding to and existing alongside the divine command or because God's reasons for legislating would equally have led the political authorities to impose the same norms if God had remained silent on the matter. However, neither of these two senses of independence undermines the possibility of acting with the intention to comply with God's commands, even when the independent basis for compliance is fully appreciated by the agent.

For just as one can act with the aim of obeying one's master even when one's appetites serve as independent basis for complying, so too can one perform a single act with the intention of satisfying two masters who independently make the same demand. Similarly, there is nothing barring a servant from acting with the intention of obeying his master, even when that servant knows that a different master would have demanded the same performance.

Still, perhaps there are other reasons that the independent credentials of the *mishpatim* might recommend downplaying the motive of obedience. For suppose there is value in complying with the *mitzvot bein adam l'chaveiro* for the reasons *in virtue of which* they are independently obligatory (e.g., as an appreciation of the value of human beings). On this assumption, perhaps compliance out of the motive of obedience is not recommended on the ground that individuals should comply for different reasons.[17] The difficulty with this suggestion is that it does not explain why the multiple motives must be seen as competing, why someone cannot, and hence should not, comply from the additional motive of obedience.[18]

Similarly, suppose there is a principle, applicable not only to *mitzvot bein adam l'chaveiro* but to obligations more generally, that requires us to comply with obligations for the reasons in virtue of which the obligation exists (as opposed to the reason *that* they are obligatory, or for some other reason altogether). It is true that, in the case of *hukkim*, such a principle would require that we act from the motive of obedience to God, since such performances are, in general, not independently obligatory. However, since God's command is *a* ground of obligation for *all* of the commandments, such a principle would hardly preclude acting out of the motive of obedience in the case of *mishpatim*. Indeed, if the principle requires that actions in accordance with duty be performed for *all of* the reasons on account of which the performance is obligatory, then it would *require* such a motive of obedience for *mishpatim* as well as *hukkim*.

Although it is lodged firmly within the consciousness of many traditional Jews, it is surprisingly difficult to justify on principled grounds Maimonides' restriction of R. Shimon's teaching. Perhaps, however, we are asking too much. Perhaps it is enough to observe that many, if not all, desires to transgress the *mitzvot bein adam l'chaveiro* would constitute desires arguably destructive to human relations in and of themselves, and that the divine rationales for this class of commandments would in any case be served by compliance that was not motivated by obedience to God, but for other reasons, such as a proper appreciation of the value of humanity.[19]

## Notes

1 The Rabbis were well aware of this risk associated with the pursuit of reasons for the commandments; see b. Sanhedrin 21b.

2 Unless otherwise noted, I have used, with very slight adaptation, R. Weiss's translation of EC from the Arabic, published in Weiss and Butterworth 1975.

3 Note that in the extant versions of the *Sifra* to Lev. 20:26, the teaching is attributed not to R. Shimon but rather to Rabbi Elazar ben Azaryah. Nevertheless, following Maimonides, I will continue to refer to it as R. Shimon's teaching.

4 b. Kiddushin 31a.

5　Maimonides, *Laws of Repentance* 7:4.

6　The tannaitic source is Sifra Ahare Mot 9:13. In translating "*din*" as "proper" I follow Twersky 1972 – with the caveat that, in this context, it is to be understood as "uniquely proper," in the sense that it would be *im*proper to fail to do what it would be proper to do, e.g., impose the *mishpatim*. Weiss 1975 translates "*din*" as "deserves to be," whereas Hayes 2015 translates it as "logical," a terminology I will occasionally use too.

7　Note that it does not follow from this that a community has acted contrary to reason if it has imposed a norm that was not "proper" or "logical" in this sense.

8　For examples of others who hold this view, see Twersky 1980, 415, n. 145; Schweid 1989, 113ff.

9　"The meaning of many of the laws became clear to me and their causes became known to me through my study of the doctrines, opinions, practices, and cult of the Sabians, as you will hear when I explain the reasons for the commandments that are considered to be without cause [i.e., the *hukkim*]" (3.29).

10　Of course, it also raises the question of why subsequent generations, in different historical conditions, should be bound by a law that is not tailored to their own circumstances.

11　Twersky 1980, 432.

12　In the fourth chapter of EC Maimonides offers a rationale for some *hukkim* (as well as *mishpatim*), which, like the rationales offered in the *Mishneh Torah*, also underdetermine the laws they are invoked to explain.

13　See, e.g., b. Shabbat 133b; b. Baba Kamma 9b; Rashi, ad loc., s.v. B'Hiddur.

14　For present purposes, we can construe this condition liberally, such that a bare inclination or impulse for the act, unaccompanied by a judgment that the act is in any way good, would count as something that makes it a contender.

15　At most one could be motivated by the absence of inclination or perceived reasons, as when someone says that they refrained from doing something *because* they didn't want to do it and/or saw no reason to do it.

16　It is worth noting that even the rabbinic view that, in general, requires an intention to fulfill the law as a condition of fulfillment suspends this requirement for *mitzvot bein adam l'chaveiro*; see, e.g., R. Ovadya Yosef, *Yabbia Omer* (YD 6:29). However, notwithstanding the absence of a strict requirement, most rabbinic authorities who have considered the question have held, in keeping with the suggestion above, that the best course of conduct is to act out of, inter alia, the motive of obedience; see, e.g., *Toldot Hazon Ish* (vol. 2), 183. Also on point is Rabbeinu Tam's restriction of the application of the Talmudic dictum *Gadol ha–metzuveh ve-osseh* ["Greater is he who is commanded and performs than he who performs voluntarily"] to the *mishpatim*; see Shitta Mekubetzet (Bava Kamma 87a). According to R. Moshe Feinstein, the basis of this restriction is that, in the case of *mishpatim* alone, the motive of obedience is a precondition of the religious significance of the performance, and R. Feinstein urges such a motivation for this reason (*Iggerot Moshe* [YD 1:6]).

17　Relatedly, R. Yechiel Yaakov Weinberg maintains that, "it is better that a person give [required gifts] of his own free will, out of a feeling of love for his fellow Jew. If he gives only because God has so commanded, he diminishes the measure of love ..." (*Seridei Esh* [I, 61]).

18　Might it explain the sense of competition if the motive that does not appeal to God's commandment is the very reason on account of which God issued the command? Perhaps acting from a motive of obedience requires that one refrain from entering the fray of first-order considerations that might have led God to issue the command. If that were the case, the wish to preserve the non-theological motive would require us to suppress any motive of obedience. The difficulty with this suggestion is that it is predicated on an unconvincing claim about the motive of obedience. I can pay taxes, for example, both out of a sense of legal obligation and also because it is, among other things, a means of transferring money to those less fortunate, even knowing that facilitating such a transfer is one of the reasons why taxes are imposed in the first place.

19 Thanks to Daniel Frank, Rachel Mannheimer, Yakir Paz, Aaron Segal, and Gideon Yaffe for extremely helpful discussion and comments.

## Further Reading on Ritual and Rationality

Goodman, L. E. "Rational Law/Ritual Law," in *A People Apart: Chosenness and Ritual in Jewish Philosophical Thought*, ed. D. Frank (Albany, NY: SUNY Press, 1993), 109–200.

Halevi, Judah. *The Book of Refutation and Proof on Behalf of the Despised Faith (The Kuzari)*, trans. B. Kogan and L. Berman (New Haven, CT: Yale Judaica Series, forthcoming), 2.59–60.

Heinemann, I. *The Reasons for the Commandments in Jewish Thought: From the Bible to the Renaissance*, trans. L. Levin (Boston, MA: Academic Studies Press, 2008).

Hirsch, S. R. *Horeb: A Philosophy of Jewish Laws and Observances*, trans. I. Grunfeld (London: Soncino Press, 1962).

Leaman, O. *Moses Maimonides* (London: Routledge, 1990), 129–161.

Leibowitz, Y. "Religious Praxis: The Meaning of Halakhah," in *Judaism, Human Values, and the Jewish State* (Cambridge, MA: Harvard University Press, 1992), 3–29.

Lichtenstein, A. "Does Jewish Tradition Recognize an Ethic Independent of Halakha?" in *Modern Jewish Ethics*, ed. M. Fox (Columbus, OH: Ohio State University Press, 1975), 62–88.

Novak, D. "The Talmud as a Source for Philosophical Reflection," in *History of Jewish Philosophy*, eds. D. Frank and O. Leaman (London: Routledge, 1997), 62–80.

Rynhold, D. *Two Models of Jewish Philosophy: Justifying One's Practices* (Oxford: Oxford University Press, 2005), 48–100.

Saadia Gaon, *The Book of Beliefs and Opinions*, trans. S. Rosenblatt (New Haven, CT: Yale Judaica Series, 1948), 3.2.

Schweid, E. *Studies in Maimonides' Eight Chapters*, 2nd ed. (Jerusalem: Academon, 1989) [Hebrew].

Sokol, M. "Mitzvah as Metaphor," in *A People Apart: Chosenness and Ritual in Jewish Philosophical Thought*, ed. D. Frank (Albany, NY: SUNY Press, 1993), 201–228.

Stern, J. "Modes of Reference in the Rituals of Judaism," *Religious Studies* 23 (1987), 109–128.

Stern, J. *Problems and Parables of Law: Maimonides and Nahmanides on Reasons for the Commandments* (Albany, NY: SUNY Press, 1998).

# 11 Repentance and Forgiveness

Human freedom and the capacity to repent provides the fuel for a classic case study in philosophical exegesis of a biblical text. Scattered throughout Exodus are remarks in which God is said to have 'hardened' or stiffened Pharaoh's heart, thus rendering him motivationally impotent, and *then* punished him for cruelty to the Israelites. The philosophical conundrum here is how to make sense of holding Pharaoh responsible, and therefore justifiably punishing him, for actions springing from a 'hardened' heart, from a will rendered unfree. After all, we hold responsible and hence liable for punishment only such agents who freely, without outside interference, choose their actions. **Maimonides** is clear in Chapter 8 of *Shemonah Perakim* (*Eight Chapters*), his introduction to Avot in his commentary on the *Mishnah*, that we are free to choose our course of action. As a result, we can be held responsible and liable for punishment for what we choose to do, and it is on account of this freedom of choice that God punishes Pharaoh by hardening his heart, by taking away his power to choose. This latter *is* the divine punishment for previously chosen evil. Indeed it provides the set-up for the ultimate destruction of Pharaoh, but the important point for Maimonides is that the divine hardening of the heart is subsumable under a libertarian theory of moral agency.

**David Shatz** canvasses the variety of philosophical readings that have been offered to make sense of the aforementioned biblical conundrum. Historically they range from the bold claim of Joseph Albo (fifteenth century) that God's intervention in hardening Pharaoh's heart does not in fact remove his ability to choose, to a naturalistic reading, which finds the biblical remarks to be compatible with the quasi-Aristotelian view that after a time character is fate and as agents we have after a while lost all ability to choose to do otherwise. The exegetical options on display are ingenious, and Shatz does not come down firmly on one side in the philosophical dispute.

In hardening Pharaoh's heart God takes away his power to choose; *a fortiori* he loses the capacity to repent, even if he wanted to. In his essay **Jonathan Jacobs** focuses on the nature and justification of repentance and forgiveness in Jewish thought, especially medieval Jewish philosophy. A moment's reflection reveals the centrality of repentance and forgiveness in Judaism. Yom Kippur is the Day of Atonement, a time for repentance and asking forgiveness for wrongs done against God (*bein adam l'Makom*) and against other human beings (*bein adam* *l'chavero*). Jacobs conscripts Maimonides, Saadia Gaon, and Bahya into service of his discussion, and emphasizes the theocentric focus of the Jewish discussion by contrast to more secular views, such as that of Aristotle, that tend not easily to find a place for repentance and forgiveness in their moral theorizing. As Jacobs notes, in Judaism both repentance and forgiveness play out against the background of humility before God and gratitude for His grace and beneficence in giving humankind a law, a way of life by which to flourish. Repentance and forgiveness are to be understood as reparation for failing to live up to the divine beneficence.

## MOSES MAIMONIDES (1138–1204)

### Commentary on the Mishnah (1168)

### Shemonah Perakim (Eight Chapters), Chapter 8 (tr. Weiss and Butterworth)

#### Free Will and Punishment

To sum up the matter, you should believe that just as God wishes man to be erect in stature, broad-chested, and to have fingers, so too He wishes him to move or be at rest of his own accord and to perform actions voluntarily. He does not force him to perform them nor prevent him from performing them. This notion was explained in the book of Truth, where He said: *Behold, the man has become like one of us, knowing good and evil* (Genesis 3.22). The *Targum* has already made clear the interpretation of His appraisal, [*like one*] *of us, knowing good and evil.* It means that he [Adam] has become unique in the world, i.e., a species having no similar species with which he shares this quality he has attained. What is this quality? It is that he himself, of his own accord, knows the good and the bad things, does whatever he wishes, and is not prevented from doing them. Since this is so, he might stretch out his hand, take from this tree, *and eat and live forever* (Genesis 3.22). Since this is necessary for human existence, I mean, that man performs good and bad actions by his choice when he wishes it, it necessarily follows that he can be instructed in the good ways and be commanded, forbidden, punished and rewarded. All of this is just. It is necessary for him to accustom his soul to good actions until he acquires the virtues, and to avoid bad actions until the vices disappear from him, if he has acquired any. He should not say he has already attained a condition that cannot possibly change, since every condition can change from good to bad and from bad to good; the choice is his. With a view to this subject and for its sake, we set down everything we discussed concerning obedience and disobedience.

Something still remains for us to explain regarding this subject. There are some verses which lead people to fancy that God preordains and compels disobedience. That is false and we shall explain these verses because people are often preoccupied with them. One of them is his saying to Abraham: *And they shall be enslaved and oppressed* (Genesis 15.13). They said: 'He preordained that the Egyptians would oppress the *seed of Abraham.* Why then did He punish them, when they necessarily and inevitably enslaved them [the Hebrews] as He preordained?' The answer is that this is like the Exalted saying that some people born in the future will be sinful, some will be obedient, some virtuous, and some bad. Now, this is correct, but it does not necessarily follow from this statement that a given bad man is bad without fail, nor that a given virtuous man is virtuous without fail. Rather, whoever is bad is so by his own choice. If he wishes to be virtuous, he can be so; there is nothing preventing him. Similarly, if any virtuous man wishes to, he can be bad; there is nothing preventing him. The prediction is not about a particular individual, so that he could say: 'It has been preordained for me.' Rather, it is stated in a general way, and each individual remains able to exercise his choice upon his original inborn disposition. Similarly, if any individual Egyptian who oppressed them and treated them unjustly had not wanted to oppress them, he had the choice about that; for it was not preordained that a given individual would oppress them...

His saying, *And I will harden Pharaoh's heart* (Exodus 14.4) – and then punishing him and destroying him – contains a subject for discussion and a major principle stems from it. Reflect upon my discourse on this subject, set your mind to it, compare it with the discourse of everyone who has discussed it, and choose the best for yourself. If *Pharaoh* and his followers had committed no other sin than not letting *Israel* go free, the matter would undoubtedly be problematic, for He had prevented them from setting [Israel] free. As He said: *For I have hardened his heart and the heart of his servants* (Exodus 10.1). Then [according to this assumption] He requested that [Pharaoh] set them free, though he was compelled not to set them free. Then He punished him and destroyed him and his followers for not setting them free. This would have been an injustice and contrary to everything we have previously set forth.

However, the matter is not like this, but rather *Pharaoh* and his followers disobeyed by choice, without force or compulsion. They oppressed the foreigners who were in their midst and treated them with sheer injustice. As it is clearly said: *And he said to his people: Behold, the people of Israel. ... Come, let us deal shrewdly with them* (Exodus 1.9–10). This action was due to their choice and to the evil character of their thought; there was nothing compelling them to do it. God punished them for it by preventing them from repenting so that the punishment which His justice required would befall them. What prevented them from repentance was that they would not set [Israel] free. God explained this to [Pharaoh] and informed him that if He had only wanted to take [Israel] out [of Egypt], He would have exterminated [Pharaoh] and his followers, and they would have gone out. But in addition to taking them out, He wanted to punish [Pharaoh] for oppressing them previously. As He said at the very outset: *And also that nation, whom they shall serve, will I judge* (Genesis 15.14). It was not possible to punish them if they repented, so they were prevented from repenting and they continued holding [Israel]. This is what He says: *Surely now I have put forth my hand ... but because of this I have left you standing, etc.* (Exodus 9.15–16).

No disgrace need be attached to us because of our saying that God may punish an individual for not repenting, even though He leaves him no choice about repentance. For He, may He be exalted, knows the sins, and His wisdom and justice impose the extent of the punishment. He may punish in this world alone, He may punish in the other [world] alone, or He may punish in both realms. His punishment in this world varies: He may punish with regard to the body, money, or both. He may impede some of man's voluntary movements as a means of punishment, like preventing his hand from grasping, as He did with *Jeroboam* (1 Kings 13.4), or the eye from seeing, as He did with the *men of Sodom* who had united against *Lot* (Genesis 19.11). Similarly, He may prevent the choice of repentance so that a man does not at all incline toward it and is destroyed for his sin. It is not necessary for us to know His wisdom to the extent of knowing why He punished this individual with this kind of punishment and did not punish him with another kind, just as we do not know the reason He determined this species to have this form and not another form. But the general rule is *that all of His ways are just* (Deuteronomy 32.4). He punishes the sinner to the extent of his sin and He rewards the beneficent man to the extent of his beneficence.

If you were to say: 'Why did He request, time after time, that [Pharaoh] set *Israel* free, although he was prevented from doing so? It is as though the plagues came down upon him for remaining obstinate, although his punishment – as we have said – was that he remain obstinate. Was it not futile, then, to request of him what he was unable to do?' However, this too was part of God's wisdom, to teach [Pharaoh] that if God wanted to abolish his choice He would do so. So He [as it were] said to him: 'I request that you set them free, and if you set them free now, you will be saved. But you will not set them free so that you will be destroyed.' [Pharaoh] would have had to respond favorably, which would have been the opposite of the prophet's claim that he was prevented from responding favorably. Thus, he was not able to. There is an important verse about that, well known to all the people. He said: *And for the sake of declaring My name throughout all the earth* (Exodus 9.16). God may punish a man by preventing him from choosing a certain action, and he knows it but is unable to struggle with his soul and drive it back to make this choice ...

We have surely explained the meaning of those difficult verses in the *Torah* and the *Bible* which make [people] fancy that God compels disobedience. It is an explanation that is correct according to the most rigorous reflection, and we preserve our principle that obedience and disobedience are in man's hands and that he is a free agent in his actions. What he wants to do, he does; what he does not want to do, he does not do. However, God punishes him for his sin by nullifying his volition, as we have explained. Acquisition of the virtues and the vices is [also] in his hands. Therefore it is obligatory and necessary that he be avid and work hard for his own sake to acquire the virtues, since there is no one outside of himself moving him toward them. This is what they say in the moral teachings of this *tractate: If I am not for myself, who will be for me?* (*Mishnah*, Avot 1.13) ...

## DAVID SHATZ

## "Freedom, Repentance, and Hardening of the Hearts" (1997, revised 1999), in D. Frank, O. Leaman, and C. Manekin (eds.), *The Jewish Philosophy Reader* (2000)

On several occasions in the Bible, God 'hardens the heart' of individuals. 'Victims' of divine hardenings include the Egyptian king Pharaoh (Exod. 4:21; 7:3; 9:12; 10:1, 20, 27; 11:10; 14:4, 8, 17, and arguably 14:5, 18), the Moabite king Sihon (Deut. 2:30), and the army of Canaan in the time of Joshua (Josh. 11:20). Proverbs 21:1 informs us, indeed, that the 'heart of a king is in the Lord's hands like streams of water; He will turn it to whatever He wants'; and without referring to hardening *per se*, the prophet Elijah insinuates that God has led the hearts of the sinning Israelites astray (1 Kings 18:37).

Cases like these generate formidable theological problems. In what follows I identify these problems, sketch a few solutions that have been offered by Jewish philosophers, and briefly assess the solutions without concluding firmly in favor of one or the other of them. As we shall see, Jewish philosophical treatments of hardening are varied and ingenious, and they stimulate considerations of challenging philosophical and exegetical issues.

### The Problems

To harden someone's heart is, apparently, to interfere in the person's motivational system so as to cause the person to act in a way different than he or she would have otherwise acted. Consequently, the most obvious problem posed by hardening of the hearts pertains to the loss of free will incurred by the hardened agent. Most philosophers subscribe to the principle that, when an agent S interferes directly to affect agent V's motivational system in a way that does not involve rational persuasion—brainwashing, hypnosis and the like—such interference will normally preclude V's freely performing and bearing responsibility for acts that the intervention caused. It would seem, therefore, that, by hardening, God deprives certain people of a significant good, free will. We may call this the 'free will deprivation problem'.

One might retort that in Judaism free will is not as great a value as the 'free will deprivation problem' and other theological stances, such as 'free will theodicies', imply. For example, authoritative Jewish sources at times justify coercion to secure correct behavior; in fact, the biblical God tries to elicit obedience to His commands by promising rewards for compliance and threatening dire punishments for disobedience. There are also doctrines in Jewish thought to the effect that having free choice is not as good a state as doing right automatically (e.g., Nachmanides, commentary to Gen. 2:9 and Deut. 30:6). Hence the free will deprivation problem we posed—'but isn't free will a significant good?'—rests on what some might regard as an exaggerated premise about the value of free will in Judaism.

Over against this argument, I maintain that the conundrum of hardening cannot be made to disappear so quickly. First of all, some Jewish philosophers address the problem of hardening precisely because they value free choice highly; regardless of how, for example, the medieval giants Saadia Gaon and Moses Maimonides would harmonize their views with the claims I alluded to, the problem of free will deprivation emerges fully and forcefully *for them*, and their views must be considered. Second, even in the absence of a specific problem posed by hardening, we need to inquire into the *purpose* of God's hardening hearts. That is to say, there is a difference between *defending* God (by saying He didn't do anything objectionable by depriving someone of free will) and *explaining His motivations.* Questioning the assumptions of the free will deprivation problem serves to defend God, but it goes no distance toward answering this query about His motivation in depriving an agent of free will.

Third and most importantly, disposing of the free will deprivation problem by altering our value judgements about free will still leaves us with—besides the questions about God's motivation—three *other* difficulties:

- The *responsibility problem*: If God causes Pharaoh to will an evil act, namely, keeping the Israelites enslaved, why should Pharaoh be held responsible for this act and be punished for it? How can free will and moral responsibility coexist with hardening?
- *The repentance-prevention problem*: Judaism teaches that God wants sinners to repent. If so, why would God prevent any individual from changing his ways for the better?
- *The causation problem*: If God causes Pharaoh to will an evil act, namely, keeping the Israelites enslaved, has God not (a) caused an evil act, (b) made a person morally worse, and (c) caused further suffering to the Israelites and Egyptians?

All of these problems are formidable, even if we are not troubled by God's taking away free will.

Before proceeding to examine responses to these problems (actually, I will not be addressing the causation problem), we should take note of another phenomenon that invites questions similar to those bred by the hardening narratives, a phenomenon for which Judaism has no convenient name. Christians call it 'sanctification', and I will here use the label 'betterment.' Consider Deuteronomy 30:6, where God promises that He will 'circumcise the hearts of you and your descendants.' This sounds as though God will remove the Jews' inclination for evil—interfering with their will. Likewise, God tells Ezekiel that He will give the people a 'new heart' and 'new spirit' and will remove their 'heart of stone' (Ezek. 36:26). The *siddur* (Hebrew prayer book) includes a plea to '*compel* our evil inclination to be subjugated to You.' Jewish philosophers who address hardening say much about hardening and little about betterment even though the latter gives rise to problems about free will and responsibility similar to the former. As we will see, the concept of betterment figures in one particular analysis of hardening.

## Some Solutions

Here are several approaches taken by Jewish philosophers to solve the problems surveyed above. A 'solution' to the hardening and betterment problems must satisfy two criteria. It must be philosophically cogent; but it also must be compatible with, if not directly supported by, the Bible's narrative and terminology and concepts found in other parts of Jewish tradition.

### Reinterpretation of the Term

Some exegetes, including Saadia Gaon (*Book of Beliefs and Opinions*, IV:6) and R. Yitzchak Arama (chapter 36 of his *Akedat Yitzchak*), deny that the term 'hardening of the heart' has anything to do with interference in motivational systems. It connotes instead keeping someone alive (as per Saadia) or providing respite (as per Arama). Most interpreters implicitly disagree with these readings.

### The Modest Solution

What I would call the 'modest' solution contends that, had God *not* hardened Pharaoh's heart, and Pharaoh would have therefore released the Israelites due to the mounting pressure of the plagues, this would not have been a free choice on Pharaoh's part anyway, and would not have constituted repentance. Rather, the decision to release would then have been *coerced*. Hence, the charge that God has 'deprived' Pharaoh of free will is false, since Pharaoh is not now *less free* than if God had not intervened. Further, because releasing the Israelites would have taken place only under pressure of the plagues, Pharaoh would not have genuinely repented had he succumbed to the plagues' pressure.

Elements of the 'modest' claim are found in Moses Nachmanides' and Obadiah Sforno's commentaries to Exodus 7:3, and in Joseph Albo's *Book of Roots*, IV:25. But all these philosophers put forth the modest claim in the context of a wider strategy, rather than present it in isolation as I have just done. And this is understandable, for the approach seems to provide at best a defense against the charge of free will deprivation and repentance prevention, not an explanation of why God hardens. In addition, more must be said if we are to explain why Pharaoh is *responsible* for the hardened act.

### The Bold Claim: Pharaoh Acts Freely

According to what I call 'the bold claim', Pharaoh's act of keeping the Israelites enslaved is in truth *free*, despite God's intervention. When God 'hardens' Pharaoh's heart, this means merely that he *strengthens* Pharaoh's heart, giving him the fortitude not to let the plagues automatically dictate a decision to release the Israelites. Thanks to the hardening, the king now has a choice: whether to release the Israelites or to keep them enslaved. Two possibilities are open to him, whereas without the hardening he had but one (to release the Israelites). The existence of this choice suggests he is responsible for his (freely chosen) hardened act, and that he has a possibility to repent. (See Albo, *Book of Roots*, IV:25.)

A different version of the bold claim runs as follows: by increasing the king's willpower (by weakening certain desires and/or strengthening others), God, *de facto*, is allowing Pharaoh to act in accordance with his already formed character, and thus to act freely. Hardening is God's way of respecting Pharaoh's own prior choices, of helping him to follow in his previously freely chosen path while imposing upon him full responsibility for those hardened acts. He has the opportunity to act in accordance with his true self. To be sure, this does not explain why Pharaoh was deprived of the opportunity to repent by releasing the Israelites; but if we accept the point made by the modest claim—that releasing the Israelites due to the plagues would not count as repentance anyway—we have a solution to the repentance prevention problem as well (cf. Psalms 81.11–12 and *BT*, Makkot 10b, Shabbat 104a).

On either construction, there is a deep concern about the bold claim. The king is like a subject who has been hypnotized, and an act performed as a result of hypnotic suggestion is widely regarded as an unfree act. Though free choice may require alternative possibilities, an objector will claim, merely having alternative possibilities is not sufficient for free choice—the aetiology of the choice's existence matters. While the force of this objection is debatable, and indeed it is in my opinion not persuasive, the issue of aetiology is surely important to determining responsibility; for absent God's intervention, Pharaoh would not have acted wickedly during those plagues. The difficulty is greater with regard to the second variant of the bold strategy, for how could God say to Pharaoh, 'You have to live with the results of your choices'? After all, Pharaoh can turn around and say, 'Granted my previous choices were bad, my choice *now*, as I witness the plagues, wouldn't have been to keep them as slaves—that's your doing.'

### Hardening as Punishment

According to yet another view, God hardens the agent's heart as a means of *punishing* him. Specifically, the hardened agent is thereby deprived of three great goods: (a) free will, along with (b) the potential to act rightly, and (c) the chance to repent. He is not punished further *for* the hardened act. Removing free will is a perfectly just punishment for a person so depraved, an appropriate tit-for-tat. The agent hardened his own heart in the earlier plagues, contrary to God's will; so now his heart becomes hardened by God, contrary to his own will. Likewise, he chose to do evil, so now his punishment (or part of it) is … that he does evil! Hardening is not only a case of the punishment fitting the crime—rather, hardening is 'a punishment that is the very sin that it punishes' (Kretzmann 1988, 205; Maimonides presents a version of the 'punishment' solution in *Eight Chapters*, chapter 8). Notice that insofar as it recognizes the value of free will by considering free will deprivation as an evil, the 'punishment' solution is compatible with, and even partially dovetails with, high assessments of free will such as those found in free will theodicies.

Unfortunately, the punishment solution, as stated thus far, is incomplete, for it falters as regards the repentance deprivation problem. The solution would claim that the hardened agent is punished precisely by losing the opportunity for repentance. But even granted the heinous character of figures like Pharaoh, some thinkers have been troubled by the implication that God actively shuts the gates of repentance to some people. (See, for example, Arama, *Akedat Yitzchak*, Exodus, chapter 36; cf. Maimonides, *Eight Chapters*, chapter 8, and *Mishneh Torah*, Laws of Repentance, chapter 6.)

## The Naturalistic Approach

Each of the analyses examined to this point takes hardening as a supernatural intervention. But the distinguished biblical scholar Umberto Cassuto (1883–1951) explains the expression 'God hardened Pharaoh's heart' in a way that contradicts the supernaturalist reading of hardening:

> In early Hebrew diction, it is customary to attribute every phenomenon to the direct action of God. ... Every happening has a number of causes, and these causes, in turn, have other causes, and so on ad infinitum; according to the Israelite conception, the cause of all causes was the will of God, the Creator and Ruler of the world. Now the philosopher examines the long and complex chain of causation, whereas the ordinary person jumps instantly from the last effect to the first cause, and attributes the former directly to God. This, now, is how the Torah, which employs human idioms, expresses itself. Consequently the expression 'but I will harden his heart' is, in the final analysis, the same as if it were worded: 'but his heart will be hard'.
>
> (1967, 56; cf. Maimonides, *Guide of the Perplexed* 2.48)

Once hardening is read naturalistically, with no implication of divine intervention, the standard problems about deprivation of free will, prevention of repentance, and assignment of responsibility become non-starters. Hardening, on this view, is not a form of direct divine action to begin with.

But if Cassuto is right, what is the difference between Pharaoh's earlier 'self-hardenings' and God's later 'other-hardenings'? Why does the Bible use differing expressions for what is allegedly the same type of event? Cassuto's reply that the terms are interchangeable seems inadequate; why wouldn't the ordinary person ascribe all the hardenings to God? At this point we should turn to the suggestion of the contemporary biblical scholar, Nachum Sarna:

> This ['God hardened Pharaoh's heart'] is the biblical way of asserting that the king's intransigence has by then become habitual and irreversible; his character has become his destiny. He is deprived of the possibility of relenting and is irresistibly impelled to his self-wrought doom.
>
> (1989, 23)

Sarna's view, as I want to reconstruct it here, interprets 'God hardened Pharaoh's heart' as follows (the wording is mine):

> In the natural order of things a person S sometimes will makes choices that subsequently cause S to disregard incentives against making that sort of choice, depriving S at that later occasion of the possibility of deciding otherwise. Pharaoh's choice not to release the Israelites in the face of plague six was due to earlier choices Pharaoh had made, choices that caused him to disregard incentives for releasing them and that rendered unavoidable the choice he in fact made, viz., to keep them enslaved.

Sarna's view is reminiscent of Aristotle's position that a person is responsible for his or her character, if the person's earlier choices led up to that character (*Nicomachean Ethics*, III:5 [1114a]). Bad people are held responsible for unavoidable bad acts when their previous choices produced those later unavoidable acts.

Returning now to the problem that confronted Cassuto—why does the Bible vary its language?—the answer is that Pharaoh's 'self-hardenings' in plagues 1–5 were not wholly determined by previous choices he had made. *Those* choices were reversible in the sense that he could choose differently. So in those cases we are told that he hardened his *own* heart. But from plague six and onward Pharaoh had no choice any more—hence the shift in the Bible's language, which reflects the operation of a natural process. Adapting a felicitous remark made by Wolfson (1979, 210–11), we may say: God gives every human being the power to sin or not sin (i.e., free will), but He does not give every human being, always, the power to repent or not repent. Some lose this ability over time as they make more and more bad choices.

A challenge to the new version of naturalism may be marshalled from the Bible's description of plague seven, where Pharaoh hardens his *own* heart. If 'God hardened Pharaoh's heart' (plague six) is really another way of saying that Pharaoh's previous choices have caused him to keep the Israelites enslaved, that his path has become irreversible, and that his character has become his destiny, why would Pharaoh in plague seven be said to harden his own heart, implying (on the present theory) that his path of plague six was not irreversible after all?

The naturalist answer to this, I suggest, is that although Pharaoh's choices in plagues 1–5 made it inevitable that in plague *six* he chose to keep the Israelites enslaved, it does not follow that his choice during plague *seven* is also due to his choices in plagues 1–5. Perhaps the incentives present in plague seven to release the Israelites were greater than those present in plague six, and even a person for whom the choice in plague six was inevitable could have acted otherwise in plague seven and could have released the Israelites. No matter how bad a person's character has become, resulting in certain acts that are fully determined by previous choices, there are circumstances in which that character does not by itself dictate a bad choice. Of course, the naturalist must go on to maintain that after plague seven Pharaoh's decision not to release was, as in plague six, the inevitable result of his previous choices. (God is thereafter again said to harden his heart.) This is odd if the plagues are assumed to escalate in severity, increasing rather than decreasing the incentive to keep the Israelites enslaved.

Another problem has to be faced, however. The Bible attributes a *motive* to God for the hardening, namely, to display the divine power and 'multiply My wonders in the Land of Egypt' (Exod. 7:3; 10:1; 12:9). But according to the naturalist account, what does it mean to ascribe a motive to God? Aren't Pharaoh's 'divinely hardened' acts explicable without reference to a motive God has for the hardening? Indeed, how does a divine motive fit in with the account altogether?

I suggest that God's 'motive' fits into the account if we return to the full statement in the Talmud we quoted earlier: 'when one comes to be declared impure, we give him an opening [to impurity]; *when one comes to be purified, we assist him*' (Shabbat 104a; emphasis mine). Even if God does not directly intervene in any person's motivational system to produce *sinful* decisions, one may still posit that (a) He does directly intervene to produce good decisions when He sees that a person is trying to do the right thing, and (b) He does this even if the person is trying to do the right thing only because he harbors fear of the consequences of intransigence. It follows that if Pharaoh wanted to release the Israelites—for whatever reason, even fear—then God *ordinarily* would assist him in doing so (by, say, intervening to stifle any inclination on Pharaoh's part to slip back into doing the wrong thing). Now suppose further that God on occasion chooses to withhold assistance because He wants to realize certain goals, the attainments of which are more valuable to Him than the sinner's repenting. Then we can say of Pharaoh something analogous to what is said by Wolfson: 'God did not think of him [Pharaoh] as meeting His auxiliary grace in assisting him to turn away from his free choice of his evil conduct' (1979, 208). As distinct from Wolfson, I am suggesting that God's withholding motivational assistance is a function not only of Pharaoh's merit, but also of God's having the special motive of manifesting His power so as to make himself known to the Egyptians and Israelites.

The 'withheld assistance' view, then, treats hardening as a non-miraculous natural process, the way things go when there is no divine intervention, while explaining betterment supernaturally. Thus, hardening, on this view, is basically the withholding of supernatural assistance. In sum, for the naturalist account to explain the Bible's reference to God's motive, it needs to combine a naturalistic view of the process of hardening with a supernatural account of the process of betterment. Transformation of personality for the better originates in self, but is completed by God.

A few tasks remain for the naturalist besides the anomaly I noted earlier about plague seven. One is to explain why someone as depraved as Pharaoh would have qualified for divine assistance, were it not for God's desire to manifest His power. (Perhaps this would have been due not to Pharaoh's merit, but to God's concern for the suffering of the Israelites.) In addition, the naturalist might want to shed light on the question of whether the bettered agent deserves credit for his bettered state. I think that in some cases the answer is yes (namely, in those cases in which the agent has solicited God's help), but in others it is no. Whatever the outcome of an exploration of those matters, it is fair to say that from the naturalist perspective keeping God out of the hardening process has certain theological advantages.

## JONATHAN JACOBS

### "The Nature and Justification of Repentance and Forgiveness"

Repentance and forgiveness are vitally important aspects of Jewish life. To admit and confront one's wrongdoing, endure genuine remorse, and undertake with real resolve to ethically reorient oneself—to repent—is to return to God. To forgive exhibits willingness to repair a damaged relationship, to forswear resentment, making it possible to restore mutual, supportive concern. That is crucial for the well-being of the community and individuals. Repentance and forgiveness, we should say, are *deep* and there are few aspects of life that go deeper or have greater significance. Both repenting and forgiving reflect concern with fundamental elements of a rightly lived life.

*I*

While there are some affinities with Christian views of repentance and forgiveness, Judaism understands these issues in a distinctive way. Judaism does not include the notion of original sin, of the depravity of human nature, wounded in a way that can be repaired only by interceding salvific power. It would be a mistake to conclude that because Judaism does not include a counterpart to Christ's suffering for humanity's sinfulness, there is no role for grace in Judaism. The giving of Torah is an act of divine grace. The commandments in Torah constitute guidance for how to live a righteous life. Fulfilling the commandments enables a person to walk in God's ways, to imitate God to the extent possible for a human being. Human beings are created in the image of God in that we possess intellect and will, and human beings can know God's ways and walk in them by the study of the commandments and fulfilling them.

Repentance and forgiveness are forms of concern for the created order with a vitally significant place in how we regard and treat other persons and ourselves. They reflect the aspiration to strive to be holy and the aspiration to love one's neighbor. Indeed, if we try to imagine moral life without repentance and forgiveness it is difficult to see how the aspiration to holiness and to love one's neighbor could be fulfilled.

One of the chief differences between religiously grounded moralities and secular or naturalistic moralities is that, in the former, there is a vitally important role for human beings' *responsiveness* to God and divine revelation. That responsiveness shapes key issues of ethics and moral psychology. Imitation of God, possible through fulfilling the commandments, can guide one's aims and aspirations. Moral life involves striving to fulfill what God's wisdom and benevolence requires of us. Moreover, there is an important relation between responsiveness and *gratitude*. Gratitude has a central place in Judaism (and in Christianity and Islam) that makes for a striking contrast with, for example, ancient Greek thought. One of the main themes of the present discussion is that there are important connections between gratitude, repentance, and forgiveness.

While there are numerous different currents of Jewish thought, we will focus on the way that medieval Jewish thought—especially Maimonides'—contrasts with ideas found in the some of the ancient sources from which medieval Jewish thought borrowed. Saadia and Bahya will also figure in the discussion. The contrasts between those Jewish thinkers and ancient Greek philosophy enable us to highlight enduringly fundamental elements of Jewish thought that are not confined to the medieval context.

## II

Aristotle's *Metaphysics* commences with, "All men by nature desire to know. An indication of this is the delight we take in our senses; for even apart from their usefulness they are loved for themselves ...".[1] Because the essential nature of a human being is a rational nature, the fundamental *telos* of a human being, and one's fundamental orientation to the world, is to seek knowledge, to attain as complete an understanding as possible. Aristotle is not asserting the plainly false hypothesis that every person does their utmost to actualize their intellect as fully as possible. Instead, he is making a claim about the kind-specific nature of human beings and the place of intellectual activity in the most complete realization of that nature.

In Jewish sources *gratitude* is an essential element of our relation to God and our acknowledgement of our dependence upon God and his wisdom and benevolence. We will see that there is an important relation between gratitude and repentance and forgiveness. Aristotle's First Cause, though it actualizes understanding of all that is, does not relate to other beings through concern, care or benevolence. Judaism holds that God is a wise, merciful, providential first cause, with an intentional relation to the created order. That makes a fundamental difference to our relation to God. An implication of that difference is that reason requires that we recognize the gratitude owed to God. Saadia writes:

> ... logic demands that whoever does something good be compensated either by means of a favor shown to him, if he is in need of it, or by means of thanks, if he does not require any reward. Since, therefore, this is one of the general demands of reason, it would not have been seemly for the Creator, exalted and magnified be He, to neglect it in His own case. It was, on the contrary, necessary for Him to command His creatures to serve Him and thank Him for having created them.[2]

And Bahya writes:

> How much, then, should a man obey, praise, and thank the Creator of all benefaction and benefactors, whose beneficence is infinite, permanent, and

perpetual, done neither for His own benefit nor for drawing away misfortunes, but is all-loving kindness and grace towards men.[3]

Maimonides argues that "we are commanded to love God (exalted be He); that is to say, to dwell upon and contemplate His commandments, His injunctions, and His works, so that we may obtain a conception of Him, and in conceiving Him attain absolute joy."[4] Unlike other natural beings, we are capable of knowledge of God and of striving to do justice, exhibit righteousness and loving-kindness, and for that we should be profoundly grateful.

While we are to be grateful to God for creating us with powers other creatures lack, we are also to be humble. Maimonides makes a point of arguing that "[i]n the case of some character traits, a man is forbidden to accustom himself to the mean. Rather, he shall move to the other [i.e., far] extreme. One such [character trait] is a haughty heart, for the good way is not that a man be merely humble, but that he have a lowly spirit, that his spirit be very submissive. Therefore it was said of Moses our master that he was 'very humble,' and not merely humble."[5] "Likewise, anger is an extremely bad character trait, and it is proper for a man to move away from it to the other extreme and to teach himself not to become angry."[6] And he tells us "The wise men of old said: 'Anyone who is angry—it is as if he worships idols.' They said about anyone who is angry: If he is a wise man, his wisdom departs from him, and if he is a prophet, his prophecy departs from him."[7] Anger, we might infer, can distract and cloud judgment, and through anger we needlessly hurt others and are tempted to act in ways that are unfair and thoughtless.

There are important connections between this view of anger and humility on the one hand, and the understanding of forgiveness and repentance on the other. Consider what Maimonides and others say about repentance. In "Laws of Repentance" Maimonides writes,

> What is Repentance? It consists in this, that the sinner abandon his sin and remove it from his thought, and resolve in his heart never to repeat it, as it is said, "let the wicked forsake his way, and the man of iniquity his thoughts" (Is. 55:7); that he regret the past, as it is said, "Surely, after that I turned I repented, after that I was instructed, I smote upon my thigh" (Jer. 31:19); that he calls Him who knows all secrets to witness that he will never return to this sin again, as it is said, "neither will we call any more the work of our hands our God, for in Thee the fatherless findeth mercy" (Hos. 14:4). It is also necessary that he make oral confession and utter the resolutions which he made in his heart.[8]

And Bahya writes, "The elements essential to repentance are four in number: contrition for one's former sins, determined avoidance of them, admitting them and asking pardon for them, and undertaking in heart and conscience never to repeat them."[9]

When addressing the question, "Is the penitent the equal of the pious man?"[10] Bahya notes that the penitent can be better than the pious man. How can this be? When the penitent repents sincerely and thoroughly, when he is "forever humble and submissive to God; when he takes no pride in any of his good deeds. … when he shuns sin and error for the rest of his life—then he is the penitent who is even better than the pious man who has never sinned in the same way or any way like it."[11] "For the pious man cannot be humble in the same way as the contrite sinner … and he is not safe from pride, haughtiness, and vanity in his good deeds."[12] Like Maimonides, Bahya is emphatic about the significance of humility.

In *The Book of Beliefs and Opinions* Saadia says that the penitent "carries out the terms of repentance,"[13] which include "(a) the renunciation of sin, (b) remorse, (c) the quest of forgiveness, and (d) the assumption of the obligation not to relapse into sin."[14] He goes on to say, "[t]o the four conditions of repentance listed previously should be added the following further aids; namely, more extensive prayer, increased charity, and the endeavor to restore [other] men to the path of virtue."[15]

For repentance to be genuine and not merely superficial, the agent may need to look closely, fearlessly into himself, to find whether there are habits, attitudes, and dispositions, which, if unchanged, are likely to lead to further sinning. Maimonides writes: "Similarly, the perfect man needs to inspect his moral habits continually, weigh his actions, and reflect upon the state of his soul every single day. Whenever he sees his soul inclining toward one of the extremes, he should rush to cure it and not let the evil state become established by the repetition of a bad action—as we have mentioned."[16]

We find nothing like repentance in Aristotle's ethical thought or moral psychology. Aristotle's interest in self-awareness is primarily a matter of guarding against acquiring bad habits and dispositions, and attending to oneself in ways that enable one to ascertain what the mean requires in one's own case. What is involved in the relevant dispositions lying in the mean in one's own case is a highly individualized matter. One person has a volatile temper and another is composed. One person has strong appetites and another's are more moderate. One person is inclined to be selfish and inconsiderate, someone else is inclined to be generous and thoughtful, and so forth. It is important to guard against doing that which one will regret, or coming to be a sort of person one regrets being. But that is not the same as the concern with repentance. Aristotle recognizes the importance of *ethically relevant self-awareness* but he does not connect it with an authority to which we are to be responsive, and from which issue specific commandments concerning what makes for a well-led life. Nor is there a concern with how we will be ultimately judged, though Aristotle does, of course, emphasize the relation between states of character and one's prospects for happiness.

Repentance involves responsiveness to commandment and awareness that judgment is based on a searching knowledge of a person's soul. God is a judge to whom nothing is obscure or unknown. It is true that Aristotle holds that a life of contemplative activity is how we can lead lives most like that of the gods, and that "the wise person more than anyone else … is most loved by the gods."[17] However, this is not a close counterpart to the Jewish notion of *imitatio Dei*. The gods to whom Aristotle refers are not creators and they are not beings with which human beings enter into deeply significant relations. Aristotle's First Cause does not have loving concern for the world.

There is no Aristotelian counterpart to *halakha* or to covenant, and there is no clear counterpart to Maimonides's conclusion of the *Guide*, where he says, directly after arguing for intellectual perfection as man's highest and most complete perfection, that God's purpose is that, "the way of life of such an individual after he has achieved this apprehension, will always have in view *loving-kindness, righteousness,* and *judgment* through assimilation to His actions ...".[18] That at least *seems* to be in tension with Maimonides's view that "the perfection of man that may truly be gloried in is the one acquired by him who has achieved, in a measure corresponding to his capacity, apprehension of Him."[19]

Without trying to resolve the apparent tension between the practical and the intellectual in Maimonides's conception of the most complete human perfection, we can see that repentance is vitally important in regard to a person's relationship with God. The individual who does not repent is, on that account, someone who is unconcerned to right himself ethically. Bahya writes, "I say that repentance is when a man is reconciled to obeying God after he has failed to do so and sinned, and when he retrieves what he has lost by sinning."[20] To sin is to disobey; to repent is to restore a morally sound disposition, needed for a morally right relation to God and to other people. Not to repent is to exhibit unwillingness to renounce wrongdoing; it is a failure to redirect oneself in the proper way. It is thereby also a failure to be humble, a failure to acknowledge how one has lapsed from the relevant standard of conduct.

That failure can undermine one's own virtue and righteousness, and also one's relations with other persons. David Hartman takes note of the connection between repentance and community when he writes:

> The individual within the Jewish community recognized the primary role of community in shaping his spiritual self-consciousness. To separate from the community was to cut oneself off from the God of history. The divine will, history, community, action were therefore dominant and interconnected organizing principles of daily life.[21]

For Maimonides, one of the chief aims of the Law is "the welfare of the body."[22] The welfare of the body "comes about by the improvement of their ways of living with one another." Repentance is an important element of "the abolition of wronging each other."[23] To repent is to be willing to endure rebuke and to follow through with striving to fulfill the point of rebuke, i.e., to morally restore and improve oneself.

The Law says, "You shall surely rebuke your neighbor and not bear sin because of him" (Lev. 19:17) and "You shall not fear the face of any man." (Deut. 1:17) This can sound like a commandment to police our neighbors and in that respect it can seem highly illiberal and intrusive. But the commandment to rebuke (without humiliating or degrading the person rebuked) is an expression of concern for one's neighbor. If our fellowman is leading a life of moral corruption or is acting wrongly unawares, that is a proper matter of concern to us. If one really cares for the welfare of the people Israel, one is obliged to actualize that in effective, practical terms, and to try to retrieve those who have gone astray.

Rebuke has a constructive role in motivating a person to repent, and repentance is a fundamental way in which a person can return to God, redirect himself to God's ways, and come closer to God. "Repentance is, therefore, not limited to the negative goal of effacing previous offense. Rather, being itself the fulfillment of a positive act of obedience, it serves to condition man to further obedience."[24] To rebuke a member of the community is not a form of condescending moral paternalism; it is a way of showing concern for one's neighbor, for the community, for the created order. "If someone sees his fellow man who has sinned or who follows a way that is not good, it is a commandment to make him return to the good and to make known to him that he sins against himself by his evil actions. As it is said: 'You shall surely rebuke your neighbor.'"[25] But one should be rebuked in private, and one "shall not at first speak harshly so to put him to shame."[26] For, "we learn it is forbidden to humiliate an Israelite; all the more [it is forbidden] in public."[27]

## III

Forgiveness, too, is vitally important to the individual and the community. By forgiving we forswear resentment and show willingness to restore relations with those who have wronged us. No one is so excellent, so superior as to be above forgiving, as though he is immune to being wronged or hurt. No one is so perfect as never to need to be forgiven. For, "a man inevitably has defects."[28] "*Solomon* said absolutely: *There is no man who is just upon the earth, who does only good and does not sin*" (Eccles. 7:20).[29] Also, "for an individual cannot but sin and err, either through ignorance—by professing an opinion or a moral quality that is not preferable in truth—or else because he is overcome by desire or anger. If then the individual believed that this fracture could never be remedied, he would persist in his error and sometimes perhaps disobey even more because of the fact that no stratagem remains at his disposal."[30]

Not to repent is to fail to acknowledge the wrong one has done and to leave it uncorrected as a part of one's action-guiding capacity. Not to rebuke is to leave a person without what may be necessary guidance. Not to forgive is to leave a damaged relationship unrepaired, at the risk of corrupting oneself through harboring resentment and anger. "Transgressions, confessed on the first Day of Atonement, are again confessed on the next Day of Atonement, even if one has continued penitent, as it is said, 'For I know my transgressions, and my sin is ever before me' (Ps. 51: 5)."[31]

Forgiveness is notably absent from the moral psychology we find in Plato and Aristotle. Considering why that should be so will help illuminate its role in Jewish thought and life. Discussing whether and why forgiveness is of interest to Aristotle, Charles Griswold writes:

Why is it that Aristotle nowhere praises forgiveness (as distinguished from pardoning and excusing) as a virtue? The core answer lies in the character of his perfectionist ethical scheme, for it is one that seeks to articulate and recommend the character of the man—and in Aristotle, it is a man—of complete virtue. The gentleman possessing the perfection of moral virtue— the *megalopsuchos*—certainly has no need (by his own lights, anyhow) for being forgiven, because by definition he is morally perfect (and in any case, his pride would not allow him to recognize himself as in need of forgiveness). He also would seem unforgiving of others, for three reasons. First, he has no interest in sympathetically grasping the situation and faults of non-virtuous persons—they are of little account to him. Second, he would judge himself immune to being injured by them morally ...[32] The third reason why forgiveness is not part of the magnanimous person's outlook is implicit in the hierarchical value scheme that is part and parcel of his perfectionist outlook, and comes across in the dismissiveness that characterizes the attitude of the *megalopsuchos* toward "inferior people."[33]

By contrast, one finds many examples of forgiveness in the Hebrew Bible, Joseph forgiving his brothers is one notable instance (Gen. 50). At Exodus 34: 6–7 God is said to forgive iniquity, transgression, and sin, and to forgive iniquity and not to maintain His wrath forever. We find forgiveness in many other passages, among them Gen. 33 (Esau forgiving Jacob), Numbers 12 (Moses forgiving Aaron and Miriam); see also Deut. 21:8, and pleas for forgiveness, in Ps. 38 and 51. David forgives Saul in Samuel 24; and God's forgiveness is highlighted in Micah 7:18.

Forgiveness is not the same as mercy though in ordinary usage the terms are often used as though they are interchangeable. Mercy is a matter of withholding punishment that is justified. It concerns electing not to impose sanction though it is deserved. To forgive is to let go of resentment, to cease to regard the other person as morally corrupt, and to be willing to restore one's relation with the wrongdoer. Whether forgiving is an *obligation* is a very difficult question, forgiveness sometimes is regarded as a requirement, sometimes as supererogatory.

In either case, forgiving makes genuine reconciliation possible. Maimonides holds that a person sinned against should "blot out the matter from his heart and not bear a grudge."[34] And, "the Torah was particularly concerned with grudge-bearing so that the wrong done be completely blotted out from a man's heart ..."[35] Forgiveness is impossible if a person succumbs to hatred of the wrongdoer. But is repentance on the part of the wrongdoer a necessary condition for being forgiven? It might seem so. Yet, isn't it sometimes the case that forgiving a person *motivates* repentance?

Maimonides holds that every person is liable to sin, as we noted above. Though sinning is inevitable, it is also the case that, because we have free will, whatever action one performed, *that* action was avoidable. We cannot excuse a sin by saying it could not be helped. (As David Shatz points out in his essay in this section, even the (unrepentant) hardening of Pharaoh's heart is compatible with free will, one that freely chose wrong repeatedly.) One cannot claim that the imperfection of human nature, the inevitability of sin, should excuse *this* particular wrong act. That is why, "whoever is bad is so by his own choice. If he wishes to be virtuous, he can be so; there is nothing preventing him. Similarly, if any virtuous man wishes to, he can be bad; there is nothing preventing him."[36] And, "if one desires to turn towards the good way and be righteous, he has the power to do so."[37] We may not be free *never* to sin, but in each case, we are free not to sin. And we are able to ethically reorient ourselves to righteousness.

If we understand that anyone, even the most pious among us, is liable to sin, we might be more willing to see the point in forgiveness, to see that each of us needs to be forgiven. "Thou shalt not take vengeance" (Lev. 19:18) is a commandment, and to forgive and to refrain from vengeance can be one way in which our humility is expressed and our anger controlled. It is also a way of guarding against long-nursed resentment, against being overcome by anger and turning another person's transgression into the motive for one of our own or lashing out inappropriately. Saadia says of the person who insists upon satisfying his vengeance, "he will still have incurred the severe punishment of God from which no one can save him except the forgiveness of him whom he has wronged, as Scripture says: *A man that is laden with the blood of any person shall hasten his steps unto the pit; none will support him*" (Prov. 28:17).[38]

### Conclusion

Repentance and forgiveness both reflect recognition of humility before God, commitment to righteousness, and concern for the created order. They do this through reflecting a willingness to acknowledge wrongs done, to seek to repair wrongful dispositions, and to restore relations with others, explicitly forswearing resentment and vengeance. Those are all consistent with a commitment to seeing that justice is done, another crucial aspect of Jewish life. Repentance and forgiveness are among the most significant ways in which, despite our finitude and imperfection, we can nonetheless strive to imitate God.

### Notes

1  *Metaphysics* 980a 22–23.
2  *The Book of Beliefs and Opinions*, in Saadia 1948, 139.
3  *The Book of Direction to the Duties of the Heart*, in Bahya 1973, 178.
4  *Book of Commandments*, in Twersky (ed.), 1972, 432.
5  *Mishneh Torah*, Laws Concerning Character Traits 2.3, in Maimonides 1975, 31.
6  Ibid., 32.
7  Ibid.
8  *Mishneh Torah*, Laws of Repentance 2.2, in Maimonides 1981.
9  *The Book of Direction to the Duties of the Heart*, in Bahya 1973, 333.
10  Ibid., 343.
11  Ibid., 344.
12  Ibid.
13  *The Book of Beliefs and Opinions*, in Saadia 1948, 220.

14 Ibid.
15 Ibid.
16 *Shemonah Perakim* (*Eight Chapters*), chapter 4, in Maimonides 1975, 73.
17 *Nicomachean Ethics* 1179a31–2.
18 *Guide of the Perplexed* 3.54, in Maimonides 1963, 638 (cf. the attributes of God, Exodus 34: 6–7).
19 Ibid.
20 *The Book of Direction to the Duties of the Heart*, in Bahya 1973, 330.
21 Hartman 1976, 5.
22 *Guide of the Perplexed* 3.27, in Maimonides 1963, 510.
23 Ibid.
24 Stern 1979, 599.
25 *Mishneh Torah*, Laws Concerning Character Traits 6.7–8, in Maimonides 1975, 48.
26 Ibid.
27 Ibid., 49.
28 *Shemonah Perakim* (*Eight Chapters*), chapter 4, in Maimonides 1975, 73.
29 Ibid. (italics in original).
30 *Guide of the Perplexed* 3.36, in Maimonides 1963, 540.
31 *Mishneh Torah*, Laws of Repentance 2 (83a), in Maimonides 1981.
32 Griswold 2007a, 7–8.
33 Ibid., 9.
34 *Mishneh Torah*, Laws Concerning Character Traits 7.8, in Maimonides 1975, 52.
35 Ibid.
36 *Shemonah Perakim* (*Eight Chapters*), chapter 8, in Maimonides 1975, 89.
37 *Mishneh Torah*, Laws of Repentance 5.1, in Maimonides 1981.
38 *The Book of Beliefs and Opinions*, in Saadia 1948, 391–2.

## Further Reading on Repentance and Forgiveness

Flint, T. P. "Divine Providence," in *The Oxford Handbook of Philosophical Theology*, eds. T. P. Flint and M. C. Rea (Oxford: Oxford University Press, 2009), 262–285.

Frankfurt, H. "On God's Creation," in *Necessity, Volition, and Love*, ed. H. Frankfurt, (Cambridge: Cambridge University Press, 1998), 117–128.

Gerondi, J. *Gates of Repentance*, trans. S. Silverstein (Jerusalem: Feldheim Publishers, 1981).

Griswold, C. *Forgiveness: A Philosophical Exploration* (Cambridge: Cambridge University Press, 2007).

Jacobs, J. "Forgiveness and Perfection: Maimonides, Aquinas, and Medieval Departures from Aristotle," in *Ancient Forgiveness*, eds. C. L. Griswold and D. Konstan (Cambridge: Cambridge University Press, 2011), 216–236.

Kretzmann, N. "God Among the Causes of Moral Evil: Hardening of Hearts and Spiritual Blinding," *Philosophical Topics* 16 (1988), 189–214.

McCann, H. J. "Divine Sovereignty and the Freedom of the Will," *Faith and Philosophy* 12:4 (1995), 582–598.

Metzger, A. B. Z. (trans.) *Rabbi Kook's Philosophy of Repentance: A Translation of Orot ha-teshuvah* (New York: Yeshiva University Press, 1968).

Morgan, M. "Mercy, Repentance, and Forgiveness in Ancient Judaism," in *Ancient Forgiveness*, eds. C. L. Griswold and D. Konstan (Cambridge: Cambridge University Press, 2011), 137–157.

Murphy, J. G. *Getting Even: Forgiveness and its Limits* (New York: Oxford University Press, 2005).

Murphy, J. G. and J. Hampton, *Forgiveness and Mercy* (Cambridge: Cambridge University Press, 1998).

Peli, P. *On Repentance: The Thought and Oral Discourses of Rabbi Joseph Dov Soloveitchik* (New York: Jason Aronson Publishers, 1996).

Pereboom, D. "Free Will, Evil, and Divine Providence," in *God and the Ethics of Belief: New Essays in Philosophy of Religion*, eds. A. Dole and A. Chignell (New York: Cambridge University Press, 2005), 77–98.

Shatz, D. "Hierarchical Theories of Freedom and the Hardening of Hearts," *Midwest Studies in Philosophy* 21 (1997), 202–224.

Stump, E. "Sanctification, Hardening of the Heart, and Frankfurt's Concept of Free Will," *Journal of Philosophy* 85 (1988), 395–420.

Stump, E. "Personal Relations and Moral Residue," *History of the Human Sciences* 17:2–3 (2004), 33–57.

# 12 Religious Pluralism and Toleration

An analysis of the grounds for religious toleration toward gentiles in the teachings of R. Menachem Ha-Me'iri (1249–1315) is the subject of **Moshe Halbertal's** essay. The rabbis of the Talmud placed restrictions on all manner of commercial and economic interactions between Jews and gentiles, but as Halbertal points out, Me'iri dramatically reformulated the notion of idolatry in such a way that gentiles, almost without exception, were not to be considered as idolaters. As "ones possessed of religion," the traditional (Talmudic) laws severely constricting Jewish relations with non-Jews are for Me'iri inapplicable to the other monotheistic religions, specifically Christianity and Islam. Me'iri's arguments thus provide for toleration and a considered ecumenism among monotheistic faiths.

**Moses Mendelssohn's** epistolary response (1769) to Lavater's request for a refutation of Christianity, on pain of conversion to it, is celebrated for its rhetorical brilliance, less celebrated for its being a non-sequitur and in its own way a paradigm of passive aggression. (David Shatz in his essay in this section on religious diversity senses a tone of "moral superiority" in the letter.) Sensing in Lavater's request a kind of proselytizing, Mendelssohn goes on the offensive. He does not address the theological issues on the table, and Lavater's demand for argument and refutation, but rather focuses upon the absence of a proselytizing impulse in Judaism and on its 'live and let live,' tolerant acceptance of other religions. Mendelssohn's response presumes an antithesis between Judaism and Christianity, though he hardly mentions the latter by name. Christianity prioritizes doctrinal truth as the path to salvation, and as a result holds non-believers as damned. By contrast, Judaism is defined by law, not doctrine, and though the written and oral laws are binding only on Jews, gentiles who live by a moral code merit "eternal bliss," according to the rabbis. Judaism does not proselytize, unlike Christianity, precisely because (exclusionary) doctrinal uniformity counts for naught and a principled pluralism is normative. For Mendelssohn, Jews and non-Jews (even "a Confucius or a Solon") can live together amicably, as the demand from the Jewish side is toleration and respect for difference.

Interfaith dialogue has been a familiar activity over the last few decades, driven especially by the Vatican II document *Nostra Aetate* (1965). As **David Shatz** notes, the discussions are not over which religion is true, but rather how people of different faiths should view each other's religion and live together in peace. Shatz's essay indexes this issue to the Jewish tradition, and its historic 'indifference' to engage in interfaith dialogue. Mendelssohn's emphasis on the manifest absence of a proselytizing impulse in Judaism can be seen as part of this 'indifference.' Why aren't Jews more eager to spread the truth as they see it? Over the ages Jews have suffered the charge of haughtiness or thinking themselves superior, stemming from a perception of Jewish exclusivism. Shatz details a variety of reasons why historically Jews have not proselytized, and many of them are grounded in a keen sense of its minority status and the dangers involved in attempting to play on the turf of a much more powerful adversary. The challenge for Judaism in a world of many different religions and cultures is to find a way to participate in the general discussion, while still retaining its identity.

## MOSHE HALBERTAL

### "'Ones Possessed of Religion': Religious Tolerance in the Teachings of the Me'iri," in *The Edah Journal* 1.1 (2000)

In dealing with relations between Jews and gentiles, Rabbi Menachem Ben Shlomo Ha-Me'iri (1249–1315) of Provence took up a subject with a long history of treatment by the halakhic authorities who preceded him. His unique approach in this area offers an instructive example of the integration of philosophy and *halakhah*.

The halakhic consideration of relations with gentiles had taken place in the eleventh century, more than two hundred years before the Me'iri's time. From the beginning of Jewish settlement in Christian Europe, Jewish communities formed economic relationships with their Christian neighbors that were inconsistent with talmudically dictated restrictions on business dealings with non-Jews, such as the ban on commerce with non-Jews on their festival days, the ban on selling their ritual objects, and the ban on commerce whose profits would accrue to the Church. These limitations foisted economic difficulties upon the Jewish communities in Christian Europe, which in turn set their own rules of conduct vis-à-vis Christians.

The German and French halakhists adopted varied and complex strategies for bridging the gulf they confronted between communal practice and *halakhah*. As a first step, Rabbeinu Gershom Me'or Ha-Golah claimed that the halakhic prohibitions remained intact, but local halakhic authorities should avoid vain efforts to enforce them: "Better that Israel sin unknowingly than knowingly." Nevertheless the communal practice gained halakhic legitimacy through various explanations offered by Rabbeinu Gershom and the halakhists who succeeded him. One position reasoned that the prohibitions had been decreed in different circumstances, at a time when the Jewish community was large enough to be economically self-sufficient—and that situation no longer existed within the small *Ashkenazi* communities. Another position, also relying on changed circumstances, sanctioned the customary conduct "because of hatred" ("*mi-shum eivah*"). Still other authorities sought to limit the applicability of these prohibitions by means of local, novel reinterpretations of the talmudic passages that had generated the restrictions. All these halakhic strategies shared a common component: Each halakhic authority refrained from drawing a distinction in principle between Christianity and the idolatrous religions toward which the halakhic restrictions had been formed. At most, they distinguished between the Christian multitudes and the Christian religion. Relying on the argument in the Talmud Bavli that, "Gentiles outside of the land of Israel are not idolaters. Rather, they adhere to their ancestral customs" (*Hulin* 13b), these halakhists determined that because the local gentiles were not devout, some of the prohibitions on commerce did not apply to them. Nevertheless, they held that even though Christians were not devout in their religion, Christianity itself was idolatrous. As Jacob Katz has shown, this complex position of the *Ashkenazi* halakhists grew out of their desire to preserve the huge disparity between monotheistic Judaism and idolatrous Christianity while simultaneously easing the economic burden that resulted from defining Christianity as idolatrous.

Religious tolerance in the Me'iri's teachings has been the subject of scholarly examination, but the nexus between his halakhic position and his general worldview and its sources has never been adequately clarified. Scholarly consideration began with a detailed analysis by Jacob Katz, who viewed the Me'iri as adopting a unique, comprehensive position based on a fundamental theological concept. The Me'iri's predecessors had proposed various solutions to bridge the gulf between widespread medieval *Ashkenazi* practice and the halakhic limitations on contact with gentiles. However, none of them took a position that distinguished fundamentally between idolatry and Christianity. If such a distinction appeared at all in halakhic literature, it was limited in its use to particular times and places, and it provided no basis for a definitive and generalized permissive ruling. The Me'iri was the first to draw this fundamental distinction, and the permissive ruling he proposed was accordingly definitive and independent. It followed neither post facto from the community's practice, nor did it depend on other permissive rulings. Finally, it extended beyond the permissive rulings issued by the halakhic authorities who preceded him...

The Me'iri's conception incorporates several important fundamental innovations. The first is the reason for his sweepingly permissive ruling with respect to the halakhic prohibitions on indirect contact with idolatrous ritual: the determination that idolatry is a phenomenon that has departed the world or been marginalized. The Me'iri extends this principle to areas unrelated to the economic interaction between the Jewish community and its Christian surroundings, permitting us to see in his view a broader conception of the historical progress made by faith.

The second innovation relates to the link between his permitting contacts with contemporary gentiles on the grounds that they are not idolaters, and the substantive change in how their juridical status is conceived. This link rests on the determination that idolatrous nations are nations lacking fear of the Divinity and, therefore, that they do not recognize the concept of sin or transgression. Thus there is a two-way causal connection between a nation's idolatry and its lack of restrictions by the ways of religion.

The third innovation is the Me'iri's concept that the Talmud's inequality between Jew and gentile with respect to personal and property rights arises from the parallel distinction between restricted nations and those unrestricted, not from any ontological distinction between Jew and gentile or even between idolaters and worshippers of the Divine. By establishing the inequality on this new basis, the Me'iri limits its application to the ancient idolatrous nations and also provides it an inner rationale. The inequality reflects a sort of measure-for-measure attitude toward the undisciplined nations: There is no obligation to treat lawless nations in accordance with legal constraints. The Me'iri applies this distinction between restricted and unrestricted nations to matters going beyond the constraints that vexed his predecessors, such as danger to life on the sabbath, as well as the preparation of food for a gentile (*Beit Ha-Behirah, Beitsah*, Linge ed., pp. 117–118) and the daring reading of "*Ein Mazal le-Yisrael*" as a statement granting direct divine concern to all who possess religion (*Beit Ha-Behirah, Shabbat*, p. 615).

To examine the philosophical and theological origins of the Me'iri's determination that idolatry no longer exists and his assumptions regarding the concept of "restricted by the ways of religion," it is necessary to study his use of the terms "possessed of religion," "ways of religion," or "religious ways" in contexts independent of the halakhic standing of gentiles. These terms appear numerous times in such contexts throughout the Me'iri's writings and those passages help illuminate his intention in coining the terms "nations restricted by the ways of religion" and nations "possessed of religion," and enable us to understand the broader context of his position.

The concept "one possessed of religion" (*ba'al dat*) has its source in a distinction widely drawn by Maimonides' philosophical heirs—Samuel Ibn Tibbon, Moses Ibn Tibbon, and Jacob Anatoli. "Possessed of religion" denotes a person whose faith and actions are based not on inquiry (*iyyun*), but on an accepted belief in a divinity that exercises providence and imposes punishment. According to the philosophers, religion is a necessary condition to the existence of the social order, for in contrast to those "possessed of wisdom" (*ba'alei hakhma*), the masses are motivated primarily by the hope of reward and the fear of punishment. Belief in *creatio ex nihilo* (*hidush*) is the central metaphysical premise that characterizes those possessed of religion and that makes religion possible. It is therefore fitting that a philosopher treat as esoteric everything connected with positions that negate *creatio ex nihilo*, providence, and recompense. A society lacking religion is a dangerous society, as stated by the philosopher whom the Me'iri quotes in his comments on those restricted by the ways of religion: "Put to death one who has no religion." Here we can recognize the influence of the concept of religion that flourished in the philosophical tradition preceding the Me'iri, and it is not surprising that he refers to the philosophical statement in what is clearly a halakhic analysis. The Me'iri differed from his predecessors in how he ranked one possessed of religion and one possessed of wisdom, yet he derived the concept of religion and its essential nature from the philosophical tradition that preceded him. For the Me'iri, the concepts "possessed of religion" and "ways of religion," when considered in broad theological contexts, are always linked to a belief in *creatio ex nihilo*, providence, and recompense, or to actions intended to strengthen that belief. These constitute the central core of the realm of religion as defined by the Tibbonides. The Me'iri uses these terms frequently, but for present purposes allow me cite only a few paradigmatic examples.

In the first part of his "Essay on Repentance" ("*Hibbur Ha-Teshuvah*"), the Me'iri describes the beliefs that allow for the existence and benefits of repentance as beliefs belonging to one possessed of religion:

> But my intention in this chapter is only to caution the sinner not to give up on repentance, whether by failing to believe in it or by fearing that it will not be accepted because of the multitude of his sins. Both of those foreign and evil notions will lead their adherents to hold fast to their wickedness. For the belief in the benefits of repentance, as described by the rabbi, the guide of righteousness [i.e., Maimonides] in one of his chapters, is among the factors without which people possessed of religion cannot get along. ... But by believing in the benefits of repentance and the damage caused by its absence, he will be strengthened in the true knowledge that God, may He be blessed, oversees our ways and has the power to punish us and cause us loss if we disobey Him and to do well by us if we serve Him; and he will then strive to mend his ways.
>
> (pp. 22–23)

The benefits of repentance assume a belief in providence and recompense, which are necessary conditions to the existence of people possessed of religion. These beliefs cannot be attained through reason, but must be received through a tradition. In his comments on the structure of the Book of Ecclesiastes, the Me'iri uses the expression "ways of religion" to describe the unprovable domain of belief, which cannot be contradicted by logic: "It is known that the intention of King Solomon, of blessed memory, in this book was to bolster the ways of religion and the received tradition and to teach that no proof can stand in its way nor any logical argument turn it aside" (p. 669). The Me'iri thus uses the concepts, "possessed of religion" and "the ways of religion," i.e., his central concepts pertaining to gentiles, in the broader context of his system as well. From contexts independent of gentiles, we learn that these concepts clearly grow out of the Maimonidean philosophical tradition. Religion does not reflect the philosophical core common to intellectuals of all religions. Its concern is rather with the domain of religious *praxis*, which grows out of beliefs that inquiry cannot prove.

A clear example showing that religion is not part of the philosophical/ analytical stratum is Ibn Kaspi's usage of the adage, "Put to death one who has no religion." In describing his opposition to scholars (*me'ayyenim*) who disparage the commandments, Ibn Kaspi says:

> My son, there are two types among our people who adopt contemporary traits. Do not walk in their path and let your foot avoid their ways. The first type are the philosophizers among our people who have not served their full

apprenticeship ... yet cast scorn on the words of our sages of blessed memory and treat casually the commandments that call for action (*mitsvot ma 'asiyyot*) ... I swear by the Eternal, that Aristotle and his associates and students all caution us to observe everything in the Torah and in the words of the prophets and especially to be careful with respect to the commandments calling for action. As Plato said: "Put to death one who has no religion."

(*Sefer Ha-Musar*, p. 67)

The philosopher must participate in the domain of religion, which is encompassed not within the analytical core shared by those possessing wisdom, but within the dimension of religious *praxis*.

The domain of religion forms the basic layer of beliefs on which the existence of a disciplined community is founded. This domain is the common province not of those possessed of wisdom but of religious believers as a whole, who have faith in a creating, overseeing, and recompensing God. The Me'iri's religious tolerance grows out of his recognition of a religious domain held in common by Jews, Christians, and Muslims, and from the fact that the value of the common domain is rooted in its necessary contribution to the creation of sound societies. The Me'iri occasionally portrays this realm in radical terminology, referring to the brotherhood of those possessing religion or to the applicability to all such people of the name "Israel." His conception of the common base of all religions is reflected most astonishingly in relation to an apostate (*mumar*) who moves from one religion to another. As Jacob Katz has pointed out, according to the Me'iri an apostate (*meshumad*) is not one who has changed his religion but one who lacks any religion. A Jew who converts from Judaism to Christianity is not subject to the rule of "one who is pushed down [into a pit to die] but is not taken out." By virtue of being a Christian, he remains within the core that is common to Judaism and Christianity: Both are possessed of religion. The apostate who must be put to death is one who has thrown off the yoke of all religion in general:

Heretics (*minim*) and non-believers (*epiqorsim*) may be directly harmed; and informers (*masorot*) are permitted [to be harmed] though their property may not [be used]; and one who apostatizes to idolatry is within the class of the heretics. But all of this is so only when the rubric of "Israel" continues to apply to them, for anyone who is within that rubric and disavows and desecrates the religion is subject to severe punishment, for he has become a heretic and is as one who has no religion. But one who has completely left the rubric [of Israel] and become a member of another religion is considered by us to be the same as any other member of the religion he has joined.

(*Beit Ha-Behirah Horayyot*, A. Sofer ed., p. 275)

Intolerance for idolaters has its source, therefore, not in their being members of another religion, but in their being members of no religion at all because they are not restricted by the ways of religion. The Me'iri is the first thinker to suggest a concept of inter-religious tolerance built on the functional value common to all religion. His tolerance thus extends to other religions, but not to people lacking any religion whatsoever.

Creating a common core shared by religious people in general requires a mind-set different from the one that distinguishes between true and false religions, which is the distinction that underlies intolerant points of view. The ability to break free of the distinction between true and false religion and create a generic rubric of "religion" that encompasses various particular traditions (including the religion of Israel) grows out of a conception of the important functional role played by religion, or the "ways of religion," in Judaism, Islam, and Christianity. This core, common to all those possessed of religion, is fundamentally independent of questions of truth and falsity. It does not arise out of any logical argument, but is distinguished primarily through its ability to create a disciplined society. It must be stressed that the Me'iri does not base his tolerance for other religions on a non-particularist core of philosophical truth, on which thinkers of all religions agree. Such a core does not engender religious tolerance, for it emphasizes the metaphysical truths of a conception of the Divine, such as the simple unity of God. Those are the possession of only a limited group, and are certainly not shared generally by Christian believers. It is precisely the focus on the religious core shared by all believers that enables the Me'iri to avoid detailed questions of metaphysical truth, which inevitably lead to intolerance of the sort manifested by Maimonides. The Me'iri derived his conception of the functional importance of the religious core from the Provencal philosophical tradition that preceded him. Again, however, he was unique in applying it to the issue of the halakhic attitude to gentiles and in concluding that discrimination with respect to rights and responsibilities extends only to those gentiles not found within the category of those possessing religion. This progression in the Me'iri forms an instructive paradigm of the interaction of *halakhah* and philosophy.

The distinction between restricted and unrestricted nations is causally connected to the more fundamental distinction between the ancient nations that worshipped idols and the nations of the Me'iri's time that did not do so ... The latter distinction was the basis for permitting contacts with gentiles of the Meiri's time that had been forbidden because they might entail indirect support for or benefit from idolatrous ritual and its apparatus. But how did the Me'iri understand the nature of idolatry? What is the source of his theory of progress that claims that idolatry has departed the world or is relegated to its margins? Just as the clarification of the concepts, "ways of religion" and "persons possessed of religion" is found in passages containing theological statements not dealing directly with prohibitions on commerce with gentiles, the Me'iri's concept of progress can be clarified by passages reflecting more general theological contexts.

In his "Essay on Repentance," the Me'iri identifies four stages of belief: the sensory (*murgash*), the self-evident (*mefursam*), the syllogistic or rationally derived (*muqash*), and the received through tradition (*mequbbal*). He identifies the ancient nations with the first two stages:

It is well known that in ancient times, false ideas were widespread, for they believed only in what was perceived by the senses or was self-evident or axiomatic; and this is the view attributed to the generation of the Tower of Babel. Because they did not conceive of the existence of anything non-corporeal (*nifrad, nivdal*), they denied the existence of God and instead worshipped the heavenly objects. Were they to see a ladder standing on the ground with its top reaching heavenward, they would not see the Lord of Hosts standing upon it, and they would not believe in His *sancta*. This is what the sages of blessed memory meant when they said that the intention of the Tower builders was to place an idol at its top with a sword in its hand to kill Him, as it were, for "killing" is the sages' way of portraying the absence of existence of something real. ... It is an allegory meaning that the Babel generation lacked any notion of the existence of things that were neither perceived by the senses nor self-evident. However one who inquires (*ba'al mehqar*) will exert the effort to believe in what reasoning generates and proves, and will thereby come to a belief in some of the firm bases of the Torah, such as the existence of God and all non-corporeal objects.

(*Essay on Repentance*, pp. 255–256)

Again, in his *Commentary on Psalms*, the Me'eri writes:

For beliefs must be arrived at through one of four ways: sense perception, self-evident claims, or received tradition [sic]. In ancient times, there were flawed opinions that believed only in what could be perceived through the senses or what was axiomatically self-evident ... and they accordingly denied the existence of God or anything non-corporeal as well as all the disciplines of religion; [only] a few such continue to inhabit some remote places. However the philosopher exerts through inquiry the effort to believe in what comes to him through syllogism and proof. Even so, man's beliefs could not be perfected until the Torah came. One who accepts it takes on the yoke of the kingdom of heaven, and believes, in addition to the foregoing, in everything that the ways of religion require him to believe in a comprehensive way that lacks nothing.

(*Commentary on Psalms*, p. 47)

The Me'iri's wording in the *Commentary on Psalms* ("they accordingly denied the existence of God or anything non-corporeal as well as all the disciplines of religion") clearly identifies the ancient nations who believe only in what the senses can perceive as the "nations unrestricted by the ways of religion" that appear in his halakhic writings.

As is evident from the foregoing passages, these nations are situated at the first stage of cognition, where there is no belief in the existence of any independent non-corporeal entity. As the Me'iri puts it, they deny "the existence of anything non-corporeal." The stage going beyond beliefs dependent on sense perception begins with the rational philosopher who comes to recognize the existence of an independent, non-corporeal transcendent cause and therefore believes in the existence of God. The ancient nations were fetishists who failed to recognize the existence of a transcendent, non-corporeal cause in the universe. That is, they lacked a concept of God.

In Aristotelian terms that the Me'iri employs elsewhere, the ancient nations' physics reached the realm of the spheres, but they failed to recognize the realm of the non-corporeal forms and the first cause. In portraying the beliefs of the ancient nations that deny the existence of anything non-corporeal, the Me'iri occasionally uses an allegorical understanding of the story of the Tower of Babel, at whose summit the builders placed an idol brandishing a sword, and he contrasts it with Jacob's ladder. Like the tower, the ladder describes the levels of existence; but unlike the fetishists of the Babel generation, Jacob saw God standing atop the ladder. The distinction between pagans and monotheists here is the distinction between a materialist worldview and a metaphysical outlook that acknowledges the existence of non-corporeal forms. On the basis of this conception of idolatry, the Me'iri determined that idolatry has departed the world, since all [contemporary] religions recognize the existence of a non-material, transcendent cause that exercises providence and recompense. The distinction between paganism and its negation lies neither in the details of the various religions' concepts of God's unity, nor in the difference between polytheism and pure monotheism. Were that the distinction, Christianity would be considered an idolatrous religion. It is because the Me'iri identifies the ancient nations with materialism and fetishism that he can determine with certainty that Christianity is not an idolatrous religion, since it too recognizes a transcendent, non-material cause. The Me'iri then argues that the idolatrous nations, which deny the non-corporeal and lack any concept of God, lack as well any fear of God that forms the basis for "the restrictions of religion."

A comparison of the Me'iri's comments on the ancient nations with those in Samuel Ibn Tibbon's essay, "*Ma'amar Yiqqawu Ha-Mayim*," reveals that the latter is the source of the Me'iri's concept of progress. One can readily enumerate their common basic elements: (1) the allegorical understanding of the Tower of Babel, whose summit reaches the heavens. This symbolizes the limit of the Babel generation's understanding, namely the world of the spheres that excludes non-corporeal forms; (2) the shared interpretation of the sword referred to in the *midrash*, and the explanation of "killing" as intellectual denial; (3) the contrasting parallelism between Jacob's ladder, on which angels ascend and descend and on whose summit God stands, and the Tower; and (4) the basic picture of a progression from a materialistic understanding to one that recognizes the existence of a transcendent reality. All of these show clearly that the Me'iri derived his concept of progress from the philosophical tradition of Provence. Samuel Ibn Tibbon used this concept to justify revealing the secrets of the Torah—an application that the Me'iri himself, as a follower of the moderate Maimonidean school, opposed. The Me'iri, however, extended the same concept of progress to the halakhic problem of how to relate to gentiles, and used it to forge an absolute distinction between the ancient nations and those of his time.

Notwithstanding the concept of progress that he developed, the Me'iri was of the opinion that idolatry had not totally departed the world. It could still be found at the "extremities" of the inhabited world: "In my opinion, all those remote places in which idolatry remains are subject to the strict rulings applicable to the early [nations]" (*Beit Ha-Behirah Avodah Zarah*, p. 214). He gave the distinction between restricted and unrestricted nations definitive geographic expression, with civilization found at the "center," and barbarian nations lacking any civilizing laws to be found at the margins.

Here, too, the Me'iri makes stunning halakhic use of a widespread medieval image. The concept that wild, lawless nations exist on the fringes of the settled world is referred to in Jewish sources that pre-date the Me'iri, and is tied to theories of climate that were widespread in the Muslim and Christian worlds during the Middle Ages. Until the Me'iri, however, no halakhist using the term had identified the gentile or idolater of the talmudic tradition with these fringe nations. After creating the juridical category of the brotherhood shared by Jews, Christians, and Muslims, the Me'iri drives the concept of the threatening "Other" away from the Jew's society. The enemy as defined in Jewish tradition continues to exist. Its existence may be required for the community's self-definition, but it is cast out to the margins of the settled world. The Me'iri's unique use of the concepts "possessed of religion" and "religious ways" and his idea of progress provide an instructive example of how a philosophical conception intertwined with halakhic analysis can lead to a changed interpretation of earlier halakhic sources.

## MOSES MENDELSSOHN (1729–86)

### Open Letter to Lavater (1769) (tr. Bowman), in M. Gottlieb (ed.), *Moses Mendelssohn: Writings on Judaism, Christianity, & the Bible* (2011)

Honorable friend of humanity!

You have deemed it proper to dedicate to me Mr. Bonnet's *Investigation of the Proofs for Christianity*, which you have translated from the French. And in the dedication you have deemed it proper to implore me, before the eyes of the public and in the utmost solemn fashion, "to refute this work, provided that I do not find the *essential* arguments in support of the facts of Christianity to be correct, but that if I find them to be correct, to do what prudence, love of truth, and honesty command me to do—what *Socrates* would have done if he had read this work and found it irrefutable." That is, to forsake the religion of my fathers and embrace the one that Mr. Bonnet is defending. For surely, even if my thinking were otherwise servile enough to allow me to regard *prudence* as a counterweight to the love of truth and honesty, in this case I would nevertheless find all three in the same scale [of the balance].

[Mendelssohn proceeds to give reasons for why he shall not be drawn into a public defense of his faith.] ... And yet for all I care, Judaism could have been razed to the ground in every polemical textbook and triumphed over in every scholastic exercise, without my ever having to be drawn into a dispute about it. Every expert or dabbler in rabbinical matters could have devised for himself and his readers, without the slightest opposition from me, the most ridiculous concept of Judaism by drawing on worthless books that no reasonable Jew reads or knows. I would be able to refute the contemptuous opinion that one has of a Jew through virtue rather than through polemical writings. My religion, my philosophy, and my rank in civil life furnish me with the most important reasons for avoiding all religious disputes and for speaking in my public writings only of those truths that must be equally important to all religions.

According to the principles of my religion, I *should* attempt to convert no one who was not born under our law. This spirit of conversion, the origin of which some people would so gladly like to charge to the Jewish religion, is, however, diametrically opposed to it. All of our rabbis unanimously teach that the written and oral laws that make up our revealed religion are binding only on our nation. *Moses* charged *us* with the law; it is an *inheritance of the congregation of Jacob*. [*BT*, Sanhedrin 59a] All of the other peoples of the earth, we believe, have been instructed by God to abide by the law of nature and the religion of the patriarchs. [*BT*, Avodah Zarah 64b] Those who regulate their conduct in accordance with the laws of this religion of nature and reason are called *virtuous men of other nations*, and they are children of eternal bliss.

Our rabbis are so unmoved by any passion for conversion that they even direct us to employ serious counterarguments to discourage any volunteer who has the intention to convert. We are supposed to point out to him that by this step he is unnecessarily taking on a very hard burden. That in his current circumstances he has only to observe the Noahide duties in order to attain salvation, but that as soon as he accepts the religion of the Israelites, he freely submits himself to all of the strict laws of this faith and then must either observe them or expect the punishment that the Lawgiver has attached to their transgression. Finally, we are also supposed to present him with a faithful picture of the misery, oppression, and contempt in which the nation currently lives, in order to keep him from taking what may possibly be an overhasty step that he could subsequently regret.

The religion of my fathers, therefore, does not *wish* to be disseminated. We are not supposed to send missions to either of the Indies or to Greenland in order to preach our religion to these distant peoples. Alas, the latter in particular observe the law of nature better than we do according to the descriptions that we have of them. According to our religious doctrines, they are an enviable people. Whoever is not born under our law may not also live under our law. We take only ourselves to be obliged to observe these laws, and this cannot offend our fellow men. Do our opinions seem absurd? It is not necessary to dispute the matter. We act in accordance with our convictions, and others may call into question the validity of laws that, by our own admission, place them under no obligation. We can leave to their own consciences whether or not they act justly, tolerantly, and philanthropically when they ridicule our laws and customs to such a degree. As long as we do not intend to convince others of our opinions, arguing is useless.

If a *Confucius* or a *Solon* lived among my contemporaries, I could, in accordance with the principles of my religion, love and admire the great man, without hitting on the ridiculous idea of wanting to *convert* a Confucius or a Solon. Convert him? For what reason? Since he does not belong to the *congregation of Jacob*, my religious laws do not bind him, and we would soon come to an agreement about doctrinal matters. Because I believed that he could attain salvation? Oh, it seems to me that whoever guides people to virtue in this life cannot be damned in the next one, and I need not fear that any venerable collegium might take me to task for holding this opinion ...

I am lucky to be friends with many an excellent man who is not of my faith. We sincerely love one another, even though we suspect and suppose that we are of entirely different opinions in matters of faith. I enjoy the pleasure of their company, which improves and delights me. Never did my heart secretly call out to me: *Too bad about their beautiful souls!* Whoever believes that no salvation is to be found outside of his church must quite often feel such a sigh rising in his breast.

It is indeed a natural obligation for every mortal man to spread knowledge and virtue among his fellow men and to blot out their prejudices and errors as much as is within his power. Given this way of thinking, one might believe that everyone is obliged to publicly dispute the religious opinions that he takes to be erroneous. But not all prejudices are equally harmful, and therefore the prejudices that we believe we perceive among our fellow men must not all be handled in the same fashion. Some are in direct conflict with the felicity of the human race; their influence on men's morals is obviously pernicious, and one ought not to expect even an accidental benefit to come of them. Every friend of humanity must forthrightly attack them. The direct way of attacking them is indisputably the best way, and any delay by taking roundabout paths is irresponsible. To this sort belong all of people's errors and prejudices that disturb their own or their fellow men's peace and contentment, and kill every seed of what is true and good in people before it can sprout. On the one hand, there is fanaticism, misanthropy, and the spirit of persecution; on the other hand, there is thoughtlessness, voluptuousness, and immoral freethinking.

Now and then, however, the opinions of my fellow men that I take to be errors belong among those higher theoretical principles that are too far removed from practical matters to be immediately harmful. But precisely because of their generality they constitute the foundation on which a people who cherishes them has built up its system of ethics and social life, and so they have accidentally become of great importance to this portion of the human race. Publicly disputing such precepts because they seem to us to be prejudices means digging up the foundation in order to investigate whether or not it is firm and secure, without shoring up the building. Whoever cares more for the welfare of mankind than for his own renown will keep a rein on his opinions concerning prejudices of this sort, and he will guard against attacking them forthrightly and without the greatest care, in order not to overturn what he deems a suspicious ethical principle before his fellow men have *accepted* the *true* one that he wants to put in its place.

Therefore, I can readily believe that I recognize the national prejudices and erroneous religious opinions of my fellow citizens, and yet am *obliged* to remain silent if these errors do not *directly* lead to the destruction of either *natural* religion or *natural* law but rather are *accidentally* connected to the promotion of the good. It is true that the morality of our actions hardly deserves this name if it is founded on error, and the promotion of the good will always be supported much better and more securely by the truth than by prejudice, *provided that it is recognized*. But as long as the truth is not recognized, as long as it has not become national, so as to be able to influence the great mass of the people as powerfully as a deeply rooted prejudice, such prejudice must be nearly holy to every friend of virtue.

Such modesty is all the more obligatory if the nation that in my opinion cherishes such errors has also made itself worthy of admiration through virtue and wisdom and contains a number of great men who deserve to be called benefactors of the human race. Such a noble part of humanity must even be shown respect and excused when it makes mistakes. Who would dare to overlook the excellent qualities of such a sublime nation and to attack it where he thinks that he has noticed a weakness?

These are the motives that my religion and my philosophy furnish me for carefully avoiding religious disputes. If you add the domestic circumstances in which I live among my fellow men, then you will completely excuse me. I am a member of an oppressed people who must beg for protection by appealing to the benevolence of the dominant nation, protection that we do not receive everywhere and that we do not receive anywhere without certain restrictions. My coreligionists gladly renounce freedoms that are granted to every other human being, and they are content if they are tolerated and protected. They must rate it no small kindness for a nation to accept them under tolerable conditions, since in many a state even *residence* is denied them. Is it not the case, given the laws of your native town, that your circumcised friend is not even allowed to visit you in *Zurich*? What gratitude do my fellow believers thus not owe to the dominant nation that includes them within its universal love of mankind and allows them, without any impediment, to pray to the Almighty in accordance with the ways of their fathers! They enjoy the most respectable freedom in the state in which I live. Should their members not shrink from challenging the religion of the dominant portion of the population, that is, from attacking their protectors in the flank that for virtuous people must be the most sensitive one?

I decided always to act in accordance with these principles, and because of them I decided to avoid religious disputes with the utmost care if no extraordinary cause should force me to change my mind. I have been bold enough to pass over in silence the private challenges of estimable men, and I thought that I might scorn the entreaties of the small minds who have thought that they could publicly attack me on account of my religion. But the solemn appeal of a *Lavater* forces me at least to reveal my convictions publicly, so that no one will take an inordinate silence for *contempt* or *confession*...

I have now indicated the reasons why I desire so very much never to engage in disputes about religious issues. ...

DAVID SHATZ

## "Theology, Morality, and Religious Diversity"

Mendelssohn's letter to Lavater, as well as the texts cited by Moshe Halbertal from the writings of Menachem Ha-Me'iri, address distinct questions, but both express what are widely called liberal or enlightened positions regarding Judaism's perspective on other religions. As commonly used, these terms refer to a set of related values—equal worth and dignity, tolerance, pluralism, diversity, and the rights of all to equal treatment.

Religious diversity has been a central topic of theology at least since the Second Vatican Council, which in the 1965 *Nostra Aetate* (*In Our Time*) introduced important changes in Catholic thought. Among them was that, after a long history of proclaiming the doctrine "no salvation outside the Church" and denying toleration to most other religions, the Church now acknowledged that other religions contain truth and holiness, urged mutual understanding and respect, and exhorted "her sons" to collaborate with other religions for the benefit of humanity.[1] As a result of Vatican II, there has been a proliferation of interfaith dialogues and an explosion of "isms" on the philosophical scene: exclusivism, inclusivism, pluralism, universalism, and relativism. These "isms" mainly represent not different approaches to which religion is true, but rather how individuals who regard theirs as "a [or the] true religion" should view other religions—their value, their truth, the consequences of believing in them, their role in the world, and more.[2]

## I

Let me elaborate on the core questions that adherents of a religion might ask vis-à-vis other religions, excluding the epistemological question of how one knows that his or her religion is correct:

1) Truth: Are there religious/spiritual truths in other religions? This question immediately must be refined, because the answer is so obvious—several religions hold overlapping beliefs, such as belief in a personal God who created the world and exercises providence over it. A non-trivial form of the question is: Do other religions have religious truths *that I don't have in mine*? And a follow-up: If they do, should I try to find these truths (through reading, conversation, lectures, or formal dialogues), or instead should I rest content with the truths I have? Especially important is whether some *core* claims of another religion that do not appear in mine are true and worth investigating.[3]

2) Salvation: Is my religion the only path to salvation?

3) Spiritual value: What spiritual benefits are enjoyed by, or are open to, people of other faiths? What about secularists—can they perhaps relate to God via ethical living despite their atheism or agnosticism?

4) Eschatology: What religious views and practices will be accepted by the world at the end of days? Will all religions become one (namely, mine)? Will

all remain as they are? Will religions as we know them disappear even while monotheism prevails? Will adherents of "wrong" religions be punished by God?

5) Explaining multiplicity: Why does God allow so many religions? Do they serve in a divine plan for history? This question is especially acute if the 'other' religions are believed to be false or harmful.

6) Practical issues: Should adherents of my religion seek proselytes, thus saving them spiritually? Should they participate in interfaith dialogues?

I cannot engage adequately with all these issues here. I propose instead to concentrate on a problem that implicates several of them and arises out of Jewish teaching, and to situate Mendelssohn and the Me'iri in the context of that problem.

## *II*

In Deuteronomy, God admonishes the Israelites not to worship "the sun, moon, stars, and the whole heavenly host . . . which your Lord God has allotted (Hebrew: *asher halak*) to other peoples everywhere under heaven."[4] Basing himself on Talmudic sources, Rabbi Shmuel ben Meir (1085–1158, known by the acrostic Rashbam) comments that the main meaning of the verse is that God allots the sun, moon, and stars to other people to worship, because "He does not care about them" (*eino hoshesh bahem*). Jolting though it is, Rashbam's comment is actually a softer version of an interpretation posed in the Talmud and glossed by Rashbam's grandfather Rashi [Rabbi Shlomo Yitzhaki, 1040–1105], the most famous of all Jewish commentators, that "*asher halak*" means "which he has made slippery."[5] That is, the heavenly bodies are means by which God makes non-Jews slip up and be punished, a kind of divine entrapment.[6]

The challenges to such material include a dual charge of unfairness. Seemingly there is divine unfairness: what could justify God in excluding the overwhelming majority of humanity from valuable spiritual experience and accomplishment, and granting this only to one group that constitutes 0.3 per cent of the world's population? And there is seemingly human unfairness: Is it right of *Jews* to be indifferent to others' spiritual welfare? Why aren't we benevolent to them by communicating and arguing for what we regard as truth—as the Church does? We may call our questions, collectively, 'the problem of indifference'.

Like many Jewish texts that present a sharp, binary Jews/gentiles division, those we have cited may be understandable reactions to persecution. Yet even without this factor, Jewish attitudes to proselytizing seem to reflect indifference to others' spiritual welfare. Although in the early centuries of Christianity Jews did proselytize,[7] and although Jewish tradition lauds great proselytes like Ruth and Onkelos, the settled, normative position is that Jews should not proselytize, and indeed prospective converts should be dissuaded unless they evince the deepest sincerity and desire.[8]

Mendelssohn invokes such teachings with pride and an implication of moral superiority. Yet we must ask: Doesn't the Church have the right attitude here?

True, it's unjust to kill those who do not accept the offer of truth and salvation, but the question of why Jews aren't more benevolent about sharing the truth as they see it is a fair one.[9]

### III

So why don't Jews proselytize? Let us consider some answers.

First, there is the realia. Historically, it was dangerous for Jews to aggressively proselytize, and the chances for success were small. In addition, Jewish proselytizing could encourage Christian proselytizing, an undesirable outcome for Jews. (Christians who proselytize will not be comparably fearful of Jews proselytizing in return since, as it has been put, they "have a larger market share.") [10]

Second is a point that has both practical and ethical dimensions. Proselytizing, even of a non-coercive kind, can, according to David Berger, "certainly damage, even poison, intergroup relations, and it renders respectful dialogue about religious matters next to impossible."[11]

Third, Judaism, unlike Christianity and Islam, is rooted not only in beliefs, practices, and attitudes, but in ethnicity. Ruth declared to her mother-in-law Naomi: "Your people are my people, and your god is my god." She both joined Naomi's people existentially, and embraced the Jewish God. Accepting some converts, those who are truly devoted and who identify with the people, is one thing. But *seeking* converts is another, because at least theoretically it threatens to pry ethnicity and religion apart on a fairly large scale.[12]

The next few arguments against proselytizing either raise ethical objections to the practice, or point to a positive ethical value achieved by desisting from proselytizing. A caveat: we are not looking for an explanation that is historically accurate, but for one that creates a coherent, compelling reason not to proselytize.[13]

One ethical objection to proselytizing, the fourth objection overall, works from considerations of reciprocity. I have noted that, practically speaking, Jewish proselytizing might induce Christian proselytizing. A further, ethical spin on reciprocity is derived from the Golden Rule, or a loosely Kantian principle: Do not proselytize others because you would not want to be proselytized yourself. This argument doesn't explain why one should not be open to being proselytized, nor why it is wrong to proselytize in cases where you yourself wouldn't mind being proselytized. Nonetheless it goes some distance toward explaining the dominant Jewish approach, especially since our questions concern individuals who wish to continue adhering to their religion and therefore are not willing to be proselytized.

A fifth explanation is that to proselytize is to jar and impair individual and group identity. Proselytizing also interferes with individuals fulfilling a duty to carry out their traditions.[14]

Sixth, proselytizing intrudes on the privacy of faith.[15] *Privacy* can mean several things,[16] but for present purposes the argument that invading privacy is wrong can be left at an intuitive level.

The seventh response is not so much an ethical objection to proselytizing as an attempt to find positive ethical significance in leaving other faiths alone.

Mendelssohn, as well as the former Chief Rabbi of the United Kingdom, Lord Sacks, suggest that aversion to proselytizing is a result of Judaism's appreciating diversity and seeking to cultivate it. The moral advantage of living with diversity, with different ways of relating to God, is that it makes possible the virtue of tolerance. The latter cannot thrive in uniformity. Mendelssohn wrote, "Brothers, if you care for true godliness, let us not pretend that conformity exists where diversity is obviously the plan and goal of Providence."[17] The existence of other religions creates a context for humility, tolerance, and respect for the other. Not proselytizing is deciding that it is more important for Jews to cultivate tolerance and respect for the other than to share with others that which one regards as truth. Readers need to judge the approach at hand partly by evaluating this proposition. It must be noted, however, that because many Jewish legal sources suggest that at least some other religions, including Christianity, are prohibited even to gentiles, as they constitute *avodah zarah* (foreign worship), the diversity argument collapses in this particular context.[18]

Eighth and finally, we come to a family of arguments I call "It's not broken" arguments.

## IV

The general idea behind "It's not broken" is that other religions are in order as is. There are several variants of this view, and all or nearly all have Jewish sources that could be cited in support. The versions are:

(1) Pluralism: all religions are true.
(2) Although not all religions are true, adherents of other religions already have a suitable relationship with God in virtue of subscribing to their religions.
(3) All people have the potential to relate to God even without conversion.
(4) Converting adherents of other religions is superfluous and pointless, because adherents of other religions can earn a share in the world to come without converting.

Let us examine each of these propositions.

(1) If pluralism is understood as affirming that all religions are true, it confronts notorious problems. Pluralism would seem to reduce to relativism:[19] How can all religions be true if they contradict one another![20] In addition, if pluralism/relativism were true, it should be a matter of indifference which religion one adopts. Not only syncretism but even apostasy, no matter how whimsical, seem all too simple to justify (since all positions will be true and of equal worth). This argument is contrary to principles of various religions and violates their self-understanding.[21] Moreover, openness to the possibility that "the accumulated wisdom of other world religions can enhance and enrich" one's spiritual life—an appealing and I think empirically verified proposition—becomes pointless, since one religion is as good as any other.[22]

(2) The notion that adherents of other religions already have a suitable relationship with God—a different form of pluralism—is stated sharply by the twelfth century Yemenite rabbi Nethanel Ibn al-Fayumi, who maintains that God sends prophets to each nation, establishing every religion's relationship with the deity.[23]

A different attempt to acknowledge that adherents of other religions enjoy relationships with God by means of their religion comes from Rabbi Abraham Isaac Kook (1865–1935) and, famously, decades later by the Christian theologian John Hick. On this view, it is impossible to know or characterize God in Himself. All religions[24] are culturally conditioned responses to the indescribable divine reality. Mendelssohn (in *Jerusalem*) makes a similar claim, paraphrased by Michah Gottlieb as follows: "[M]ultiple representations of religious truth help prevent people from imagining that their particular religious symbols adequately signify the unconditional."[25] Diversity is therefore desirable.

Now, even granting that other religions possess truth and enjoy God-human relationships because they are responses to the unknowable divine being (the evidential basis for this claim of responsiveness is not clear), the Kook-Hick strategy comes with the following limitation as regards proselytizing: it does not appear to explain why Jews should not attempt to bring *secularists* to religion. This problem disappears in Rabbi Kook's mystical framework, however; for him, divinity and religious value inhere in *all* phenomena and viewpoints, including secularism, and in this regard his position has an advantage over Hick's. But there is another problem: both Hick and Rabbi Kook concede that some religions are better than others in their representations of the divine and in their ethical conduct.[26] Why, then, shouldn't Jews proselytize to give others a *better* religion? And is it fair that only Jews have this superior religion? Jews "proselytize" non-religious Jews, so why not proselytize non-Jews?[27]

(3) The next form of "It's not broken," closely related to the preceding one, refers to spiritual *possibilities*—potential connections to God—for non-Jews. A *midrash* tells us, "If a person wishes to be a *tsaddik* (a righteous one), he may be one even if he is a gentile, because it is not a title determined by ancestry."[28] Maimonides affirms that

> Each and every human being, from anywhere in the world, whose spirit has moved him and whose knowledge has given him understanding to set himself apart in order to stand before the Lord, to serve Him, to worship Him, and to know Him, who walks upright as God created him to do, and releases himself from the yoke of the many foolish considerations which trouble people— such an individual is as sanctified as the Holy of Holies (*kodesh kodashim*), and his portion and inheritance shall be in the Lord forever and ever.[29]

Apparently such an individual need not adopt a formal religion. In fact, Maimonides did not wish for individuals to invent their own religions.[30]

(4) The argument against proselytizing that Mendelssohn gives in his letter to Lavater can be represented as yet another variant of "It's not broken." Non-Jews

are already guaranteed salvation by their ethical conduct and observance of the seven Noahide laws, even if they have the wrong theology. "Convert a Confucius or a Solon? What for? . . . It seems to me that anyone who leads men to virtue in this life cannot be damned in the next." The support here is a view in the Talmud, codified by Maimonides, that "pious gentiles have a share in the world to come."[31] One need not be Jewish to achieve spiritual heights. In fact, since Jews have more *mitzvot* to observe and more heresies to avoid if they are to earn salvation, non-Jews have a better chance to receive the rewards of the afterlife than do Jews. This point could explain why Jews do proselytize other Jews.

Rabbi Israel Lipshitz (1782–1860), the author of a well-known commentary on the Mishnah, gives striking expression to the idea that ethical conduct, sans correct theology, is sufficient for the salvation of non-Jews:

> Many [non-Jews] made especially great improvements for all people, such as Jenner who created the smallpox vaccine. . . . and Drake who brought the potato to Europe, which at times has prevented famine, as well as Gutenberg who invented printing. Many did not receive reward in this world, such as the pious one Reuchlin, who endangered his own life to prevent the burning of the Talmud. And could one possibly think that these great benefactors will not be recompensed in the next world after death—is it not the case that God does not withhold the reward from any creature?[32]

Let us return to the argument that, because righteous gentiles deserve and receive a share in the hereafter, there is no point in converting them. But, one may ask, what if Judaism affords a higher level of relationship with God than do other religions, or at least some other religions, and with it a correspondingly higher reward? The argument from salvation makes it appear that people take religion pass/fail rather than for a letter grade reflecting their level of achievement. Gaining access to the hereafter doesn't hide the fact that while alive the non-Jew did not gain all that he or she could have spiritually. Why aren't there more opportunities for non-Jews to embrace the "true" religion in this life? The notion that we can lower the demands for gaining reward (allowing the Noahide laws as the criterion) does not address the question of why we do not focus on bringing the non-Jew up to an optimal level.[33] By way of reply, according to some classical texts (midrashic and Maimonidean), non-Jews can rise to spiritual levels such as "tsaddik," "God-fearer," and "Holy of Holies." So one is not bringing X to a higher spiritual level by converting X. Maimonides seems committed to this position; becoming "Holy of Holies" suggests that non-Jews can reach the highest spiritual levels. Yet even if they cannot, some of the other considerations against proselytizing are strengthened if non-Jews can attain salvation without converting.[34]

There are still other classically-rooted answers to our question, "Why not proselytize?" Consider the view, held by a number of prominent Jewish thinkers, that Christianity and Islam have produced positive effects for world and/or Jewish history—spreading discussion of Torah and the commandments, and (this was said of Christianity) providing Jews with ethically protective surroundings during the exile.[35] This would explain why God allows the other (monotheistic) religions to flourish. Arguably we can turn this claim into a reason for not proselytizing: perhaps God implements His ends by means of *other* religions because, for reasons we do not fully understand, these religions can best produce positive effects if they operate as gentile enterprises, rather than as Jewish ones (assuming that only a small part of the gentile world would convert to Judaism if Jews would proselytize). But having already raised numerous possibilities, I now leave our discussion of why Jews might choose not to proselytize and turn to Me'iri.

## V

Mendelssohn seeks to level the field, to make Christianity and Judaism equal in a particular respect: conduciveness to salvation. Halbertal shows that Me'iri also sought to level the field, but in a different respect: equality of *treatment*. Judaism contains a variety of laws that limit Jewish commerce with gentiles, distinguish between Jews and non-Jews as regards juridical rights and obligations, and distance Jews from gentiles as regards social interaction. Although Me'iri kept the third type of law largely in place, he drew a groundbreaking distinction, unmatched in medieval rabbinic literature, between "nations that are restricted by the ways of religion" and nations that are not. For Me'iri, the critical legal distinction is not between Jew and gentile, but between people who possess religion and people who do not. Paralleling Mendelssohn, Me'iri does not require correct theology for salvation; individuals with a wrong theology, such as Christians, are within the category "restricted by the ways of religion."[36] Halbertal notes that Me'iri is the first to suggest a notion of inter-religious tolerance built on the functional value common to all religion, namely creating "a disciplined society." At the same time, Me'iri believes that adherents of the religion in question must have faith in what Halbertal calls "a non-material, transcendent cause that exercises providence and recompense."

Halbertal notes that for Me'iri only nations at the "extremities" of the world qualify as "not restricted by the ways of religion." But whereas Me'iri posits, as a condition for ethical behavior, belief in a providential God, we must recognize that theistic religions may be deistic; they may leave the creator uninvolved with the world. Moreover, some religions have forms that are not theistic and even atheistic (for instance, Buddhism). Finally, what about secular humanists—eminently ethical people, more ethical than some theists? Read in a strict constructionist way, Me'iri's tolerance would have limited scope.

Me'iri's assumption that only religion (indeed, only non-deistic religion) can ensure ethical behavior does not seem plausible. In his time and place, ethics might have accompanied religion because secularism was not a significant phenomenon. In our time, by contrast, there is much godless goodness. Moreover, many traditional Jews have absorbed and live according to modern values such as autonomy and equality.[37] By extension Me'iri's principles would seem compatible with treating moral secular individuals on a par with Jews with respect to juridical rights and responsibilities.[38] Strictly speaking, we should recall that Me'iri speaks about "*nations* that are restricted by the ways of religion." Perhaps, therefore, a particular individual who is unethical but belongs to an ethical *nation* should receive equal treatment with Jews. However that may be, it should come as no surprise that Me'iri's views weigh heavily in contemporary Jewish efforts to treat other religions with a level of respect not generally accorded them in the past and to value non-religious ethical paradigms. In circles that respect Me'iri's views, theology has been replaced by ethics as the crucial criterion. In this way Mendelssohn's and Me'iri's views converge.[39]

## Notes

1 Changes in Christian attitudes and actions vis-à-vis Jews since *Nostra Aetate* are described in Korn 2011.
2 For formulations of the "isms", see Brill 2010 (which cites many Jewish sources), McKim 2012, and Runzo 1988.
3 Some would go further and ask whether some claims of another religion that *conflict* with claims in my religion, perhaps even core claims, are true; but cf. Gellman 2013, 31–6.
4 Deuteronomy 4:19.
5 See Babylonian Talmud [BT] *Megillah* 9b, *Avodah Zarah* 55a, and Rashi to the relevant lines.
6 Reinforcing the notion that God gives worthwhile laws only to Jews (whether due to indifference or to a desire to deprive non-Jews) are Psalms 147:19–20 and *Exodus Rabbah* 15 (esp. 15:23) and 30:9. However, the dominant idea in Judaism, the locus classicus for which is BT *Sanhedrin* 56aff., is that God gave seven laws to Noahides (gentiles).
7 On the history of rabbinic attitudes, see Goldenberg 1997 and Novak 1999.
8 See BT *Yevamot* 47a. Jewish law goes further by prohibiting gentiles from adopting the most prominent Jewish practices; but cf. Hirschman 2000 and Linzer 2005.
9 The benevolence argument, along with others for (and against) proselytizing, are assessed in Thiessen 2011 and Marty 1999.
10 See Berger 2010, 367–70. Berger notes that because of persecutions, some Jews may have wanted gentiles to remain unconverted in order that they not be saved.
11 Berger 2010, 376. Berger adds that "the question is whether they [these concerns] are serious enough to set aside the salvific advantage of conversion to Christianity," but also that "In dealing with Jews, the moral objections to conversionary efforts increase exponentially" because of Christianity's majority status and because of the history of Christian treatments of Jews.
12 See also Berger 2010, 368. Jewish thinkers have grappled with the doctrine of chosenness, presenting accounts that dissociate it from racist doctrines; see Frank (ed.), 1993, Gellman 2013 (and his essay in this volume; cf. Carmy 2013), Kaminsky 2007, Kellner 1991, Novak 1995; also, Wyschogrod 1983 and Soloveichik 2005.
13 I have elaborated on the next three objections in Shatz 2011 and 2013.
14 See Montefiore 1997; cf. Shatz 2011, 508–10 and Shatz 2013, 177–86.
15 See Soloveitchik 1964.
16 See Shatz 2013, 167–77.
17 As quoted in Gottlieb 2013, 112. Given Gottlieb's analysis, it must be said that Mendelssohn's argument is more complicated than my introduction of it here suggests.
18 This was pointed out by David Berger, who suggested replacing the usual translation of *avodah zarah* as "idolatry" with the literal translation "foreign worship", particularly when characterizing Christianity; see Berger 2010, 381–2.

19  See Kellner 2006b, 110–11, 146–147; cf. Jospe 2012 and the reply by J. Kellner and M. Kellner 2012.
20  See Margalit 1998.
21  But cf. McKim 2012, chap. 8.
22  Gellman 2013, 32–3.
23  See Jospe 2012, 107–9.
24  For Rabbi Kook, presumably, with the *exception* of Judaism, based as it is on the Sinaitic revelation.
25  Gottlieb 2013, 100.
26  See Rappoport 2004 and Hick 2004.
27  See Broyde 1999. This question requires more analysis than I can give it here.
28  *Be-Midbar Rabbah*, 8:2; see also *Tana de-Bei Eliyahu* 10.
29  *Mishneh Torah*, Laws of Sabbatical and Jubilee Years 13:12, translated, with slight alteration, from Kellner 2006a, 247.
30  See Maimonides, *Mishneh Torah*, Laws of Kings 10:9.
31  Tosefta *Sanhedrin* 13:2 and BT *Sanhedrin* 105a (a contrary view is cited too); Maimonides, *Mishneh Torah*, Laws of Kings 8:11. Maimonides however imposed a qualification that distressed Mendelssohn and undercut his own salvation argument; see Korn 1994, Kellner 2006a, 241–50.
32  Lipshitz, *Tiferet Yisrael* to Avot 3:14 (Boaz #1), as translated (mostly) by M. Miller; see also *Tiferet Yisrael* to *Sanhedrin* 10:1. Rabbi Lipshitz goes on to remark that non-Jews have an advantage over Jews because they arrive at God by their own free will and effort.
33  Mendelssohn's views about religious pluralism can defuse these objections, but I am here addressing the "conversion is superfluous" argument more broadly.
34  David Berger makes this point.
35  Maimonides, *Mishneh Torah*, Laws of the Sabbatical and Jubilee Years 13:13; Halevi, *Kuzari* 4:23 (see also 2:36); Abarbanel, commentary to Deuteronomy 4:23; Arama, *Akedat Yitzhak, va-Ethanan* 88; Emden, commentary to *Avot* 4:11.
36  The Noahide laws prohibit *avodah zarah*, but rabbinic authorities in the modern period argue that Christianity is *avodah zarah* for Jews but not for non-Jews. (How what is 'foreign worship' for one individual is not for another needs explication, but I shall not enter into that question here.) Almost all relevant rabbinic sources maintain that Islam does not constitute *avodah zarah*. For another nuanced analysis of Me'iri, see Berger 2005.
37  For a fuller listing, see Brody 2014.
38  See Berger 2005, 96–9.
39  My thanks to David Berger and Aaron Segal for comments on an earlier version of this paper.

## Further Reading on Religious Pluralism and Toleration

Gellman, J. *God's Kindness Has Overwhelmed Us: A Contemporary Doctrine of the Jews as the Chosen People* (Boston, MA: Academic Studies Press, 2013), 31–42.
Halevi, Judah. *The Book of Refutation and Proof on Behalf of the Despised Faith (The Kuzari)*, trans. B. Kogan and L. Berman (New Haven, CT: Yale Judaica Series, forthcoming), 4.23.
Hick, J. "Religious Pluralism and Salvation," *Faith and Philosophy* 5:4 (1988), 365–377.
Hick, J. *An Interpretation of Religion: Human Responses to the Transcendent* (New York: Macmillan, 1989).
Kolitz, Z. *Confrontation: The Existential Thought of Rabbi J. B. Soloveitchik* (Hoboken, NJ: Ktav, 1993), Part 2.

Plantinga, A. "Pluralism: A Defense of Religious Exclusivism," in *The Philosophical Challenge of Religious Diversity*, eds. K. Meeker and P. Quinn (New York: Oxford University Press, 1999), 172–192.

Maimonides. *Mishneh Torah*, Laws of Kings 11.4, ed. S. Frankel, (Bnei Brak, 1975).

van Inwagen, P. "Non Est Hick," in *God, Knowledge, and Mystery: Essays in Philosophical Theology* (Ithaca, NY: Cornell University Press, 1995), 191–216.

# Bibliography

## Primary Texts and Translations

Albo, J. *Book of Roots* (Jerusalem: Feldheim, 2011) [Hebrew].

Arama, I. *Akedat Yizhak* (Jerusalem: Ofset Yisrael-Amerika, 1961).

Averroes (Ibn Rushd). *On the Harmony of Religion and Philosophy* (*Fasl al-Maqal*), trans. and comm. G. F. Hourani (London: Gibb Memorial Trust, 1961).

Bahya Ibn Pakuda. *The Book of Direction to the Duties of the Heart*, trans. M. Mansoor (Oxford: Littman Library of Jewish Civilization, 1973).

Bland, K. (ed. and trans.). *The "Epistle on the Possibility of Conjunction with the Active Intellect" by Ibn Rushd with the Commentary of Moses Narboni* (New York: Jewish Theological Seminary of America, 1982).

Cohen, H. *Ethik des reinen Willen*, in *Werke*, Hermann-Cohen-Archiv am Philosophischen Seminar Zürich, dir. H. Holzhey (Hildesheim: G. Olms, 1984).

Cohen, H. *Religion of Reason Out of the Sources of Judaism*, trans. S. Kaplan (New York: Frederick Ungar Publishing Co., 1972; Atlanta: Scholars Press, 1995; orig. 1919).

Crescas, H. *Or Hashem*, ed. S. Fisher (Jerusalem: Sifre Ramot, 1990).

Crescas, H. *The Light of the Lord*, trans. W. Z. Harvey (1973) [brief selection from Book 2 in D. Frank, O. Leaman, and C. Manekin (eds.), *The Jewish Philosophy Reader* (London: Routledge, 2000), 265–270].

Eisenstein, J. D. (ed.), *Ozar Midrashim: A Library of Two Hundred Minor Midrashim*, 2 vols. (New York: Bloch, 1915).

Frank, D., O. Leaman, and C. Manekin (eds.), *The Jewish Philosophy Reader* (London: Routledge, 2000).

Gersonides. *The Wars of the Lord*, 3 vols., trans. S. Feldman (Philadelphia, PA: Jewish Publication Society, 1984–1999).

Gottlieb, M. (ed.), *Moses Mendelssohn: Writings on Judaism, Christianity, and the Bible* (Waltham, MA: Brandeis University Press, 2011).

Halevi, J. *The Kuzari*, trans. H. Hirschfeld (New York: Schocken, 1964).

Halevi, J. *The Book of Refutation and Proof on Behalf of the Despised Faith* (*The Kuzari*), trans. B. Kogan and L. Berman (New Haven, CT: Yale Judaica Series, forthcoming).

Heschel, A. J. *God in Search of Man* (Philadelphia, PA: Jewish Publication Society, 1959; New York: Farrar, Straus and Giroux, 1976).

Heschel, A. J. *Moral Grandeur and Spiritual Audacity*, ed. S. Heschel (New York: Farrar, Straus and Giroux, 1997).

Hirsch, S. R. *The Nineteen Letters*, trans. K. Paritzky, rev. and comm. J. Elias (Jerusalem and New York: Feldheim, 1995).

Hyman, A., J. J. Walsh, and T. Williams (eds.), *Philosophy in the Middle Ages,* 3rd ed. (Indianapolis, IN: Hackett, 2010).

James, W. *Varieties of Religious Experience*, lecture XVII, in W. James, *Writings: 1902–1910* (New York: Viking Press, 1987).

Josephus, F. *The Jewish War*, trans. G. A. Williamson (Harmondsworth: Penguin, 1959).

Kant, I. *Religion Within the Limits of Reason Alone*, trans. T. M. Greene and H. H. Hudson (New York: Harper, 1960).

Kant, I. "On the Failure of All Attempted Philosophical Theodicies," in *Kant on History and Religion* ed. and trans. M. Despland (Montreal: McGill-Queen's University Press, 1973), 283–297.

Kant, I. *On the Old Saw: That It May Be Right In Theory But It Won't Work In Practice*, trans. E. B. Ashton (Philadelphia, PA: University of Pennsylvania Press, 1974).

Kant, I. *Groundwork to the Metaphysics of Morals*, in *Immanuel Kant, Practical Philosophy* ed. and trans. M. Gregor (Cambridge: Cambridge University Press, 1999).

Levinas, E. *Du sacré au sainte* (Paris: Les Editions de Minuit, 1977).

Levinas, E. *Ethics and Infinity*, trans. R. Cohen (Pittsburgh, PA: Duquesne University Press, 1985).

Levinas, E. *Difficult Freedom: Essays in Judaism*, trans. S. Hand (Baltimore, MD: Johns Hopkins University Press, 1990).

Luzzatto, M. H. *Da'at Tevunot*, ed. Y. M. Spinner (Jerusalem: Hamesora, 2012).

Maimonides, M. *The Code of Maimonides [Mishneh Torah]*, Book Fourteen, The Book of Judges, trans. A. M. Hershman (New Haven, CT: Yale University Press, 1959).

Maimonides, M. *The Guide of the Perplexed*, 2 vols., trans. S. Pines (Chicago, IL: University of Chicago Press, 1963).

Maimonides, M. *A Maimonides Reader*, ed. I. Twersky (New York: Behrman House, 1972)

Maimonides, M. *Ethical Writings of Maimonides*, ed. and trans. R. Weiss and C. Butterworth (New York: New York University Press, 1975).

Maimonides, M. *Mishneh Torah, The Book of Knowledge*, trans. M. Hyamson (Jerusalem: Feldheim Publishers, 1981).

Maimonides, M. *Mishneh Torah, The Book of Knowledge*, trans. H. M. Russell and J. Weinberg (New York: Ktav, 1983).

Maimonides, M. *Epistles [Iggrot ha-Rambam]*, 2 vols., ed. I. Shilat (Jerusalem: Ma'aliot, 1987–8) [Hebrew].

Maimonides, M. *Crisis and Leadership: Epistles of Maimonides*, trans. A. Halkin and comm. D. Hartman. (Philadelphia, PA: Jewish Publication Society, 1994).

Maimonides, M. *The Guide of the Perplexed*, abridged J. Guttmann and trans. C. Rabin (Indianapolis, IN: Hackett, 1995).

Malebranche, N. *The Search after Truth*, ed. and trans. T. M. Lennon and P. J. Olscamp (Cambridge: Cambridge University Press, 1997).

Manekin, C. (ed.), *Medieval Jewish Philosophical Writings* (Cambridge: Cambridge University Press, 2007).

May, H. and B. Metzger. (eds.), *The Oxford Annotated Bible Revised Standard Edition* (Oxford: Oxford University Press, 1962).

Nahmanides. *Kitve Ramban,* vol. 2, ed. C. D. Chavel (Jerusalem: Mosad Harav Kook, 1964).

Nietzsche, F. *Human, All Too Human: A Book for Free Spirits*, trans. P. V. Cohen and H. Zimmerman (Amherst, MA: Prometheus Books, 2009).

Rosenzweig, F. *Jehuda Halevi* (Berlin: Verlag Lambert Schneider, 1927).

Rosenzweig, F. *Franz Rosenzweig: Der Mensch und sein Werk: Gesammelte Schriften* (Boston, MA and The Hague: Martinus Nijhoff, 1974–1984).

Rosenzweig, F. *Briefe und Tagenbucher,* vol. 2 (The Hague: Martinus Nijhoff, 1979).

Rosenzweig, F. *Philosophical and Theological Writings*, ed. and trans. P. Franks and M. Morgan (Indianapolis, IN: Hackett, 2000).

Saadia Gaon. *The Book of Beliefs and Opinions*, trans. S. Rosenblatt (New Haven, CT: Yale Judaica Series, 1948/1976).

Saadia Gaon. *The Book of Doctrines and Beliefs*, abridged and trans. A. Altmann (Indianapolis, IN: Hackett, 2002).

Scherman, N. (ed. and trans.), *The Chumash: The Stone Edition* (New York: Mesorah Publications, 1993).

ben-Sheshet, Y. *Shut ha-Ribash* (Jerusalem: Machon Yerushalayim, 1993; orig. 1547).

Shneur Zalman of Liady. *Ma'amare Admor Hazaken 5572* (New York: Kehat Publication Society, 2006).

Soloveitchik, J. B. "Confrontation," *Tradition* 6 (1964), 5–29.

Soloveitchik, J. B. "Moses and the Redemption," in J. B. Soloveitchik, *Festival of Freedom: Essays on Pesach and the Haggadah*, ed. J. Wolowelsky and R. Ziegler (Jersey City, NJ: Ktav, 2006), 149–159.

*Soncino Babylonian Talmud*, ed. I. Epstein (London: Soncino Press, 1952).

Spinoza, B. *Opera,* 4 vols., ed. C. Gebhardt (Heidelberg: Carl Winter Verlag, 1925).

Spinoza, B. *The Collected Works of Spinoza*, 2 vols., ed. and trans. E. Curley (Princeton, NJ: Princeton University Press, 1985 and 2016).

Spinoza, B. *Spinoza: Complete Works*, trans. S. Shirley and ed. M. Morgan (Indianapolis, IN: Hackett, 2002).

Spinoza, B. *Theological-Political Treatise*, trans. M. Silverthorne and J. Israel (Cambridge: Cambridge University Press, 2007).

Spinoza, B. *Theological-Political Treatise*, in *The Collected Works of Spinoza*, vol. 2, ed. and trans. E. Curley (Princeton, NJ: Princeton University Press, 2016).

Strauss, L. *Persecution and the Art of Writing* (Chicago, IL: University of Chicago Press, 1952).

Strauss, L. *Natural Right and History* (Chicago, IL: University of Chicago Press, 1964).

Strauss, L. "The Mutual Influence of Theology and Philosophy," *Independent Journal of Philosophy* 3 (1979), 111–118.

Strauss, L. "On the Interpretation of Genesis," in L. Strauss, *Jewish Philosophy and the Crisis of Modernity*, ed. K. H. Green (Albany, NY: SUNY Press, 1997), 359–376.

*Talmud Bavli Hashalem Vehamefoar* (Jerusalem: Oz VeHadar, 2000).

*Torat Hayim* (Jerusalem: Mosad Harav Kook, 2006).

## Other Books and Articles

Ashkenazi, T. H. *Shut Hacham Tzvi* (Jerusalem, 1981).

Bell, D. A. *The Cult of the Nation in France: Inventing Nationalism, 1680–1800* (Princeton, NJ: Princeton University Press, 2001).

Bellah, R. *Beyond Belief* (Berkeley, CA: University of California Press, 1991).

Benjamin, W. "On the Concept of History," in W. Benjamin, *Selected Writings*, vol. 4, ed. H. Eiland and M. Jennings, trans. H. Zohn (Cambridge MA: Harvard University Press, 2003), 389–400.

Berger, D. "Jews, Gentiles, and the Egalitarian Ethos: Some Tentative Thoughts," in M. Stern (ed.), *Formulating Responses in an Egalitarian Age* (Lanham, MD: Rowman & Littlefield, 2005), 83–108.

Berger, D. *Persecution, Polemic, and Dialogue: Essays in Jewish-Christian Relations* (Boston, MA: Academic Studies Press, 2010).

Bernfeld, S. *Knowledge of God* (Warsaw: Ahiasaf, 1897) [Hebrew].

Bloch, E. *The Spirit of Utopia* (Stanford, CA: Stanford University Press, 2000).

Bodoff, L. "Was Yehudah Halevi Racist?" *Judaism* 38 (1989), 174–184.

Brill, A. *Judaism and Other Religions: Models of Understanding* (New York: Palgrave Macmillan, 2010).

Brody, B. "Modern Orthodoxy: A Philosophical Perspective," *Hakirah* 17 (2014), 31–67.

Broyde, M. "Proselytism in Jewish Law: 'Inreach, Outreach and the Jewish Tradition'," in *Sharing the Book: Religious Perspectives on the Rights and Wrongs of Proselytizing*, eds. J. Witte Jr. and R. C. Martin (Maryknoll, NY: Orbis Books, 1999), 45–60.

Carlyle, T. *The Works of Thomas Carlyle,* vol. 4, ed. H. D. Traill (London: Chapman and Hall, 1837/1903).

Carmy, S. "Love's Scandal: A Review of [Gellman] *God's Kindness Has Overwhelmed Us,*" *First Things* 238 (2013), 51–54.

Cassuto, U. *Commentary on the Book of Exodus* (Jerusalem: Magnes Press, 1967).

Code, L. *Epistemic Responsibility* (Lebanon, NH: University Press of New England, 1987).

Cohen, R. (ed.), *Face to Face with Levinas* (Albany, NY: SUNY Press, 1986).

Crisp, O. and M. Rea (eds.), *Analytic Theology: New Essays in the Philosophy of Theology* (Oxford: Oxford University Press, 2009).

Currie, G. *The Nature of Fiction* (Cambridge: Cambridge University Press, 1990).

Davidson, D. "What Metaphors Mean," *Critical Theory* 5 (1978), 31–47.

Davidson, H. "Maimonides on Metaphysical Knowledge," in *Maimonidean Studies*, vol. 3, ed. A. Hyman (New York: Michael Scharf Publication Trust of Yeshiva University Press, 1992–3), 49–103.

Dewey, J. *A Common Faith* (New Haven, CT: Yale University Press, 1934).

Dostoevsky, F. *The Brothers Karamazov,* trans. C. Garnett (New York: Modern Library, 1950).

Fackenheim, E. *Encounters Between Judaism and Modern Philosophy: A Preface to Future Jewish Thought* (New York: Basic Books, 1973).

*Faith and Philosophy* (vol. 14.4, October 1997): Philosophy of Religion and Jewish Religious Thought.

Feinstein, M. *Igrot Moshe Orach Hayim,* vol. 4 (Bene Berak: n.p., 1982).

Fenton, P. B. "Jewish Attitudes to Islam: Israel Heeds Ishmael," *Jerusalem Quarterly* 29 (1983), 84–102.

Frank, D. (ed.), *Autonomy and Judaism: The Individual and the Community in Jewish Philosophical Thought* (Albany, NY: SUNY Press, 1992).

Frank, D. (ed.), *A People Apart: Chosenness and Ritual in Jewish Philosophical Thought* (Albany, NY: SUNY Press, 1993).

Frank, D. (ed.), *Commandment and Community: New Essays in Jewish Legal and Political Philosophy* (Albany, NY: SUNY Press, 1995).

Frank, D. "Prophecy and Invulnerability," in *The Jewish Philosophy Reader*, eds. D. Frank, O. Leaman, and C. Manekin (London: Routledge, 2000), 79–83.

Frank, D. and O. Leaman (eds.), *History of Jewish Philosophy* (London: Routledge, 1997).

Frank, D. and O. Leaman (eds.), *The Cambridge Companion to Medieval Jewish Philosophy* (Cambridge: Cambridge University Press, 2003).

Gallois, A. *Occasions of Identity: The Metaphysics of Persistence, Change, and Sameness* (New York: Oxford University Press, 1998).

Gellman, J. *Experience of God and the Rationality of Theistic Belief* (Ithaca, NY: Cornell University Press, 1997).

Gellman, J. *God's Kindness Has Overwhelmed Us: A Contemporary Doctrine of the Jews as the Chosen People* (Boston, MA: Academic Studies Press, 2013).

Goldenberg, R. *The Nations That Know Thee Not: Ancient Jewish Attitudes toward Other Religions* (Sheffield: Sheffield Academic, 1997).

Goodman, L. E. *God of Abraham* (New York: Oxford University Press, 1996).

Goodman, L. E. *On Justice: An Essay in Jewish Philosophy* (New Haven, CT: Yale University Press, 1991; 2nd ed. Oxford and Portland, OR: Littman Library of Jewish Civilization, 2008).

Goodman, M. *The Dream of the Kuzari* (Or Yehudah: Dvir, 2012) [Hebrew].

Gordis, R. *The Book of God and Man* (Chicago, IL: University of Chicago Press, 1965).

Gottlieb, M. "Moses Mendelssohn's Metaphysical Defense of Religious Pluralism," in M. Gottlieb, *Faith, Reason, Politics: Essays on the History of Jewish Thought* (Boston, MA: Academic Studies Press, 2013), 98–121.

Graetz, H. "The Stages in the Evolution of the Messianic Belief," in H. Graetz, *The Structure of Jewish History and Other Essays*, trans. I. Schorsch (New York: Jewish Theological Seminary, 1975), 151–171.

Griswold, C. *Forgiveness: A Philosophical Exploration* (Cambridge: Cambridge University Press, 2007a).

Griswold, C. "Plato and Forgiveness," *Ancient Philosophy* 27 (2007b), 269–287.

Griswold, C. and D. Konstan (eds.), *Ancient Forgiveness* (Cambridge: Cambridge University Press, 2011).

Gutting, G. *Religious Belief and Religious Skepticism* (Notre Dame, IN: University of Notre Dame Press, 1983).

Guttmann, J. *Philosophies of Judaism* (New York: Schocken Books, 1973; orig. 1933).

Halbertal, M. and A. Margalit. *Idolatry* (Cambridge, MA: Harvard University Press, 1992).

Halper, E. C. "Torah as Political Philosophy: Maimonides and Spinoza on Divine Law," in *Judaic Sources and Western Thought: Jerusalem's Enduring Presence*, ed. J. A. Jacobs (Oxford: Oxford University Press, 2011), 190–214.

Hartman, D. *Maimonides: Torah and Philosophic Quest* (Philadelphia, PA: Jewish Publication Society, 1976).

Hartman, D. *A Living Covenant: The Innovative Spirit in Traditional Judaism* (New York: Free Press, 1985).

Hartshorne, C. *A Natural Theology for Our Time* (LaSalle, IL: Open Court, 1967).

Harvey, W. Z. "R. Hasdai Crescas and his Critique of Philosophic Happiness," *Proceedings of the Sixth World Congress of Jewish Studies* (Jerusalem: World Union of Jewish Studies, 1977), 3: 143–149 [Hebrew].

Hayes, C. *What's Divine about Divine Law? Early Perspectives* (Princeton, NJ: Princeton University Press, 2015).

Hick, J. *Death and Eternal Life* (Louisville, KY: Westminster, 1994).

Hick, J. *An Interpretation of Religion: Human Responses to the Transcendent* (New York: Macmillan, 1989; 2nd ed. Basingstoke: Palgrave Macmillan, 2004).

Hirsch, E. "Identity in the Talmud," *Midwest Studies in Philosophy* 23 (1999), 166–180.

Hirsch, E. "Rashi's View of the Open Future: Indeterminateness and Bivalence," *Oxford Studies in Metaphysics* 2 (2006), 111–136.

Hirschman, M. "Rabbinic Universalism in the Second and Third Centuries," *Harvard Theological Review* 93 (2000), 101–115.

Husik, I. *A History of Mediaeval Jewish Philosophy* (New York: Atheneum, 1976; orig. 1916).

Idel, M. "Defining Kabbalah: The Kabbalah of the Divine Names," in *Mystics of the Book: Themes, Topics, and Topologies* ed. R. A. Herrera (New York: Peter Lang: 1993), 97–113.

Jacobs, J. *Law, Reason, and Morality in Medieval Jewish Philosophy* (Oxford: Oxford University Press, 2010).

Johnston, M. *Surviving Death* (Princeton, NJ: Princeton University Press, 2010).

Jospe, R. "Teaching Judah Ha-Levi: Defining and Shattering Myths in Jewish Philosophy," in *Paradigms in Jewish Philosophy,* ed. R. Jospe (Cranbury, NJ: Associated University Presses, 1997), 112–128.

Jospe, R. "Pluralism Out of the Sources of Judaism: The Quest for Religious Pluralism without Relativism," in *Jewish Theology and World Religions,* eds. A. Goshen-Gottstein and E. Korn (Oxford and Portland, OR: Littman Library of Jewish Civilization, 2012), 87–121.

Kadushin, M. *The Rabbinic Mind* (New York: Jewish Theological Seminary, 1952).

Kahana, M. and M. K. Silver. "Deists, Sabbateans, and Kabbalists in the Prague Community: A Censored Sermon by Rabbi Yehezkel Landau, 1770," *Kabbalah: Journal for the Study of Jewish Mysticism* 21 (2010), 349–384.

Kaminsky, J. S. *Yet I Love Jacob: Reclaiming the Biblical Concept of Election* (Nashville, TN: Abingdon, 2007).

Katz, J. *Exclusiveness and Tolerance: Studies in Jewish-Gentile Relations in Medieval and Modern Times* (London: Oxford University Press, 1961).

Kavka, M., Z. Braiterman, and D. Novak (eds.), *The Cambridge History of Jewish Philosophy: The Modern Era* (Cambridge: Cambridge University Press, 2012).

Kellner, J. S. and M. Kellner. "A Respectful Disagreement: A Response to Raphael Jospe," in *Jewish Theology and World Religions,* eds. A. Goshen-Gottstein and E. Korn (Oxford and Portland, OR: Littman Library of Jewish Civilization, 2012), 123–133.

Kellner, M. *Maimonides on Judaism and the Jewish People* (Albany, NY: SUNY Press, 1991).

Kellner, M. *Maimonides' Confrontation with Mysticism* (Oxford and Portland, OR: Littman Library of Jewish Civilization, 2006a).

Kellner, M. *Must A Jew Believe Anything?* 2nd ed. (Oxford and Portland, OR: Littman Library of Jewish Civilization, 2006b).

Kogan, B. "Who Has Implanted within Us Eternal Life: Judah Halevi on Immortality and the Afterlife," in *Judaism and Modernity: The Religious Philosophy of David Hartman* ed. J. W. Malino (Aldershot: Ashgate, 2004), 445–463.

Korn, E. "Gentiles, the World to Come, and Judaism: The Odyssey of a Rabbinic Text," *Modern Judaism* 14 (1994), 265–287.

Korn, E. "Orthodoxy, Modern Pluralism, and the Christian Other," in *Mishpetei Shalom: A Jubilee Volume in Honor of Rabbi Saul (Shalom) Berman* ed. Y. Levy (New York: Yeshivat Chovevei Torah Rabbinical School, 2011), 307–339.

Kreisel, H. *Prophecy: The History of an Idea in Medieval Jewish Philosophy* (Dordrecht: Kluwer, 2001).

Kretzmann, N. "God Among the Causes of Moral Evil: Hardening of Hearts and Spiritual Blinding," *Philosophical Topics* 16 (1988), 189–214.

Kroll, N. "Teleological Dispositions," *Oxford Studies in Metaphysics* (forthcoming).

Lebens, S. "The Epistemology of Religiosity: an Orthodox Jewish Perspective," *International Journal of Philosophy of Religion* 74 (2013), 315–332.

Lebens, S. "Why so Negative about Negative Theology? The Search for a Plantinga-proof Apophaticism," *International Journal of Philosophy of Religion* 76 (2014), 259–275.

Lebens, S. "God and his Imaginary Friends: a Hassidic Metaphysics," *Religious Studies* 51 (2015), 183–204.

Leibowitz, Y. "Min ha-Leumiyut el ha-hayatiyut" [From Nationalism to Bestiality], *Haaretz*, Oct. 5, 1984.

Levenson, J. *Resurrection and the Restoration of Israel: The Ultimate Victory of the God of Life* (New Haven, CT: Yale University Press, 2008).

Levin, Y. "Tefilot Ara'iyot lare'aya Kook" [Occasional Prayers by Rabbi Kook], *Akdamot* 9 (2000).

Lewinsohn, J. "Philosophy in Halacha: The Case of Intentional Action," *The Torah u-Madda Journal* 14 (2006–7), 97–136.

Lewis, C. S. *Mere Christianity* (New York: Simon and Schuster, 1980).

Lichtenstein, A. "Law and Spirituality: Defining the Terms," in *Jewish Spirituality and Divine Law* eds. A. Mintz and L. Schiffman (New York: Yeshiva University Press, 2003), 3–33.

Lichtenstein, A. "Communal Governance, Lay and Rabbinic: An Overview," in *Rabbinic and Lay Communal Authority* ed. S. L. Stone (New York: Yeshiva University Press, 2006), 19–52.

Linzer, D. "On the *Mitzvot* of Non-Jews: An Analysis of *Avodah Zarah* 2b–3b," *Milin Havivin* 1 (2005), 25–37.

Manekin, C. and M. Kellner (eds.), *Freedom and Moral Responsibility: General and Jewish Perspectives* (College Park, MD: University Press of Maryland, 1997).

Manekin, C. and R. Eisen (eds.), *Philosophers and the Jewish Bible* (College Park, MD: University Press of Maryland, 2008).

Margalit, A. "The Ring: On Religious Pluralism," in *Toleration: An Elusive Virtue,* ed. D. Heyd (Princeton, NJ: Princeton University Press, 1998), 147–157.

Marty, M. "Introduction," in *Sharing the Book: Religious Perspectives on the Rights and Wrongs of Proselytizing* eds. J. Witte Jr. and R. C. Martin (Maryknoll, NY: Orbis Books, 1999), 1–14.

McKim, R. *On Religious Diversity* (New York: Oxford University Press, 2012).

Meister, C. *The Oxford Handbook of Religious Diversity* (New York: Oxford University Press, 2011).

Melamed, Y. "Salomon Maimon et l'échec de la philosophie juive moderne," *Revue Germanique Internationale* 9 (2009), 175–187.

Melamed, Y. "Spinoza's Anti-Humanism: An Outline," in *The Rationalists,* eds. C. Fraenkel, D. Perinetti, and J. Smith (Dordrecht: Kluwer, 2010), 147–166.

Melamed, Y. "He is the Place of the World, yet the World is not His Place" (unpublished manuscript).

Michelet, J. *Journal*, 4 vols., ed. P. Viallaneix (Paris: Gallimard, 1959).

Montefiore, A. "Ecumenical Movements and Truth," *Midwest Studies in Philosophy* 21 (1997), 145–158.

Morgan, M. *Discovering Levinas* (Cambridge: Cambridge University Press, 2007).

Morgan, M. *Fackenheim's Jewish Philosophy: An Introduction* (Toronto: University of Toronto Press, 2013).

Morgan, M. and P. Gordon (eds.), *The Cambridge Companion to Modern Jewish Philosophy* (Cambridge: Cambridge University Press, 2007).

Morris, T. V. *Our Idea of God: An Introduction to Philosophical Theology* (Downers Grove, IL: InterVarsity Press, 1991), 47–64.

Nadler, S. *Spinoza's Heresy: Immortality and the Jewish Mind* (Oxford: Clarendon Press, 2001).

Nadler, S. and T. M. Rudavsky (eds.), *The Cambridge History of Jewish Philosophy: From Antiquity through the Seventeenth Century* (Cambridge: Cambridge University Press, 2009).

Nagel, T. *Mind and Cosmos* (Oxford: Oxford University Press, 2012).

Neusner, J. "Messianic Themes in Formative Judaism," *Journal of the American Academy of Religion* 52 (1984), 357–374.

Novak, D. *The Election of Israel: The Idea of the Chosen People* (Cambridge: Cambridge University Press, 1995/2007).

Novak, D. *Natural Law in Judaism* (Cambridge: Cambridge University Press, 1998).

Novak, D. "Proselytism in Judaism," in *Sharing the Book: Religious Perspectives on the Rights and Wrongs of Proselytizing*, eds. J. Witte Jr. and R. C. Martin (Maryknoll, NY: Orbis Books, 1999), 17–44.

Novak, D. *Zionism and Judaism: A New Theory* (Cambridge: Cambridge University Press, 2015).

O'Brien, C. C. "Nationalism and the French Revolution," in *The Permanent Revolution: The French Revolution and Its Legacy, 1789– 1989*, ed. G. Best (Chicago, IL: Fontana Press, 1988), 17–48.

Olson, E. *What are We? A Study in Personal Ontology* (New York: Oxford University Press, 2007).

Petuchowski, J. J. *The Theology of Haham David Nieto: An Eighteenth Century Defense of the Jewish Tradition* (New York: Ktav, 1970).

Pines, S. "The Limitations of Human Knowledge According to Al-Farabi, ibn Bajja, and Maimonides," in *Studies in Medieval Jewish History and Literature*, ed. I. Twersky (Cambridge, MA: Harvard University Press, 1979), 82–109.

Plantinga, A. *God and Other Minds* (Ithaca, NY: Cornell University Press, 1968).

Plantinga, A. *Does God Have a Nature?* (Milwaukee, WI: Marquette University Press, 1980).

Plantinga, A. *Warranted Christian Belief* (Oxford: Oxford University Press, 2000).

Putnam, H. *Reason, Truth, and History* (Cambridge: Cambridge University Press, 1982).

Rappoport, J. "Rav Kook and Nietzsche: A Preliminary Consideration of Their Ideas on Religions, Christianity, Buddhism, and Atheism," *The Torah u-Madda Journal* 12 (2004), 99–129.

Rawls, J. *A Theory of Justice*, revised edition (Cambridge, MA: Harvard University Press, 2001).

Rea, M. "Introduction," in *Analytic Theology: New Essays in the Philosophy of Theology*, eds. O. Crisp and M. Rea (Oxford: Oxford University Press, 2009), 1–30.

Ricoeur, P. "Evil, A Challenge to Philosophy and Theology," *Journal of the American Academy of Religion* 53 (1985), 635–648.

Roth, L. *Is There a Jewish Philosophy? Rethinking Fundamentals* (London: Littman Library of Jewish Civilization, 1999).

Rudavsky, T. M. *Maimonides* (Oxford: Wiley-Blackwell, 2010).

Runzo, J. "God, Commitment, and Other Faiths," *Faith and Philosophy* 5 (1988), 343–364.

Russell, B. and T. Branch. *Second Wind: The Memoirs of an Opinionated Man* (New York: Random House, 1979).

Rynhold, D. *Two Models of Jewish Philosophy: Justifying One's Practices* (Oxford: Oxford University Press, 2005).

Sacks, J. *The Dignity of Difference: How to Avoid the Clash of Civilizations* (London: Continuum Books, 2002).

Sarna, N. *The JPS Torah Commentary: Exodus* (Philadelphia, PA: Jewish Publication Society, 1989).

Scholem, G. *The Messianic Idea in Judaism and Other Essays on Jewish Spirituality,* (New York: Schocken Books, 1971; 2nd ed., 1995).

Schwarzschild, S. *The Pursuit of the Ideal*, ed. M. Kellner (Albany, NY: SUNY Press, 1990).

Schweid, E. *Studies in Maimonides' Eight Chapters*, 2nd ed. (Jerusalem: Academon, 1989) [Hebrew].

Seeskin, K. *Jewish Philosophy in a Secular Age* (Albany, NY: SUNY Press, 1990).

Seeskin, K. "Jewish Philosophy in the 1980s," *Modern Judaism* 11 (1991), 157–172.

Seeskin, K. *Autonomy in Jewish Philosophy* (Cambridge: Cambridge University Press, 2001).

Seeskin, K. *Jewish Messianic Thoughts in an Age of Despair* (Cambridge: Cambridge University Press, 2012).

Shach, E. M. *Mikhtavim Uma'amarim*, vol. 1 (Bene Brak: n.p., 1988).

Shatz, D. "Worship, Corporeality, and Human Perfection: A Reading of *Guide* 3.51–54," in *The Thought of Moses Maimonides,* eds. I. Robinson, L. Kaplan, and J. Bauer (Lewiston, NY: Edwin Mellen Press, 1990), 77–129.

Shatz, D. "Hierarchical Theories of Freedom and the Hardening of Hearts," *Midwest Studies in Philosophy* (1997), 202–224.

Shatz, D. *Jewish Thought in Dialogue: Essays on Thinkers, Theologies and Moral Theories* (Boston, MA: Academic Studies Press, 2009).

Shatz, D. "Morality, Liberalism, and Interfaith Dialogue," in *New Perspectives on Jewish-Christian Relations: In Honor of David Berger*, eds. E. Carlebach and J. J. Schacter (Leiden: Brill, 2011), 491–519.

Shatz, D. "On Undermining the Beliefs of Others: Religion and the Ethics of Persuasion," in *Faith: Jewish Perspectives,* eds. A. Sagi and D. Schwartz (Boston, MA: Academic Studies Press, 2013), 137–187.

Silman, Y. *Philosopher and Prophet: Judah Halevi, the Kuzari, and the Evolution of His Thought* (Albany, NY: SUNY Press, 1995).

Sirat, C. *A History of Jewish Philosophy in the Middle Ages* (Cambridge: Cambridge University Press, 1985).

Soames, S. *Philosophical Analysis in the Twentieth Century, vol. 1: The Dawn of Analysis* (Princeton, NJ: Princeton University Press, 2003).

Soloveichik, M. "God's Beloved: A Defense of Chosenness," *Azure* 19 (2005), 59–84.

Spero, S. *Morality, Halakha and the Jewish Tradition* (New York: Ktav, 1983).

Stahl, N. *Twentieth Century Jewish Literature: Conceptions of the Divine* (New York: Routledge, forthcoming).

Steiner, M. "Rabbi Israel Salanter as a Jewish Philosopher," *The Torah u-Madda Journal* 9 (2000), 42–57.

Stern, J. *Problems and Parables of Law: Maimonides and Nahmanides on Reasons for the Commandments* (Albany, NY: SUNY Press, 1998).

Stern, J. *The Matter and Form of Maimonides' Guide* (Cambridge, MA: Harvard University Press, 2013).

Stern, M. S. "Al-Ghazzali, Maimonides, and Ibn Paquda on Repentance: A Comparative Model," *Journal of the American Academy of Religion* 47 (1979), 589–607.

Stroumsa, S. *Maimonides in His World: Portrait of a Mediterranean Thinker* (Princeton, NJ: Princeton University Press, 2009).

Stump, E. *Wandering in Darkness* (Oxford: Oxford University Press, 2010).

Swinburne, R. *The Existence of God* (Oxford: Clarendon Press, 1991; orig. 1979).

Tamres, A. S. *Keneset Yisrael Umilhamot Hagoyim [The Synagogue of Israel and the Wars of the Gentiles]* (Warsaw, 1920).

Teitelbaum, Y. *Vayoel Moshe* (Jerusalem: Yerushalayim Press, 1982).

Thiessen, E. *The Ethics of Evangelism: A Philosophical Defense of Proselytizing and Persuasion* (Downers Grove, IL: InterVarsity Press, 2011).

Twersky, I. *Introduction to the Code of Maimonides (Mishneh Torah)* (New Haven, CT: Yale University Press, 1980).

van Inwagen, P. "The Possibility of Resurrection," *International Journal for Philosophy of Religion*, 9 (1978), 114–121.

Wainwright, W. (ed.), *God, Philosophy, and Academic Culture: A Discussion Between Scholars in the AAR and the APA* (Atlanta, GA: American Academy of Religion, 1996).

Wasserman, E. B. *Ikveta Demeshiha* (Jerusalem: Makhon Or Elhanan, 2002).

Wettstein, H. "Poetic Imagery and Religious Belief," in *Philosophy and Faith: A Philosophy of Religion Reader*, ed. D. Shatz (New York: McGraw-Hill, 2002), 106–114.

Wettstein, H. *The Magic Prism* (New York: Oxford University Press, 2004).

Wettstein, H. "The Significance of Religious Experience," *The Modern Schoolman* 86 (2011), 381–398 (reprinted in H. Wettstein, *The Significance of Religious Experience*).

Wettstein, H. *The Significance of Religious Experience* (New York: Oxford University Press, 2012).

Williams, B. "The Makropulos Case: Reflections on the Tedium of Immortality," in *Problems of the Self* (Cambridge: Cambridge University Press, 1973), 82–100.

Williams, B. "Descartes and the Historiography of Philosophy," in *The Sense of the Past* (Princeton, NJ: Princeton University Press, 2006), 257–265.

Williams, R. *Teresa of Avila* (New York: Continuum, 2000).

Wolfson, H. *Repercussions of the Kalam in Jewish Philosophy* (Cambridge, MA: Harvard University Press, 1979).

Wyschogrod, M. *The Body of Faith: Judaism as Corporeal Election* (New York: Seabury Press, 1983).

Zimmerman, D. "The Compatibility of Materialism and Survival: The 'Falling Elevator' Model," *Faith and Philosophy* 16 (1999), 194–212.

Zimmerman, D. "Three Introductory Questions," in *Persons: Human and Divine,* eds. P. van Inwagen and D. Zimmerman (Oxford: Clarendon Press, 2007), 1–32.

Zimmerman, D. "Personal Identity and the Survival of Death," in *Oxford Handbook of Philosophy of Death*, eds. B. Bradley, F. Feldman, and J. Johansson (Oxford: Oxford University Press, 2012), 97–154.

# Index